DWELLINGS, SETTLEMENTS AND TRADITION
CROSS-CULTURAL PERSPECTIVES

INTERNATIONAL ASSOCIATION FOR THE STUDY OF
TRADITIONAL ENVIRONMENTS, BERKELEY

DWELLINGS
SETTLEMENTS
AND TRADITION

CROSS–CULTURAL PERSPECTIVES

EDITED BY

JEAN–PAUL BOURDIER
NEZAR ALSAYYAD

**UNIVERSITY
PRESS OF
AMERICA**

Lanham • New York • London

Published by
University Press of America
4720 Boston Way
Lanham, MD 20706 U S A

3 Henrietta Street
London WC2E 8LU England

Co-published with
International Association for the Study of Traditional Environments   [I A S T E]
Center for Environmental Design Research
University of California Berkeley
Berkeley, CA 94720 T E L : (4 1 5)   6 4 2 - 2 8 9 6   U S A

Printed in the United States of America.
Book Design: Annabelle Ison, Nezar AlSayyad

Library of Congress Cataloging-in-Publication Data

Dwellings, settlements, and tradition : cross–cultural perspectives / edited by
Jean–Paul Bourdier, Nezar AlSayyad.
p.   cm.
1. Dwellings—Cross–cultural studies.   2. Human settlements—Cross–cultural studies.
3. Vernacular architecture—Cross–cultural studies.   I. Bourdier, Jean–Paul.
II. AlSayyad, Nezar.
GN413.D84   1989   307.1'4—dc20   89–34496 CIP

ISBN 0–8191–7523–4 (alk. paper)
ISBN 0–8191–7524–2 (pbk.: alk. paper)

CONTENTS

PREFACE

The idea behind this book stemmed from discussions Jean-Paul Bourdier and I had in 1985 and a course we co-taught in 1987 entitled "Traditional Habitat." This graduate seminar was primarily concerned with identifying linkages between two separate and usually distinct areas of study: vernacular rural dwellings, which interested Jean-Paul, and contemporary urban squatter settlements, which interested me. From the outset of our work together it was obvious that we disagree on some issues, not only because we had different concerns, but because we used different area-study jargon. As I look back on our early discussions, I am reminded that we basically agreed that these two types of habitat were both the product of traditional cultural processes and that these processes had not received their fair share of attention from scholars in either area. We also came to recognize that there was an apparent lack of communication between scholars working on different aspects of what we termed "traditional dwellings and settlements."

In thinking about ways to deal with what we perceived to be an excessive disciplinization of the subject, we decided to organize a meeting of specialized scholars. We decided that this meeting should include all scholars involved in studying traditional dwellings and settlements without regard for discipline or the variety of labels that they attached to their research subjects. Believing that specificity in an interdisciplinary discourse may be a vice rather than a virtue, we decided to keep the theme of the meeting deliberately general.

Before we had secured total funding for the project, we took the bold step of circulating a call for papers. We had expected to receive no more than fifty submissions from scholars we thought we already knew, but we were astonished by the overwhelming interest in our announcement. What we had initially envisioned as a small seminar brought more than four hundred abstracts, and we were faced with the awesome task of administering the First International Symposium on Traditional Dwellings and Settlements in Comparative Perspective.

Our primary task was to screen the wide assortment of submissions. While reading the abstracts, we made a preliminary classification of content based on an extensive computerized keyword index. We then asked the advice of a committee of reviewers assembled from related disciplines. This blind review resulted in the selection of 125 papers for presentation at the symposium. We then set about trying to organize a program that would maintain our interdisciplinary focus and cross-cultural perspective. We invited in addition five distinguished scholars representing different disciplines to address the symposium in plenary sessions. These were folklorist Henry Glassie, architectural historian Spiro Kostof, vernacularist Paul Oliver, environment-behavior expert Amos Rapoport, and cultural geographer Yi-Fu Tuan.

Following the symposium it became clear that we had compiled a considerable amount of excellent unpublished research. We also realized that publishing it in the form of an oversized proceedings volume might not be the best way to disseminate it. Fortunately, the establishment of the International Association for the Study of Traditional Environments (I A S T E) during the symposium enabled us to compile most of the papers presented in the Traditional Dwellings and Settlements Working Paper Series (see Appendix). Drawing on the themes which we had asked some of our keynote speakers to address, we then decided to assemble a book that would represent the various concerns covered by the symposium. Authors of the different chapters included in the book were accordingly asked to revise their work for publication in this new format.

As with the symposium, we decided that the book should be devoted more to raising questions than to providing answers, that it should be comprehensive without being conclusive, and that it should concentrate on restructuring what we already know rather than augmenting the great store of existing knowledge. We felt the book would have some merit if it forced us to examine our biases and form new research questions that go beyond the boundaries of our own disciplines.

No book with a title like *Dwellings, Settlements and Tradition* can claim to be comprehensive or to do justice to such a rich topic. Consequently, we are not concerned here with presenting an exhaustive view, nor with unifying terminology or agreeing on paradigms. In fact, we are seeking acceptance of the multiplicity of definitions and meanings contained in the idea of traditional dwellings and settlements. In the process of putting this book together we have tried to avoid proposing grand theories. And yet, recognizing that the worst type of research problem is one that is ill-defined, we did adopt some basic theoretical positions. One of these was that tradition must not be interpreted simply as the static legacy of the past but rather as a model for the dynamic re-interpretation of the present. It is precisely this approach which contributors to this book take: to formulate new, more appropriate questions instead of offering answers to old, long-held ones.

Throughout this endeavor we have received the support and encouragement of many individuals and institutions. We would like to acknowledge the support of the Graham Foundation for Advanced Studies in the Fine Arts, Chicago, the National Endowment for the Arts, Washington, D.C., and the College of Environmental Design at the University of California, Berkeley. Many of our colleagues contributed to the review process and acted as chairs or discussants for the symposium sessions, and many of our students participated in the actual day-to-day operation of the event. Without help from both groups our task would have been impossible. We also wish to acknowledge the encouragement and advice of the former dean of the College of Environmental Design, Richard Bender, and the current dean,

Roger Montgomery. Their support and advice was very valuable in bringing about this book and the activities which preceded it. We are deeply indebted to the staff of the Center For Environmental Design Research at Berkeley, particularly Nora Watanabe and Kellie Crockett, whose help and friendship were invaluable. Finally, we would like to thank those who participated directly in the project, especially Gulsum Nalbantoglu who worked on it from its inception, coordinated the symposium activities and assisted us with the organization of the book. Both David Moffat, as assistant editor and copy editor, and Annabelle Ison, as graphic editor and production coordinator, brought a dedication without which this book would not have appeared in its present form. Our final note of thanks should go to our contributors for making it all possible.

Nezar AlSayyad
Berkeley, April 1989

DWELLINGS, SETTLEMENTS AND TRADITION: A PROLOGUE

JEAN-PAUL BOURDIER
NEZAR ALSAYYAD

What can a book on dwellings, settlements and tradition hope to achieve? What are traditional dwellings and settlements? How do they arise and why do they persist? How do we in academia study them and to what end? These are a few of the questions contributors to this volume address.

Traditional dwellings and settlements are the built expression of a heritage that continues to be transmitted from one generation to another. Usually the product of common people without professional intervention, they provide the habitat for much of the world's population. According to one estimate, traditional dwellings and settlements house between eight and nine million households in a variety of urban and rural settings.[1]

In recent years interest in the social and cultural values, images and perceptions underlying traditional dwellings and settlements has become widespread among scholars in various disciplines. Specific labels such as "vernacular," "indigenous," "primitive," "tribal," "folkloric," "popular" and "anonymous" have been introduced to describe the subjects of a variety of inquiries. Many of these qualifiers originated from particular disciplinary bases and may not be interchangeable. For example, vernacular architecture in many parts of today's world often cannot be considered indigenous, because it relies on imported materials to achieve local styles. Nevertheless, the inability to come up with a single appropriate label should not prevent us from talking about these dwellings and settlements as one group. One thing common to all the above qualifiers is that they describe a process that becomes a norm when enough people in a given society adopt it. Since this is one of the more apparent qualities of tradition in built form,[2] we have decided to use "tradition" as an all-encompassing umbrella term. Used in this way, the term may also be useful in an age when scholars are beginning to recognize that the study of those dwellings and settlements whose form originated out of cultural processes rather than specialized aesthetic judgements is an open and irrevocable inter-disciplinary arena.[3] The term has limitations; there are, for example, traditions in medicine, science and high-style architecture. But in the context of this work, a *thing* is "traditional" if it satisfies two criteria: it is the result of a process of transmission, and it has cultural origins involving common people. Professional traditions satisfy the former but not the latter condition. This book will deal with buildings and spaces which are deliberately non-academic, which provide for the simple activities and enterprises of ordinary people, which strongly relate to place through respect for local conventions, and which are produced by a process of personalized thought and feeling rather than utilitarian logic.[4]

The study of traditional dwellings and settlements as so defined is not new. But between the pioneering works by Morgan and Morse in the nineteenth century[5] and Rudofsky's *Architecture Without Architects*, the exhibition and accompanying book that brought a resurgence of scholarly interest in the 1960s, there was a paucity of work on the subject -- albeit some excellent monographs on the dwellings of specific ethnic groups. The late sixties witnessed the publication of Rapoport's *House Form and Culture* and Oliver's edited volume *Shelter and Society*. And more recently we have seen Guidoni's *Primitive Architecture* and Oliver's *Dwellings: The House Across the World*.[6] All these studies have made a significant contribution to the field.

This book differs from earlier studies in its use of the cross-cultural approach, its concentration on the dichotomies of traditional societies in the non-Western world, and its attempt to include contributions that represent a variety of approaches to the subject. Individual chapters cover a wide territory from Korea, Japan, Indonesia, Thailand and India to Egypt, Jordan, Palestine and Botswana, from the Old World of the Mediterranean to the New World of the Australian continent.[7] Contributors representing a variety of disciplines include architects, anthropologists, art and architecture historians, folklorists, geographers and sociologists.

Defining vernacular architecture less by subject than by method, Dell Upton identified four "avenues of inquiry": object-oriented studies, socially oriented studies, culturally oriented studies and symbolically oriented studies.[8]   While the first type tries to interpret the intention of a dwelling's creator and the second is concerned with overall social history, the third and fourth suggest a shift towards a typologized study of dwellings within certain socio-cultural and historic contexts, with the purpose of uncovering the enduring values of their builders and the symbols that signify deeper structures of society.   Although Upton was mainly concerned with the Anglo-American vernacular, his categories could easily be applied to the larger field of traditional dwellings and settlements.   To its credit, and also possibly to its detriment, this book contains examples of each of the four types of approaches defined by Upton.   There is, however, another area that needs to be discussed in addition to the four types, one that cannot be merely categorized as "aesthetic trickle-down theories."[9]   This is what we called design-oriented studies, and these include the work of those people who seek better ways of understanding the past without accepting a simplistic return to earlier traditions.   The design-oriented study which is concerned with redefining and reaffirming regional identity is among the few remaining avenues for exploring contemporary alternatives to tradition, and contributors to this book present some ideas about how this could be achieved.

As most of the contributions to this volume exemplify, no study whose approach privileges either physical, formal, metaphysical or socio-cultural factors can account for the aesthetic, symbolic and polysemic richness of traditional dwellings and settlements. Valuing one factor over another, which may be useful as counter strategy in exclusionary contexts, often leads to the conversion of the particularity of approach into a universal practice, persuading researchers that it is the "best" way to proceed and the only one validated in the field.

In the past there has been a tendency among researchers interested in the dwellings and settlements of the Third World to focus exclusively on the formal and structural dimension of the building process. Nowadays it is more common to encounter sociohistorical and material-cultural approaches which allow a better exploration of architectural form in its relation to systems of values, even though this often results in aesthetics being equated with mere formalistic concern, and architecture being used only as illustrative evidence of other inquiries.

Initially this book and the activities that preceded it were intended to explore three aspects of traditional environments: the dwelling unit, the larger settlement, and methodological interpretations. The dwelling unit is the basic architectural component of the traditional environment; the physical determinants, climatic constraints, aesthetic meanings and social practices are all important aspects of concern at this level. Settlement layouts represent a larger scale of analysis at which one can discover much about spatial organization, design symbolism and social hierarchy. The concern for methodologies of interpretation is intended to raise questions about modes of representation. It calls attention to the very element that makes research findings communicable, and thereby to the way knowledge is produced, translated and circulated.

As the outline of the book started to take shape, it became obvious that this general structure, which worked well for organizing the symposium, was not appropriate for a book which would attempt to relate the three independent, yet clearly linked concepts of dwelling, settlement and tradition. Talking about dwellings alone without placing them in the context of settlements, or without recognizing that content is limited by method, no longer seemed as reasonable a practice as it had during the symposium.

There are, of course, many ways by which an edited book like this can be put together. The table of contents represents one such way, the sequence of this introduction represents another. This book begins with a survey of the different conceptions of "tradition" in the built environment as examined by authors from different disciplines. It then moves to another group of authors, who challenge the relevance of our conventional research paradigms and question the validity of our research assumptions and the value of our disciplinary boundaries. Contributors in the following sections present a variety of case studies of traditional dwellings and settlements. Again, there is a good mix of regions and disciplinary approaches. Here the concentration is on the meanings, forms and ritual practices which may be symbolic of larger societal values. The question of whose values are being expressed arises in the process, hence the necessity in subsequent chapters to address the dichotomy between the social construction of traditional realities by those who live them and the academic representation of those realities by those who study them. The issues present in this dichotomy are further explored in the last two sections of the book. The concentration here, however, is on the problems that arise when two different world views are involved -- whether these be the views of the colonizer and the colonized, the native and the immigrant, or the modernist and the traditionalist. These final contributions highlight the importance of break points in the history of nations and people when new traditions are born out of hybridization and the struggle to achieve and maintain a national identity.

The book opens with the contributions of Yi-Fu Tuan, Amos Rapoport, Paul Oliver and Jean-Paul Bourdier. Although very different discussions, they all attempt to unravel the meaning of "tradition," and at times cross one another in the definitions advanced. "Handed-down architecture," as well as the problem of meaning construction, are the shared subjects of inquiry.

"We wish to pass on what we value, and one way to assign value to something is to say that it is traditional, sanctioned by history . . . or nature itself." Yi-Fu Tuan encapsulates in this short statement both the positive and negative connotations of "tradition," its active dimension and passive assumptions, its authority as well as uncertainty, and, last but not least, the self-reflexive position of the speaking/writing subject. It is this latter quality that contributes to the distinctive tone of the paper, whose voice lays open the personal play of a social self caught between tradition and modernity. Inviting the reader to venture into a philosophical inquiry that scans across the un-modernized country-side of Europe, Africa and China, Tuan leads us swiftly from carpenters, farmers and tribal chiefs to great lords, kings, emperors and duchesses. Tradition, as low and high, past and present, is discussed in relation to creativity, choice, power, consumerism and time. Choice, which Tuan considers to be "at odds with the traditional" and "an ideal of modern times made possible by material plenty," is in a first stage treated as an attribute of freedom, a transcendence of local condition, a state of unnaturalness, and a privilege of those in power. As such, it is contrasted with constraint, which is associated with regard for the lay of the land, with being bound to the availability of local materials and to life's irreducible essentials. In a second stage, however, choice leads from freedom to boredom. "[It] was at one time the burden of kings, . . . [but it] is now available to everyone with a major credit card." The return to something "more funda-mental, more traditional is [therefore] a constant temptation." And constraint takes on a variety of meanings; it could become a form of salvation. "At a deeply serious level, constraint implies waiting. To yield control of one's time to another is perhaps the hardest part of bondage, for the passage of time is the passage of life." Unique to such a statement is the introduction of notions of time and of waiting to the concept of tradition. One may argue with Tuan on his development of the concept of choice by drawing distinctions between freedom or liberation, and the practices of freedom or of liberty. An act of liberation does not necessarily guarantee the practice of liberty, and the latter may have great importance and autonomy in a traditional context. But, ultimately, one would have to agree with Tuan that today, "every consumer is a potentate, shocked by having to wait for what s/he wants. Yet without waiting there is no value."

In the complex age in which we live the growing interest in traditional architecture is perhaps symptomatic of a desire to address the past architectural heritage in terms other than those set up by the reductive opposition between tradition and modernity. The attempt to erode this old divide does not lead necessarily to a redefinition of tradition, but rather to a *reading* (and re-reading) activity, as in the chapter "Reading Tradition" which emphasizes how tradition continues to be made, as the meanings attributed to it are constantly produced according to the contexts perceived and the relations drawn. This reading activity explores, for example, tradition in the context of and in relation to postmodernity. It calls for a practice of interdisciplinarity that requires the modifying of established boundaries, and it leads to an understanding of dwelling as the materialization of the bond between people and the means by which they choose to transmit "handed-down" knowledge and social practices. The question of representation that arises here is dealt with through a discussion of the graphic image. Drawing is thus analyzed as a tool for thinking and representing that is socially determined and, therefore, subject to critique as well as open to research.

It is also in an attempt at re-reading that Paul Oliver writes: "It can be argued that there is no such thing as a 'traditional building,' and no larger field of 'traditional architecture.' There are only buildings that embody traditions." This conclusion is provocatively arrived at after Oliver has made a substantial effort to elaborate on the term, concept and context of tradition and traditional architecture with particular attention to the question of transmission. Oliver's claim that this study is of pressing importance because of earlier neglect is justified. The task of listening to and retrieving people's sayings and comments as related to their built environment is highly valued by field researchers. The emphasis on transmission in the making of material culture leads Oliver from Kazimierz Dobrowski's narrow view in his study of the culture of peasants to Jan Vansina's more comprehensive interest in the historical information of oral testimonies. It is here that

Oliver's contribution seems most significant. In a lively section of the chapter, "Voices of the People," he sets out to exemplify the five types of oral transmission proposed by Vansina: Formulae, Poetry, Lists, Tales and Commentaries. The examples provided in the frame of Vansina's typology are most insightful, as they highly enrich our understanding of the processes whereby buildings "come to be." What remains questionable in the end, however, is Oliver's assertion that, "whatever the means of communication and the social circumstance in which it takes place, it is the message which is of ultimate importance." Such an assertion would place Vansina's typology and its use as a framework in the sphere of cumulative knowledge where classification is carried out as an end in itself rather than a means to move beyond the dichotomy between form and content (how and what). The attempt at structuring oral transmission could thereby remain largely illustrative if it does not displace the preconceived categories. Oliver is not unaware of the limitation of Vansina's typology. As he remarks in his conclusion, it "lays the emphasis on formulaic oral transmission and . . . places a low premium on creativity, [and] also omits any kind of exchange or argument."

In Amos Rapoport's investigation of the attributes of "tradition," the basic questions of "what" and "why" in the study of traditional dwellings and settlements are posed with the aim of providing clear answers and offering potential lessons. The need for a new definition of traditionality underlies the chapter, whose inclusive sets of attributes are presented as being useful "in clarifying what traditional environments are all about." Examining in detail the potential relationships involved in traditionality of process and traditionality of product, Rapoport not only seeks to confirm intuitive assumptions common to researchers on typical traditional environments, to clarify their use, and apply them in discussion on popular design, but he also endeavors to lay the foundation for a whole research program in which these assumptions would be questioned, changed, developed or refined. That "traditional" is not a given, that it does not denote natural, self-evident qualities, is indeed a necessary point of re-departure for all studies in the field, and Rapoport's insistence on this point is certainly helpful.

However, whether a better understanding of the traditional reality and a more appropriate determination of its properties could be achieved through skillful dissection, exhaustive accumulation and thorough cataloguing is another fundamental question. Attributes in the sense of predicates can easily become *attributions*, hence the necessity to recognize the limit of systems of classification. Therefore, after suggesting that this approach "allows more subtle classification;" that it has "methodological advantages and avoids reliance on ideal types;" that it "provides a conceptual framework for the topic and promises to lead to the development of a theory;" and that it can also provide, among other things, specific lessons "about designing for developing countries;" Rapoport carefully concludes that "comparative research on traditional environments . . . is a treasure house of human experience." Traditional environments, according to this view, are "an essential part of what design must become now and in the future. The question is how to go about studying them." This chapter presents one possible answer to this problem.

The contributions of Rapoport and Oliver certainly open the door to a thorough evaluation of definitions and methods. Also of importance in the study of traditional dwellings and settlements are the issues of boundaries and the problems involved with accepting conventional research assumptions and pre-set limits. This is what the second section of the book deals with. All three chapters in it suggest that both continuities and broader methodological settings should be given greater emphasis in the study of traditional environments.

Spiro Kostof starts the section by calling on those studying human settlement to consider town and country not solely as opposites, but as points on a single continuum. He reminds us that although the two landscapes have always been interdependent, the overriding preoccupation of historians has been to consider the city as "a remarkable artifact," separate from the countryside in which it is set. This way of thinking has parallels in the division of architecture into high style and common style. Obviously, looking at the human environment in such terms can be counterproductive, especially when it results in consideration of the city as a distinctive unit. Kostof asserts that the study of physical continuity between the rural and urban landscape would begin to unearth a new "history of settlement patterns," one that engages the total landscape and "eases the anxieties rampant in those many parts of the world that are trapped between tradition and the present." Kostof goes on to suggest that tradition has no end and that in today's world we should be seeking tradition in everything "modern."

Sophie Clement-Charpentier's contribution provides additional examples of the argument posed by Kostof. She tells us about research which shows how the same structures that govern the spatial organization of villages can be present in towns. Understanding the structure of relatively simple villages, therefore, can be of great assistance in understanding the far more complex fabric of towns. In Thai, the word *ban* can mean a "dwelling," a "village" and even a "quarter" of a town, without any distinction between the rural or urban character of the unit. This linguistic continuity has its physical counterpart in the organization of traditional Thai settlements. Clement-Charpentier explains how Thai villages initially appear unorganized, but upon further inspection reveal a definite structure. This structure is based on rules of organization that are in turn based on religious belief, social custom and economic necessity. The rules embody principles such as overall linearity, respect for the orientation of neighboring houses and general organization of neighborhoods around Buddhist monasteries, or *wats.* Many of the same organizing principles are evident in towns, Clement-Charpentier claims, so that whole quarters can sometimes look like villages. The traditional process of urbanization among the Thai, especially in Laos, is one of rural agglomeration. Alternatively, where a town is designed as the symbolic center of a region, large areas inside the city walls can retain a rural character. The importance of Clement Charpentier's chapter lies in its reminder that rural infiltration helps retain tradition in the more complex and modernized fabric of urban areas. Perhaps the central question raised is whether tradition urbanizes rural areas or vice-versa.

Jo Tonna writes about a different type of infiltration, what he calls the "interpenetration" of high and folk styles in traditional buildings. He challenges another classical dichotomy, one that is as significant that between town and country. We are told that it is difficult in Malta to make the usual distinction between "high" and "low" style building. This may be a common quality of the architecture of countries under the influence of various cultural spheres, but the particularity of it in Malta is that a two-way interaction developed between high and folk styles. On the one hand, high-style notions migrated out of towns to the important buildings of villages such as parish churches. On the other, a folk tradition developed in the use of high-style ornament in the towns, and traditional stone building techniques were adapted to cater to more complicated high-style forms. In addition, European Baroque and Islamic ideas competed over the years. For example, the Islamic idea of the street as a barrier between private realms was challenged by Baroque ideas of the street as a place of public spectacle. Tonna's chapter demonstrates the complex ways in which a high tradition" originating outside a culture can interact with the little tradition that springs up from inside it."

Also challenging the dichotomy between "high" and "low" architecture is Amr Abdel Kawi's attempt at problematizing the prevailing professional attitude by relating the story of the oasis of Farafra, not as viewed by the professional, but as told to him by its inhabitants. The professional attitude in which Kawi initially partook is criticized as, "always objectifying what I saw so as to fit it within my preconceived set of classifications that ordered the world for me," reducing it thereby to a world of objects divested of meanings. This attitude is successfully exposed in Kawi's analysis, "as simply another tradition of explaining the world; one that is different from the tradition adopted by the inhabitants of Farafra." Kawi's method of engaging "the others as co-searchers" is undeniably enriching, especially when it is clearly presented at the start of the chapter not as a new method but as "an experience that brought about an onslaught of critical self-reflexive questions" concerning our professional attitudes as architectural researchers. The opposition set up between the symbolic (meanings) and the physical aspects, the people's eye and the professional eye, the authentic maker's testimony and the architect's adopted observation, and the insider's position and the outsider's view is, however, another question that needs to be problematized. Furthermore, how the inhabitants' own words are recorded, used and quoted in the text, written for an audience of outsiders, points back to Kawi's work and the way he "re-tells" and understands -- that is, a "professional" relating of the people's story.

More attention to the problems of representing traditional realities would enrich reflections on the nature of traditional dwellings. Michael Linzey's discussion of the notions of "speaking to" and "talking about" in relation to Maori architecture is another engaging attempt at tackling this problem while inducing us to reflect on its own basic dualistic stance (we/they; Europeans/Maori). At one level this chapter offers a literal reading of New Zealand's Maori dwelling experience. What distinguishes the Maori experience from the European one is that Maori people directly address the house in tribal occasions and public gatherings; "architecture for them is a living tribal presence in the hearts of people." At another level the chapter points to its own mode of address -- common to other chapters as well: that of *talking about* a traditional phenomenon while *speaking to* an international audience. Exploring the subject/object relation, it sets out to compare the "likely mytho-poetical foundations of Maori behavior" with "related figures within traditions of European education." Within this framework, the two modes of address take on an allegorical dimension as they also connote different world views. "To talk about something is to *see* something as an It, as a mere thing. To speak to something is to *see* a person, or to *see* something personified . . . . To talk about something is to deliberately place semantic distance between oneself and the other." Thus talking about "secures for the human being the mastery of his essence" -- "I" is the midpoint of a constituted world, the "other" is the sphere of having. Speaking to, by contrast, is a relation of mutuality. "[It] is not centered on the I nor on the You, but it is symmetrical and equal."

It is often difficult to resist talking about -- that is, posing cultural facts as things observed rather than heard, transcribed, constructed in dialogue and reconstructed in memory, for the critical practice involved in this speaking to architecture requires that we remember the "freedoms" of interpretation which are also its constraints. Reading (which includes transcribing, translating and interpreting) is properly symbolic, as Roland Barthes reminded us. It is symbolic not because it is tied to an image, but because it is capable of always pointing to the very plurality of meanings. This is particularly significant in studies like the one by Suzanne Preston Blier which "combines an analysis of African aesthetic with an exploration into related features of architectural symbolism." The translation of the terms used in aesthetic valuation by the Batammaliba, the insertion of some of the architect's/builder's comments and fragments of conversation related to the house, are here skillfully woven with Blier's own explanations into a consistent and insightful interpretation of Batammaliba aesthetics. The uniqueness of Blier's study resides both in the wealth of local oral sources she provides and in her skill in elaborating symbolic readings of the data gathered. Thus, such a term as *yala*, identified with "evenness," is placed, for example, within a sign system as a criterion for the beauty of a building, a link between house and family (people and architecture), and an expression of ideals of political power, social harmony and ancestral order. In its investigation of architectural symbolism, however, the chapter contributes more to fortifying and unifying the meanings arrived at, hence with building a language of certainties (factualities), than to incorporating uncertainties in this process of unification. The necessity to expose, while speaking, the aleatory aspects of the voice of knowledge is part of the constraints that the freedoms and rigors of cultural interpretations engender.

The way one constructs meaning and understands semantically how a house is conceived, like the way one builds a house, is often indicative of either an ideology or a world view. Botond Bognar remarks, "today, in our increasingly prosaic world of instrumental reality with the inevitable tendency to reduce reality to scientifically measurable and exploitable certainty, the qualities of the 'invisible' yet poetically sensible world, rather than the visible but often senseless formalistic attributes of the Japanese house are the most significant legacies of its unique tradition." In trying to understand, describers and analyzers like ourselves have to remain alert to "what the cultural patterns of perception of the times let [us] see." This is particularly useful when it is a question of grasping the immaterial through the material in the context of a (modern) civilization exclusively centered on the "visible" world. Bognar's exploration of the place of no-thingness in the Japanese house retraces the history and evolution of the house, emphasizing how architecture not only reflects a philosophical tradition and a family system, but also helps to shape the Japanese way of life. The significance of the Japanese house "points beyond the immediately obvious, the factual, the formal." Thus, one of the concepts, for example, that characterizes the Japanese house in its centripetal space structure is that of *oku*. Defined as "innermost core," *oku* does not really refer to the concept of core in the sense of a *substantial* center, as the Western metaphysics of Presence formulates it. Rather, it is the invisible center, or more precisely, "it is a convenience devised by a spirit and climate which deny absolute objects or symbols such as a notion of center."[10] Thanks to it, "the Japanese have been able to give an illusion of depth to spatial compositions, regardless of their physical, usually small and shallow dimensions." In an architecture where "totality as such is never (re)presented visually in the state of completeness and perfection," it is hardly surprising that not only lightness and "insubstantiality" (spatiality) are effortlessly achieved, but that they are also brought out in a way that both reinterprets and challenges the past. The importance of tradition, Nyozekan Hasegawa argues, "lies not so much in the preservation of the cultural properties of the past in their original forms as in giving shape to contemporary culture."[11]

Although characteristic of modern Japanese culture in its ability to transmit and perpetuate its traditions, the above statement, understood in its plural meaning, can be found in many other cultural contexts where tradition is still "coherence in every aspect of life," and where "every act of creation is real or meaningful only insofar as it repeats the initial act of creation." For Ismet Khambatta, "constant renewal and regeneration is the essence of 'tradition.'" In this cyclic concept of time, the act of building is a remembering of the creation of the universe, and the traditional dwelling based on the Hindu canon of architecture reflects in its rituals and physical structure the Supreme Principle or *Brahman*. Exploring the meaning of "residence" in traditional Hindu society, Khambatta invites us to follow an open metaphysical and architectural itinerary from *residence* to *residue*, interlinking the three houses: man, building and cosmos. The itinerary starts with the metaphysical construct which affirms that "every existing thing is a 'residence,'" and it moves on to the Ritual Diagram of the Building (the *Vastupurusamandala*), the Rite of Impregnation (*Bhumi Pujan*), and the Domestic Sacrifice (*Vastu Santi*). It eventually reaches the Building (the residue, or "the immanent cause of all that exists") and its architectural features: base (plinth), shaft (courtyard), and threshold (doorway of ingress and egress).

Religious rituals also associated with the construction and use of domestic space are commonly practiced in traditional cultures, as Eleftherios Pavlides and Jana Hesser's study of the traditional Greek house shows. Their chapter also examines a variety of objects used in the house and the yard to protect against "the evil eye," and it explores two ritual focii of the house (rather familiar to the students of traditional dwellings): the entrance door, and the small shrine or *iconostassi* which connects the house with the village church. Unlike the island-house of modern individualist society, the traditional Greek house discussed here as a primary domain for family worship is linked with the religious life of the larger community. Sang Hae Lee gathers comparable conclusions with a more comprehensive scope in his analysis of the siting and organization of traditional Korean settlements. "The association of architectural or landscape elements with the sense of spiritual solidarity and oneness lead to a better understanding of the spatial organization of the village." The selection of a site for the house and the village is said here to be determined by four main factors of which *feng-shui*, or geomancy, is the most important. Of great interest in household siting and organization, for example, is the chain of factors determined by *feng-shui* that relates the location of the gate (decided according to the maximum receivability of the incoming *ch'i*, or "cosmic breath") to the direction of the principal room and the kitchen, and to the classification of house-types into two categories. Lee also suggests that the criteria which determine the general organization of Korean settlements can be looked upon as a culturally sensitive theory of physical order with inherent symbolic purposes.

The house as a miniature cosmos, and as a totality of natural environment, community and family, is at the heart of both Jerome Feldman's description of the great chief's house in the South Nias village of Bawomataluo and Gunawan Tjahjono's discussion of center and duality in Javanese dwellings. Nature, writes Tjahjono, "is a source of danger as well as a blessing. Duality dominates the day-night cycles, dry-wet seasons, mountain-sea dissimilarity, and sky-earth contrast." Thus the dwelling, which materializes the relation between nature and community in the Javanese environ-ment, "accommodates the actual and the ritual, the known and the unknown, the factual and the spiritual." The emphasis put on the notion of center and duality in the chapter may at first sight seem to contrast the Javanese dwelling with the Japanese house mentioned by Bognar. A more careful reading, however, shows the two chapters to be much closer in spirit than they first appear. Tjahjono's notion of duality is in many ways more comparable to the Chinese concept of *Yin* and *Yang*, with its indispensably fluctuating to-and-fro movement, than to Cartesian dualism, which often connotes categorical conflicts and contradictions (mind/matter; good/evil). For example, the idea of center points to both a centrifugal and a centripetal place in the Javanese world view. It is said to be manifested in diverse elements of the house, and "in the figure of the ruler who represents the state, which in turn symbolized the cosmos. The cosmic power was oriented to, stored in, and radiated from the ruler." Worth mentioning also is the related gender determination of space arrangements and architectural forms, such as that between *omah* and *pendopo* with the *peringgitan* structure as mediator. The distinction in usage between *pendopo* and *omah* is particularly significant when the shadow play is performed during a ritual feast. "On that occasion, the screen which spreads at the middle of the *peringgitan* divides the audience into two domains, the male in the *pendopo* and the female in the *omah*. Since the puppeteer sits facing the *omah*, only the females have the honor to watch the shadow while the males watch the puppets. Hence *peringgitan* links the two different worlds conceptually through a dramatic ritual performance."

In sharp contrast to these views are the following three chapters which show how traditions were formed under conditions of colonization or immigration. The section starts with John Webster's analysis of European cottage settlements in Tasmania which he claims can be examined as a "colonization process on a *tabula rasa*." Webster is suggesting that Tasmania offers ground to examine the development of dwelling and settlement forms "under almost laboratory conditions." He explores ways in which emigrants from the British isles adapted a cottage tradition they brought in their memories to a new land and a new climate. In a Glassie-like fashion, Webster demonstrates that by adapting a basic Georgian box formula for housing and a basic grid for settlement patterns, settlers unskilled in the building trades created a new traditional system flexible enough to allow for both variation and extension. Here we have to remember that this was aided by the fact the settlers shared a system of values, an image of the world, and a colonial administration that did not shy from providing leadership, setting rules and establishing a framework for development. The lessons from the Tasmanian *tabula rasa* experiment may be useful in our search for a new "attainable vernacular that takes into consideration the emerging needs of our contemporary society," Webster suggests.

Aharon Ron Fuchs and Michael Meyer-Brodnitz's contribution deals with a different type of colonized environment. They demonstrate how the revival of the stagnant economy of Palestine under the Ottoman administration in the mid-nineteenth century caused a new building form to emerge. This form was at once the result and the expression of socio-economic changes. Rarely can context be so directly related to the rise of a particular house-type as in the case of the central hall house in Palestine, which transformed the urban environment of the region, they claim. After a period of economic growth, a new class of rich landlords and city notables emerged in the region. The building activity of these new rich gave rise to a new house-type whose form was determined by trade with the Western world, and building materials that resulted from emerging industrial processes. The authors, however, are convinced that the central hall house-type, with its tiled roof and glazed windows, should not be viewed as a step toward Westernization, but toward modernization. This research about how the Arabs of Palestine, struggling under colonial Ottoman rule and European imperialism, introduced a new house form which in time became traditional may provide a lesson for contemporary Palestinians living on the West Bank under similar circumstances.

Interestingly enough, in the next chapter Norma Evenson argues that colonial rule greatly complicates the matter of determining a country's traditional building practices. Such has been the case in Indian metropolises such as Bombay, Madras and Calcutta. The complex ways British and Indian cultures have mixed over the years make it extremely difficult to render the usual value judgements about the origin of local traditions. Local adoption of imported ideologies and attempts at stylistic revival have further muddied the water. The contemporary Indian city began its life as a cultural hybrid. Founded as an instrument of colonial domination, it became a center for change and modernization. New building forms were invented in the dense new environment, and architectural styles imported by the British became associated with progress and were copied by the Indian elite. But Westernization was challenged by the very colonizers responsible for it. Some British residents, concerned for the inappropriateness of their imported styles, tried to integrate traditional Indian design into contemporary architecture, even though many of their attempts remained superficial. We can conclude from Evenson's chapter that the question of tradition may be irrelevant in the Indian city because the concept of a metropolis is alien to Indian culture. Cities embody a way of life that has become international, and those seeking tradition will not likely find it in the city. In a sense Evenson's views complement those of Tonna regarding the interpenetrations of imposed and local styles and conflict with those of Clement-Charpentier about the ruralization of cities.

When traditional lifestyles and ways of building come into contact
with forces of change and modernization, conflicts are bound to
exist. In Seteney Shami's chapter, these forces were present in the
late nineteenth century in Jordan when changes in Ottoman tax and
land-registration law forced a semi-nomadic people to settle in one
place. The example of the Jordanian village of Umm Qeis focuses
on the period 1880-1930, a time when state intervention caused a
semi-nomadic people to develop a more permanent building style.
As part of an attempt to record a settlement slated for demolition
after the Jordanian government decided to excavate an important
Greco-Roman building site, Shami's work shows how socio-
economic forces were as important as environmental ones in
shaping a traditional community. In particular, she focuses on the
impact of Ottoman laws that introduced a new tax and land-
registration system. Before the laws were implemented, the lands
around Umm Qeis were farmed seasonally and sporadically. But
afterwards a new settlement pattern emerged, as pastoralists were
forced to create villages and group themselves into teams to farm
large areas. This also brought a division into social classes and a
refinement of building types. The result was that the landowning
class in Umm Qeis developed a particular style of inhabiting large,
secure dwelling compounds. It is impor-tant to note that just as a
record of inter-family relationships can be seen in the relation of
buildings to one another, the changing intra-family dynamics can
equally be read in the disposition of temporary mud walls used to
divide up the interior of each compound. Shami's contribution
clarifies the connection between material remains and social life in
a premodern era and shows how the study of the layout of a
settlement can elucidate the socio-economic forces behind its
development.

In another vein, Roxana Waterson's chapter reviews how the
forces of change and material progress have had a variety of
effects, not all detrimental, on traditional building styles in
Indonesia. She focuses on three tribal groups, the Toraja of South
Sulawesi, the Minangkabau of West Sumatra and the Toba Batak
of North Sumatra. Here the phenomenon of internal migration, in
particular, is examined to see how it has allowed these groups to
re-evaluate their building traditions. Migration in search of

worldly experience and better job opportunities has long occurred in many parts of the world. In Indonesia it recently has allowed various tribal groups to regroup in the city. The attendant awareness of each group's cultural heritage brings about a reaffirmation of ethnic identity. Together with the new wealth generated in these far-off cities, this has led to a sort of traditional building boom back on tribal homelands. In Indonesia this phenomenon seems to be aided by the special significance accorded the clan origin-house; rebuilding these origin-houses is a way for families to gain prestige. In all three of Waterson's cases the resurgence of traditional building has had little to do with the functional qualities of the building tradition, but with its expression of tribal values.

This idea of what tribal immigrants would build in their home villages after their exposure to city life is also present in the last contribution, that of Anita Larsson. In Botswana, as in many developing countries, Larsson brings our attention to the fact that traditional ways of building are being abandoned on account of government action and changes in the availability of building materials. These changes seem not to have always been for the better, since they have often caused poor people to do with less. Larsson remarks that changes in the style of Tswana housing, which began during colonial times, continued after independence, as the national administration sought to provide government-subsidized low-income housing. She notes that this new housing did not reconcile people's desires for modern living with traditional forms. In comparing traditional and modern housing, she notes that while traditional houses made great use of outdoor spaces, especially for women's domestic activities, they lacked certain amenities necessary for modern living. Modern housing, on the other hand, requires capital expenditure, and this meant that the responsibility for providing housing, traditionally a women's role, was transferred to men. This profound shift seems to have caused the form of housing and the cultural system in which it is valued to be more reflective of men's concerns, and it has ultimately contributed to the further domestication of women. Larsson, like many contributors to this book, remarks that modernization that is insensitive to traditional roles and responsibilities may disrupt social patterns. This in turn may change the form and meaning of housing and may dictate for us new models for studying traditional dwellings and settlements.

As people, it is said, we make our environments and then they make us. As academics, we believe there is a parallel: we make our disciplines, and these in turn determine our views. It is our hope that this book will allow us to temporarily set aside our specialized jargons, and engage in a cross-cultural and interdisciplinary review that will enrich our knowledge and redirect our vision.

REFERENCE NOTES

1. Paul Oliver, *Dwellings: The House Across the World* (Austin: University of Texas Press, 1987), p. 7.
2. For more on the general question of tradition, refer to Edward Shils, *Tradition* (Chicago: University of Chicago Press, 1981).
3. Walter Goldschmidt, "Foward," in Labelle Prussin, *Architecture in Northern Ghana* (Berkeley: University of California Press, 1969).
4. This classification is very similar to R.W. Brunskill's definition of vernacular building in his *Traditional Buildings of Britain: An Introduction to Vernacular Architecture* (London: Victor Gollancz Ltd., 1981), pp. 2,4.
5. Lewis H. Morgan, *Houses and Houselife of the American Aborigines* (Chicago: University of Chicago Press, 1965 -- original 1881) and Edward Morse, *Japanese Homes and Their Surroundings* (New York: Dover 1961 -- original 1896).
6. Bernard Rudofsky, *Architecture without Architects* (New York: Museum of Modern Art, 1964); Amos Rapoport, *House, Form and Culture* (Englewood Cliffs, NJ: Prentice-Hall, 1969); Paul Oliver, *Shelter and Society* (New York: F. Praeger, 1969) and *Dwellings: The House Cross the World*, and Erico Guidoni, *Primitive Architecture*, R.E. Wolf, trans. (New York: H. Abrams, 1978). At the time this book went to press another relevant volume, *Housing, Culture and Design*, edited by Setha Low and Erve Chambers, was released by the University of Pennsylvania Press.
7. Unfortunately, the Americanists are visibly absent from this volume. The initial announcement of the Symposium which brought in 400 abstracts attracted only twenty submissions relating to American vernacular subjects, none of which could be included in this book.
8. Dell Upton, "The Power of Things: Recent Studies in American Vernacular Architecture," *American Quarterly* Vol. 35 no. 3 (1983), pp. 262-279.
9. *Ibid.*
10. Fumihiko Maki, as quoted in Bognar's chapter.
11. Nyozekan Hasegawa, as quoted in Bognar's chapter.

TRADITIONAL:
WHAT DOES IT MEAN?

YI-FU TUAN

"Tradition" or "traditional" is a common word and is frequently used in both sociological and architectural literature. As a result, its meaning has become rather vague.[1] Is it the equivalent of "folk" or "premodern"? Does it signify a work produced by a specialist who uses materials from no-matter-where so long as they serve the purpose of realizing a preconceived dream or design? Can the word "traditional" ever be a neutral term? When we say of a building that it is traditional, do we intend approval or, on the contrary, criticism? Why is it that the word "traditional" can evoke, on the one hand, a feeling of the real and the authentic and hence some quality to be desired, but, on the other hand, a sense of limitation -- of a deficiency in boldness and originality? These are large and difficult questions. I believe, however, that we can acquire new insight and greater clarity as to their true import if we couple the idea of tradition with the idea of constraint-vs-choice. Is choice bad because it has the flavor of arbitrariness, or is it good because it implies creativity?

Let us begin with tradition's literal meaning, namely, "that which has been handed down". Everything that we see in the present landscape has had a past, however brief, and is in that literal sense traditional. Only a small proportion of what we see and have today will be passed on to the future -- and the more distant the future the smaller that proportion will be. We wish to pass on what we value, and one way to assign value to something is to say that it is traditional, sanctioned by history, by a Golden Age, by the immemorial ways of one's ancestors or by nature itself. Although these are different reasons, they share the impress of objectivity. Objectivity gives prestige to the traditional. We do not see the traditional as arbitrary, the whimsy of an individual human creator.

The traditional that is opposed to the arbitrary seems to us desirable or good. But it is also opposed to -- at least, not fully compatible with -- the idea of creativity. The traditional can, of course, accommodate small changes, but not radical innovation. This is the prerogative of the gods or of culture heroes. Only they can be truly creative without seeming capricious. Choice is also at odds with the traditional. Like creativity, choice is an ideal of modern times made possible by material plenty; it is an ideal of freedom rather than of constraint or restraint, an ideal of will rather than objectivity.

Choice is limited in nonliterate and folk societies. People have to make do with whatever is at hand. The form and arrangement of dwellings, for example, are constrained by the availability of local materials, the nature of the local climate and the socioeconomic facts of life. To a modern observer, the material world thus created can have enormous appeal because everything in it has a purpose, and because its aesthetic qualities emerge unobtrusively out of the serious business of living. Folk artifacts are often able to project an image of elemental power or stark elegance that modern aestheticians value. By appearing to address life's irreducible essentials, they exude an air of import. In Europe's unmodernized countryside, a carpenter's bench or a farmer's plow, a barn or a cottage are some of the commonplace objects that have a deeply human as well as aesthetic appeal. The American poet Theodore Roethke (1908-63) said that his favorite author is anonymous.[2] Well, peasant artifacts and dwellings have anonymous "authors". By virtue of this anonymity, they can seem as necessary as the meadows and the hills.

Western experts may judge certain African villages and Chinese rice terraces to be among the most beautiful of human works.

Whoever built them must have been very creative. But the makers of these forms do not necessarily see themselves thus. Creativity, as that term is understood in the modern West, suggests prideful assertiveness -- a quality not highly valued in traditional culture. To traditional African or Chinese farmers, the places they live in have always existed more or less in their present form, and are just about as natural as the materials from which they are made. If there is creativity, it lies not in the dwellings of humble folk but in those of their more powerful chiefs, and in communal houses, although even the monumental and decorative elements in them are grounded in religious symbolism and are intimately tied to the timeless cycles of life and death. In advanced traditional societies, great lords -- unlike mere tribal chiefs -- enjoy enormous power. The resources at their command give them real freedom to choose -- to transcend the local condition. They can build a whole new geometric city in disregard of the lay of the land in a mere year or two -- almost "overnight" on the historical time scale. And of course they do not depend on local materials. Potentates such as Queen Hatshepsut, King Solomon, and China's First Emperor Ch'in Shih Huang-ti have sought to bring to their capitals exotic plants and animals from the most distant parts of their known world. A Chinese poet described the fabulous garden of the First Emperor as containing

Unicorns from Chiu Chen,
Horses from Ferghana.
Rhinoceros from Huang Chih
Birds from T'iao Chih.[3]

What the First Emperor created was unnatural. The plants and animals in his garden did not belong there. They were uprooted from their native habitats, transported over great distances, and then willfully juxtaposed. Chinese moralists, outstandingly Mencius, have been critical of such extravagances.[4] They seem to say that great architectural projects not only impose hardship on ordinary people but are to be condemned for going beyond the limit natural to mortals.

Power manifests itself convincingly by transcending the local. When potentates use power this way, they are fully conscious of having created something that stands out and that does not blend with local life. As an example, I have drawn your attention to the microcosmic garden. Power can, however, also be used to do the opposite -- to *spread* rather than to garner. Here are a few illustrations of what I mean. A group of people, let us say, has created a form of life suited to their condition; they then seek to impose it -- either by force or with the help of prestige -- on other parts of the world. An example from China would be the diffusion of the rectangular grid-pattern city, invented in the North, to the rest of the empire. In the West, an outstanding example from classical antiquity is the architecture of cities throughout the Roman Empire. As Kenneth Clark and other scholars have observed, wherever you go in what was once the Roman Empire, you are likely to encounter the same insignia of Roman power.[5] The Romans built the same type of forum, coliseum and public bath whenever they sought to establish a major city, just as under the American imperium, Holiday Inns and shopping malls are ubiquitous. There was little or no desire on the part of the Roman conquerors to heed the genius of place, to incorporate local materials and traditions in their buildings. And even if in their formal projects Roman architects did incorporate local materials and styles, they probably did so for reasons of policy or for self-conscious aesthetic reasons rather than because they had to make do with what was immediately at hand. An analogy with the International Style of architecture in our time is irresistible. Skyscrapers command attention in almost all the major metropolises of the world -- New York, San Francisco, Hong Kong and soon (perhaps) Beijing. If we think of the International Style as quintessentially untraditional, then so was at one time the geometric city of China beyond its place of origin, and so was the Roman city of Britain.

At this point, I anticipate objections. Critics will object to my idea that microcosmic gardens, Chinese geometric cities, and skyscrapers are all in the same sense modern -- that is, they all exemplify the exercise of choice, the deliberative use of creative power. They will say that the microcosmic garden and the geometric city are timeless, inspired not by any personal desire to be original and creative, but rather by bowing to the paradigmatic pattern inscribed in the sky. Religion and ritual have played a necessary part in them that is not at all the case in the building of skyscrapers. I defer to the criticism and confess that I have exaggerated to make a point. Nevertheless, I would note that the founders of the modern style were inspired by a vision of human brotherhood that has its roots -- if traced back far enough -- in religion, that their desire for stark honesty and simplicity was moral as well as aesthetic, that what they urged on others did not seem to them willful or arbitrary, for the modern functional style emerged in part out of a desire to combat the eclecticism and self-indulgence of bourgeois architectural taste in the late Victorian period.[6]

Power makes it unnecessary to defer to the constraints of locality. In the past, only a few people had such power. Now, in a prosperous country, almost everyone has. Although I live in a small town called Madison, the food I eat comes from all parts of the world. On State Street, which is only a few blocks long, are American, Chinese, Greek, Indian and Hungarian restaurants. My home is a hodge-podge of styles, decorated with things from just about everywhere. I may not, like China's First Emperor, have unicorns in my garden, but the world I have created through my buying power is almost as packed with odd, incompatible things. Potentates of the past, such as Louis XIV, appear to have suffered from periodic attacks of surfeit and boredom, relieved by ever greater extravagances and faster tempos of changes -- putting in a forest one year, removing it the next.[7] Choice was at one time the burden of kings. Their dilemma lay in having to choose among the dozen or so concubines and mistresses, all more or less beautiful. As modern consumer, my dilemma consists in having to pick one brand of toothpaste among half a dozen, all more or less desirable and good for my dental health.

There is, however, an important difference. Potentates of the past, no matter how free and wayward they were in behavior, could always fall back on the eternal verities which they honored if only in transgression. I, for my part, have to live in a world without such verities, guided in my choice of home and possession by the unanchored shifting values of society, propagated -- more often than not -- in short frenetic disjointed bits, through the advertising media. By the eternal verities, I mean primarily religion, its world-view and rituals. But I also have in mind certain social assumptions and practices, such as kinship obligations and the hierarchical ordering of men and women that are taken completely for granted and provide a firm anchor for the exercizing of choice in the less essential areas of life. When Teresa of Avila visited the home of the Duchess of Alba, she was shocked by the clutter and heterogeneity of the duchess' possessions, all thrown together in her gallery without apparent rhyme or reason.[8] The gallery, however, was only a small part of the duchess' life. In furnishing it, she exercised her freedom. Despite the heterodoxy of her gallery, her general mode of living could still be deemed traditional because much of it was still dictated by necessity. Now, in a prosperous modern society, the whole arena of life, and not just as it were the playroom, seems open to choice. I can more or less choose where to live, what style of home to have and how to furnish it from cellar to attic. Even social practices and moral behavior are no longer firm, but are subject to negotiation, defined by context. Even religion has become a question of personal preference and convenience. "Attend a church of your choice," is a common exhortation by the liberal-minded pastors of our time.

An immediate consequence of having the means to make choices is a sense of liberation. At last, we can more or less do what we like. Choice, once the prerogative of kings, is now available to everyone with a major credit card. But in the long run a consequence of unlimited choice is boredom, induced by the feeling that nothing really matters if all that matters is personal taste. People who have known affluence and who have found it curiously unfulfilling after the first flush may yearn for a past that is not cornucopian Eden but rather some iron age of constraint. The return to something simpler, more fundamental, more traditional is a constant temptation.

Constraint has a variety of meanings. It could mean hardship in wrestling a livelihood from the land. People in the back-to-land movements of our time see physical hardship itself as a form of salvation. Constraint could mean a return to unquestioned customs and moral codes. This is the simple-minded path taken by fundamentalists. At a deeply serious level, constraint implies waiting. To yield the control of one's time to another is perhaps the hardest part of bondage, for the passage of time is the passage of life. Louis XIV was shocked into saying, "J'ai failli attendre" (I almost had to wait). Now, every consumer is a potentate, shocked by having to wait for what he wants. Yet without waiting there is no value. Finally and importantly, the appeal of constraint might have a profound psychological source, namely, the experience that often the best things in life come to us unexpectedly, beyond our conscious control. Think of the difference between the ecstasy of falling in love and the mere pleasure of having to pick among a set of more or less desirable dates, or of an idea that strikes us out of the blue to one that we have artfully built. The one sweeps us off our feet and gives us an overwhelming sense of import. The other is seldom more than pleasant.

I have associated tradition with constraint. I have also said that its literal meaning is "that which has been handed down." Out of all the things that have been handed down to us and that we now possess, what do we wish to pass on? This is a truly challenging question. In a large, dynamic, and pluralistic society such as ours, there can be no clear answer. Perhaps what we must seek to retain are not so much particular artifacts and buildings (though we should try to do so in exceptional instances), but rather the skill to reproduce them. If we retain the skill, then no human work is irrevocably lost.

REFERENCE NOTES

1. Edward Shils, *Tradition* (Chicago: University of Chicago Press, 1981).
2. David Wagoner, ed., *Straw for the Fire: From the Notebooks of Theodore Roethke 1943-1963* (Garden City, NY: Doubleday & Co., 1972), p. 251.
3. E.R. Hughes, *Two Chinese Poets: Vignettes of Han Life and Thought* (Princeton, NJ: Princeton University Press, 1960), p. 27.
4. Mencius, *The Four Books*, James Legge, trans. (New York: Paragon Book Reprint Corp., 1966), pp. 674-75.

5. Kenneth Clark, *Civilization: A Personal View* (New York: Harper & Row, 1970), p. 3.

6. Anthony Heilbut, *Exiled in Paradise: German Refugee Artists and Intellectuals in America from the 1930s to the Present* (New York: Viking Press, 1983), p. 16.

7. Lucy Norton, *Saint-Simon at Versailles* (London, Hamish Hamilton, 1958), p. 265.

8. See Victoria Sackville-West, *The Eagle and the Dove* (London: Michael Joseph, 1943).

READING TRADITION

JEAN-PAUL BOURDIER

We are living in a period variously called the decline of the new, the age of mass media; an age of postindividual, postindustrial, poststructuralist and postmodern society. These labels can be quite deceptive, for the absolute new has never really existed, "mass" no longer equates with "people," and "post" in contemporary theory does not merely mean "after," but also implies "with" and "before."

The growing interest in traditional architecture among architects may be viewed as a desire to seek better ways for understanding their heritage, hence for transmitting and re-creating without having to accept a simplistic return to earlier architectural traditions or abide by a mere rejection of cultural pasts. Generally speaking, in the United States and in Europe there is a need to subject modernization and its exclusive emphasis on optimized technology to critical scrutiny, while in Third World countries there is an imperative to solve the paradox of how to benefit from modernization while returning to the wisdom of non market-dependent values. These are processes that are different because they are context-specific, but they are also tightly related to each other.

AN INTERDISCIPLINE

In recent years the study of traditional and vernacular dwellings and settlements has expanded beyond the limits of antiquarian and nostalgic interest into a discipline of its own (albeit a discipline always-in-the-making) and a critical practice concerned among other things with reaffirming regional/cultural identities and breaking the monotony, if not the oppression, of standardization. Its nature has also allowed it to extend beyond the limits of any single field to become a focus for research that cuts across the boundaries of a great number of disciplines, involving scholars in the arts, the humanities and the social sciences. A feature of postmodernism itself, this cutting across established boundaries remains plural; it manifests itself differently through a number of key notions today, including those of interarts, interculturalism, and interdisciplinism. The erosion of the old divide between high culture and popular culture has made it increasingly difficult to draw any clear-cut line of separation. It is therefore also of importance that in studying traditional dwellings, emphasis be given precisely to the interpenetration of classic and folk traditions, to the interdependency of towns and the countryside in the morphology of settlements, and to the continuity from rural to urban areas in house-types and groupings. These three approaches are found in this book in the chapters by Jo Tonna, Spiro Kostof and Sophie Clement-Charpentier, respectively.

On interdisciplinary work, Roland Barthes made an observation that may well apply to the study of traditional dwelling. He wrote: "*Interdisciplinary* studies, of which we hear so much, do not merely confront already constituted disciplines (none of which, as a matter of fact, consents to *leave off*). In order to do interdisciplinary work, it is not enough to take a 'subject' (a theme) and to arrange two or three sciences around it. Interdisciplinary study consists in creating a new object, which belongs to no one."[1] Research on dwelling traditions belongs, therefore, no more to architecture than to anthropology, archeology, geography or art and architecture history -- to name just a few. To avoid reiterating the values that legitimize each of the disciplines involved, perpetuating thereby the conventions carried within their established boundaries, the work would have to go beyond the mere assembling of these different fields. This is where the challenge is issued. By asking potentially far-reaching questions about professional divisions and about the security and hierarchy they imply, attempts at understanding the traditional vernacular reality and eventually at revitalizing the roots of contemporary design practice will necessarily re-examine some basics that may now be taken for granted. I propose to contribute here to two questions that always need to be raised, the questions of tradition and representation.

TRADITION AND POSTMODERNITY

Much has been and continues to be said on the question of tradition, as many of the contributions to this volume evidence. Some of these contributions tackle the problem of defining the idea, exploring at length its denotations as well as positive and negative connotations, while others investigate its meanings in relation to specific built environments. But the issue, as some of us see it, is not so much to accumulate attributes of traditionality to come up with *a* better definition, or even to circumscribe the field. Nor is it to simply invalidate the notion because of the many specific negative connotations often implied in its use. The issue is more to question certain fundamental assumptions so as to open up the concept of tradition from a number of points of departure. Definitions are made in order to be remade and to invite further modifications of their limits.

Tradition is a term that has often been used in opposition to modernity. As such, it has been situated within a system of binary oppositions (nature/culture; beliefs/science; mythic/historic; low style/high style; change/stagnancy) whose use even as an analytic tool is often reductive. In this period of the decline of the new it is certainly not new to say that modernization can no longer prove to be liberative *in se*. Much has been written on the failure of the modern architectural project and its participation in the principle of unlimited self-realization; much also on its participation in the idea of progress achieved with universal rationality and of emancipation at the scale of humanity, of which the colonial enterprise was a comprehensive manifestation. Never has the rejection of the belief in the need to break with tradition in order to install an entirely new way of living and thinking been so widely and diversely voiced. As the philosopher Jurgen Habermas puts it, "modernism is dominant but dead."[2] What can be read in such a statement is that modernism is still considered to be expanding, but it is no longer creative. We can't negate modernism, for it infects our environment. Yet we can't simply work against it either, because the modernist project has made us aware of the limits of merely "working against."

To reflect on the postmodern condition is to rethink the relation between the traditional and the modern. Our conception of modernity creates its own self-enclosed canons of traditionality. Tradition identified as the past is a modernist idea. The same holds true for the concept of vernacular when it is equated with low technology. In a context where the relation between traditional and modern has lost a fixed temporal reference, tradition perceived as a settled body of knowledge that can be objectively transferred, uncovered, mastered and laid claim to is at best reactive and at worst mortuary. Dead and circular answers feed endlessly on dead and circular interrogations. To say this, however, is not to say that one can simply deny or surpass the modernist values that condition existence today. One often partakes in perpetuating them even while dismantling them, for the question, "where does modernity begin and where does it end?" necessarily remains unanswerable. And it is this very unanswerable quality that constitutes the condition of postmodernity.

If the modernist concept of tradition remains problematic to all studies of traditional dwelling, it is all the more so to those carried out by Westerners like myself whose research focuses on non-Western architectural traditions (although I am no less fond of those existing in the West). "Nostalgic," "antiquarian," and "romantic" are adjectives that may rightfully be applied to the many works we produce, anthropological or architectural, that offer in their interpretations not a mode of transmitting a knowledge but, supposedly, the knowledge itself. Instead of trying to bypass, deny or censor the problems raised, we would have to work with them -- critically. The question, as I started out saying with regard to the prefix "post" that accompanies the word modern, is not that of excluding or legitimizing what comes "before," but that of working with difficulties and uncertainties within a continuum of past, present and future.

In discussing tradition and postmodernity, I am not referring to the "pure technique, pure scenography" postmodernism promoted by Charles Jencks, as Frampton has put it;[3] nor to the one termed "neoconservative" by Hal Foster, which resorts to pastiche in the name of style and history -- in other words which is marked by an eclectic historicism that reduces historical periods to ruling-class styles and relates to history mainly as "a store of styles and symbols to plunder."[4] Rather, I find more creative the postmodern condition as analyzed by Jean-Francois Lyotard, who wrote: "A work can only become modern when it is first postmodern. Postmodernism thus understood is not modernism at its ending, but at its nascent stage, and this stage is constant."[5] It is interesting to relate this statement to one by Yi-Fu Tuan, who writes in this book: "Everything that we see in the present landscape has had a past, however brief, and is in that literal sense traditional." Although very different, these two statements do meet on a certain level, since they both defy the modern tendency to view relations in time and space in term of simple successions or linear chronology. Postmodernism as bearer of *old* truths that have emerged in the last two decades in particular is a way of seeing into the already-existing cracks in the modern project. It is, again, a way of rethinking the relation between the traditional and the modern.

TRADITIONAL AND VERNACULAR: DWELLING AS BEING ON EARTH

If the study of traditional dwelling is an important one, it is not only because the world's population by and large is accommodated in traditional dwellings, but also because it is necessary to rethink the dwelling-as-living reality in housing contexts where the problem of alienation still prevails. The juxtaposition of the terms traditional and dwelling can be criticized for carrying a normative attitude specifying what architecture is and what it is not. However, one can also argue that if architecture mostly stands for eminent edifices and monuments that are urban and aesthetically imposing, it also qualifies the practice of a profession and the product of a professional -- the architect. "Architecture without architects," "indigenous architecture" or "vernacular architecture" are possibilities, but they are in no way free of specific connotations. Furthermore, not every building is a dwelling place. Dwelling radically means "being on the earth." This is the well-known definition Heidegger brought back to us from Old English and High German: "The way in which you are and I am, the manner in which we humans *are* on the earth is *Buan*, dwelling . . . . Building as dwelling, that is, as being on the earth, . . . remains for man's everyday's experience that which is from the outset 'habitual.'"[6] Dwelling therefore needs not be reduced to an activity that one performs alongside others, or to "having a roof over our head and a certain number of square meters at our disposal," as Norberg-Schulz has written.[7] The terms traditional and vernacular meet where vernacular goes back to its Latin meaning as "things that are homemade, homespun, home-grown, not destined for the marketplace, but are for home use only."[8] "The relationship of traditional man with the world," wrote a traditionalist in African matters, "was a living relationship of *participation*, not of pure utilization."[9] John Turner made the now classic distinction between housing as the provision of a commodity and housing as an activity,[10] while Ivan Illich went on to rename this activity *dwelling*, tracing it back to such notions as "be," "exist" and "live" -- that is "to be alive." In the vernacular context dwelling coincides with living. "To dwell means to live in the traces that past living has left."[11]

TRANSMISSION: THE QUESTION OF REPRESENTATION

The African scholar Cheikh A. Hampate Ba defines oral tradition as "the bond between man and the spoken word." He calls it "the living tradition."[12] If one takes this definition as a further point of departure for rethinking the relation between the traditional and the modern, then tradition, generally speaking, would be the bond between men, women and the material they choose to work with in transmitting a knowledge or world view -- be this material speech, earth, writing, photography or drawing.

In the definition advanced above, several questions are implied. One relates directly to the context from which it is excerpted and in which Hampate Ba carries on the now familiar argument: "Nothing proves *a priori* that writing gives a more faithful account of a reality than oral evidence handed down from generation to generation . . . . What is involved . . . is the actual value of the man who is giving the evidence, the value of the chain of transmission he is part of, the trustworthiness of the individual and collective memory." The cultural bias that values the written word over the spoken word speaks for a specific ideology of control, one in which "the signature becomes the sole recognized commitment, while the deep sacred bond that used to unite man and word disappears, to be replaced by conventional university degrees."[13] This bias has many faces. On the one hand the written word takes on the weight of fact, accounting for the convenient classification of societies into those with history and those without; on the other hand there is a marked general tendency among scholars to neglect or to underrate all other representational structures. The written word is unproblematically valued as the most reliable source of information as well as the most capable of describing and analyzing accumulated data. The question of whether one should place more trust in one representational structure than in another is obviously not where the problem lies. Each structure generates its own sets of problems that need to be dealt with; moreover, as Hampate Ba points out, "written or oral evidence is in the end only human evidence and it is worth what the man is worth."[14]

What is emphasized in this living tradition is the mode of handing down or passing on what we value. As Bruno Queysanne has relevantly pointed out, handing down is also handing over, and tradition is thus less an act of conservation than of transmission.[15] In the worthiness of the person who is carrying on the task of transmitting, Hampate Ba also sees "the value of the chain of transmission" that this person is part of. This "bond between man and the spoken word" thus implies more than one link: it implies the bonds that tie one person to another, one generation to another and one people to another; the bond that ties the subject to his or her making; and the bond that ties one making or one mode of transmission to another.

It is in the context of handing over, or of the value of the chain of transmission a person is part of (whether this person is a member of the society in question or an outsider), that representation occupies a central role. There has been, with the works of poststructuralist critics, an important process for exposing the limits of representation, which render more and more untenable claims of objectivity of observation, transparency of description or immediacy of experience. To say that the simplest cultural accounts are intentional fabrications, and that interpreters constantly construct themselves and their products through the subjects they study, is to repeat what may already sound evident. But to incorporate and materialize this in the creative process of understanding and interpreting -- the living tradition -- is to open a ground that offers no ready-made solutions or methodologies.

THE GRAPHIC IMAGE

Three means of representation prevail for the time being in the study of traditional dwellings. These are verbal language, the photographic image and the graphic image. A number of critical examinations have been and will continue to be made of the uses of the first two in the areas of writing, cinema and photography. But the last is perhaps the least debated yet the most relevant to my own work and to architectural depiction in general. What I constantly have to face and explore is precisely the language of drawing, or drawing as a tool for thinking and representing. One could mention here, for example, the tendency in many cultural research works to resort to drawing as a mere instrument of communication, and an inadequate one at that. This often results in schematic drawings that are neither fully conceptual nor

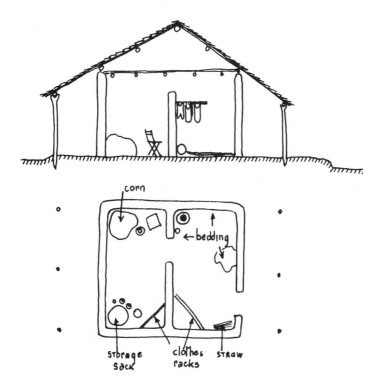

F I G U R E 1. Neither conceptual nor representational, drawing as mere instrument of information.

representational (FIG. 1). Endless efforts are often spent in bringing out the subtleties of verbal language, but little attention is given to the way a line, the tone of a line, a surface rendering, the choice of a view angle, or the choice of type and mode of drawing can structure our experience (FIGS. 2, 3). Shape, volume, light, texture, shade, depth, movement (FIGS. 4, 5), kinaesthetic experience of space: a drawing is not simply visual or mental. If a schematic drawing appears merely instrumental, and neither conceptual nor representational, it is in most cases because it has reduced the dwelling experience to a simplistic sketch or outline. In other words, it has represented the experience poorly without fully realizing the function of the conceptual drawing. This function is not the neutral printing out of a previous concept, but an interactive process that involves eye, mind, heart and hand. A drawing that takes a reality as a given and is effected for information's sake is bound to remain fixed instead of constituting a site for reading. It does not allow itself to grow on the reader, nor does it allow him or her to follow and retrace its itineraries. Conceptual and representational drawings -- diagrams and elaborate line and surface drawings -- may both be used in a single case to interpret the dwelling reality. They expand one another but their functions are not interchangeable.

To think with drawings is not a question of drawing well, or an aesthetic-formalistic concern, although such a skill is certainly helpful to produce sensitive drawings. It is rather to explore the

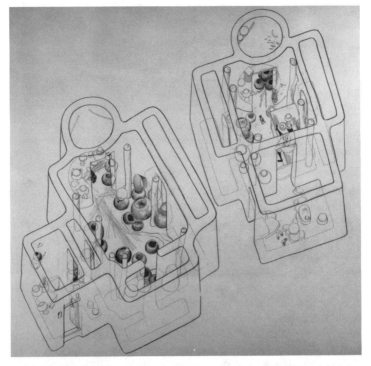

F I G U R E S 2, 3. Dogon dwelling, Mali (left); Joola dwelling, Senegal (right). Lines do speak a language. Different modes of drawing structure the viewer's experience differently.

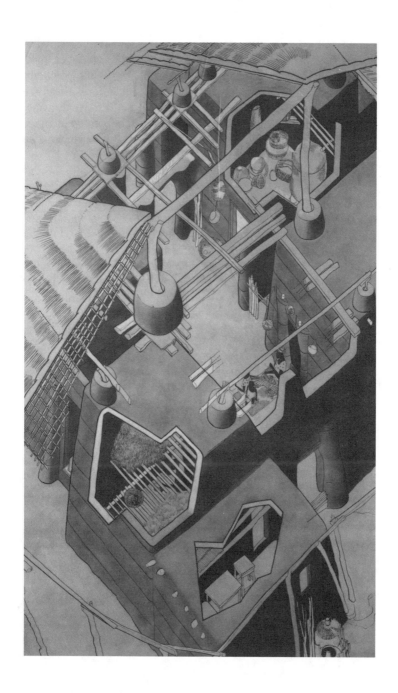

limits and potentials of drawing as a structure in itself. The representation of three-dimensional space in a two-dimensional drawing is commonly done with plans, elevations, sections, perspectives and axonometrics. There is therefore already a primary range of possibilities within representational drawing. Here I would like to give just a few examples of what is involved in the choice of making a perspective as compared to drawing an axonometric.

The position of the drawer is one of centrality in the perspective, for it can easily be located through the eye level and vanishing points (FIG. 6). What a perspective presents is a temporary and fragmented spatial experience from a static point of view. In other words, what the drawer offers is what the reader gets. It is a one-way reading in which only one or a maximum of two spaces can be viewed; showing more spaces behind through the device of transparent walls will certainly clutter the drawing. Furthermore, the perspective organizes knowledge in function of what is immediately visible. The involvement it requires from the reader is passive, since it presents reality in a form he or she is already accustomed to.

FIGURES 4, 5.
Joola dwelling (left) and Mandinka dwelling, Senegal (right). Representational drawings can go beyond realistic and aesthetic concerns. They can constitute a complex layered site for reading, and their function is not interchangeable with that of the conceptual diagram.

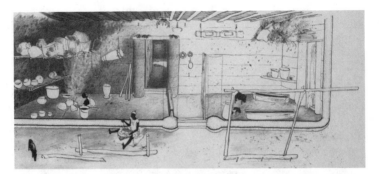

F I G U R E 6. Joola dwelling, Senegal. The cutaway perspective drawing usually offers spatial experience from a static point of view.

The axonometric (or bird's-eye view), more specifically the cutaway axonometric (FIG. 7), requires much more initiative on the part of the drawer as well as the reader. It gives an overall aerial perspective of the dwelling while playing with the norms of realist representation. To open a parenthesis here, what immediately comes to mind regarding the bird's-eye overview is the familiar military spirit, with its aerial photography and its precise mapping of habitats and surrounding terrain. The desire to perceive a phenomenon in its entirety is certainly not unrelated to the tendency to equate vision with control, knowledge and power. Apprehending a non-professionally built environment with the eye of a professional architect or anthropologist -- as plan, section, elevation and perspective, or as decipherment, dissection, classification and kinship-mapping -- is to partake in such a desire. Surely enough, I find myself pleading guilty at almost every step on the path, because I have a particular affection for maps -- although only the very old ones that bear the traces of previous voyages or the very elaborate ones that inscribe the physical quality of the terrain. To say this, however, is not to say that all birds' eye-view representation bears the same degree of totalizing control and omniscience. There are ways of resisting the all-governing and maximal overseeing military spirit as well as the modern consumer's desire for fast appropriation and immediate gratification. And there are differences to make between aerial

FIGURE 7. Joola dwelling, Senegal. The cutaway axonometric solicits the drawer's creative ability. It invites the viewers to read the reality of a house by reconstituting a personal visual path through the spaces and objects drawn.

graphic document. These differences lie precisely in the how and why of the chain of transmission, in the readings that result from the production and circulation of the photographed or drawn materials. Here I come back to the use of perspective and axonometric views.

The cutaway axonometric has the potential to acknowledge its status as representation and to play with the norms of realist representation in several ways. The position of the drawer is imaginary and constructed. His or her intervention is constantly acknowledged. This occurs first through the fact that the axonometric does not built itself on the realistic standard of the perspective with its vanishing points, and hence all objects are reproduced at the same scale and may be said to be slightly distorted -- although this may not be immediately evident to the untrained eye. Second, the cutting away of a space is a deliberate decision of the drawer and hence the process of assembling a cutaway axonometric is creatively demanding. In addition to demanding drafting and recording skills such as time-consuming measurements for precise scale, it actively solicits the initiative of the drawer. Where should one cut into a space and why would one open up the wall(s) or roof(s) of a house? Furthermore, although the cutaway axonometric offers an above-ground view, it allows the reader to reconstitute an on-the-ground experience by putting to use such devices as simultaneous views of spaces through transparent walls. The drawing thereby suggests an understanding of how the spaces interact, while inviting the reader to imagine the experience of walking through several spaces with their offered and hidden views. The active involvement of the reader is provoked not only by the unusual angle of view but also by the range of reading possibilities and itineraries suggested. The reader is not presented with one point of departure, and must choose and make up a personal reading path. Needless to say, although I often find the cutaway axonometric more creative and challenging than the perspective, there is no tool of representation that cannot be used differently, and one can easily imagine the potential of a series of perspectives that reconstitute an array of fragments of reality, while leaving the work of assemblage to the reader (FIG. 8).

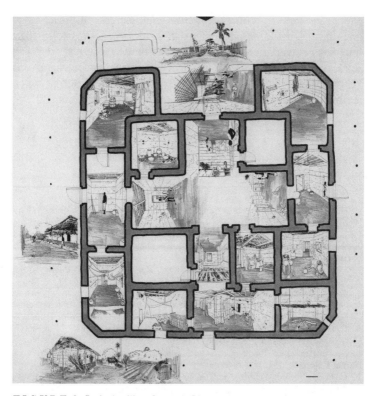

F I G U R E 8. Joola dwelling, Senegal. Plan-perspective. An example of the many possible alternatives that also involve the creative participation of the viewer.

For tradition to remain a creative concept it is important, as quoted earlier from Hampate Ba, that "the deep sacred bond that used to unite man and word" does not disappear. In the context of the language of drawing, this statement could mean that whenever a drawer sets out to draw a dwelling, especially when the dwelling is from a different culture, the drawer should not only keep alive those things that informed the drawing (what he or she sees -- including local constraints, cultural specificities and professional obligations), but also what has inspired the drawing (how he or she sees and reconstructs the experience, and materializes its *punctum* -- the mutual designation between drawer and dwelling in this intersubjective and intercultural encounter). Drawing not as mere expression but as production enables the functions of preservation and change, qualities inherent to all work of transmission. "The time has come to gather the old into the new," remarked Aldo van Eyck sometime ago. "We can meet 'ourselves' everywhere -- in all places and ages -- doing the same things in different ways, feeling the same differently, reacting differently to the same."[15]

REFERENCE NOTES

1. Roland Barthes, *The Rustle of Language*, R. Howard, trans. (New York: Hill and Wang, 1986), p. 72; Hal Foster, ed., *The Anti-Aesthetic. Essays on Postmodern Culture* (Port Townsend, WA: Bay Press, 1983).
2. Jurgen Habermas, "Modernity -- An Incomplete Project," in Foster, ed., *The Anti-Aesthetic*, p. 6.
3. Kenneth Frampton, "Towards a Critical Regionalism: Six Points for an Architecture of Resistance," in Foster, ed., *The Anti-Aesthetic*, pp. 16-30.
4. Hal Foster, *Recodings* (Port Townsend, WA: Bay Press, 1985), p. 2.
5. Jean-Francois Lyotard, *Le Postmoderne explique aux enfants* (Paris: Edition Galilee, 1986), p. 30. See also Jean-Francois Lyotard, *The Postmodern Condition: A Report on Knowledge*, G. Bennington and B. Masumi, trans. (Minneapolis: University of Minnesota Press, 1984).
6. Martin Heidegger, *Poetry, Language, Thought*, A. Hofstadter, trans. (New York: Harper Colophon, 1975), p. 147.
7. Christian Norberg-Schulz, *The Concept of Dwelling* (New York: Electra-Rizzoli, 1985), p. 7.
8. Ivan Illich, *Gender* (New York: Pantheon, 1982), p. 68.
9. Cheikh Amadou Hampate Ba, "The Living Tradition," in J. Ki-Zerbo, ed., *General History of Africa. Volume I: Methodology and African Prehistory*, (Berkeley: University of California Press, 1981), p. 183.
10. John Turner, *Housing by People* (New York: Pantheon, 1977).
11. Illich, *Gender*, pp. 119-20.
12. Hampate Ba, "The Living Tradition," p. 167.
13. *Ibid.*, p. 167,
14. *Ibid.*, p. 166.
15. Bruno Queysanne, "Architecture and Tradition," paper presented at the International Symposium on Traditional Dwellings and Settlements, Berkeley, CA, April 1988.
16. As quoted in Arnolf Luchinger, *Structuralism in Architecture and Urban Planning* (Stuttgart: Karl Kramer Verlag, 1980), p. 20.

HANDED DOWN ARCHITECTURE: TRADITION AND TRANSMISSION

PAUL OLIVER

Over the past century there has been a growth of interest in the buildings of "non-literate," "pre-literate" and "unsophisticated" societies. But with an increase in academic studies such terms have come to seem pejorative in the face of the variety and complexity of the cultures and communities considered, and phrases such as "architecture without architects" have become wholly inadequate to define the nature, or quality, of their buildings. While "traditional architecture" has been frequently employed as a substitute term, its suitability, or the implications of accepting it, has not been subjected to much scrutiny.

In this chapter I discuss how the term "tradition" has been interpreted by anthropologists, and how the implied meanings in its use have a bearing upon our comprehension of building concepts and processes. Principal among these is the recognition that the establishment and maintenance of a tradition requires the passing of its essential elements from the members of a group to their successors. This may often be conducted verbally, and there are a number of vehicles of oral tradition, often formulaic in nature, some examples of which I cite. Other, non-verbal means are of no less importance. It is my contention that in the study of tradition in architecture it is the transmission of traditions that is least researched and yet most essential to its understanding.

Recently we have seen the gradual adoption of the adjective "traditional" to describe buildings that have previously been termed "primitive," "folk," "indigenous" or "vernacular."[1] (We might also note the broad acceptance of the word "architecture" to describe buildings in which architects as designers played no part.) Implicit in the titles and texts of recent works is the assumption that we are agreed as to what traditional means in terms of architecture. There is little in the way of explanation of the word's use and application.

The word tradition is defined *The Concise Oxford Dictionary* as "opinion or belief or custom handed down from ancestors to posterity," as "doctrine supposed to have divine authority but not committed to writing," and as "artistic or literary principles based on accumulated experience or continuous usage."[2] The problem with these definitions, insofar as they are relevant to architecture or to the uses to which buildings are put, is that they are as applicable to a Mayan temple or a Gothic cathedral as they are to any of the kinds of buildings represented in the books mentioned above. We may observe though that belief, custom, doctrine or principles refer to concepts about the traditional, rather than to material artifacts.

Edward Shils, in one of the very few works devoted to the subject, argues however, that "Tradition -- that which is handed down -- includes . . . all that a society of a given time possesses and which already existed when its present possessors came upon it and which is not solely the product of physical processes in the external world or exclusively the result of ecological and physiological necessity. The *Iliad*, in a recently printed English translation is a *traditum*; so, is the Parthenon."[3] In this all-embracing definition everything that is cultural and inherited is a *traditum*, an exemplar of tradition. Whereas this means that every vernacular building, every indigenous tool with which it was built, is an element of the tradition, it also means that every painting, every poem and every product of former architects and engineers are also *tradita*. Here too, "traditional architecture" becomes a term to describe all buildings from the past that survive to the present.

TRADITIONAL CONTEXTS

Of course, we may argue that traditional architecture is that which is built by the members of traditional societies, a designation which Shils averred "has come about by misdirection; 'traditional' has seemed to be a less pejorative term than 'primitive,' 'heathen,' 'savage,' 'backward,' 'pagan,' 'barbarian,' and 'simple.'"[4] Whether the term is used for this reason or not, it begs the question as to what is meant by a traditional society.

A somewhat uncomfortable distinction was made by Robert Redfield between the "Great Tradition" and the "Little Tradition." Explained by his co-worker Milton Singer, these terms "distinguish the *cultural content* of those aspects of a culture that are regarded as 'higher' from those that are considered 'lower.' The higher aspects are usually more reflective and more systematically presented and embody the greatest intellectual and aesthetic achievements of the culture. As such, they tend to be stored in 'texts' of various kinds -- oral, written, inscribed, carved and painted, sung and acted."[5] Redfield wrote that he thought of the "two traditions not as ideal-types . . . I think of them as concepts for separating out, in any old-established civilization with important orthogenetic features, the content, roles and offices, media and process of one system that cultivates a reflective component with other unreflective systems in local communities."[6] With urbanization, Redfield and Singer argued, the Little Tradition becomes transformed into a Great Tradition. While we may feel less than happy with the qualitative and hierarchical implications in Redfield's formulation, the concept of an elite tradition, reflective and self-aware, and a popular or "folk" tradition, which shares much of a common culture but which is non-reflective and unselfconscious, is helpful in broad outline.

To some extent Redfield's formulation corresponds with Max Weber's views. Weber perceived a level of authority or a system of "imperative coordination" which he considered traditional "if legitimacy is claimed for it and believed in on the basis of the sanctity of the order and the attendant powers of control as they have been handed down from the past, 'have always existed.'"[7]

He also recognized a level of "strictly traditional behavior" which lay "very close to the borderline of what can be justifiably called meaningful action, and indeed often on the other side. For it is very often a matter of almost automatic reaction to habitual stimuli which guide behavior in a course which has been repeatedly followed." But he was aware that "attachment to habitual forms can be upheld with varying degrees of self-consciousness and in a variety of senses."[8]

We can recognize that what we term traditional architecture falls more into the realm of the unreflective, unselfconscious sector of the total culture than that of the reflective elite. Fixity and persistence in plan, the sanction and legitimacy of precedent in design, the formalization of techniques and processes in construction, and the use of spaces in accordance with the dictates of custom, typify traditions in buildings which operate as a coordinated system. Adherence to known and tried techniques, the codification of behavior and the pursuit of building methods because "this is how they are done," all crystallize as norms of behavior. Eventually, they are accepted uncritically, becoming matters of habit and of established values.

TRADITION AND CHANGE

Dependency on tradition is a bulwark against change. A Luddite mentality which protects the *status quo* and is in conflict with innovation out of fear of displacement is far from uncommon. But this is not the only reason for resistance to change. The isolation of remote communities in many parts of the world insulates them from outside influence and reinforces their dependence on what they know and have inherited. The alien is a source of suspicion and the new is an affront to the values of the elders. Hence we may find building methods and types in, let us say, Borneo or West Irian which have remained the same over many centuries and have only been subject to change in recent decades.

While resistance to major changes in conservative societies persists, variations from common practice are frequently encoun-

F I G U R E 1. Tradition, custom, and change: Two Yemeni builders using a traditional technique of stone walling, though their method of mud mortaring has been adapted to cement in order to make their house walls more resistant to earthquakes. (P h o t o : Yasemin Aysan.)

tered, though they may be modest departures from the traditional norms. In an introduction to a study of deliberately invented traditions, the historian Eric Hobsbawm drew a distinction between tradition and custom:

> The object and characteristic of "traditions" is invariance. The past, real or invented, to which they refer imposes, fixed [normally formalized] practices, such as repetition. "Custom" . . . does not preclude innovation and change up to a point . . . [it] cannot afford to be invariant because even in "traditional" societies life is not so.[9]

Stated in semiological terms, tradition as interpreted here is the rule system, the *parole*, while custom is the manner in which it was practiced or exercised, the *langue*. It can be argued that there can be no change without tradition, that tradition provides the matrix within which any changes may be introduced. Even so, the rate of change may be virtually imperceptible, as small innovations and modifications are tried, repeated and proved to be effective and gradually incorporated into customary practice or are found wanting and dropped. The deliberate solution of problems encountered in specific construction contexts, and the devising of skills to meet them, occur in every part of the world. As Malinowski demonstrated fifty years ago, all societies change, however slowly.[10]

Yet if some changes are brought about by subtle influence or modest innovation, others may be sudden and brutal. Military conquest may bring in its wake dramatic changes which may lead to the colonization of building styles. One need go no further for examples than the pervasive Turkish architecture in Albania or the presence of Venetian houses on Greek islands. There may be change as a result of religious conversion, such as the adoption of North African plans and forms by Islamicized West Africa. Change may be induced by edict, Henry VIII's requirement that timber houses should be built with box frames so that more trees could be saved for building the fleet being one such case. Or it may be the result of the deliberate initiation of a new technology like the introduction by the British in the Sudan of fired bricks made with the clamp kiln. While such forms of induced change may be effected through conflict with local traditional practices, eventually they are likely to become accepted traditions in themselves.

Isolation notwithstanding, the processes of borrowing and adaptation by contiguous societies of elements which are acceptable or seem appropriate to their needs may be traced in many cultures. They may be of a purely practical or structural nature, or they may be of symbolic or decorative import; sometimes they are a combination of both, like the distribution of saddle roofstructures in Southwest Asia.[11] "Culture is transmitted geographically as well as chronologically, in space as well as in time, by contagion as well as by repetition," wrote A.L. Kroeber. "The spread in area is generally called *diffusion*, as the internal handling through time is called *tradition*."[12]

Kroeber, in fact, placed less importance than some writers on the *traditum*. "The terms 'social inheritance', or 'tradition' put the emphasis on how culture is acquired rather than what it consists of." Culture, he argued, "consists of conditioned or learned activities (plus the manufactured results of these); and the idea of learning brings us back again to what is socially transmitted, what is received from tradition, what is 'acquired by man as a member of societies.' So perhaps *how it comes to be* is really more distinctive of culture than what it *is*."[13]

ORAL TRADITIONS

Definitions of the word tradition have much in common. "Generally speaking, 'tradition' covers the total cultural heritage handed down from one generation to the next,"[14] summarized Kazimierz Dobrowolski when writing on peasant culture in Southern Poland. Like many other writers, including some quoted above, he used the phrase "handed down" to describe the process whereby the continuity of tradition is maintained.

Though it is persistently used to describe the process whereby tradition is maintained (there is hardly any definition of "tradition" in which it does not appear), "handing down" is almost always used metaphorically. With the exception of certain ritual contexts, such as the transfer of a symbol of office or rule -- a scepter perhaps -- to a new political or spiritual leader, or the gift of a trousseau or dowry in a society where parents pass on family heirlooms, little is literally handed down. Even here, "handed on" might be a better term. Yet even if the metaphor is overworked and often thoughtlessly applied, there is general agreement that a fundamental characteristic of tradition is that it is transmitted from one group to another or from one individual to another. The process is usually assumed to have a temporal rather than a spatial dimension and to be diachronic rather than synchronic. Diffusion apart, the transmission of a tradition, or *traditum*, is most often seen to be from its guardians to their successors.

If transmission is the essence of tradition, it would seem imperative that its nature be given serious attention. "In all the great cultural undertakings of the human race, the oral transmission of tradition plays a great role," Edward Shils observed.

> In the production of material objects such as sculptures, paintings, and buildings, the instruction of the novice must to a large extent be oral, even though observation and empathy also provide guidance, as do written manuals, drawings, and models.15

But Shils has far less to say on the subject of oral transmission than he has on transmission through texts, and less to say on the traditions of the common people than on the esoteric knowledge of priesthoods and intellectual elites.

With his concern for the culture of the peasantry, Kazimierz Dobrowolski gave more attention to the processes of transmission, noting that the passing of the social heritage by speech or other stimuli which are received by the sense of hearing, or by visual demonstrations of actions and objects, always involves direct human contact. Transmission media of a mechanical character, including print, musical scores and phonographs, relieve the producers and receivers from such contact and establish only an indirect and impersonal relationship. Observing that the term

F I G U R E 2. Persistence of tradition: The technology of house building in the Haute Vienne, France, may change, with concrete block used in place of stone. But the traditional leafy bush is tied to the "roof tree" until the house is completed. (P h o t o : Paul Oliver.)

"traditional culture" is customarily used by ethnographers to mean "cultural contents and values which are *transmitted orally*,"16 Dobrowolski noted the conservatism and stabilizing "propensity for the preservation and maintenance of the existing social order," within peasant traditional culture. The past "supplies a pattern for living and provides a model for human action." Oral transmission in his view had a limited capacity for cultural transfer from one generation to its successors, affecting the quantity and quality of what was passed on. This resulted in a decline in the public memory, opening the way for the slow processes of change and replacement, older usages falling irrevocably into the "limbo of social oblivion."

Against this loss of folk memory, peasant craftsmen had their own defenses. The village carpenters of Podhale used neither drawn plans nor written calculations; "their entire technological knowledge was based exclusively on memory and was reduced to the repetition, in practical action, of a few basic models . . . a larger, two-roomed house, and a smaller one having one room only, with certain variants which consisted of adding summer-rooms and stores (*kamora*)." The family likenesses between arti-facts and buildings, so frequently noted and admired in the architecture of preliterate societies, is thus seen as the outcome of the need for the survival of a technological tradition and a control against change. Dobrowolski concluded that there was a relative paucity of different examples of material culture when these were compared with the highly developed system of behavioral patterns. "On the one hand we have a limited number of such material arrangements as type of houses, plans of the interior, furniture, dress, ornaments, etc., and on the other, a great number of highly differentiated social situations, each demanding a special, customarily prescribed form of conduct."[17] Though some may not agree with this view, Dobrowolski's analysis of the effectiveness, strengths and limitations of the transmission of tradition in peasant societies is a key text in an inadequately studied field.

Oral transmission was of the essence of peasant traditional culture in Dobrowolski's discussion; and it may also be seen as a distinguishing characteristic of most traditional societies. Yet, in spite of the large number of volumes and articles on such peoples and their cultures, the nature, kinds and extent of oral transmission -- or indeed any other form of the transmission -- have seldom been researched in any depth. Though there is an increasing literature on "oral history" (there is an Oral History Association in the United States and an Oral History Society in Britain), the bulk of the material gathered and discussed has been the result of oral transmission between interviewer and interviewee. Its purpose is the documentation of the culture of the non-literate, which "offers a challenge to the accepted myths of history, to the authoritarian judgement inherent in its tradition. It provides a means for a radical transformation of history," Paul Thompson writes. He claims that "oral history gives history back to the people in their own words. And in giving a past, it also helps them towards a future of their own making."[18] It is a proud claim, but a dubious one. Oral history is not about oral transmission *within* a culture, where history does not need to be "given back." It is through internal oral transmission that the people move towards a future of their own making, and not through documentation by scholars. Even when they describe their techniques of building to specialists in vernacular architecture, craftsmen may use neither the means nor the terminology that they employ when instructing a novice.

Oral and other forms of transmission of tradition within cultures have vehicles about which we know little. The Belgian historian and anthropologist Jan Vansina is alone in having devoted a complete work to the subject. Even he is largely concerned with oral traditions as historical sources and is interested in the reliability of "historical information that can be derived from oral testimonies."[19] Perhaps for this reason he does not make a clear enough distinction between transmission among members of a society and transmission from informant within a society to external interviewer. Nevertheless, the extent of his fieldwork and the breadth of his study make his work a valuable guide to the processes of oral transmission.

Important sections of Vansina's work identify many of the characteristics of oral transmission: the chain of transmission, the structure of testimony, esoteric traditions and mnemonic devices. He also identifies many of the problems: failure of memory, the personality of the informant, the bearing of cultural values on informant and testimony. But these are factors which may differ in diverse contexts. Overriding them are the vehicles used to communicate testimony. Vansina proposes a typology based on criteria that include the purpose, significance, form and manner of transmission. He divides oral tradition into five categories: Formulae, Poetry, Lists, Tales and Commentaries. Some of these have sub-categories (for example, official and private roles for poetry; historical, didactic, artistic and personal sub-categories for tales), and each category has a number of types. Though his list does not encompass all that might be employed in the passing on of traditions in the making or use of buildings, it is sufficiently relevant to warrant summarizing.

"Formulae" consist of stereotyped phrases which may contain archaic elements but which are transmitted with accuracy. They include titles, slogans, didactic formulae such as proverbs or riddles, and ritual formulae such as spells or oaths. "Poetry" also has fixed forms but the form and content have artistic merit (in the values of the society). Historical songs and poems (whether accurate or idealized records), panegyric poetry often incorporating stereotypical phrases, and religious poetry in the form of prayer, hymns or dogmatic texts, all have official functions. Personal poetry, such as laments, may be of a private nature. "Lists" of place names may record migration routes, or may be used to defend land rights, while lists of personal names include genealogies. "Tales" are narratives characterized by prose composition. They may recount the general history of a people, the local history of a community or family history. Myths are didactic tales, of a religious character and with a moral purpose, whereas aetiological myths explain origins in other terms. Vansina identifies as sub-types local legends, tales accounting for natural phenomena, popular etymologies and stories about cultural traits. Tales told for artistic merit form a separate category, while personal recollections constitute another. Finally, "Commentaries" are supplementary information to other data, or are transmitted in a particular context. Legal precedents, explanatory commentaries and occasional comments given as brief observations or answers fall within this category.

As Vansina acknowledged, his categorization was a "rough outline," but it served to emphasize the "diversity of types which exist, and to show that each type has its own usefulness, and provides one particular kind of information only."[20] These types often have distinct structures and sequences. They do not constitute all the means of oral transmission used or available but rather those that are in themselves traditions. A few examples must suffice to illustrate the relevance of some of these types of oral transmission to the processes whereby buildings "come to be" or are used.

VOICES OF THE PEOPLE

Although Jan Vansina's draft of a typology of oral transmission was compiled with anthropological and, particularly, historical

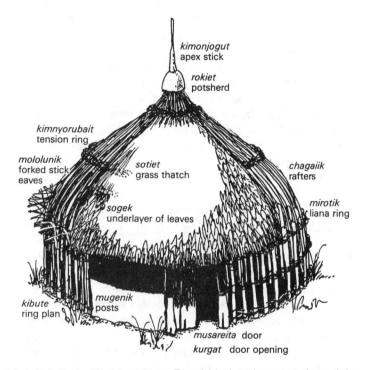

F I G U R E 3. Naming of Parts: Essential both to the preservation and the passing on of a building tradition is the naming of components and processes. Illustrated are some of the elements of the Kipsigis (Kenya) hut. From Paul Oliver, *Dwellings: The House Across the World*, p. 65.

purposes in view, it offers a framework on which a typology related to the workings of tradition in architecture might be directed. By applying some examples of oral transmission with architectural significance to his typology, its applicability and its shortcomings may be observed. For this reason it is necessary to follow his sequence, giving examples within each category and some, if not all, of his types. As noted above, "Formulae" is the first category, with "titles" the initial type. House names might be a suitable architectural equivalent of the latter.

"The name of the house (*inoa paito*) remains; the names of individual men (*inoa tanata*) disappear," said the people of Tikopia. The inhabitants of the island gave their houses permanent names, such as Ratia or Niukapu, which were related to the names of kinship groups. When a house collapsed, its name remained associated with the site, and a new house would bear it. Lying somewhere between an honorific title and a place name, such an identification of a house-site was, in Raymond Firth's words, "a valuable mechanism for the preservation of social continuity."[21] The permanence of the site and the transitory nature of the family has a corresponding sentiment in the Maori slogan, "the home is permanent, the man flits."

In many societies "didactic formulae" such as proverbs, aphorisms and sayings, draw upon building to point a moral. "Never think a home is yours until you have made one yourself," said the Winnebago; while the Yoruba of Nigeria favored gradualism with the proverb, "if you are not able to build a house at once, you first build a shed." In Ethiopia the Gurage warn that "you cannot build a house for last year's summer." Sayings directed to the craftsman himself have many counterparts to the English aphorism, "a bad workman always blames his tools." But if the meaning here is clear enough, proverbs and sayings may often be deliberately obscure. One Swahili pithily explained: "When they do not want a person to understand, they use a double meaning, saying for example, 'if you pass elephant's dung you will split your anus,' meaning, if you see someone build a fine house, and you want one like it but have not the money to build it, you will steal and get into trouble. This is what it means."[22]

"Ritual formulae" in particular may be couched in oblique or esoteric language, fully known and learned only by the initiated. They may be used in religious or magic rites associated with, for example, the selection of sites, the dedication of house posts or the blessing of the dwelling. The efficacy of the ritual is usually considered to be dependent on the precise repetition of the incantations and rites of the ceremonial. For instance, among the Lao Song of Thailand the builder of a new house celebrates its completion with the *sen phi* ceremony to the ancestors with appropriate rituals, recitations from the scriptures, blessings and consecration. With the *liang phra*, the ritual "feeding of the monks," he gains *tham bun ban*, "merit making in the house," with which he seeks to ensure the security of the dwelling.[23]

In Vansina's classification "Poetry" embraces types which may often overlap, both with the function of ritual and within the category itself. He does not accommodate song in his classification, though many kinds of poem are sung just as formulae may be chanted. Apart from revealing the values of a society towards the building, songs may be instructive of the processes of making it. A song cycle translated from the Riradjingo of the Goulburn Island, northeastern Arnhem Land, described the raising of stilt houses:

> Erecting forked sticks and rafters, posts for the floor, making the
>   roof of the hut like a sea-eagle's nest:
> They are always there, at the billabong of three goose eggs, at the
>   wide expanse of water . . .
> As they build, they think of the monsoon rains -- rain and wind
>   from the west, clouds spreading over the billabong . . .
> They cover the sides of the hut, placing rails on forked sticks.
> We saw the heaving chests of the builders, calling invocations for
>   the clouds rising in the west . . .
> Making the door of the hut, preparing it within . . .
> They think of the coming rain, and the west wind . . . wind
>   bringing the rain, spreading over the country.
> Carefully, therefore, prepare the hut,
>   with its roof and its posts . . . .[24]

Other songs speak of living in the dwelling, of happiness, domesticity or sometimes of the struggle for shelter. "The Rainman's Praise Song of Himself" was noted among the Aadonga of Angola:

> No house is ever too thick-built
> To keep me, the rain, from getting in.
> I am well-known to huts and roofs,
> A grandson of Never-Been-There.
> I am mother of the finest grasses,
> Father of green field everywhere.
> My arrows do not miss their aim,
> They strike the owner of huts.
> I am terror to clay walls and the architecture of termites . . . .[25]

"Lists" follow poems. Locations on migration routes and place-names may have some relevance to the study of traditional architecture, providing information that may indicate patterns of diffusion and influence. But within popular culture they can have other functional purposes. The stone roofs of the Cotswold houses in England are clad with thin, flat slabs or "tiles," split by frost and drilled to take wooden pegs. As a young "slatter," or roof-maker, Gilbert Peachey of the village of Chadworth when aged fourteen started to "pick up the rubbish and sort all the tiles out . . . when you sort a few thousand out to go on a roof you very soon learn the names of the measurements but you never finish learning the tiling itself." Like other apprentices to the craft, he learned the list of traditional dimensions on the "slatter's rule," starting with the smallest: "short-cocks, middle cocks and long-cocks; short cuttings, long cuttings; muffeties; bachelors; short nines and long nines; short whippets and long whippets; short elevens and long elevens; short becks and long becks . . . ."[26] the numerals indicating the introduction of Imperial measurements. Lists of measurements may also be learned by heart, and systems other than Metric and Imperial have persisted until recently, among them the Swahili units: *shabiri*, a hand-span from thumb-tip to fourth fingertip; *dhiraa*, a cubit or half a yard (also called *mkono*); *pima*, four *dhiraa* or a fathom; *jora*, sixty *dhiraa* or a bolt of cloth. More recently, Imperial measurements have their Swahili equivalents, the *inchi, futi, yadi* and *maili* (mile).[27]

Both the methods of building and the values associated with it may be present in "Tales" told after dark. Through them the young may be prepared for their future roles, as well as be entertained. The "Glaistig Lianachan," a local folk tale from Lochaber in the Scottish Highlands, for example, tells of Big Black Gillie Mac-Cuaraig who was abducted by mythical Glaistig at a river ford. To secure her freedom she promised him "a big house, well-built, into which spells of fire, or water, or arrow of iron could not penetrate and that he would get it dry, sheltered, and with a blessing upon him against armed men and the fairies" -- all in a single night. With a loud scream she summoned the fairies to her aid. As Mrs. Ryan, born Clementine MacDonell of Keppoch, retold the legend,

They brought flags and stones from the Fall of Clainaigh, and they were passing them from hand to hand. And on the inch they were cutting cabers and the taobhan -- the long rafters, smooth and flat from the Wood of Caoranach. And she was saying without a pause, 'One stone on the top of two stones. Two stones on the top of one stone, sharp sticks, turves, wattle, pins from every tree but the wild cherry.' And in the graying of the day, there was turf over the ridge and smoke out of it . . . .

When the Glaistig denied Big Black Gillie her freedom, she put a curse on him "that he should wither like the bracken and grow old like the rushes . . . and he should have no sons in his own place. And it is still said in that country that this curse came true indeed."28

Though the purpose of the aetiological myth is to account for the origin of phenomena and may therefore refer to non-historical time, it may still be revealing of values related to quite specific aspects of building -- even to the unlikely theme of the origin of the "privy." According to one Maori aetiological myth, the first *heketua*, or latrine, was made by Mauima, the eldest of the Maui brothers, the ancestral culture heroes. Hunting for his sister, he learned from one Rehua that she was held on the island of Motutapu. Turning himself into Rupe, a pigeon, he rescued her and bore her to Rehua's village, which was polluted by excrement as its people were too lazy to clean it. Unaided, Rupe cleaned the village and, as the verse-myth explained:

Also made by him
Was the latrine for disposing
Of the filth.
Also erected was the post
For the hand hold,
The name of that post
Being the Post-of-Whaitiri.
And all was finished.

The myth goes on to describe how Kaitangata, the son of Rehua, saw the latrine, which was built on the edge of a cliff, and decided to try it out. "When he reached the side of that cross beam, he lifted one of his feet onto that cross beam and squatted." Stretching out his hand he grasped the Post-of-Whaitiri and strained back, "thinking vainly that it was firm, but no, the post pulled up, that man fell, was killed immediately, and did not recover." As he fell his blood stained the sky, and thereafter a red streak in the sky was called *Ka tuhi Kaitangata*. Many Maoris concluded that Rupe deliberately loosened the post so that Kitangata would be killed as a punishment to Rehua because his people failed to help clean their village.[29]

The final category, "Commentaries," includes legal statements, explanations and brief comments. These, Vansina argues, have a legal or didactic purpose and are therefore invaluable micro-traditions. Such accounts, though frequently noted by researchers, are usually reworked for subsequent incorporation in a paper. A description given by a Portland quarry-man, Harry Hounsell, while splitting a large rock prior to breaking it up for building stone, is an example:

> Well, we're trying to ream this rock off the bed, a piece of rock of about two hundred tons, approximately. Well, the process is puttin' in pig placers, that's pieces of cast steel about inch and a half thick, fifteen inches long and about six inches wide. And you work your placers up under the rock, what you call on the risin'. Well after you got your placers in you fix your pigs in, nice and tight. Then you knock these wedges in and the wedges is about fifteen inches long and two inches wide and they're tapered down to a very sharp -- taper. Well you might have five placers under this rock here, now, and you knock all your wedges in. And you have a chant -- somebody give you a chant for to keep in time. The rock must be struck altogether, not one after the other, for to get your weight behind your wedges, what they call reamin' your rock out before you start cuttin' out.

And the quarry-men returned to work, with Harry Hounsell leading them with a work-chant.[30]

TOWARDS A THEORY OF TRANSMISSION

In considering these examples of oral transmission in the frame of Jan Vansina's typology, it is clear that some have been driven in like Harry Hounsell's wedges; they were not a natural fit. In part this is due to the typology itself which lays emphasis on formulaic oral transmission and does not include informal or spontaneous observations and narratives. This limitation which places a low premium on creativity also omits any kinds of mutual exchange or argument. Even in the notes to the final category, which includes brief comments, Vansina stresses their formulaic nature. Though I have included examples of song to illustrate the categories, in fact he makes no reference to song as such -- only to poetry. Ballads, folk song, popular verse, children's rhymes are among the kinds of oral tradition which find no place among the types -- even though many are highly formulaic in structure and have proven longevity.

These omissions notwithstanding, the typology has been useful in demonstrating some of the kinds of oral transmission that throw light on aspects of popular involvement in architecture. It also reveals, if incidentally, a number of other facets of the subject. Among these is the question of the identities of the transmitters and the receivers of the "testimonies." Unfortunately, many of the sources of the examples cited are by no means clear on this point, and it cannot be assumed that these are evidence of oral transmission in process. In some instances they may have been heard and noted in the act of transmission; in others they may have been heard and subsequently repeated at the interviewer's request, and in still others they may be the record of direct oral transmission between informant and interviewer.

Traditions are reputedly handed on from generation to generation, but the nature of the generation is seldom identified. A generation may be considered as the average period that elapses before children are in a position to replace their parents. Three to five generations might span a century. It is sometimes believed that it takes three generations to establish a tradition, though members of a club will know that a tradition can be accepted in a cycle of three meetings. Elders to youth, priests to initiates, fathers to sons, mothers to daughters, masters to apprentices, craftsmen to novices, children to their juniors -- the generations who transmit traditions differ according to their age, gender, role and function.

The occasion of transmission is significant: some traditions are passed in secret, some in formal circumstances, some in anger, some in affection. They may be thought of as a part of ritual, as a means of acquiring skills, as entertainment, as learning through

F I G U R E 4. Transmission: A man learns from his father the skills of applying *kar-ghel* (mud and straw plaster) to an adobe wall. His son watches and learns. Isfahan, Iran. (P h o t o : Paul Oliver.)

play or as socialization within family or community. The kind of society, its cultural identity and its location may all affect the nature of the traditions transmitted and the importance placed upon them. It is perhaps worth drawing attention to the fact that the examples cited above were recorded in tribal, folk, peasant and popular communities (acknowledging that, for the present, these terms are unqualified). The contexts included day labor, house-building, tale-telling and ceremonial.

All the foregoing discussion has been related to oral transmission, but many of the circumstances indicated apply equally to other forms of transmission. Mimicry, mime, acting, dance, music, play, gesture, painting, carving, modelling and model-making are some of the kinds of non-verbal communication which carry and sustain traditions. Many of these have direct bearing upon architecture in building, decoration, occupation and use.

Whatever the means of communication and the social circumstances in which the transmission of tradition takes place, it is the message which is of ultimate importance, and this is related to the specific purpose for which it is intended. In architecture this involves a great many issues, too many to detail here. But we are aware that they include the physical environment and the site, natural resources and the nature of the economy. They involve settlement pattern and orientation, location and spatial organization, social structure and family type, territory and inheritance. Structural systems, preparation of materials, construction methods, skills and technologies are fundamental to building. But the cycle of the seasons, age and gender, concepts of public and private space, and the properties of behavioral norms can all be reflected in occupation and utility, while religion and belief, symbols and signification may be implicit in the use of space or explicit in detail and ornament. All are defined or influenced by tradition and are subject to change, however subtle.[31]

It would seem obvious therefore that the nature, purpose and content of oral and non-verbal forms of transmission would be fundamental to the study of traditional architecture. Yet such is not the case. In spite of the vast quantity of studies of vernacular buildings -- measured, drawn in plan, section and elevation, or described in technical detail, the fewer, but still numerous, studies of their use, and the occasional analyses of their symbolism, the verbatim record of how the traditions involved in them were transmitted is exceptionally rare.[32] With the partial exception of the account of the Lao Song ritual, none of the examples cited above was specifically recorded to illuminate the transmission of tradition in architecture.

In one sense it can be argued that there is no such thing as a traditional building, no larger field of traditional architecture. There are only buildings which embody traditions. This most neglected area of study is also the most pressing and, ultimately, the most important. As yet we have no general theory to encompass it, because the paucity of research does not justify it. But this chapter is intended as a step towards that end.[33]

REFERENCE NOTES

1. T. Itoh, *Traditional Domestic Architecture of Japan* (New York and Tokyo: Weatherhill/Heibonsha, 1972); S. Denyer, *African Traditional Architecture* (London: Heinemann, 1978); S. Hallett and R. -Samizay, *Traditional Architecture of Afghanistan* (New York: Columbia University Press, 1980); F. Schwerdtfeger, *Traditional Housing in African Cities* (New York: John Wiley, 1982); A. and V. Larsson, *Traditional Tswana Architecture* (Stockholm: Swedish Council for Building Research, 1984); K. Andersen, *African Traditional Architecture* (London: Oxford University Press, 1977); R. Lewcock and Z. Freeth, *Traditional Architecture in Kuwait and the Northern Gulf* (London: Archaeology Research Papers, 1978); and others.
2. *The Concise Oxford Dictionary*, rev. 4th ed., (Oxford: Clarendon Press, 1954), p. 1353.
3. E. Shils, *Tradition* (London: Faber and Faber, 1981), p. 12.
4. *Ibid.*, p 293.
5. M. Singer, *When a Great Tradition Modernizes* (New York: Praeger, 1972), p. 4.
6. *Ibid.*, letter to M. Singer by R. Redfield (1956), p 10.
7. M. Weber, *The Theory of Social and Economic Organization* (London: Collier-Macmillan, 1947), p. 341.
8. *Ibid.*, p. 116.
9. E. Hobsbawm and R. Ranger, *The Invention of Tradition* (London: Cambridge University Press, 1983), p. 2.
10. B. Malinowski, *The Dynamics of Culture Change* (New Haven: Yale

University Press, 1945, 1965).

11. G. Domenig, *Tektonic in Primitiven Dachbau* (Zurich: ETH, 1980).

12. A. Kroeber, *Anthropology: Culture Patterns and Processes* (Harcourt Brace and World, 1923, 1963), p. 219.

13. *Ibid.*, p. 61.

14. K. Dobrowolski, "Peasant Traditional Culture," *Ethnografia Polksa* Vol. 1, reprinted in T. Shanin, ed., *Peasants and Peasant Societies* (Harmondsworth: Penguin Books, 1977), p. 277.

15. Shils, *Tradition*, p. 91.

16. Dobrowolski, "Peasant Traditional Culture," p. 278.

17. *Ibid.*, p. 284.

18. P. Thompson, *The Voice of the Past: Oral History* (Oxford: Oxford University Press, 1978), p. 226.

19. J. Vansina, *Oral Tradition: A Study in Historical Methodology* (London: Routledge and Kegan Paul, 1961, 1965), pp. 1-18.

20. *Ibid.*, pp 141-164.

21. R. Firth, *We, The Tikopia* (London: George Allen and Unwin, 1936, 1957), pp. 82-87.

22. Proverbs, various sources; J. Allen, *The Customs of the Swahili People: The Desturi za Waswahili* (Berkeley: University of California Press, 1901, 1983), p. 289.

23. L. Pedersen, "The Influence of the Spirit World on the Habitation of the Lao Song Dam, Thailand," in K. Isikowitz and P. Sorenson, eds., *The House in South-East Asia*, pp 119-122.

24. R. Berndt, *Three Faces of Love: Traditional Aboriginal Song-Poetry* (Melbourne: Thomas Nelson, 1976), pp. 11-12.

25. A. Pettinen, "Sagen und Mythen der Aadonga" (1926), reprinted in W. Trask, *The Unwritten Song* Vol. 1 (London: Jonathan Cape, 1969), pp. 71-72.

26. G. Peachy (interview with J. Turner 1970?), *Cotswold Craftsmen*, Saydisc SDL247. For other slatter's terms, see P. Oliver, "Vernacular Know-How," *Material Culture* Vol. 18 no. 3, pp 113-26.

27. C. Zaslavsky, *Africa Counts: Number and Pattern in African Culture* (Westport: Lawrence Hill and Co, 1973), pp. 88-89; see also J. Allen, *The Customs of the Swahili People*, p 232.

28. I. Grant, *Highland Folk Ways* (London: Routledge and Kegan Paul, 1961), pp. 147-49.

29. Sir P. Buck, *The Coming of the Maori* (Wellington: Whitcomb and Toombs, 1950), pp. 140-42.

30. H. Hounsell (interview with P. Kennedy, 1954), *Knock, Ream and Bash: Work Chants and Stoneworkers Shanties*, Folktracks FSC-30-203.

31. P. Oliver, *Dwellings: The House Across the World* (Oxford: Phaidon Press, 1987).

32. Two recent and important exceptions are D. and S. McAllester, *Hogans: Navajo Houses and Songs* (Middleton: Wesleyan University Press, 1980), and S. Blier, *The Anatomy of Architecture: Ontology and Metaphor in Batammaliba Architectural Expression* (New York: Cambridge University Press, 1987).

33. I am interested in receiving any examples of oral transmission in which aspects of architectural tradition have been noted or recorded in the course of fieldwork.

ON THE ATTRIBUTES
OF "TRADITION"

AMOS RAPOPORT

In dealing with the relationship between dwellings and settlements, four major issues are addressed: what is meant by "tradition," what is meant by "dwellings" and "settlements," why this topic should be addressed, and what lessons, if any, such study can provide.

Since I have frequently discussed how dwellings and settlements are best conceptualized and how the link should be made between them, and also why traditional, vernacular, historical and other environments should be studied and how one learns from them, these topics will be discussed only briefly. This chapter will emphasize the question of what is meant by "traditional" -- both generally and specifically in connection with built environments. This will be done by identifying the attributes of the concepts "tradition" and "traditional."[1]

DWELLINGS AND SETTLEMENTS

Dwellings and settlements are both forms of built environments which can themselves be conceptualized in different ways. Minimally, they involve relationships between people and people, people and things, and things and things. Their design is usefully conceptualized as the organization of four variables: space, time, meaning and communication.[2]

Common to all such conceptualizations is the essential point that built environments are more then artifacts. Since they are particular types of built environments, so are dwellings and settlements. Moreover, it is sometimes difficult to separate dwellings and settlements, particularly in the extreme case of communal dwellings, where dwelling and settlement are one.

This, and the use of many outdoor settings, leads to a conceptualization of housing as systems of settings within which certain systems of activities take place. These systems can comprise different settings arranged in different ways with different linkages and separations. The dwelling and its parts are linked to many other settings in the neighborhood, the settlement and beyond.[3] It is the cultural landscape which needs to be studied; and while this can be analyzed, it cannot arbitrarily be split into components. The specifics of such systems of settings, one of which is the house-settlement system, vary greatly with culture. This is why this conceptualization is essential for valid cross-cultural comparisons to be made; otherwise non-comparable units may be compared.[4]

Housing can also be conceptualized in terms of environmental quality, i.e., the many attributes which characterize any system of settings and which are seen as undesirable, or, alternatively, are sought and chosen within the constraints operating for any group at a given time. Environmental quality can in turn be conceptualized in terms of an environmental quality profile in which four things can vary: the components, their ranking, their importance vis-a-vis other qualities, needs or wants, and whether they are positive (pulls) or negative (pushes).[5]

While these conceptualizations will not be used much explicitly in this paper, they need to be borne in mind; they also play a crucial role in any comparative studies.

REASONS FOR STUDYING THE TOPIC

I will not develop the rationale for studying traditional environments in any detail, but would summarize the argument I have often made as follows. One may ignore traditional environments; one may acknowledge their existence but deny that they have any value, interest or lessons; or one may romanticize them and try to copy them. I argue that the only valid approach is to analyze them in terms of concepts, and derive lessons which are applicable to research, theory-building or design. Not only is it important to study traditional environments, it is essential.

The full range of environments available must be studied -- all types, in all cultures, across the full time span as well as the whole environment (the system of settings or cultural landscape). Any generalizations made and any patterns identified (these are essential to the development of any worthwhile theory) must be based on the largest and broadest (i.e., the most varied) body of evidence. Most environments ever built were not designed by architects, are not in the Western tradition, and go back a long time -- approximately two million years. They are, in other words, those commonly described as traditional. They must, therefore, be studied and are bound to have lessons; after all, they represent the bulk of examples of human ingenuity in creating built environments, the record of the full range of environment-behavior interactions.[6] Of course, this subject, like any other, can be studied simply because one likes it; but one needs to go beyond that -- to learn from it. This learning can be of different kinds, all potentially valuable. The lessons can be about specifics or about process or product characteristics; or the topic can be studied as an entry point to Environment-Behavior Studies.[7]

THE MEANING OF "TRADITIONAL" --
IDENTIFYING ITS ATTRIBUTES

The term traditional is often used unselfconsciously, as in discussions contrasting modernization with traditional ways. Yet, like many such terms, it is clearly complex. For example, a one and one-half page abstract of an unpublished paper used the terms "tradition" or "traditional" fifteen times to refer to physical entities, communities, cultures, values, activities, lifestyles, etc. The only explicit meaning given was "rural," which implies a contrast with "urban." This indicates the word can also be taken to mean "old" or "of the past" (urban meaning "modern").[8] Most commonly, when traditional is used without explicit definition it means "of the past."

Reference to traditional decor or furniture (e.g., copies of Colonial, Louis XIV, Chippendale and the like) or houses (Colonial, Tudor and the like) also implies "old," "of the past." But while this is an important element of the concept, it is not sufficient. One can ask: What is "old"? When is "old"? When does a thing become "old"? Does this mean preliterate, pre-contact, pre-colonial, pre-industrial, pre-World War II, pre-independence? Or can the term mean any of these? These are difficult questions to answer, since traditional seems to be a relative term, as is "primitive."[9] A more adequate definition or description is needed. Since it is clearly a rather complex term, it seems necessary to dismantle it, as I have done for other terms like "culture" and "environment."[10]

Moreover, equally complex concepts such as "vernacular" cannot be defined on the basis of a single characteristic or even a small set of characteristics. Such concepts need a larger number of attributes which need not be present in every member of the class.[11] Rather, a range of variations within defined limits allows every member of the type to possess many of the characteristics, and allows each characteristic to be shared by many members of the type. Thus, *no single characteristic or attribute is both sufficient and necessary for membership in the type.*[12]

Similarly, the concept of tradition or traditional needs to be defined by a large number of attributes or characteristics, not all of which need be present in any given case. At the very least this rather large set of attributes is needed to check one's often intuitive sense of what a given "thing" is.[13] Such an approach helps to clarify the concept by making its attributes more specific, and it also makes it possible to identify subsets of attributes relevant to different domains. It is possible, for example, that traditional may mean different things when applied to economic behavior than when applied to environments.

The purpose of the key section of this paper thus becomes to derive a set of attributes which characterize the concepts of tradition and traditional. This was done through an informal content-analysis of literature on the topic, which does not discuss it much explicitly -- a point also made in the one major study of the concept.[14] However, scattered in various publications are many uses of the term, including explicit definitions. Attributes of tradition or traditional were identified, whatever the domain to which they referred. In all cases implicit attributes were made explicit, whether these referred to tradition *per se* or to its most commonly used antonym -- modernity. This approach was taken because the most common unselfconscious attribute, "old" or "of the past," contrasts with "modernity," "contemporary," "of now," etc.[15] The concern was both with what tradition *is* and what it *does*.[16]

From this analysis it proved possible to derive a set of descriptors about which there seems to be agreement in spite of a few minor contradictions. These contraditions are often due to what is considered or left out, since generally only a few aspects are discussed.[17] In general I will identify the list of attributes without judging their validity or usefulness, merely trying to clarify what the term means in general. This work is also preliminary, and it will require more systematic searches and content-analyses to sharpen, refine and improve our understanding of the concept.

One should note that tradition can be seen as a positive or a negative concept, the latter being more common.[18] It can also be neutral. This is the position I adopt. Also, tradition does not need to be rejected or embraced *in toto*; it is possible to admire traditional artifacts while rejecting the tradition that produced them, an attitude commonly found among designers.[19]

There is one exception to my neutrality. There can be different kinds of traditions, so that while contemporary science and modern culture generally are seen as hostile to traditional ways of thinking and acting, they have their own traditions.[20] Thus there is some selection among the attributes that follow; they tend to center on the relation of those terms that are potentially relevant to built environments in what Redfield has called the "little tradition."

The statements that were content-analyzed were found both in academic literature from a variety of fields and in the popular press. The content-analysis was done in two stages. First, the attributes were left embedded in the phrases or sentences in which they appeared so as to retain some of their context, qualifications and elaborations. Their respective sources were also identified. The list consisted of 98 items varying in length from single short phrases to sentences and paragraphs to passages of more one-half page. These served as the material for the second stage of analysis. At this level attributes that were implicit were made explicit, distinct attributes included in single passages were separated, and overlap, repetition and redundancy were eliminated. The result was a more succinct set of 128 attributes, not identified individually as to source. These were organized into five major categories, one of which was further divided into six subcategories.[21]

One recurring meaning of tradition, a common thread in the way the word is commonly used in everyday speech and in the attributes identified in the literature review, could be characterized as *conservatism* in the sense of accepting the past, continuity and repetition.[23] This sense is most succinctly and effectively captured by the phrase, "*what makes a tradition is meaningful repetition.*"[24] Much of the literature is concerned with what is repeated, through what mechanisms it is repeated, and what, if anything, makes it meaningful.

Although the list of attributes is greatly condensed, and there is a considerable loss of detail and subtlety, the list still captures a clear consensus in the literature. As already emphasized, one would not expect all attributes to apply in any one case. Recall

NATURE OF GROUPS

A. Non-Western
Non-European
Indigenous
Pre-Contact
Pre-Colonial
Grass-Roots
Vernacular

B. Small Scale
Relatively isolated
(physically and/ or
socially)
Strong links to place
High local autonomy
(vs "center")
No orientation to state
or other large entities
Rely on social
conventions
Informal social
institutions
Informal controls
Tight constraints
Strong constraints
Little individual choice
Little individual selection
(much "pre-selection")
Accepting things
generally (comfort,
well being, status,
rewards, technology etc.)
Rule bound (especially
old rules)
Unquestioned rules
Social sanctions
Collective control
Collective sharing
Strong kinship
Ascriptive status
Consensual
Normative (strong norms)
Obligatory
Strongly shared
schemata, values, beliefs,
models etc.
Unified world view
Customary
Accepting religious and
familial authority

C. Preliterate (hence oral)
Non-literate
Working by example
Depending on
socialization and
enculturation

D. Group oriented
Strong group identity
Non-individualistic
Little individual freedom
Anonymous
Little individual
motivation

Egalitarian[22]
Affectivity
Consensus
Communality
Strong social bonding
Homogenous
Few constituent parts
Constituent parts highly
coincident
Membership and
boundaries of group very
persistent and coincident
Accepting hierarchy
Low conflict

E. Pervasive religiousity
Ritualistic (ritual
important)
Magical beliefs
Strongly "symbolic"
Sacred relationship to the
land

F. Rationality non primary
Non rationalistic
Unquestioning
Non-critical
Emphasis on accumulated
wisdom and experience
Non empirical science
Non reflective
Self-evident
"Natural" way of doing
things
Things as given

TEMPORAL

Old
Of the past
Accepting the past
Respecting the past
The past "substantively
present"
Non modern
Contrasting with
modernity
Past orientation
Non future-orientation

CONTINUITY

Emphasizing continuity
Providing continuity
Feeling connected
with the past
Linking past and present
Linked across generations
Conservative
Persistent
Recurrent

Repetitive
Constant action
Respect for past patterns
Reproducing past patterns
Guided by past patterns
Habitual
Received models
Replacing particular
things, not patterns
or models.

CHANGE

Slow change
Slow growth (population,
economy etc.)
Enduring
Long lasting
Low novelty
Slow obsolescence
Constancy (vs. change)
No deliberate or
continuous search
for improvement
Static ideals
Stable
Non-innovative
Accommodating change
conservatively
Little variability
Gradual modification

ECONOMY/ TECHNOLOGY

Preindustrial
Limited material resources
Conservative/prudent use
of resources
Not "economically
rational"
Emphasis on "non-
productive activities"
Not market oriented
Land seen in terms of
social relations
Non hedonistic
Non consumerist
Accepting of resource,
reward "income" etc.,
distribution
Non-technological
Slow technological growth
Diffuse knowledge
and skills
Dispersed modes
of production
Low specialization
(in work, activities,
behavior etc.)
Low differentiation

T A B L E   1.
Attributes of Traditionality.

that at this point I am not judging the utility, validity or consistency of any attribute. However, one could suggest in a preliminary way that what are called traditional societies, environments and so on, tend to exhibit many or most of these attributes, and in very strong form; traditionality is tradition -- only more so.

TRADITIONALITY AND BUILT ENVIRONMENTS

The point is often made that there can be different kinds of traditions. Since anything can become a tradition by being transmitted over time, tradition is a very general concept potentially applicable to many domains: lifestyles, behaviors, institutions, law, art, philosophy, built environments, monuments, cultural landscapes, settlements, physical objects and artifacts; beliefs about all sorts of things, events, places, groups or meanings; cultural constructs, values, images, practices, technology, government, politics and administration, and so on. It follows that different mechanisms of transmission may be used, although all involve people; only people transmit traditions (as they do culture), and only people pass on artifacts or shape them by translating schemata and patterns into built form.[25] Also, as already suggested, some parts of tradition (e.g., artifacts) may be accepted and others (e.g., lifestyles or social arrangements) may be rejected. Thus different parts of tradition may change differentially and in different ways so that certain essential elements continue and are combined with new ones, as is often the case in developing countries.[26]

It thus becomes necessary to relate the attributes of tradition as a general concept to built environments. The question is how this can be done.

Intuitively, it seems that reference to "traditional built environments" includes reference to those typically described as primitive or vernacular. Contemporary, high-style design and popular design (suburbs, roadside strips and the like) are both excluded. The place of pre-modern, high-style, (traditional!) design is rather ambiguous. I will, however, arbitrarily exclude it from consideration and confine myself largely to preliterate and vernacular design.[27]

This is frequently the case in the literature. For example, *Tradition*, a publication of the Missouri Cultural Heritage Center (University of Missouri-Columbia), deals with the "heritage of the state," meaning historical folk or grass-roots (i.e. vernacular) arts and environments. Traditional thus means belonging to local groups, and, by implication, to the periphery. Similarly, Algerian vernacular design (also called "spontaneous" or "popular"), contrasted with high-style buildings which represent elite culture, has been equated with traditional.[28] It is defined as comprising those constructions produced by a group for itself; these are rarely the work of specialists, serve as a setting for daily life, express the needs and wants of the group and, to the extent they are differentiated, the individual as well.

The intuition that preliterate and vernacular design are, in fact, the prototypes or exemplars of what most people call traditional design,[29] the closest thing to an ideal type, becomes clear from my discussion of these environments in *House Form and Culture*.[30] The attributes of these types of environments discussed at various places in that book, in most detail on pp. 6-7, parallel quite closely many of the attributes of traditionality identified in Table 1. There seems to be some circularity involved. Since definitions of traditionality are based on the same types of societies studied in folk design, the same assumptions apply: the values, social arrangements, economies and built environments are products of the same groups.

One needs a way to break this circularity, to be able to deal with less clear-cut cases and with other types of environments. As already mentioned, my analysis of tradition is based on some recent work (the most complete of which is not yet published) that argues that the concept of vernacular design is not self-evident and is, in fact, rather difficult to define. A new definition is needed, based on identifying a large set of attributes, which are meant not only to help define preliterate and vernacular design and distinguish one from the other, but to help distinguish them from high style, popular and other types of design, and to help define these other concepts as well. Clear-cut ideal type definitions are as unlikely as monothetic ones. In effect, a more general taxonomy for classifying environments is proposed, meant to help locate environments on a continuum.[31]

A preliminary set of attributes was developed comprising seventeen process and twenty product characteristics. These are not definitive, are not arranged in order of importance; neither have scales or ways of evaluating environments according to them been developed. The attributes have, however, proved useful in teaching a course on vernacular design. They have also proved useful in trying to locate spontaneous settlements in developing countries on the continuum. While spontaneous settlements differ from traditional vernacular settlements, they also seem to be the closest thing to them today.[32]

This second set of attributes, listed in Table 2, is potentially useful, together with the attributes of traditionality in Table 1, in clarifying what traditional environments are all about. It is also potentially useful in dealing with less clear-cut cases and with other types of environments.

It is suggested that the use of both sets of attributes will not only break the definitional circularity, but -- by dismantling a complex and overly broad term -- will allow the emergence of a clearer, stronger and more precise notion of what traditional design is, how it comes about and what it does. This is the more likely considering the fact that the attributes of traditionality comprise social, economic, symbolic, affective and other characteristics, and that the attributes of environment comprise a wide range of both process and product characteristics. Through the different interactions among these two sets of attributes, a large -- even if incomplete -- range of issues can be clarified.

At the same time the rather large number of attributes involved presents a problem. The potential number of relationships that

PROCESS CHARACTERISTICS

1. Identity of designers
2. Intention and purposes of designers.
3. Degree of anonymity of designers.
4. Reliance on a model with variations.
5. Presence of a single model or many models.
6. Extent of sharing of model.
7. Nature of schemata underlying the model.
8. Consistency of use of a single (same) model for different parts of the house-settlement system.
9. Type of relationships among models used in different types of environments.
10. Specifics of choice model of design.
11. Congruence of choice model and its choice criteria with shared ideals of users.
12. Degree of congruence and nature of the relation between environment and culture/lifestyle.
13. Use of implicit/unwritten vs. explicit/legalistic design criteria.
14. Degree of self-consciousness/unselfconscious of the design process.
15. Degree of constancy/invariance vs. change/originality (and speed of change over time) of the basic model.
16. Form of temporal change.
17. Extent of sharing of knowledge about design and construction.

PRODUCT CHARACTERISTICS

1. Degree of cultural and place-specificity.
2. Specific model, plan forms, morphology, shapes, transitions, (e.g., inside/outside, interface, entrances), etc.

3. Nature of relationships among elements and the nature of underlying rules.
4. Presence of specific formal qualities: complexity, solid-void relations, fenestration, massing and volumes, articulation, level changes and how handled, the nature, complexity and articulation of urban spaces and degree of variations in their use of light and shade, use of vegetation, etc.
5. Use of specific materials, textures, colors, etc.
6. Nature of relation to landscape, site, geomorphology, etc.
7. Effectiveness of response to climate.
8. Efficiency in use of resources.
9. Complexity at large scale due to place specificity.
10. Complexity at other scales due to use of a single model with variations.
11. Clarity, legibility and comprehensibilty of the environment due to the order expressed by the model used.
12. Open-endedness allowing additive, subtractive and other changes.
13. Presence of "stable equilibrium" (vs. the "unstable equilibrium" of high style).
14. Complexity due to variations over time (changes *to* model not *of* model [as in *process* characteristics No. 15]).
15. Open-endedness regarding activities: types, numbers, overlaps, multiple uses, etc.
16. Degree of multisensory qualities of environment (large range of non-visual qualities).
17. Degree of differentiation of settings -- number, types, specialization, etc.
18. Effectiveness of environment as a setting for lifestyle and activity systems (including their latent aspects) and other aspects of culture.
19. Ability of settings to communicate effectively to users.
20. Relative importance of fixed-feature vs. semi-fixed feature elements.

T A B L E 2 . Process and Product Characteristics of Built Environments.[33]

need to be discussed is very large and cannot possibly be done here. I can merely suggest the approach and give a very few examples of relationships between a selected few attributes from the two lists. Note that since both sets of attributes are provisional, both may change. In particular, the attributes of traditionality are open to revision in light of knowledge of attributes of built environments. This is because few discussions of traditionality have been based on this domain.

A more detailed examination of the potential relationships involved in traditionality of process and traditionality of product would, I believe, reveal several things. First, it would tend to confirm the intuition that the phrase "traditional built-environments" typically refers to the exemplars of preliterate and vernacular settings -- the "exotic" examples so frequently used.[34] Second, the specific reasons for this intuitive use would be greatly clarified. Third, these insights would become applicable to other, less clear-cut examples. They would prove useful for discussing the difference between high-style design in the past and today, and also for discussing popular design, possibly the most neglected topic. This approach also has the advantage of suggesting a research program; many of the assumptions made about environments and traditionality would be questioned, changed, developed or refined, and problems and questions would be suggested which would become important starting points for research.

Table 1 suggests that most of the attributes of tradition concern the "Nature of Groups," and refer to six different aspects of groups and their members. Three other major sets of attributes concern time, and I have labelled them "Temporal," "Continuity" and "Change." One last set is related to "Economy/Technology."   A more systematic and technical derivation of the major factors or dimensions of the attributes would be useful as part of the research program. It would also be useful to assign relative importance to attributes, both generally and relative to built environments, and to identify additional attributes.

The few examples which follow relate a few attributes of environments to the major categories of attributes of traditionality, with scattered reference to individual attributes. The object is to demonstrate the approach rather than to provide conclusions.

TRADITIONALITY OF PROCESS

The attributes of traditionality in general have little to say directly about *the identity of designers*, although a number of attributes (e.g., "diffuse knowledge and skills," "dispersed modes of production," "low specialization," "anonymity" and so on) seem to bear on that topic. At the same time recent work suggests that these attributes may be overstated, at least in the case of those built environments commonly regarded as traditional.

The attributes in "Nature of Groups (D)" imply that designers are anonymous, have little individual motivation and are not ranked in any way. "Economy/Technology" would suggest that there should be no specialist designers (or builders). This indeed is the accepted view, and one might conclude that these attributes of traditionality seem to throw no new light on traditional environments. The contrary is the case: recent work on the design of material culture in traditional societies suggests that there were well-known designers. These people are often unknown or anonymous only to us as outside observers. For example, the facade decorations and patterns of the Sepik River men's houses in New Guinea were "copyrighted." This was also the case elsewhere, and there were frequent and strong sanctions against alienation of designs, payment for their use and so on.[35] The point that specialists occasionally built important structures was made in *House Form and Culture* and is now more generally accepted. Thus, while all men in the Gilbert Islands could build, specialists built meeting houses; and in parts of Oceania there were specialists in the building of Canoe houses, some of whom were known to be much better than others, and were regarded as artists.[36] In the eastern Solomon Islands and in parts of New Guinea artists were very important and influential. While working with strict patterns (an attribute of traditionality), they clearly competed with one another; this was also the case in parts of Africa. In northern Nigeria mud mosque builders were often celebrated in songs, and these master masons were endowed by popular opinion not only with creativity and genius but with supernatural powers; some of them became folk heroes.[37]   Similarly, the creators of canoes, paintings and songs in Aboriginal Australia were also known, celebrated and held in high esteem.   It thus appears that the anonymity of traditional designers may have been exaggerated.

It is also possible that these views about traditional design are over-sgeneralized; they may only apply in some situations, or only to dwellings and not to other settings. It may also be an artifact of our lack of knowledge (i.e., it may only be apparent at the etic level), and in the societies in question the designers may be very well-known and may even be ranked, with some enjoying major reputations.   Little seems to be known about how common or prevalent specialization and fame were, and whether there were any commonalities among settings (or artifacts) so designed. As far as I know, these issues have not been studied systematically. This discussion suggests fruitful topics for research in the literature and in the field, and it illustrates the value of this type of analysis both in generating research questions and in bringing disparate bodies of work to bear on one another.

The attributes of traditionality shed much more light on the *nature of the models* used in design.   Moreover, the study of built environments does not seem to alter the analysis of traditionality. Taken together, the two sets of attributes greatly clarify the nature of the models or schemata, their persistence, their provenance, their characteristics, the extent to which they are shared, and many other topics.   The attributes in "Nature of Groups (B)," "(D)," "(E)" and "(F)" clearly have a major bearing on such models; so do the specific attributes in "Continuity" and "Change." "Economy/Technology" seems to contribute less.

In fact, most attributes of traditionality bear on the nature of schemata, models and the like, suggesting that these are critical aspects of traditional design.   This, and the fact that they are central to all design, is a point I have made frequently; environments are thought before they are built, and design tries -- however imperfectly -- to reach some ideal embodied in an image, schema or model. This is the purpose of the choices made in the choice model of design.[38] It follows that *traditional environments are those that result from traditional models or schemata*, from traditional beliefs and modes of thinking and acting. This may be the key. The question then becomes: What are the characteristics of traditional models?

Even the "Nature of Groups (A)," which in general is the least useful, does make several points. Models used will be unlike those typical of the Western tradition of the last two hundred years, and they are also likely to be found in their clearest form among "exotic" groups. As a result, such built environments will be difficult to understand, because the underlying schemata are foreign, and they will therefore be difficult to understand without first understanding the culture.[39]

This implies that such models and schemata are likely to be highly culture-specific and variable. The nature of the systems of settings, the activity systems in them, and the environmental quality profiles will also be highly variable and unlike "ours." This is reinforced by the content of "Nature of Groups (B)," which suggests great local variability. In effect, traditional environments are likely to be highly place-specific (more correctly, group-specific), i.e., to exhibit major variation over space and little variation over time, see "Temporal." This is, of course, a major attribute of "folk environments" according to Glassie, whereas both high-style and popular environments vary little over space, but a great deal over time.[40] Thus it is suggested that the patterns of vernacular (i.e. traditional) environments lead to identity by regions, while the patterns of high-style and popular style lead to identity by periods.[41] This is reinforced by another attribute of traditional societies -- that land in them is not just space to be subdivided and sold. Rather, it is seen in terms of social ralationships, history and intimate links between the land and the group; the identity of the group is bound up with that land, which is sacred. Thus, Australian Aborigines belonged to the land, not vice versa.[42]

Such models persist because of tight constraints, "pre-selection," limited choice, consensus, strong norms and social sanctions, and all the other attributes of "Nature of Groups (B)." The attributes in "Nature of Groups (D)" further reinforce this, and also have things to say about the uniformity of models, their low individual variability, relation to group identity and so on. Individual differences within traditional groups are less than within contemporary groups, i.e., there is less individuality.[43] Recent empirical studies have shown this increase in individuality with modernization, with a consequent break in the given tradition.[44] Attributes in "Nature of Groups (E)" lead one to hypothesize that schemata will emphasize meaning (the latent or symbolic aspects of function) and will tend to embody religious, cosmological and similar beliefs; this will be both an important aspect of them and a major point of difference with more modern schemata.[45] Such schemata will also tend to be repeated, because of the attributes in "Nature of Groups (F)" and also those in "Continuity," "Temporal" and "Slow Change."[46]

It can, I think, be seen that a detailed discussion of the various linkages and mutual clarifications, and the use of and search for empirical data bearing on them, would be very useful. This also, once again, begins to suggest questions and problems. Since these are the critical first steps in research, this approach becomes a starting point for a research program. Finally, even in the current undeveloped state, this discussion makes certain findings (such as place specificity of traditional design) predictable from the interaction of various attributes. The discussion of group- and place-specificity also makes an important point: at least some product characteristics emerge "naturally" from a consideration of process; these also become "predictions" -- a most useful and important point that suggests that one may be on the road to theory development.

Limitations of space preclude any more examples of the interaction between attributes of traditionality and process characteristics of environments. I will, therefore, turn to a few examples related to product characteristics.

PRODUCT CHARACTERISTICS AND TRADITIONALITY

Scanning the two sets of attributes in question again shows the importance of the types of schemata or models and how they are used: many characteristics of environments as product follow from this concern: complexity, formal qualities, and ability to communicate effectively, and many others, for example.[47] A high degree of specificity also becomes evident; qualities present in some cases are absent in others. For example, in some cases the open-endedness and stable equilibrium of many traditional environments are absent because the model is not varied at all; in others the adjustments to the model do lead to these qualities. The question then concerns the extent to which the model is varied, and the point at which it becomes a different model (i.e., a change *of* the model rather than *to* the model). This question is more operational, and it has implications for the study of other types of environments and for design (i.e., it leads to potential lessons).

One attribute of traditionality (in "Economy/Technology") suggests a product characteristic of environments which Table 2 omits. This is the "non-hedonistic" and, particularly, "non-consumerist" attribute of traditionality. Comparisons of slides of traditional and contemporary house interiors in the same culture suggest the extraordinary impact on the latter of the proliferation of possessions. In general, members of traditional societies tend to have few possessions; dwellings are bare and the objects owned can be stored out of sight or in various odd corners or places. In contemporary dwellings the extraordinary growth of possessions of various sorts has instrumental implications, such as creating a need for storage space or special display facilities, greater security and greater differentiation and specialization of settings. This reinforces the general tendency towards more types of settings, which are few in traditional environments.[48] This in turn, leads to a greater need for separations -- reinforced by increasing individuality and other changes in group attributes such as status, homogeneity, egalitarianism and many others. This relates to the latent implications of possessions -- owned objects are displayed and become indicators of status.

I have personally observed among the Bedouin that the first modern buildings are meant for safe storage of possessions rather than for dwelling. In the case of the Kalahari Bushmen the impact of the individual ownership of possessions on social organization and culture (i.e., on group attributes such as individualism, cohesion, cooperation, conflict, etc.), and on the built environment (both dwellings and settlements), has been well documented.[49] Greater individualism means more and varied models and schemata. It also leads to greater attempts to communicate identity, since individual status is both more important and less clear.[50] The relation between more possessions and the need for more space, more different kinds of space, security for objects and more privacy all lead to more separation from the outside and from other people and to more differentiation internally.[51]

Such changes in the number of possessions also have another consequence. They lead to the much greater importance of semi-fixed feature elements in communicating meaning which, I have argued, characterizes present-day built environments. Other changes in meaning also follow. For example, with changes of traditional attributes to modern ones, individual meanings tend to become more important than group meanings. Thus in traditional situations meanings are shared (lexical) within the group and tend not to be shared at all by other groups; the boundary is as strong in this respect as in others. Meanings are never idiosyncratic, or individual, as they tend to become with modernity.[52] It has even been suggested that ethnic identity itself becomes a way of establishing *individual* identity.[53]

The change in other attributes of traditionality, for example the development and increase in literacy (and possibly also what Popper calls World Three), and the consequent great availability of a variety of symbolic systems, means that built environments communicate considerably fewer high-level meanings (e.g., symbolic, cosmological, etc.) than do traditional built environments.[54] This is reinforced by changes in attributes such as religiosity. Moreover, as a result of literacy, examples become less important, and patterns, schemata, models and the like tend to lose continuity. Tradition is, therefore, less likely to be transmitted by artifacts and more likely to be transmitted by other, symbolic means -- to the extent that it is transmitted at all. Also, as a result of certain changes in the attributes of traditionality, some of which have been discussed above, middle-level meanings --status, identity and the like -- become more important. Environments communicate less effectively; at the same time societies become larger in scale and less homogeneous, and they come to have more constituent parts, many more schemata, values, ideals and lifestyles, and more diversity and conflict. As a result everyday lower-level meanings, communicating ways to behave and the purposes of settings, tend to require greater redundancy, with a consequent impact on the built environment. This need is further reinforced by the lesser influence of norms, customs, rules, sanctions, etc., both at the societal level -- which studies of traditionality emphasize -- and at the level of settings. In traditional settings the rules for ongoing behavior are very strong, and the response to the cues (in themselves very clear and unequivocal) is largely unquestioned and habitual.[55]

Attributes such as "small-scale," "slow population growth" and "slow change" have many direct and indirect effects on the built environment, as do the changes in scale and heterogeneity which come with modernization. This not only makes relevant the large and sophisticated literature in human ecology, but suggests specific impacts. For example, the increase in population not only has an impact on economic and institutional behavior.[56] These, in turn, affect the built environment. Population increase also typically means less land, reduced mobility and other changes in privacy mechanisms and conflict-resolution mechanisms.[57] Higher density also has an impact on housing and settlement form. There is also evidence, although not unequivocal, that changes in scale have major impact on social networks, relationships, interaction communication, the nature of groups and so on.[58] These, in turn, significantly influence the nature of built environments. All of these also interact with many other attributes such as "slow economic and technological growth," "low innovation," "low obsolescence" and so on. Schemata and models in traditional societies can be repeated over long periods. Techniques remain usable and valid and setting types do not proliferate, there is very limited choice: continuity and links with the past typical of traditionality and traditional environments are not only possible but extremely likely.

Once again there seem to be major benefits in approaching the topic in the manner suggested. Starting with just two attributes, one from each table, one is quickly lead to a cascade of interactions, suggested influences, insights, questions, research problems and so on. Such an approach also begins to lead into discussions of changes in attributes with loss of tradition, modernization and so on. This leads one to the final issue which I will address briefly in conclusion: the value of studying the topic and the potential lessons that might come out of it.

CONCLUSION

The "exotic" examples of preliterate and vernacular environments and the societies that produce them do seem to be what most people mean by traditional environments. This identity is usually taken for granted -- as I did in *House Form and Culture*. It also appears that the characteristics which I attributed in that book to designers of such environments seem to correspond to some rather widely held views. A fairly detailed review of recent literature does not change that in any major way. The review does, however, achieve several things. It provides a large set of attributes which clarify the concept of traditionality and, if considered to be a polythetic set, allow more subtle classifications and distinctions to be made, and various present-day and other groups to be ranked in terms of their traditionality -- either generally or in terms of values, lifestyle, religion -- or in terms of built environments. This approach has methodological advantages and avoids reliance on ideal types. It also makes it possible, at least in principle, to rank various groups of attributes or single attributes in terms of their utility for our domain.   One thus discovers that attributes of tradition have little to say about the identity of designers but a great deal to say about the nature of schemata or models. As we shall see, other gaps can also begin to be identified.

A similar argument led to the use of a set of attributes relevant to built environments. Using these two sets of attributes (or, more generally, two such sets) should lead to a more detailed, useful and insightful discussion. This should not only greatly clarify the topic, but could quickly lead to a research program. It could also draw attention to, and make potentially useful, a number of bodies of literature -- not in general (when they can become overwhelming) -- but regarding specific attributes or sets of attributes (e.g., human ecology, anthropology, modernization, development economics and others). Moreover, by linking many concepts, drawing attention to mechanisms and so on, this approach provides a conceptual framework for the topic and promises to lead to the development of theory. Only a very few undeveloped examples of the approach could be given, but even these provided a number of implicit lessons. For example, it appears that the attributes in "Nature of Groups (A)" are less useful than other attributes, although even these draw attention to certain potentially useful characteristics, for example, that schemata may not be easily comprehensible. This is a common problem; many environments seen as chaotic are only incomprehensible to, disliked by, or inappropriate for the outside observer.[59] Other implicit lessons are conceptual, about the need to dismantle concepts, about over-generalization and so on. Others are about methodological.

Other lessons are more specific, for example about designing for developing countries or deriving ideas about climatic and energy efficiency.[60] Others concern environmental quality profiles, for example that high-level meanings are likely to be less important in contemporary situations, whereas lower-level meanings and, above all, middle-level meanings are likely to gain in importance.[61] This suggests that *different* latent functions become important in different traditional or non-traditional situations. It also appears that comfort, apart from being a highly variable concept, becomes more important in non-traditional environments, although, once again, this is place- and group-specific. Attention is drawn to changes from group to individual phenomena and increased choice, diversity, etc., although such changes need not be unilineal; they have major implications for design, especially of dwellings and neighborhoods.[62]

Other lessons are about the nature of tradition itself. Among these are that certain attributes relevant to built environments, some of which have already been mentioned briefly, are missing. Another emerges from a point about tradition ignored by the literature: that many definitions and attributes of tradition seem very close to attributes of culture.[63] In some ways this makes sense, because both concepts are seen as patterns for behavior and actions; both provide continuity, identify groups and so on. At the same time, this similarity is puzzling and presents a problem. Since all human groups possess culture, but only some are described as traditional, this identity seems difficult to resolve. It may be attributed partly to the fact that the concept of culture was defined by anthropologists largely on the basis of traditional societies (another example of the circularity found with respect to vernacular design). In any case, this is an issue that requires more thought and research.

There is another gap in the attributes of traditionality which is of the greatest importance with regard to built form. Given that environments are supportive of lifestyles and activity systems, and that a culture is best dismantled to just those (as well as to social structures and institutions),[64] it follows that "traditional lifestyle" would be a useful attribute. While many of the attributes in Table 1 do bear on social structures and institutions and, to some extent, on lifestyle, much more detail would be desirable. This is another area that requires research.

Another lesson is that there are many traditions, only some of which we call traditional.[65] Also, one can like some aspects of tradition and not others, so that traditions do not disappear or change all of a piece; some aspects may persist, while others disappear or are modified.[66] Even when traditions continue rather than being rejected, adherence to them today is not as it once was. Both rejection and fervent attachment to pastness, as well as acceptance of only some aspects of tradition, are the result of choice, of decisions. These responses are no longer non-reflective, "natural" or self-evident, qualities which constitute one of the major attributes of traditionality.

This raises questions about different contemporary traditions and about attempts to preserve past environments, the meaning of traditional decor, furniture and dwellings, liking a traditional built environment while disapproving of all other aspects of a tradition, and so on. These become potential lessons since they are problems for research.

Other such questions, and hence lessons, concern the fate of traditional groups in large complex societies, their relative survival in more centralized states such as France in comparison to their survival in less centralized states such as the United States. Questions are also raised about the nature of vernacular environments in the New World, for example, whether approaches developed to study traditional vernaculars can be at all valid in the United States (a question which J.B. Jackson has recently emphasized).

I will conclude with one final lesson regarding process which bears on the nature of design and the role of Environment-Behavior Studies (EBS).

Many of the attributes of traditionality in Table 1 relate to a particular process of preliterate and vernacular design whereby slow, incremental changes over long time periods lead to congruence with various aspects of culture and ecological setting. This I have recently called "selectionism."[67] In terms of what I call the choice model of design,[68] the criteria are widely shared and developed over long time periods by the actions of many. In any given design they are applied with minimal reflection, in a customary, self-evident way to approach an accepted model or schema. There are also few, unspecialized and undifferentiated settings, a fact which makes this process even easier, as do slow change and obsolescence, low novelty, and many of the other attributes discussed.

In traditional high-style design the schemata or models change more frequently.[69] They are, however, still used for considerable time periods. Also, most settings are still vernacular and only a few are designed by professionals who, moreover, share values and beliefs with clients, who are also the users. The knowledge and experience of designers is still applicable, even though the process is changing.

At present none of these conditions apply. There are very many, highly specialized and differentiated settings which continually proliferate, and professionals are expected to design types of environments which their traditions did not address in the past. Moreover, changes and innovation are rapid and continuous, obsolescence comes quickly, and novelty has high value. Designers as a group are quite different from users as a whole -- and there are many and diverse groups of users whose schemata, lifestyles, environmental quality profiles and systems of settings are incomprehensible to designers because they are quite foreign and exotic. Moreover, single designers, or teams of designers, are expected to produce designs in short time periods for clients who are not users, to be built by other teams. Designers, in effect, produce sets of instructions; I call this process "instructionism."[70]

For this to be feasible, design must undergo major change primarily by becoming a science-based profession (i.e., by having a research- and theory-based disciplinary foundation, a major component of which must be EBS.[71] Such research and theory require generalization and hence that body of evidence to which I referred earlier so that an essential component of it must be comparative research on traditional environments, which comprise the bulk of what humans have designed and built. Traditional design is a treasurehouse of human experience -- of successes and failures, of ways in which built environments have interacted with ecological settings and culture.[72] Such environments are an essential part of what design must become now and in the future. The question is how to go about studying it. This paper presents one possible answer to that question.

REFERENCE NOTES

1. This is a greatly edited version of a keynote paper presented at the International Symposium on Traditional Dwellings and Settlements, Berkeley, CA, April 1988.
2. A. Rapoport, *Human Aspects of Urban Form* (Oxford: Pergamon Press, 1977), pp. 8-9.
3. A. Rapoport, *House Form and Culture* (Englewood Cliffs, NJ: Prentice-Hall, 1969); "Sociocultural Aspects of Man-Environment Studies," in A. Rapoport, ed., *The Mutual Interaction of People and their Built Environment* (The Hague: Mouton, 1976), pp. 7-35; "Urban design and human systems: On ways of relating buildings to urban fabric," in P. Laconte, J. Gibson and A. Rapoport, eds., *Human and Energy Systems in Urban Planning* (The Hague: Martinus Nijhoff, 1982), pp. 161-184; "Thinking about home environments: a conceptual framework," in I. Altman and C.M. Werner, eds., *Home Environments (vol.8 of Human Behavior and Environment)* (New York: Plenum, 1985), pp. 255-286; "The use and design of open spaces in urban neighborhoods," in D. Frick, ed., *The Quality of Urban Life (Social, Psychological and Physical Conditions)* (Berlin: de Gruyter, 1986), pp. 159-175.
4. A. Rapoport, "Towards a cross-culturally valid definition of housing," in R.R. Stough and A. Wandersman, eds., *Optimizing Environments (Research, Practice and Theory)* (EDRA 11) (Washington, D.C.: EDRA, 1980), pp. 310-316; "Systems of activities and systems of settings," in S. Kent, ed., *Domestic Architecture and Use of Space -- an Interdisciplinary Perspective*, (in press), especially Fig. 5.
5. Rapoport, "Thinking about home environments"; "On Diversity" and "Designing for Diversity," in B. Judd, J. Dean and D. Brown, eds., *Design for Diversification (Housing Issues I)* (Canberra: Royal Australian Institute of Architects, 1985), pp. 5-8, 30-36.
6. For a comparable argument on the need to study traditional patterns of resource use in neotropical forests, see *MAB Bulletin* Vol.12 no. 1 (April 1988), p. 3.
7. A. Rapoport, "An approach to vernacular design," in J.M. Fitch, ed., *Shelter: Models of Native Ingenuity* (Katonah, NY: Katonah Gallery, 1982), pp. 43-48; "Environmental Quality, Metropolitan areas and traditional settlements," *Habitat International*, Vol. 7 no. 3/4, (1983), pp. 37-63; "Development, culture change and supportive design," *Habitat International*, Vol. 7 no. 5/6, (1983), pp. 249-268; "Culture and built form -- a reconsideration," in D.G. Saile, ed., *Architecture in Cultural Change (Essays in Built Form & Culture Research)* (Lawrence: University of Kansas, 1986), pp. 157-175; "Settlements and energy: historical precedents," in W.H. Ittelson, M. Asai and M. Ker, eds., *Cross-Cultural Research in Environment and Behavior* (Proc. 2nd US/Japan Seminar, 1985) (Tucson: University of Arizona, 1986), pp. 219-237; "Spontaneous settlements as vernacular design," in C. Patton, ed., *Spontaneous Shelter* (Philadelphia: Temple University Press, 1988); "Defining vernacular design," in M. Turan, ed., *On Vernacular Architecture: A Collection of Essays* (in press); "Systems of activities and systems of settings."
8. L. Subanu and B. Setiewan, "The Role of traditional values in a high density marginal settlement in Yogyakarta," (Mimeo, September 1987); J.-L. Bourgeois, *Spectacular Vernacular -- A New Appreciation of Traditional Desert Architecture* (Salt Lake City: Peregrine Smith Books, 1983), also uses the words "traditional," "traditions," etc., without defining them.
9. Rapoport, *House Form and Culture.*
10. R.A. Rappaport, *Ecology, Meaning and Religion* (Richmond, CA: North Atlantic Books, 1979), devotes a whole chapter to "unpacking" the term "ritual."

11.   Rapoport, "An approach to vernacular design"; "Spontaneous settlements as vernacular design"; and especially "Defining vernacular design."

12.   Slightly more technically, this is equivalent to moving from a monothetic definition to a polythetic approach. The former is based on a unique set of attributes which is both necessary and sufficient to assign a thing, e.g. a society or a type of environment, to a class. It is frequently an ideal type definition in which every member of the class must have all the qualifying attributes. A polythetic approach uses a larger set of attributes so that things fit into groups based on a range of variation between defined limits, a high proportion of the attributes being shared among individual members of the class. Thus in a polythetic approach no single attribute, or even set of attributes, is both sufficient and necessary for membership in the class. This formulation is based on D.L. Clarke, *Analytical Archaeology* (London: Methuen & Co., 2nd ed 1978), pp. 35-37; as developed in much more detail in Rapoport, "Defining vernacular design."

13.   K.Z. Lorentz, *The Foundations of Ethology* (New York: Springer Verlag, 1981), p. 83; cf. Rapoport, "Defining vernacular design."

14.   E. Shils, *Tradition* (Chicago: University of Chicago Press, 1981).

15.   X. Zhao, "Attributions of Architectural Forms (Models for understanding and inheriting characteristics of traditional Chinese architectural form)" (Ph.D. dissertation, School of Architecture, University of Lund, 1987); B.S. Hakim, "Recycling the experience of traditional Islamic built environments: a proposed framework and notes for generating principles" (Mimeo, College of Architecture and Planning, King Faisal University 1987); E. Rochberg-Halton, *Meaning and Modernity (Social Theory in the Pragmatic Attitude)* (Chicago: University of Chicago Press, 1986); Shils, *Tradition*.

16.   This is analagous to my discussion of approaches to culture in "Culture and built form -- a reconsideration."

17.   Shils, *Tradition*,is one notable exception.

18.   See Shils, *Tradition*; Rochberg-Halton, *Meaning and Modernity*.

19.   See Shils, *Tradition*, p. 2. I suspect that many of those who admire traditional built environments visually would reject attributes of tradition such as lack of choice, acceptance of authority, force of normative rules, lifestyle, etc. One of my students, while studying Rumanian village vernacular, was horrified at the traditional behavior and lifestyle which went with it; the conflict was acute, and the student found it very distressing.

20.   Shils, *Tradition*; Rochberg-Halton, *Meaning and Modernity*. See also *The Religion and Society Report*, Vol. 5 No. 2 (February 1988), pp. 1-4, especially 1-2.

21.   These are derived mainly from F. Bartlett, *Remembering* (Cambridge: Cambridge University Press, 1967; originally published 1932); H. Goldberg, "The Changing Meaning of Ethnic Affiliation" *The Jerusalem Quarterly* 44 (Fall 1987), pp. 39-50; Hakim, "Islamic built environments"; B. Hoselitz, *Sociological Aspects of Economic Growth: an Adaptation* (New York: Feffer and Simons, 1960); G. Hunter, *Modernizing Peasant Societies* (London: Oxford University Press, 1960); A. Inkeles and D. Smith, *Becoming Modern* (London: Heinemann Educational Books, 1974); summarized in M.T. Munarriz, "Traditional vs. modern behavior in a housing development (The Tondo Foreshore development)," *Habitat International*, Vol. 10 no. 3 (1986), pp. 143-152; W.H. Isbell, "Cosmological Order Expressed in Prehistoric Ceremonial Centers," in *Actes du XLIIe Congres International des Americanistes* vol.4 (Paris, 1986), pp. 269-297; M. Jacobi and D. Stokols, "The Role of Tradition in Group-Environment Relations," in N.R. Feimer and E.S. Geller, eds., *Environmental Psychology (Directions and Perspectives)* (New York: Praeger, 1983), pp. 157-179; R.G. Knapp, *China's Traditional Rural Architecture*

(A Cultural Geography of the Common House) (Honolulu: University of Hawaii Press, 1986); A. Meir, "Comparative Vital Statistics Along the pastoral nomadism-sedentarism continuum," *Human Ecology*, Vol. 15 no.1 (March 1987), pp. 91-107; Rapoport, *House Form and Culture*; Rochberg-Halton, *Meaning and Modernity*; D. Seamon, "Phenomenology and Vernacular Lifeworlds," in Saile, ed., *Architecture in Cultural Change*, pp. 17-24; D. Stokols and M. Jacobi, "Traditional, present-oriented and futuristic modes of group-environment relations," in K. and M. Gergen, eds., *Historical Social Psychology* (Hillsdale, NJ: Lawrence Erlbaum Associates, 1984), pp. 303-324; J. Yellen, "Bushmen," *Science 85* (May, 1985), pp. 40-48; Zhao, "Attributions of Architectural Forms"; above all, Shils, *Tradition*.

22. This clearly only applies to some, since others are described as authoritarian and hierarchical.

23. This is clearly the sense in which it is used in a recent book on a U.S. culture region, J.W. Glass, *The Pennsylvania Culture Region (The View from the Barn)* (Ann Arbor: UMI Research Press, 1986), especially pp. 225-226.

24. From a special Holiday Gift Guide of the *Los Angeles Times* (Nov. 15, 1987).

25. Rapoport, "Culture and built form -- a reconsideration."

26. Rapoport, "Development, culture change and supportive design."

27. Such design is briefly discussed in Rapoport, "Culture and built form -- a reconsideration." This seems to provide an interesting topic for research, as would popular design.

28. C. and P. Donnadieu and H. and J.-M. Didillon, *Habiter le Desert (Les Maisons Mozabites)* (Bruxelles: P. Mardaga, 1977), p. 9.

29. E. Rosch, "Principles of Categorization," in E. Rosch and B.B. Lloyd, eds., *Cognition and Categorization* (Hillsdale, NJ: Erlbaum, 1978), pp. 27-48.

30. This is also the case with Bourgeois, *Spectacular Vernacular*, and Donnadieu and Didillon, *Habiter le Desert*.

31. Rapoport, "An approach to vernacular design"; "Spontaneous settlements as vernacular design"; in most detail, "Defining vernacular design."

32. Rapoport, "Spontaneous settlements as vernacular design."

33. From Rapoport, "Defining vernacular design."

34. Rapoport, "Culture and built form --a reconsideration."

35. R. Gardi, *Tambaran* (London: Constable, 1960); S.M. Mead, ed., *Exploring the Visual Arts of Oceania* (Honolulu: University Press of Hawaii, 1979); A. Rapoport, "Identity and Environment: A cross-cultural perspective," in J.S. Duncan, ed., *Housing and Identity (Cross-Cultural Perspectives)* (London: Croom-Helm, 1981), pp. 6-35; "Culture and built form -- a reconsideration."

36. J. Hockings, "Built Form and Culture (A Case Study of Gilbertese Architecture)" (Unpublished Ph.D. dissertation, Dept. of Arch., University of Queensland (Australia), 1984); P.W. Staeger, "Where does art begin in Puluwat," in Mead, ed., *Exploring the Visual Arts of Oceania*, pp. 342-353.

37. H.T. Saad, "Between Myth and Reality: the Aesthetics of Traditional Architecture in Hausaland" (Unpublished D. Arch. dissertation, University of Michigan, 1981).

38. Rapoport, *Human Aspects of Urban Form*.

39. Rapoport, "Spontaneous settlements as vernacular design." Also A. Rapoport, "Culture and the Urban Order," in J. Agnew, J. Mercer and D. Sopher, eds., *The City in Cultural Context* (Boston: Allen and Unwin, 1983), pp. 50-75.

40. H. Glassie, *Pattern in e Material Folk Culture of the Eastern United States* (Philadelphia: University of Pennsylvania Press, 1968), pp. 33-34.

41. E.g., D. Swaim, ed., *Carolina Dwelling* (Raleigh: N.C. Student Publication, School of Design, N.C. State University, Vol. 28, 1978); W.C. Miller, "Vernacular

influences in Modern Finnish Architecture," in Saile, ed., *Architecture in Cultural Change*, p. 147.

42. A. Rapoport, "Australian Aborigines and the definition of place," in P. Oliver, ed., *Shelter, Sign and Symbol* (London: Barrie and Jenkins, 1975) pp. 38-51; P. Brown, *Highland Peoples of New Guinea* (Cambridge: Cambridge University Press, 1978); E.K. Agorsah, "Evaluating settlement and behavior patterns of traditional societies: an ethnoarchaeological perspective," in *Archaeological "Objectivity" in Interpretation* (Preprinted Papers of World Archaeology Congress) Vol. 2 (Portsmouth, England: September 1986).

43. Rapoport, "Systems of activities and systems of settings," especially Fig. 2.

44. E.g., P. Weissner, "Style and changing relations between individual and society," in *Archaeological "Objectivity" in Interpretation* Vol 2; cf. Goldberg, "The Changing Meaning of Ethnic Affiliation."

45. A. Rapoport, "Levels of Meaning in the built environment," in F. Poyatos, ed., *Cross-Cultural Perspectives in Nonverbal Communication* (Gotingen: Hogrefe, 1988); "Systems of activities and systems of settings."

46. Note that there is currently some disagreement with the received view about this and research as thus indicated. E.g., N. Williams and D. Mununggurr, "Understanding Yolngu signs of the past," in *Archaeological "Objectivity" in Interpretation*, Vol. 3. Their summary of the received view is very similar to the attributes I have identified for "Temporal"; this material, read after completing this chapter, fits the schema. ("Traditional": timeless, cyclic, changeless, concrete, time not internalized, time obedience, task-oriented time. "Modern": time-based, linear, changing, abstract, time internalized (punctuality), time discipline, work-oriented time.)

47. E.g., Rapoport, *Human Aspects of Urban Form*. Also, A. Rapoport, *The Meaning of the Built Environment (A Non Verbal Communication Approach)* (Beverly Hills, CA: Sage, 1982); "Spontaneous settlements as vernacular design."

48. Rapoport, "Systems of activities and systems of settings."

49. Yellen, "Bushmen."

50. J.S. Duncan, "Landscape and the Communication of Social Identity," in A. Rapoport, ed., *The Mutual Interaction of People and Their Built Environment* (The Hague: Mouton, 1976), pp. 391-401; "From container of women to status symbol: the impact of social structure on the meaning of the house," in Duncan, ed., *Housing and Identity: Cross-Cultural Perspectives*, pp. 36-59.

51. In this connection there seems to be a problem with Munarriz's (1986) argument that with the loss of traditional behavior consumption goes down in favor of savings. At least at the microlevel of individuals, consumption (in the sense of acquisition and ownership of things) goes up rapidly and, as we have seen, has a major impact on dwellings and, through social relationships, also on settlement form.

52. Rapoport, *The Meaning of the Built Environment*.

53. Goldberg, "The Changing Meaning of Ethnic Affiliation."

54. J. Goody, *The Domestication of the Savage Mind* (Cambridge: Cambridge University Press, 1977); Rapoport, "Culture and built form -- a reconsideration"; "Levels of Meaning in the built environment"; "Systems of activities and systems of settings." I have also discovered since writing this chapter that this point was made in C. Tilley, "Interpreting material culture," in *Archaeological "Objectivity" in Interpretation*, Vol 2.

55. Rapoport, *The Meaning of the Built Environment*; "Culture and built form -- a reconsideration"; "Levels of Meaning in the built environment"; "Systems of

activities and systems of settings."
56. E.g., Meir, "Comparative vital statistics."
57. A. Rapoport, "Nomadism as a Man-environment system," in *Environment and Behavior*, Vol. 10 no. 2 (June 1978), pp. 215-246.
58. G.D. Berreman, "Scale and Social Relations," *Current Anthropology*, Vol. 19 no.2 (June 1978), pp. 225-249; E.K. Sadalla, "Population size, structural differentiation and human behavior," *Environment and Behavior*, Vol. 10 no. 2 (June 1978), pp. 271-291; cf. Rapoport, *Human Aspects of Urban Form.*
59. Rapoport, *Human Aspects of Urban Form;* "Culture and the Urban Order."
60. Rapoport, "Development, culture change and supportive design"; "Settlements and energy: historical precedents."
61. Rapoport, "Levels of Meaning in the built environment."
62. Rapoport, "Thinking about home environments: a conceptual framework"; "On Diversity"; "Designing for Diversity."
63. A. Rapoport, "Cross-cultural aspects of environmental design," in I. Altman, A. Rapoport and J.F. Wohlwill, eds., *Environment and Culture (vol.4 of Human Behavior and Environment)* (New York: Plenum, 1980), pp. 7-46; "Culture and built form -- a reconsideration."
64. Rapaport, *Human Aspects of Urban Form;* "Cross-cultural aspects of environmental design"; "Development, culture change and supportive design"; Thinking about home environments: a conceptual framework"; "On Diversity"; "Designing for Diversity"; "Systems of activities and systems of settings."
65. Shils, *Tradition,* calls these "substantive traditions."
66. Rapoport, "Development, culture change and supportive design." This implies that there are different rates of change for different components of the built environment, which is of great importance for situations of culture change. Glass, *The Pennsylvania Culture Region,* points out that barns changed less and were more uniform (traditional) than houses because of higher criticality. One can predict that since farm structures are related to economics, and these change rapidly, barns will now change more, and houses will remain more traditional. It seems from Glass' book that this is happening.
67. Rapoport, "Culture and built form -- a reconsideration."
68. Rapoport, *Human Aspects of Urban Form.* Also, A. Rapoport, "Debating Architectural Alternatives," in *Transactions of the Royal Institute of British Architects* 3, pp. 105-109.
69. Rapoport, "Spontaneous settlements as vernacular design"; "Defining vernacular design."
70. Rapoport, "Culture and built form -- a reconsideration."
71. Rapoport, "Debating Architectural Alternatives." Also, A. Rapoport, "Studious Questions," *Architects' Journal,* Vol. 178 no. 43 (26 Oct., 1983), pp. 55-57 (reprinted in *Architectural Record* (October 1984), pp. 100-103); "Statement for the ACSA 75th Anniversary (Jubilee) issue," *Journal of Architectural Education,* Vol. 40 no. 2, (1987), pp. 65-66.
72. I have just completed a rather large book which develops this topic in great detail (*History and Precedent in Environmental Design*).

JUNCTIONS OF TOWN AND COUNTRY

SPIRO KOSTOF

The prevailing sentiment, popular as well as scholarly, has always been to consider town and country one of the classic dichotomies of culture. In my own discipline, the history of architecture, the visual contrast of the two is ineluctable (FIGS. 1, 2). Primal images of the walled city, a densely packed structure of buildings and streets, are among our commonest documents. The open countryside with its patterns of field and cottages, has never held the same interest, save for the architecturally distinguished villa and its landscaped setting. Even in the study of cities, architectural historians have been overwhelmingly preoccupied with urban design in the sense of self-conscious and formal solutions of city-form -- a preoccupation which parallels, of course, our long-held exclusive claim to pedigreed buildings, to architecture as art. The more recent fascination with what urban designers like Gordon Cullen call "townscape" is equally conditioned by visual incident, albeit of a more informal, and anonymous sort.

My own professional scrutiny for some time now has been directed, instead, at physical continuities -- continuities of time and place. I am interested in the built environment as a whole: in all buildings, the commonplace and the fancy, and their arrangements into landscapes of form subject to perennial change. For this effort, it has increasingly become evident, the disjunction of town and country is counterproductive, and the habit of viewing the city as a distinctive unit of analysis quite possibly wrong-headed. We

F I G U R E S 1, 2. Ambrogio Lorenzetti, Effects of Good Government in the
Town and Country. Siena, Palazzo Pubblico ca. 1340.

should be in the business of studying the history of settlement patterns, in which cities are merely accents, spontaneous or imposed by origin, that possess uncommon size and complexity. Physically, we should recall, city-form is most insistently beholden to prior systems of land division and settlement, farming practices and the disposition of common fields and pastures.

A PREAMBLE: THE CASE OF SIENA

To introduce some of the themes I wish to address in the chapter, it might be useful to start in *medias res*, with a well-known and beloved specimen of urban form -- the medieval commune of Siena.[1]

Siena, at the end of the thirteenth century, was a powerful and well-run North Italian city-state, locked in fierce competition with its neighbor, Florence, to the north, and holding its own. Its territory stretched south and west almost to the edge of the Tyrrhenian Sea and the swampy coastal lowlands of the Maremma, in total an area of about a thirty-mile radius from the city. This hilly, poorly-watered area included forests, good farmlands, pastures, and more than three hundred small towns, rural communities and feudal castles that recognized Siena's authority.

The city lay on the Via Francigena or Romea, a branch of the great Roman highway, the Via Emilia, connecting Parma with Rome. This tract ran right through the city, forming its north-southeast spine, and was dotted with inns and hospices which served the crowds of pilgrims and other travelers who came down from the north and, under Sienese protection, headed toward the papal city. With another leg of this spine in the direction of the southwest, the city had the shape of an inverted Y whose tips were marked by three hills -- the domed Castlevecchio and San Martino, and the linear stretch of Camollia (FIGS. 3, 5). The story of the city of Siena as we know it begins with the merger of the communities on these three hills and the transformation of the harboring dip in their midst, the Campo, into a civic center -- a process that started in the

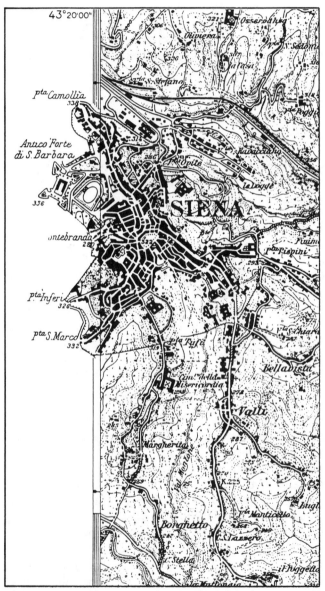

F I G U R E 3. Siena, plan of the city. (Source: Istituto Geografico Militare, reprinted from Benevolo, *Storia della Città*, 1976.)

F I G U R E 4. Siena city wall of 1326.

sixth or seventh century but was not formalized politically until the eleventh.

The walls were expanded several times as they grew. The last set, begun in 1326, loosely hugged the city. There was a lot of agricultural land within, and even the built-up area was liberally punctuated with vegetable gardens and orchards (FIG. 4). In prominent locations all over the hilly townscape, the principal families, many of them feudal nobility, had their *castellari*, fortified compounds with towers and other defensive appurtenances. These were rambling households with servant quarters, stables and warehousing facilities. The type was essentially the land-based feudal nucleus of the countryside, brought within the urban fabric by the magnates when the action moved from the countryside into the city and the agrarian economy of the earlier medieval centuries was superseded by an urban economy of banking and long-distance trade. To force these feudal lords to live within the walls, subject to the law of the city-state, was a main goal of the communal government. The defensible *castellare*, however, was a threatening unit for the city's self-government -- an undigested lump in the urban body. The commune in time will run streets right through these enclaves, forcing them to open up and front the public space civilly with perforated facades.

The example of medieval Siena, and the few points I have selected to mention about its physical appearance, help me to introduce several abiding lineaments of the mutual dependence of town and country.

First, both administratively and politically, the structure of human settlement has frequently engaged total landscapes. In this case, the Sienese commune itself is an extended pattern of townships, villages and cultivated rural land. Second, the agricultural and pastoral uses of towns have always been important, especially in the so-called pre-industrial city. Third, the issue of topography is indeed central -- not only in the primary sense that hills and valleys determine the configuration of settlements, which Siena's Y plainly demonstrates, but also in the additional and more significant sense that pre-extant rural order inevitably affects the developing city-form. In the case of Siena, urban morphogenesis is traceable to the coming together of three independent villages and their network of roads. The final lineament is that acclimation of rural housing patterns to city streets is an enduring theme of urban process for which the example of the Sienese *castellare* provides a dramatic illustration.

There are other aspects of my subject, coming to maturity in relatively recent times in the context of the modern city, which do not find prototypes in Siena. Chief among these is the history of Western experiments in urbanism that try to reconcile town and country, experiments that range form the Anglo-American picturesque suburb to the various formulations of the linear city.

RURAL/URBAN RELATIONSHIPS

I must make clear before I take up these themes for a more detailed look that it would be futile to attempt to deny the very real differences between cities and the countryside. The traditional labor of the farmer and the husbandman, set in the plains and pleats of the land and subject to seasonal rhythms, stands in millennial juxtaposition to the affairs of the city. The sociologist's distinctions must retain their qualified validity. It is surely not idle to recognize the informal social organizations of villages, with their static slow-changing ways, their low level of labor-division and their elemental sense of community or *Gemeinschaft*, and to set this against the city's enterprise, its *Gesellschaft*, impersonal and dynamic, with a refined division of labor and a dependence on advanced technologies and industrial processes.[2]

Long before sociology was born, these contrasts were eloquently articulated and enjoyed. The Renaissance in Italy, for example, set great score by the perfect life of the privileged classes balanced between *negotium* and *otium philosophicum*. That philosophical calm, for the rich and powerful Florentine merchants, could only be had in the country, where the villa engaged Nature, her flowers and trees and meadows, her secret springs and scurrying creatures. At Poggio a Caiano, at Careggi and Caffagiolo, friends of Plato, lovers of his soul and students of his text, gathered to contemplate Truth. These were *good* men who had to be merchants and bankers and politicians in the city, but who slipped away here to a rustic, basic age, where pleasures were simple and thoughts deep. "Blessed villa," Alberti rhapsodized, "sure home of good cheer, which rewards one with countless benefits: verdure in spring, fruit in autumn, a meeting-place for good men, an exquisite dwelling." Many cultures put score by this restorative balance between one's trade and one's sanity.

By the same token, the arguments of the present day which see a thorough interdependency between town and country, between agriculture and industry, and which point to the decline of the farming population, to the mechanization of farming processes and to the leveling influence of radio, television and tourism, also are well-taken. And like Alberti's celebration of the country, they are also, for the purposes of this chapter, largely beside the point.

My own concern here is man-land relations as they are manifested in physical planning, and my point is prismatic. How do we record the continuous processes of settlement and analyze its patterns?

How do we resist seeing urban form as a finite thing, a complicated object, pitted against an irreconcilable, and allegedly inferior, rural context?

The architectural historian, I have already acknowledged, is congenitally handicapped in these matters. He or she is unwilling to accept that in the study of the built environment we are all recorders of a physicality akin to that of a flowing river or a changing sky.

Come the urban geographers, who are also fascinated with the city as an intricate artifact. Their methods and traditions are sufficiently different, however, to make their analysis of the form and internal structure of cities at once more comprehensive and more specialized. At the very least, their insistence that we pay attention to land parcels and plots and the particular arrangement of buildings within them, that the street system and plot pattern belong together, has enabled them to study urban fabric and its transformations with more thoroughness than the conventional approach of the architectural historian -- to go beyond formal questions, to a discussion of land use. And the steady interest they have shown in the distribution pattern of towns, and the flow of goods and people within that pattern, has led them to consider larger physical frames than the city itself. For the case I am pleading here, this of course is good.

But the emphasis is mistakenly on cities, and the preoccupation is with generating theory. The urban geographer is intent on discovering standard behavior, independent of particular historical circumstance. The chapter headings in Harold Carter's *Study of Urban Geography* (London, 1972) make the point: "The Process of Urbanization," "The Growth of the City System," "Urban Functions and the Functional Classification of Towns," "The Ranking of Towns," etc.

The historian of the rural landscape, on the other hand, has long been fascinated with methods of farming, enclosure, estate ownership and the like, all of which stop short at the city gates. As for other allied fields, it is symptomatic of what I am proposing we redress that there should be a Rural Sociological Society with a journal called *Rural Sociology*, even though, in the fifties at least, there were occasional papers in it on the "rural-urban continuum."[3]

In the fifties, that phrase meant primarily the rural-urban fringe in the parlance of the sociologists, or the "rurban" fringe as they liked to call it. They inherited this interest from land economists who recognized the dynamic mixture of agricultural and urban (mostly residential) uses as something vital and worth studying. Sociologists in their turn, most notably those at the Storrs Agricultural Experiment Station in Connecticut, set out to observe trends in this fringe. It was Walter Firey, who first saw this band as a "dead center" between two conflicting ecologies. In a pioneering paper of 1946 in the *American Sociological Review* he described it rather eloquently:

> There exist, side by side, blocks of subdivided lots lined with sidewalks and dwellings, numerous vestigial commercial farms standing off the side roads and to the rear of platted frontages, trailer camps and squatter towns, great expanses of land grown up to weeds, well tended country estates owned by corporations and city business men -- all spottily distributed in clusters and in string-along-the-road patterns.[4]

To the sociologist, he wrote, this was "a valuable laboratory for the study of urbanization as an agricultural process."

The time frame here is recent. What is being observed is the result of changes in the American city since about the middle of the nineteenth century, specifically the history of suburbanization. Now the urban geographers, J.W.R. Whitehand foremost among them, were soon to seize on this urban fringe as a general principle of urban development throughout history.[5] Their term was the "urban fringe belt." The German equivalent, applied first to Berlin by H. Louis, is *Stadtrandzone*. This area contains a heterogeneous collection of land uses, and shows a large-scale, low-density building pattern that contrasts with the thickly woven fabric of its core. What kind of uses? Well, horse and cattle markets, for example, noxious manufacturing processes like tanning, institutions deemed a health hazard like suburban leper houses of medieval London, Leicester and Stamford, and religious houses like those of mendicant orders. In time, the city would incorporate this first, or inner, fringe belt, alter some of its character with an overlay of residential development, and give rise to a new fringe belt further out.

Alternating irregular rings of fringe belts and residential districts can be detected on the plans of many European cities. Each, according to its time, embodies distinct land uses. Parks do not predate the Baroque centuries; cemeteries, unless we are dealing with a distinct pre-Christian period like that of the Roman cities, are likely to start with the Enlightenment. More recently, we would find heavy industry, golf courses, universities, and in the outermost fringe, slaughterhouses, junkyards, sewage plants and oil refineries.

All of this is useful, but limited in application and method. The rural-urban continuum I am advocating as a perspective here is broader in scope, and intends to encourage the consideration of large social systems and urban-rural interdependence in the morphology of settlements. I am, in other words, anxious to extend to our own professional domains of the built environment the seamless world that the United Nations presumed in terms of population when it asserted in its *Demographic Yearbook* of 1952 that "there is no point in the continuum from large agglomerations to small clusters or scattered dwellings where urbanity disappears and rurality begins; the division between rural and urban populations is necessarily arbitrary."

SETTLEMENT SYSTEMS AND THEIR MUTATION

It is time I became more specific, and elaborated upon the thematic lines I suggested at the beginning of this chapter.

First, and at the broadest scale, we have to insist that human settlement is almost always continuous or concatenated, which means that towns and the countryside are subject to a responsive chain of design acts. If we think of cities alone, we tend to think of constellations based on some pretext or other, whether it is Walther Christhaller's or Auguste Losch's central place diagrams, or various systems of identifying urban spheres of influence like those advanced by A.E Smailes, C.R Lewis and others. There are other ways to group cities based on geographical logic: river or canal links, for example. Land routes and modern transportation means, like the railroad or the streetcar, are an equally effective basis of linkage. We could also cite political hierarchies of specific historical incident, for example the designation in China of urban hierarchies by means of suffixes added to the names of towns -- *fu* for a town of the first order, *chu* for a town of the second, *hieu* for a town of the third, and that is without counting elementary towns lower still.

But beyond the simple fact that a town can never exist unaccompanied by other towns, it is equally true, as Fernand Braudel put it, that "the town only exists as a town in relation to a form of life lower than its own. . . . There is no town, no townlet without its villages, its scrap of rural life attached."6 And it is precisely this interdependence, as a physical phenomenon most of all, that has suffered scholarly neglect because of our persistent interest in a dualism of town and country.

We will need to distinguish here between two kinds of processes. Let us call them *spontaneous* and *planned*, realizing of course that there is no aspect of human settlement that is not at least in part the result of premeditated action.

The planned process is easier to see. It is a common device of colonial enterprises when an alien land is readied for settlement by the colonizing power or agency. The city of course is the major vehicle of control and exploitation, but often the countryside is surveyed at the same time and distributed equitably and methodically. This is especially the case when the main colonial resource is agriculture rather than trade, say, or mining.

Both the Greeks and the Romans systematically divided the farming land at large, and matched urban plots for the settlers with corresponding extra-urban allotments. The gridded order of the new cities was extended to the regional scale, or rather a standard matrix of all arable land provided the setting within which the cities themselves were accommodated. In the Roman system of centuriation, the module unit was 20 by 20 Roman *actus* (or 750 by 750 meters), further subdivided among farmer-colonists. An intersection of boundary lines for the *centuriae*, or squares, could serve as the crossing point for the main axes -- the *cardo* and *decumanus* -- of the city.[7]

The same possibilities for a uniform system of town and country planning existed for Spanish colonial rule in America, and later still for the opening up of the territories in the United States under the Land Ordinance instigated by Thomas Jefferson. And side by side with the *sitios* of New Spain and the townships of Jefferson's grid, we can recite the Japanese *jori* system, introduced in the seventh century, and the land division, or *polders*, applied by Dutch engineers to land reclaimed from the sea. In the Netherlands, where the very land is a result of human design, distinctions between town and country are particularly vacuous.

Once again, we as students of environmental design have done very little with these comprehensive schemes, and much with the cities themselves which are only highlights within a larger coordinated design. We have written entire books on the ingenious 1732 plan of Savannah in colonial Georgia masterminded by James Oglethorpe, for example; but beyond a descriptive sentence or two we have left unexamined the extraordinary complement to this famous grid with its wards and squares -- the outer zone of farming lots, the five-acre gardens further in, the "Common round the Town for Convenience and Air," and the town proper along the Savannah River. It is only because the orthogonal distribution applied uniformly, even when the garden squares might be shared by two colonists, each with a triangular lot, that Savannah could maintain the ward and square arrangement of the original town plat as it grew in the next century and moved into its cultivated land.

By spontaneous settlements, I mean a natural promotion of towns within a previously even, unaccented landscape. I am aware that this may sound very much like a return to the old favorite, the rise of cities, that has sustained those urban historians and geographers

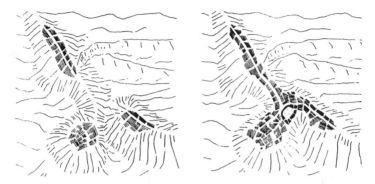

F I G U R E 5. The process of synoecism, illustrated by the merging of the villages of Castelvecchio (Città), Camollia, and Castelmontone (San Martino) to form the city of Siena. (D r a w i n g: R. Tobias.)

concerned with the pre-Classical world or the Middle Ages for several generations. But I am less interested here in the vast literature about when a town is a town (questions of size, density, economic activity, administrative function or occupational structure, etc.) than I am in those rare studies like those of Robert Adams concerning Mesopotamia.[8]

Adams' meticulous and demanding fieldwork to chart the ancient watercourses in the consensual "birthplace of the city" (which, as we would expect, turned out to be totally different than the present pattern of rivers and canals) is, in my opinion, as important for the physical history of human settlement as the more spectacular and photogenic archaeological discoveries of Leonard Wooley and his confreres have been for the history of Mesopotamian civilizations. I would also go so far as to claim, for our purposes, that the hesitant, tentative dotted lines of Adams' maps, carefully plotting ancient levees, variations of river discharges and settlement patterns, are far more critical than the diagrams of Christhaller or Thyssen.

To my knowledge this sort of documentation and analysis does not as yet exist for that other period of nascent urbanization that has intrigued urban historians of Europe, namely the several centuries in the Middle Ages when, after the subsidence of Roman urban order around the Mediterranean and the northern provinces of the empire, new towns emerged out of non-urban cores in the rearranged countryside. We have a lot of theory, an increasing volume of case studies, especially for England, and promising new directions based on the archeology of early settlements.[9] What we don't have is a scanning of regions, small or large, through that combined perspective of physical, political and social inquiry, to document and interpret transformations of the historic landscape of Europe.

Fieldwork may not be as helpful in writing the other aspects of the spontaneous process. Synoecism, the process behind the creation of medieval Siena, is one of these (FIG. 5). The term, according to Aristotle, describes the administrative coming together of several proximate villages to form a town. In his words: "When several villages are united in a single complete community, large enough to be nearly or quite self-sufficing, the *polis* comes into existence." This is how Athens was born and Rome and Venice and Viterbo and Novgorod and Calcutta, and a number of towns in Muslim Iran like Kazvin, Qum and Merv. In fact, synoecism is beginning to figure as one of the commonest origins of towns coming out of a rural context, and it is therefore unfortunate how little there is to read about the process.

The case of Islam is especially interesting in this context. Throughout its history, the Islamic city has given proof that it was conceived not so much as a tidy walled package contrasting with the open countryside, but as a composite of walled units. Twin cities, where the two settlements slowly grew together across the intervening space, were not uncommon (e.g. Isfahan, Raqqa). Ira Lapidus suggested some time ago that in some Iranian oases, entire regions might be considered composite cities, "in which the population was divided into non-contiguous, spatially isolated settlements." However you choose to categorize this constellation, it was indeed a fully self-conscious system of settlement, in that the entire region would be surrounded by an outer wall, and "urban functions were not concentrated within the walls of the largest settlement, but were often distributed throughout the oasis."[10]

The form of a synoecistic town absorbs the shapes of the original settlements, along with their road systems, and the open spaces that existed among the settlements are turned into marketplaces and communal centers. This is the origin of the Roman Forum and the Athens *agora* and Siena's Campo. In German lands during the Middle Ages, towns sometimes absorbed an adjacent rural parish, or *Landgemeinde*, in order to acquire common pasture for their flocks. The peasant inhabitants of the parish in some cases "shifted their homes into the town and became fully privileged townsmen."[11]

In Africa, traditional Black cities can be described as groups of village-like settlements with shared urban functions rather than a single center. These cities were very spread out. They consisted almost entirely of one-story structures arranged in residential compounds, no different an arrangement than the village. These compounds were often located with no particular care for alignment with the streets.[12] Sudanese Muslim cities, Al Ubayyid for example, have this same Black African pattern. In the nineteenth century Al Ubayyid was a city made up of five large villages, originally separated by cultivated areas which the Ottoman regime (ca. 1820-1884) partially filled in with barracks, mosques, a prefecture building and government worker's housing.[13]

RUS IN URBE

The next two themes I set for myself at the start of this chapter follow logically from this discussion. One has to do with the agricultural and pastoral uses of urban land, the other with the impact of rural land divisions on urban form in those spontaneous cases where an orderly regional matrix like Roman centuriation or the American Land Ordinance grid does not predetermine the pace and shape of suburban development.

I need not say much about the first of these themes. The urban accommodation of cattle has a history that stretches from Nineveh, where large open areas within the walls were set aside for the daily use of herds and "into which herds were probably driven in times of war,"[14] down to the New England common. Little need be said, too, about agriculture in the city, except to underline its prevalence and to point out again how radically an agricultural presence within the city challenges any strict separation of urban and rural domains. Sometimes a city would make its gardens and fields a walled component of the urban structure, as in the old nucleus of Cahors in a meander of the river Lot.[15] In Yoruba cities, farmers are city-dwellers, and the urban edge consists of a farm belt as much as fifteen miles wide.[16] At other times, the producing garden is a regular component of houses throughout the city. In China, not only was intensive truck-gardening found within the city, but most houses devoted a small portion of their yards to gardening. We have only spotily written the history of the transformation of producing gardens into idealized pleasure gardens. For Europe, the critical time for this was the sixteenth century.[17]

LAND DIVISION

The relation of rural land divisions to the urban form that supersedes them is a vast, critical subject, and we have not scratched much beyond the surface. I can point to some exemplary case studies to demonstrate how much we miss by neglecting this line of inquiry.

One instance is Pierce Lewis' classic study of New Orleans, entitled *New Orleans -- The Making of an Urban Landscape*, (1976) where we are shown, besides much else, the transformation of the narrow fan-shaped French plantation lots within the convex meander of the Mississippi into the radial boulevards of the expanding city (FIG. 6).

Another instance is a 1979 article by Michael E. Bonine on "The Morphogenesis of Iranian Cities," where the loose grid of towns like Shiraz and Yazd, detectable through the so-called organic city form, and the long linear streets with their rows of courtyard houses, are derived by him from the channels of subterranean

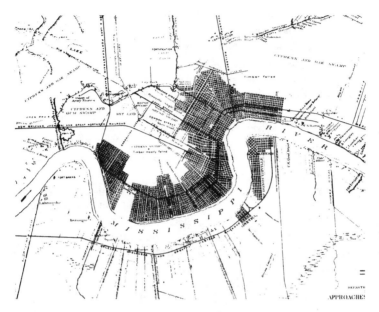

F I G U R E 6. New Orleans, Banks Map, 1863. Reprinted from Lewis, *New Orleans: The Making of an Urban Landscape*, 1976.

watercourses, or *qanat*, and a system of strip irrigation and rectangular field division.[18]

Now the documentation of this process whereby an antecedent rural landscape translates itself into urban form is exceedingly difficult, because in most cases it is impossible to reconstruct this landscape except in relatively recent history. The English have started to rediscover, for example, how the common lands and open fields which surrounded towns were first alienated to individual ownership, beginning in the mid-nineteenth century, and were then transformed into a belt of urban extension. We can see there, if we know how to read the evidence, the medieval footpaths and the furlongs of the old open fields underneath the modern network of streets.

The English have also been able to take advantage of two invaluable field surveys of the nineteenth century. The tithe maps were produced after the Tithe Commutation Act of 1836 in connection with changing the tax system on land holdings from tithes to a money payment -- that is, to a fixed rent on each holding. Most parishes in England and Wales were surveyed for this purpose, and the maps give us a precise picture of the configuration of fields. These one can superimpose on the famous Ordnance Survey maps of nineteenth century towns, drawn to a uniform scale. By matching the same segments in the tithe and Ordnance maps of Leeds, for example, it is possible to show how the pre-urban cadaster determined the lines of the urban fabric.[19]

We have still, within the context of the pre-industrial city, to comment on the acclimation of rural housing types to city streets. The evidence, never easy to gather, is steadily disappearing and scholarly interest remains marginal. The Burgerhaus of the Swiss town is a classic case of a farmstead being brought within the urban boundaries, and changing over time under pressures from urban economy, lack of building space and new architectural styles. In Sweden too, the adaptation of the rural farmstead to the city-form was slow and not complete until the late nineteenth century. My illustrated example, from the Malardalen towns of central Sweden, shows the grouping of household buildings around a central yard before a single large house facing the street would sabsorb these scattered, individually sheltered functions (FIG. 7).[18]

Let me site two other examples, one Western and the other Islamic. The medieval fortified court, or *curia*, has an urban apotheosis in more than one cultural sphere. Jacques Heers delved into the material in his classic study of medieval family clans.[21] The Islamic *haws*, on the other hand, was a large open courtyard with lodging on all four sides. The frequent location of this habitat on the outskirts of cities, and the reported presence of cattle, underscores the fact that we are dealing with the urban adaptation of a rural settlement form.[22]

Then there are those historical situations where no such adjustment was necessary, because the environmental order of the countryside and that of the city were made of the same cloth, both in terms of architecture and its arrangement into landscapes of form. This

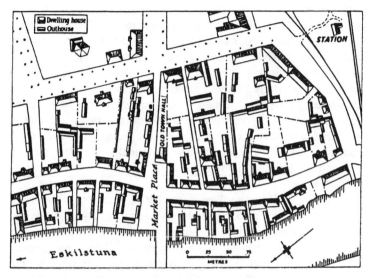

F I G U R E 7. Eskilstuna, Sweden. Distribution of buildings in the older quarter of town. Leighley, "The Towns of Malardalen in Sweden: A Study in Urban Morphology," *University of California Publications in Geography*, 3.1, 1928.

book contains several historically dispersed instances that demonstrate these continuities. The most explicit is Sophie Clement-Charpentier's "Permanence of Rural Settlements in Thai Towns," in which she presents linguistic and physical evidence for the continuity from rural to urban areas in house types and groupings, comments on the extended linear layout along a river which describes both villages and towns, and shows neighborhoods of a patently rural character ensconced within walled towns like Chiengmai.

There are two points I want to pick up and emphasize from this chapter. The first is the self-conscious survival of village settlement patterns within the fabric of a city. The second is the seeming finality of city walls, and the contradiction this implies for the rural-urban continuum here espoused.

The first of these issues entails both atavistic holdovers on the part of urbanized country folk and administrative control on the part of state authority. A striking modern example of the former is in squatter settlements like those of Zambian towns. The pattern may not be obvious at first, but the units are soon discovered -- twenty huts or so around a common space and a physical grouping resembling a circle.[23] In fact, squatter settlements would be a critical unit of study for those junctions of town and country under review in this essay. Are these ubiquitous formations best viewed as places in which rural people lose their traditional identity in preparation for city life, as it is so often maintained? Or do they, rather, represent a spontaneous opportunity for the city to regenerate its sense of tradition?[24]

The administrative control has a number of rationales, all more or less coercive. In China, especially under the Han Dynasty, the aim was to integrate the lineage community into the administrative system. The same word -- *li* -- designated a village, a city quarter and a measure of length. The initial restructuring of the countryside may well have entailed a form of synoecism, where a number of adjacent villages were converted into market towns. The subsequent divisions of cities into *li* was probably intended to keep a check on the largely agricultural population by preserving village organization. How physical this affinity continued to be is hard to know. A recent study of some Florentine new towns in the fourteenth century showed how villages were forcefully de-mapped, and their inhabitants brought to live in separate corners of the new towns which, in their strictly gridded layouts, bore little physical relation to the original village nuclei.[25]

As to the second point raised by Clement-Charpentier, we may note that the role of the walled edge as an emphatic divider of town and country has been overdrawn. Let me cite China. Despite the fact that any administrative town of consequence would be expected to be walled, the uniformity of building styles, and the layout and the use of ground space, carried one from city to suburb to open countryside without any appreciable disjunction, as F.W. Mote and other Sinologists have persuasively argued. "The basic cultural cleavages in China were those of class and occupation . . . and of region . . . , not those between cities and their hinterlands," wrote G. William Skinner.[26] Indeed, we can go further and argue that the unchanging rural environment, not the city, was the dominant component of Chinese civilization.

MODERN PARADIGMS

Under its present system of government, the walls of Chinese towns would have come down for ideological reasons even were they not functionally obsolete. It may have been Rousseau who first insisted that city walls artificially segregate crowds of urbanites from the peasants spread thinly over vast tracts of land. He urged that the territory be peopled evenly, that humans were "not meant to be crowded together in ant hills, but scattered over the earth to till it."[27] But it was the Communists who will give their own gloss to this injunction of the Enlightenment. It is they who, through their Marxist forefathers, would object to the idea of and urban/rural dichotomy: city walls artificially severed the mighty proletariat into an urban and a rural contingent, thus eviscerating its strength.[28]

The fear of a conspiracy to weaken the masses by dividing them is behind Marxist doctrines of disurbanization. The Marx-Engels Manifesto of 1848 prescribed the "gradual abolition of the distinction between town and country, by a more equitable distribution of the population over the country." This was at the core of the great debate in Russia in the twenties between the urbanists, led by the planner L. Sabsovitch who advocated the construction of urban "agglomerations," vast communes that would hold four thousand people each in individual cells, and the disurbanists, N.A. Milyutin chief among them, who proposed the abandonment of the old cities and the dispersal of the population by means of linear cities in free nature -- first along the great highways that linked Moscow with its neighboring towns, and eventually across the whole extravagant spread of Russia (FIG. 8). The agricultural and industrial workers would live together, building a common proletariat, the new Communist aristocracy.[29]

The Russian debate thus appropriated one of the great settlement theories of modern times which sought to erase the deprivations of

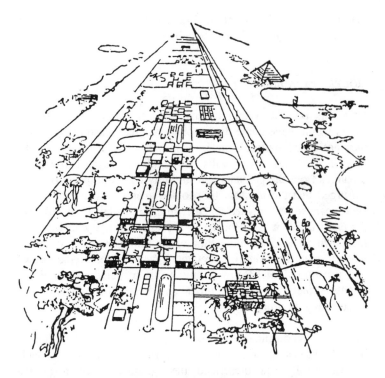

FIGURE 8. Plan for Magnitogorsk, Ernst May, 1930, aerial view. A linear scheme that reflects Lenin's goals for Soviet development: "We must aim at the fusion of industry and agriculture . . . by means of a more diffused settlement pattern for the people." Reprinted from D. Lewis, ed., *Urban Structure: Architects' Year Book 12*, 1968.

the big city by bringing everyone close to nature along an open-ended transportation spine. The idea did not need Communism to support it. It was invented by a Spanish civil engineer in the 1880s, and was elaborated by the likes of Chambless, Richard Neutra and Le Corbusier for anyone who would buy it. We see its ultimate manifestation in the linear development along our freeways today, which, like the rurban fringe with its slurbia, dissolves the city in open land.

The only other modern settlement concept of comparable power and seduction is the garden city, an English anti-urban dispersal fantasy of the turn of the century which astonishingly was adopted

F I G U R E 9. View of Glendale, Ohio, ca. 1860. Planned by Robert C. Phillips
in 1851, Glendale is probably the first American picturesque suburb designed in
sympathy with the rural landscape ideals later popularized by Olmsted.
(Source: Glendale Heritage Preservation.)

as national policy after World War II. This is not the place to
speak about Ebenezer Howard and Raymond Unwin, of
Letchworth and Welwyn. In that circle, garden city and garden
suburb were severely juxtaposed. Letchworth was a self-sufficient
town of 30,000, a model for the future reconstruction of the
capitalist/industrial environment; Hampstead Garden Suburb was a
dependency of London, nothing more. For us, and for the case we
are pleading, these elegances of dogma are unpersuasive. What is
central to our argument is that from at least the middle of the
nineteenth century, the history of the Anglo-American picturesque
suburb, not to say suburbia in general, firmly established an
intermediate environment between town and country, or as
Frederick Law Olmsted was to phrase it, "sylvan surroundings . . .
with a considerable share of urban convenience" (FIG. 9). So
durable has this intermediate environment proved that it alone
should persuade us of the futility of ever seeing urban and rural as
two distinct worlds, but rather as two aspects of a single
continuum.[30]

TOWN AND COUNTRY: BEYOND DUALISM

This paper has a modest aim. In the context of a book that provides a broad-based discussion of traditional dwellings and settlements, which freely moves across the man-made environment, it seemed worthwhile to emphasize that this physical canvas not be rent because of ideological or scholarly agendas. For too long we have extolled the city as a remarkable artifact, and urban life as an elevated form of engagement with the forces of progress, enterprise and an entire range of civilities. A polar opposite was needed, one that was easy-to-hand -- the countryside. The village and its ways acquired many friends of its own in time, but also a heavy aura of sentiment that had to do with naturalness and honesty and enduring values.

Today, given the radical changes in the traditional landscapes of the world, we can hardly seek comfort in such antipodes. And yet the urge is irresistible to lament a paradise lost, a sad disjunction between a time-honored way of doing things and the arrogant, disrespectful arrivism of the new.

To see the interdependence of two landscapes and two ways of life, to study the environment as one, not as village versus town or high style versus low, is an urgent scholarly strategy. It could also be a healing thing that softens obstinate prejudices, and eases the anxieties rampant in those many parts of the world that are trapped between tradition and the present.

The land spreads out as one: time flows. The breaks, barriers, and divorces are of our own making. Our charge now, I venture to suggest, is to find tradition in the central business district of the metropolis, to see the old irrigation ditch beneath the fancy tree-lined avenue, to recognize the ancient process of synoecism that brought villages together to form cities at work still in our modern conurbations. Tradition has no end: it cannot be superseded. The only enduring truth is in the seamless continuities of time and place.

REFERENCE NOTES

1. For a fuller version, see S. Kostof, "Urbanism and Polity: Medieval Siena in Context," in *International Laboratory for Architecture and Urban Design Yearbook*, 1982, pp. 66-73.
2. See, for example, H. Kotter, "Changes in Urban-Rural Relationships in Industrial Society," in N. Anderson, ed., *Urbanism and Urbanization*, (Leiden: E.J. Brill, 1964), pp. 21-29.
3. E.g., I.A. Spaulding, "Serendipity and the Rural-Urban Continuum," *Rural Sociology* 16 (1951), pp. 29-36.
4. See C.E. Lively, et al., "The Sociological Significance of the Rural-Urban Fringe," *Rural Sociology* 18 (1953), pp. 101-120, with a full bibliography. Firey's article was entitled "Ecological Considerations in Planning for Rurban Fringes."
5. The key essay is Whitehand, "The Changing Nature of the Urban Fringe: A Time Perspective," in J.H. Johnson, ed., *Suburban Growth* (London: Wiley, 1974), pp. 31-52. The pioneering Lewis essay referred to in the next paragraph is "Die geographische Gliederung von Gross-Berlin," in *Landerkundliche Forschung* (Krebs-Festschrift), 1936, pp. 146-171.
6. F. Braudel, *The Structures of Everyday Life* (English edition) (New York: Harper and Row, 1981), p. 481.
7. See O.A.W. Dilke, "The Planning and Building of Roman Towns," in F. Grew and B. Hobley, eds., *Roman Urban Topography in Britain and the Western Empire*, CBA Research Report 59 (1985), pp. 6-13.
8. See R.McC. Adams and H.J. Nissen, *The Uruk Countryside: The Natural Setting of Urban Societies* (Chicago, University of Chicago Press, 1972); R.McC. Adams, *The Heartland of Cities: Surveys of Ancient Settlement and Land Use on the Central Floodplain of the Euphrates* (Chicago: University of Chicago Press, 1981).
9. Refer to the studies collected in B. Cunliffe and T. Rowley, eds., *Oppida in Barbarian Europe* (Oxford: Oxford University Press, 1975); and to M.W. Barley, *European Towns: Their Archaeology and Early History* (London: Academic Press, 1977).
10. I. Lapidus, *Middle Eastern Cities* (Berkeley: University of California Press, 1969), p. 68.
11. R.E. Dickinson, *The West European City*, 2d ed., (London: Routledge and Kegan Paul, 1961), p. 331.
12. See C. Winters, "Traditional Urbanism in the North Central Sudan," *Annals of the Association of American Geographers* 67 (1977), pp. 500-520; A. O'Connor, *The African City* (New York: Holmes and Meier, 1983).
13. Winters, "Traditional Urbanism," p. 517.
14. H. Frankfort in *Town Planning Review*, 21.2 (1950), p. 103.
15. See P. Claval, *La logique des villes* (Paris: Litec, 1981), p. 307.
16. See W. Bascom, "Urbanization among the Yoruba," *American Journal of Sociology* 60 (1955), pp. 446-454, especially 448.
17. J.B. Jackson, "Nearer than Eden," in *The Necessity for Ruins* (Amherst: University of Massachusetts Press, 1980), pp. 19-35.
18. The article appeared in *Annals of the Association of American Geographers* 69 (1979), pp. 208-224.
19. See D. Ward, "The Pre-Urban Cadaster and the Urban Pattern of Leeds," *Annals of the Association of American Geographers* 52 (1962), pp. 150-166.
20. The standard work on these towns is J. Leighley, "The Towns of Malardalen in Sweden. A Study in Morphology," *University of California Publications in*

Geography, 3.1 (1928), pp. 1-134.
21. Heers, *Family Clans in the Middle Ages*, B. Herbert, trans. (Amsterdam: North-Holland Publishing Co., 1977).
22. See A. Raymond, *The Great Arab Cities in the 16th-18th Centuries* (New York: New York University Press, 1984), pp. 86-87.
23. See P. Andrews, M. Christie and R. Martin, "Squatters and the Evolution of A Lifestyle," *Architectural Design*, 1973 no. 1, pp. 16-25.
24. This query springs from discussions I have had with Nezar AlSayyad.
25. For the Chinese case, see, e.g., an unpublished thesis by Yung-Cheng Kao, "The Unit-of-Place in the Planning of Chinese Cities" (University of California, Berkeley, 1981). The Florentine new towns are the subject of David Friedman, *Florentine New Towns in the Late Middle Ages* (Cambridge, MA: MIT Press, 1989).
26. G.W. Skinner, *The City in Late Imperial China* (Palo Alto: Stanford University Press, 1977), p. 269 and passim.
27. Cited by A. Vidler in S. Anderson, ed., *On Streets* (Cambridge, MA: MIT Press, 1978), p. 46.
28. An interesting, ruthless application of these theories is underway in Ceausescu's Romania. A decision taken at the Communist Party congress in 1972 to "systemize" Romania's villages is now vigorously being implemented. The aim is to dismantle by the year 2000 6,500 ancient villages, the setting of ethnic minorities like Hungarians and Germans, and move the inhabitants to agro-industrial centers made of prefabricated slabs. "We start from the fact," Ceausescu explained in a recent speech, "that socialism must create the best conditions of life for all inhabitants without distinction, that we cannot divide the country into two, with one part in modern developed housing [in the cities], and other parts in shabby unhealthy housing." In fact, the condemned rural environment is guilty of one failing -- that it is a unique collection of traditional vernacular architecture.
29. See chiefly A. Kopp, *Town and Revolution. Soviet Architecture and City-Planning, 1917-1935* (New York and London: Braziller, 1970); Milyutin, *Sotsgorod. The Problem of Building Socialist Cities*, English translation (Cambridge, MA: MIT Press, 1974).
30. The literature on the Anglo-American suburb is vast. Good places to begin are A.M. Edwards, *The Design of Suburbia* (London: Pembridge Press, 1981); the special issue of *Architectural Design* (October/November 1981) devoted to the subject; K.T. Jackson, *Crabgrass Frontier. The Suburbanization of the United States* (Oxford: Oxford University Press, 1985). It is well-known, and significant, that the chief consequence of suburbanization, the blurring of visual distinctions between town and country, has recently come under attack. The displeasure is not, of course, new. Unwin, himself, struggled with the design consequences of density within the garden city, advocating groupings of houses that would ensure volumetric effects akin to midieval towns. From the outside, Thomas Sharp, in *Town and Countryside* (London: Oxford University Press, 1932), p. 162, inveigled against the garden city concept, insisting that town and country were "two fundamentally different things, capable of two fundamentally different types of beauty . . . . We must strive for sheer urbanity in one place as we strive for sheer rusticity in the other." And the post World War II flood of "townscape" literature came at the same issue from several fronts. What is new is the attempt to preserve the traditional rural landscape by revising our practics of suburban planning. An English case is that of Essex and the *Design Guide for Residential Areas* issued by its county council in 1973. This is a detailed indictment of suburbia. The council

minutes specify that "new housing areas shall create a visually satisfactory environment, achieved by employing either the principles of: i) buildings set within a dominant landscape of a character indigenous to Essex; or ii) buildings set to satisfactorily enclose spaces of individual identity" (from Edwards, *The Design of Suburbia*, pp. 249-250). A comparable instance in the United States is the design manual issued by the Center for Rural Massachusetts, *Dealing with Change in the Connecticut River Valley: A Design Manual for Conservation and Development* (January 1988). It establishes (p. 13) "a new discipline . . . call[ed] Rural Landscape Planning." Rejecting standard zoning and subdivision practices, it proposes by-law amendments "which would require all new developments proposed on open fields or pastures to be laid out so that no more than 50% of the farmland is consumed by streets and lots."

THE PERMANENCE OF RURAL
SETTLEMENTS IN THAI TOWNS

SOPHIE CLEMENT-CHARPENTIER

Can an anthropological approach to the spaces found in Thai
villages be helpful for understanding the layout of Thai cities and
towns? Do rural settlements have any influence on the spatial
organization of pre-industrial towns? This chapter will first
explain what the words village and town mean within Thai culture.
Then it will describe the physical layout of villages (their location,
enclosures and general morphology) and try to determine whether
underlying structures can be detected in their spatial organization.
Finally, it will attempt to discover whether these same structures
are present in towns. The structures are defined by the rules of
spatial orientation and by rules governing the layout of a house in
relation to the layouts of neighboring houses. In the patterns of
grouping dwellings, we will try to determine whether there is a
transmission of form from rural to urban contexts.

The above topics will be dealt with by recounting research that the
author and Pierre Clement have undertaken since 1969 on
populations belonging to the same Thai linguistic group. These
populations include the Lao from northern and central Laos, the
Thai from northern Thailand (mainly the Yuan or Khon Muang
from the Chiengmai region), and the Shan of the Mae Hong Son
area west of Chiengmai (FIG. 1). Through close links over several
centuries, these groups have kept a very similar culture as well as

FIGURE 1.
Map of Thailand and
Laos with the places
where the research
took place.

an almost identical language. All of them can be called Thai, and
we shall use this generic appellation in the following pages.

The villages and the towns studied can still be referred to as
traditional settlements. But here a question arises: What is the
meaning of tradition in terms of spatial layout, architecture and
urban planning? The author believes tradition in this context
means a way of organizing space from the scale of the house to the
scale of the village and the town using models and practices which
are a legacy of the past. This means transmitting the same
meanings or knowledge from one generation to the next through
building or planning practices.

We can speak of traditional built form if the following conditions
prevail:

* The economic context belongs to a wider system that we can call
pre-industrial or pre-capitalist. Everywhere in Thailand and Laos
we have seen how the replacement of a subsistence economy by a
merchant economy has influenced the organization of labor and
the ownership of land. For instance, building techniques have
changed as new tools have been imported, building materials are
no longer the same now they can be bought from a sawmill rather

than cut in the forest, and mutual aid for buildings has been replaced by hired labor. Similarly, all the land in Thailand once belonged to the King of Thailand and was granted to its occupants. Now the land is owned by common people and can be rented or sold, allowing land speculation to become widespread.

* The social organization is preserved. The layout of dwellings is strongly related to the rules of kinship and residence. These rules are very important for the transmission of architectural types within a settlement. Traditions are maintained by social cohesion around a monastery, or *wat*. This is true for both villagers and residents of a quarter in a town.

* The ideologies and religious beliefs are still alive, either as Buddhist faith, animist belief coexisting with Buddhism, or astrology. Among Thai peoples cults based on the protective spirits of the house, village and town are widespread. The whole conception of space among the Thai depends on certain specific beliefs or practices, for instance respect for correct orientation and a hierarchy from high to low or upstream to downstream. The conception of space also depends on different values attributed to the cardinal orientations, east being auspicious, west inauspicious.

Of these criteria, the economic condition is the one that changes most quickly, mainly in towns. But change does not necessarily involve a complete overthrow of social structures or of underlying beliefs. Social structures and belief systems have an inertia that helps keep tradition alive.

GENERAL PHYSICAL LAYOUT OF VILLAGES AND TOWNS

What do the words village and town signify in Thai culture? First of all, let us describe several of their general characteristics -- their general aspect, their location, their enclosures. Then let us emphasize the uniqueness of several towns. Two towns, Louang Prabang in Laos and Chiengmai in Thailand, will be singled out for our purposes.

It is essential to begin by determining whether the words village and town represent the same concepts in Thai that they do in our own, very different culture. From one culture to another there can often be erroneous interpretations based on misunderstanding of words. Also, as in the present case, our vocabulary sometimes impoverishes certain concepts which are rich with meanings in another culture.

Let us analyze what the actual words denote. The word for a village or for a quarter in a town, *ban*, also means "house" or "dwelling." One word indicates the basic unit as well as the whole settlement without drawing any distinction between whether such a dwelling or settlement is in a rural or an urban area. For "town," we can use several words: either *chieng*, originating from the Chinese *vieng* and *kamphaeng*, signifying "wall" or "rampart," or *muang*, involving the idea of a political center or principality. *Muang* denotes the territory of the province as well as the capital, its chief town. These Thai words reveal a fundamental continuity from rural to urban areas.

Now let us examine where Thai villages and towns are located. Scholars currently agree that Thai populations were already settled in the Indochinese peninsula during the thirteenth century.[1] The Thai peoples came down from southwestern China and spread out, moving along the rivers in the area, which flow mainly north to south. They settled in valleys and on plains near the water that was necessary for irrigating paddy fields. Streams were used as a means for transporting men and merchandise until the first half of the twentieth century, since a road network was almost nonexistent.

Many towns and villages were erected near such streams. This is relevant chiefly for regions where the hydrographic network is extensive or where small cultivated plains allowed low population densities. Thus, for example, the region of Louang Prabang in northern Laos came to have villages scattered along the Mekhong river and its tributaries. The Thai claim that the most valuable sites for villages are at the junction of two rivers. This is the case for the town of Louang Prabang, for instance, and for such surrounding villages as Ban Pak Thai and Ban Pak Sa (*pak* meaning "mouth").

Location along a stream gives such settlements a linear layout, a pattern that is most striking when one arrives by a waterway, as is often the case. The linear layout is also characteristic of villages settled along a canal and of more recent villages set up along roads. Of course, on large rice-growing plains such as those around Chiengmai or Vientiane, villages located among the rice fields do not present this linear layout.

As for towns, it is clear that the most important ones in northern Thailand were set up along streams. Among them are Chiengrai, Chiengsen, Fang, Chiengmai, Lampang and Nan. This follows for the chief towns in Laos as well: Louang Prabang, Vientiane, and farther south, Savannakhet and Pakse. Such positioning gives these towns their generally elongated layout, with surrounding villages scattered upstream and downstream from them the same way that houses are scattered upstream and downstream in a village.

Should we conclude that the sites of villages and towns are the same? Indeed not, because their scale is radically different. The data on the foundation of Southeast Asian ancient towns is scarce and exists as legend rather than historic fact. However, we can surmise that ancient towns did not arise at random. Their emergence depended on a political program, a prince's desire to create them. Even if a ruler chose an already inhabited location, as for instance occurred in the founding of Chiengmai in the thirteenth century, the site had first to be examined to determine whether it was suitable for a city. Knowing the care that Asian people have taken for centuries in choosing locations for their houses, we can well imagine the amount of care that must have gone into choosing the site of a town, particularly since the destiny of the town depended on what the Chinese call *fengshui*, the propitious or non-propitious configuration of a site.[2] In the case of Chiengmai, we know through ancient chronicles that the site was carefully examined before construction of the new town began.

But let us come back to the present day. Differences between villages and towns are manifest in several realms, among them demographics, social class, economic opportunity and infrastructure. It is beyond the scope of this article to discuss all of these, therefore we shall focus on one which is of particular interest for us, built form.

The Thai, like many of the populations in Southeast Asia, group their dwellings in clusters. There are no isolated houses, except for huts in the rice fields which are used only as temporary dwellings during times of work. Houses are gathered into villages, the size of which can vary from a few houses to nearly a hundred. If villages became too big, they split in two, each with its own monastery, or *wat*.

Dwellings generally rise out of groves of trees and bamboo, as houses are often surrounded by enclosures. In traditional villages houses are rather homogeneous both in terms of size and building materials, the latter being almost solely of vegetal origin.[3] Here it should be noted that Laotian rural society has always been egalitarian, a condition reflected in its built form. The only village buildings normally made with masonry were the primary school and the *wat*. The former is a recent institution, as teaching was done by monks until about the 1930s. In villages, commercial activities are limited to a few small shops kept by villagers selling food. Clothes are bought at the market in the nearest small town.

Before the spread of imported building materials, urban domestic architecture was not fundamentally different from its rural counterpart; both consisted of wood and bamboo pile dwellings. A few urban houses might have been larger, more decorated and more suitable to modern comfort. One of the reasons for this similarity could have been an old regulation prohibiting ordinary people from using masonry for their dwellings. Masonry was reserved for palaces and temples.

Socio-economic changes have brought an evolution of materials, and new transportation facilities and a new wage-labor system have allowed residents of towns to build new types of houses. These are set on concrete pilings and have a level floor enclosed by brick walls. They are similar to dwellings we see in urban areas or in areas immediately surrounding urban areas.

So it is not the nature of building materials alone that allows us to make distinctions between villages and towns. It has been the availability, or lack of availability of materials, that has been crucial. Many villages, mostly in Thailand, were well served by transportation, while many small towns in Laos used to be without transportation access.

In these Southeast Asian countries, as in many other countries, every human settlement used to be enclosed by a wall. The seats of power and religion, palaces and monasteries, are still surrounded by walls. The reasons for such enclosure must initially have been defensive, but later became symbolic. Villages were formerly surrounded by palisades of stakes, bamboo defensive works or sometimes ditches. These enclosures lost their justification at the end of the nineteenth century when local fighting ceased. Towns used to be protected by large earthen walls, frequently covered with bricks and surrounded by moats. In Chiengmai the remains of such ramparts are still visible, with sections of wall, gates and hexagonal corner bastions still skirted by moats full of water.

The traditional towns expressed the power of the princes, the *Chao*, who settled in a centrally located palace. They expressed also the supremacy of the Buddhist faith by means of their great number of *wats*. Bruneau states that apart from the aristocracy and their servants, "there was not an urban population, but a densification of villages, and a market a little more important than elsewhere. Hence there was no discontinuity between rural and urban, that is, these two categories had no justification."[4]

The towns of Laos that we studied before 1975 still suited this description for the most part, and we defined them as a collection of villages. Their walls had disappeared, but in the case of Louang Prabang, for instance, we knew where these used to be. The only distinct elements were a few colonial buildings scattered in the town centers, vestiges of the French occupation of 1893-1940. These were occupied by the Lao administration.

Thus the urban and rural fabrics used to be quite similar. The most significant factor in the changing aspect of Thai towns is the development of commercial activities since the end of the nineteenth century. From the point of view of an external observer sensitive to built form, the principal feature of a town compared to a village is now the increasing encroachment of commercial areas. Streets of shophouses are owned mainly by Chinese; they are still rather less developed in Laos, but they are flourishing in Thailand. It is a paradoxical feature of Thai towns that much of their urban character is actually not of Thai origin. The other buildings which are specifically urban, such as markets, administrative buildings and tertiary facilities, are more localized.

Before comparing rural and urban fabrics, it is necessary to explain the context into which urban fabric was inserted. To do so, certain elements of the urban morphology of Louang Prabang and Chiengmai will be stressed: their site and position in relation to the stream, what is left of their defensive walls, their main axes, their centers (each with a palace and several principal monasteries) , and their commercial areas and main markets.

Louang Prabang was the capital of the former Northern Laos Kingdom. Until 1975 it was a royal town where the King of Laos and his court used to live. Its population was 7,596 in 1958, growing to 21,179 in 1970 as a result of the arrival of refugees from the Indochina war.[5] It is situated in a mountainous region where the Mekhong and the Nam Khan rivers join to form an elongated peninsula that contains the sacred hill of Phousi in its middle. The old wall to the south of the town, now demolished, formed an irregular line linking the bank of the Mekhong to the bank of the Nam Khan (FIG. 2).

The town stretches parallel to the Mekhong. The principal thoroughfare runs through the built-up area from upstream to downstream. It is bordered by old-style masonry shophouses of Chinese merchants. Elsewhere in the town the houses are wooden pile dwellings. Pagodas and monasteries line the main street, with as many as fourteen on its upper eight hundred meters. The Royal Palace lies across the street from the Phousi. Around the town's

F I G U R E 2. The town of Louang Prabang at the junction of two streams, with its main street running from upstream to downstream, and the sacred hill of Phousi located in the middle of the peninsula. (S o u r c e : Pierre Sylvain Dore, *Contribution ethno-historique a la connaissance de la culture Louang Phrabanaise*, Doctorat d'Etat thesis, Paris V, 1987.)

main intersection are gathered administrative buildings, the town hall, the general post office, restaurants and cinemas. Beyond are residential areas, refugee quarters and, farther on, rice fields. The market, busy only in the morning, lies along the main transverse axis. Away from the banks of the Mekhong there are areas which were settled more recently.

In many parts of the town, Mogenet noted, "the quiet way of life reminds one of the countryside, the activities are extremely limited, a few coffee-houses and small shops."[6] In 1970 it was a

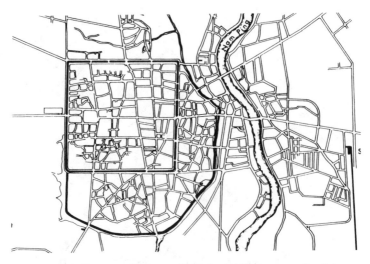

FIGURE 3. The town of Chiengmai with the river, the square wall and the principal axes. (S o u r c e : Department of Fine Arts, Bangkok.)

town with green areas everywhere, with natural ponds in its heart. There was almost no automobile traffic. One could hardly find as non-urban a town anywhere. This can be explained by the fact that Louang Prabang suffered from the political and military insecurity that prevailed in Laos for many years. It was isolated and practically cut off from the main economic activity circuits of the Indochinese peninsula.

The second town is Chiengmai, the capital of the former Northern Thailand Kingdom, the Lanna Thai.[7] Chiengmai had a population of 104,910 in 1982. It is located on a plain, bounded on its western edge by mountains. It has grown on the western bank of the southward-flowing Mae Nam Ping River, and since the 1920s on the eastern bank as well. Chiengmai is said to have been founded in 1296 by King Mengrai. The walled or square town, a quadrilateral area 1.7 kilometers by 1.6 kilometers, was previously protected by a moat that still exists and by a wall with five gates. The present rampart, largely in ruins, dates to 1796 when the old walls were rebuilt by King Kawila after two centuries of Burmese occupation. A second curving wall previously protected the town from the east and south (FIG. 3).

The square town could be considered a symbolic town, with the main palace as the headquarters of political power and the nobles' and courtiers' dwellings, the principal *wat* and the post *lak muang* symbolizing the territorial unit. Formerly ordinary townsmen could not live inside the square town, which must have seemed rather empty. The market bordered the main west-east axis, Tapae Street. Later it was moved out of the square town to a place near the river which was the core of a very prosperous commercial area held by Chinese traders. The railway first arrived in Chiengmai in 1921. Around the station on the left bank of the river arose a new quarter with wholesale trade buildings. Since the nineteenth century Western religious missions, consulates and trade establishments have been built close to the Nam Ping, on both its banks. The first bridge, a wooden one, was built by an American.

Thus the general morphology of Chiengmai is the following: a quiet area in the center inside the square wall, a busy commercial town on the east, and new peripheral extensions to the north and northwest. Large expanses of green residential areas can still be found in the square town, in the area south of it, and along the river upstream and downstream from the commercial areas. In other towns in Thailand, such as Bangkok, this phenomenon is apparent: the residential zones are kept green and quiet, while the zones devoted to economic activity become denser and more noisy and are characterized by chaotic urban development.

SPATIAL STRUCTURES

Having described the general morphology of villages and towns, we should now compare the fabric of villages and towns. It is important to uncover the structures which determine the choice of sites. Among the Thai we found these to be rules governing orientation. Orientation is influenced either by an adjacent stream or by points of the compass. The layout of some houses is fixed by the layout of neighboring houses, thus generating a regular pattern in the organization of settlements.

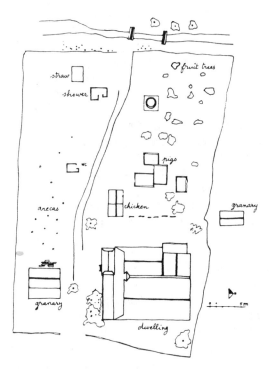

FIGURE 4.
A compound in Ban San Sai, in the rice-growing plain of Chiengmai.

Thai villages look like clusters of houses scattered among the vegetation; at first no ordered layout is apparent. And yet one aspect of village order struck us from the beginning: the villages of the Vientiane region in the center of Laos did not have the same features as those of the Louang Prabang region in the north. Initially, we categorized these villages as possessing either loose order or tight order. However, further research was necessary to understand the reasons for the difference. The two types doubtless had profoundly different natures. For instance, the population of the Vientiane region was said to be of Phoueun origin, having come from Xieng Khouang at the end of the nineteenth century. This could have caused slight cultural variations. Nevertheless, the factor which we now consider crucial is the pattern of production. This has had an influence on whether the layout of houses in the villages is more or less tight.

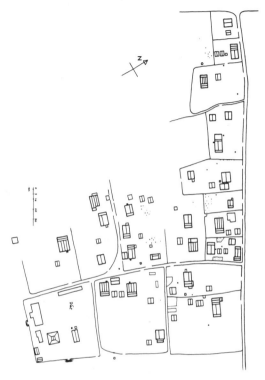

FIGURE 5.
A loose order village,
Ban Done Noun on
the Vientiane plain,
with all of the houses
nearly parallel.

In the regions where rice growing is prevalent the house is an agricultural tool as well as a dwelling. It is set in a compound that includes many outbuildings of which the rice granary is the most important (FIG. 4). Compounds are linked by footpaths and tracks wide enough to allow passage for a cart. In this type of village houses are sited fairly far from each other (FIG. 5). This type of village is numerous on the Vientiane and Chiengmai plains, both prosperous rice-growing areas.

In northern Laos there is another kind of general layout. Where the landscape is hilly and where there is less land for rice fields, the subsistence of the villagers is based less on rice and more on fishing or handicrafts. Compounds in these villages are less justified, and houses are set closer to each other with their narrow sides turned toward the path. In this connection, we did evoke a

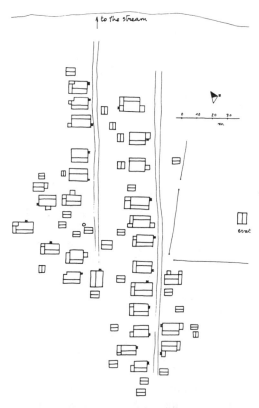

FIGURE 6.
A tight order village,
Muang Nan near
Sayaboury, northern
Laos, with its houses
lining the path.

"pre-urban structure," for instance in the village of Ban Pak Suang andr in the large but remote village of Muang Nan near Sayaboury (FIGS. 6, 7).   The Lao themselves gave this last village the appellation *muang*, "town." In Muang Nan many villagers used to practice such handicrafts as blacksmithing, weaving or spinning on the lower level of their houses.

This ordered layout is a function of the rules for orientation. These rules are not always easily readable. In the village of Ban Mae Mai in Thailand's Lampang Province, Haagensen observed: "There is no conceivable pattern in the village lay-out. The houses appear to have been sited at random and are not oriented in any particular direction."[8] But in the same article the author repro-

F I G U R E 7. A street in Muang Nan showing the gable ends of the houses.

duced a village plan in which houses are oriented in more or less the same direction to within a few degrees.

Our research did not corroborate Haagensen's statement. We concluded that all houses in the Thai villages we visited had a clearly determined orientation. We cannot claim this for other Southeast Asian populations; but among the Thai we studied, Lao, Yuan, Shan and Lu houses did not have a random orientation. Moreover, even if the rules vary from one population to another, each population had a well-stated rule which appears to have been widely followed.[9]

It is true that the positions of houses sometimes do not seem to be part of an ordered pattern, yet their orientations are defined. This can be observed in a Thai village, because houses are almost always oriented parallel to one other. Of course houses may not be rigorously parallel; their orientation may vary by a few degrees. In Thai culture, which is influenced by Buddhism, people are not compulsive about rules. They are accustomed to following rules, but they feel free to interpret them in their own way.

The rules are different in Laos than in northern Thailand. In Laos houses must be built with their ridgepoles parallel to a stream if the village is situated near one, or parallel to a road if it is not. In villages isolated in rice fields the ridgepole must be oriented east-west. It seems that the Lao wish to place themselves parallel to a direction of flow, either of a stream, a road or the course of the sun. It would be inadmissible to lie perpendicular to such a course.[10] All houses are parallel since all are parallel to the river (FIG. 6).

In the Louang Prabang region, where rectangular houses are set closer to each other, we noted a second rule. Houses turn their narrow sides toward the path, and the entrance is placed in the front part of the house. Furthermore, the front of the house cannot face the back of an opposite house. As a result, front gables face one another across the path, and the back of the houses, where the kitchens are, face each other at the rear (FIG. 8). When walking in a street, one sees only the entrance sides. A further refinement of this second rule is that two houses cannot be sited exactly opposite one another. This can be explained by the fact that Southeast Asian peoples believe that evil spirits move in straight line. As a consequence, they never line up openings.

A third rule involves the interior layout of a house. The first part of this rule is common to Laos and northern Thailand; this is that inhabitants, when sleeping, must lie perpendicular to the ridgepole. The second part of the rule is specific to Lao people and is based on the hierarchy of values the Lao attribute to different parts of the body (the head being high and noble, the feet being low and vulgar). Since it would be impolite to turn one's feet toward someone else's head, the reclining dweller must place his head opposite his neighbor's head, and his feet opposite his neighbor's feet (FIG. 9). Usually there are a few exceptions, but these only occur when a new house is built between two others. Also, when a child decides to live next to his or her parents, the heads of dwellers in the child's house face the feet of the parents to obey the customary hierarchy.[11]

FIGURE 8.
The front gables of
Lao houses face one
another across the
path, and the backs
face each other at the
rear.

FIGURE 9.
Inside the Lao house,
the head of a reclining
dweller is in the
opposite direction to
that of his neighbor's
so that the feet are
together.

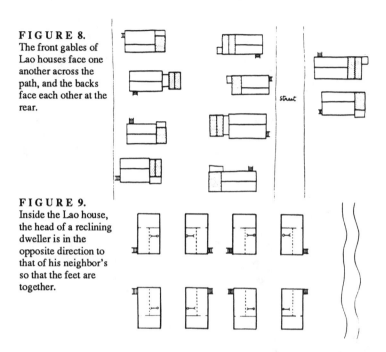

It became clear that this rule did structure neighboring groups of houses, and we concluded that it did determine the entire spatial organization of a village in a very precise way.

These rules structuring space are specific to the Lao. Among the Yuan and the Shan of northern Thailand the rule is in a way more simple -- ridgepoles must be oriented north-south. Thus villages offer a regular order with all houses nearly parallel (FIG. 10). The front side can face the south or the north, but south is the more frequent direction. The inhabitants, as in Laos, lie down to sleep in a direction perpendicular to the ridgepole. But here the neighbor's position has no influence on the interior layout. Everyone must turn his head toward the east, the auspicious direction in Buddhism.

Another rule is also based on the values that the Thai attribute to the cardinal orientations. This rule prescribes that a staircase must not face west, since west is thought to be inauspicious, the direc-

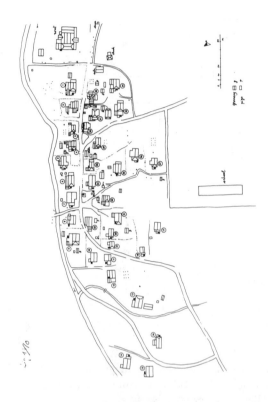

FIGURE 10.
The Shan village of
Ban Mae Sakud with
its houses oriented
north-south.

tion of death and evil spirits. When we asked house-dwellers
about this, usually they could not answer. They would speak
easily of the east, the direction of Buddha, but their beliefs
concerning the west were fraught with superstitions. In any event,
most houses in the village of Ban Mae Sakut near Mae Hong Son
complied with this rule regarding stair orientation. This was
verified primarily in the older, northern part of the village. A few
exceptions were found in the southern part, consisting of more
recent houses (FIG. 10).

Can we recognize these patterns of spatial organization in towns?
Is there a comparison to be made at this level between rural and
urban settlements? Until World War II, towns looked like rural
agglomerations, except for their markets, administrative buildings
and palaces. Since the 1960s their appearance has changed,

F I G U R E 11. The fabric of a quarter in Louang Prabang, with its dwellings
regularly oriented parallel to the Mekhong river. (S o u r c e : Luc Mogenet, *Atlas
de Louang Phrabang* Vientiane: Vithagna, 1973).

however, particularly in Thailand. In commercial streets the
scenery is radically different from that in villages. But even in the
town centers, as soon as one walks in an adjacent street, one can
suddenly find oneself surrounded by a built form that recalls rural
areas.

Such is the case in Vientiane, for instance, where whole quarters,
particularly near the Mekhong, look like villages. The density may
be a little higher here, but almost all houses lie parallel to the river.
In Louang Prabang, behind the commercial facade of the main
street one finds a village fabric, with small streets going down to
the river (FIG. 11). The houses are regularly oriented parallel to the
Mekhong except in areas near the Nam Khan, where they lie
parallel to this major tributary. However, the rules determining the
layout of two neighboring houses are not always followed.
Because of demographic pressure new houses were built in
traditional quarters, filling empty spaces and often breaking the
continuity established by rules of neighborliness. This relaxing of
rules perhaps constitutes the most obvious difference between
Laotian villages and traditional quarters in towns. It seems that the
collective rules, such as that prescribing that every house must

FIGURE 12.
A seemingly rural
neighborhood in a
block of the walled
town of Chiengmai.
(Source:
Students' work in
CEAA, Thailand
Studio, 1985.)

orient its ridgepole in a certain direction, persist to a greater degree
than the more tenuous rules, such as those requiring the layout of
new houses to take into account the layout of neighboring houses.

In the towns of northern Thailand one finds apparently rural areas
within residential quarters, but the rules of orientation apply only
to a low percentage of the built form. In Chiengmai, for instance,
some quarters in the walled town look like villages (FIG. 12). The
wooden dwellings on piles are surrounded by gardens and linked
by lanes that make right-angle turns. The compounds have
become smaller. They have lost their agricultural function and
have been converted into gardens, sometimes with vegetables and
fruit trees. Yet a few town compounds still enclose some of the
imposing rice granaries characteristic of the Chiengmai region.
These bear witness to the fact that a short time ago townsmen used
to garner their own rice crops from fields at the town's outskirts.
These people lived inside the town even though their way of life
was fundamentally rural.

Houses oriented north-south can be found in low density quarters or in the core of blocks. In Chiengmai, for instance, many blocks that are edged by shophouses have green, residential areas inside. Generally the street is the determining factor in their orientation. Dwellings and shophouses turn their entry facades towards the street, and cardinal directions do not dominate. For houses inside blocks, requirements of access determine the direction of the entrance. In towns, where densities are higher and lands scarcer, even if the rules of orientation have not completely disappeared, they have been made flexible. Municipal regulations, which appeared mainly during the twentieth century and which often contradicted traditional rules of orientation, were one of the reasons for this surrender.

THE GROUPING PATTERNS

Having observed the location and the rules of orientation for Thai settlements, an examination of the patterns of house grouping follows. In Thai settlements the dwellings are gathered according to kinship rules. On a larger scale, other clusters are formed around *wats* in villages as well as in towns.

Houses are situated as a function of residential patterns. Family links imply physical proximity. Among the Thai we have studied, houses shelter a nuclear family and sometimes the grandparents. The residence tends to be uxorilocal, a daughter living for a few years in her parents' house after marriage before building a house in the vicinity. In Laos we can see houses of married daughters very close to parents' houses. There is no physical link, but there is often a similarity in architectural typology.

Grouping patterns can be more easily read in northern Thailand. Several houses of one family can be gathered in the same compound. Family links are directly translated into built form. For instance, a familial compound in the Shan village of Ban Pang Mu enclosed the parents' house, a daughter's house and a grand-daughter's house. The oldest dwelling, the parents', was situated near the street; the most recent, the granddaughter's, was the farthest back. Such spatial organization denotes the place of a house in the kinship diagram as well as the age of the house. The rice granary was shared by all three houses.

Rice granaries are useful in discerning links between neighboring houses, for granaries often are common to several houses. A young married couple having built its own house can go on using the parents' granary for several years. A household becomes really independent only when it builds its own granary.

A single well often supplies water to several houses, and this can also reveal relationships between houses which are not apparent at first sight. In towns granaries are now unusual, yet looking at who uses which well can help in understanding groupings of houses inside a block. In Chiengmai, for instance, well water is still used as a supplement to piped water supplied by the town. The wells, located in private or semi-private spaces, can supply sets of houses.

A house by house knowledge of kin relations among the dwellers of a village is essential to understanding family groupings. In the village of Ban Mae Sakud most houses had family links to each other; only six out of thirty-four had no such links. An inquiry as to kinship relations between dwellings in a quarter of a town doubtless would give interesting data if it were made in a fairly homogeneous quarter with a relatively stable population.

Usually family links have become looser in urban areas, and because of the complexity of modern neighborhoods, it is very difficult to detect kinship relations among inhabitants. In more residential areas, some compounds still include the houses of members of a single family. Some examples can be found in Chiengmai inside the walled town (FIG. 13). The grouping of several houses belonging to the same family is still a pattern in towns when households share the same mode of production, such as when household members participate in the same handicraft or commercial activity, selling plants and flowers or preparing small amounts of ready-made food for takeout. These business activities are performed on the premises, near or beneath the pile dwellings.

FIGURE 13.
A compound in the
walled town of
Chiengmai.
(D r a w i n g:
K. Jintavorn.)

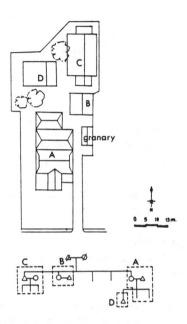

If a village usually gathers together several neighborhood units, a town usually gathers together several quarters. There is a similarity between villages and quarters in a town, but since this kind of pattern has less direct influence on built from than do rules of orientation, for instance, it is the subject here of only brief discussion.

Villages and quarters have the same core for social and spiritual cohesion, the monastery *wat*. The strong feeling of belonging to a religious community is common to villagers and townsmen. The symbolic importance of the *wat* for a quarter is revealed by the fact that the quarter is often designated simply by the name of its *wat*. In Louang Prabang, for instance, there is a Wat Mai quarter called Ban Wat Mai.

Another similarity which we have already noted is that of designation. Villages and quarters are both called *ban*, and their administrative functions are closely related. A royal ordinance claimed that "administrative divisions in Laos, except for the highest level, are identical in town and in the country."[12] In 1973 the town of Louang Prabang contained 79 *ban*. Villages and quarters were ruled by a *nay ban* elected by the council of elders.

A CONTINUITY OF TOWN AND VILLAGE

One can observe a strong continuity of culture between rural and urban areas. In villages one can perceive the structure of settlements more easily, because the rules exist and are still followed. This must have been the case formerly in towns, but the rules are no longer respected as a result of demographic, economic, and land-use pressures.

The similarities between rural and urban areas are quite apparent in Laos, where we found specific examples of traditional towns almost without industry and with precarious means of communication. The current situation in Laos and the country's recent history have resulted in the almost complete isolation of its towns. We saw that Louang Prabang looked like a collection of villages. Its principal street was paved only in the 1960s.

As for Thailand, one can discern a continuity between rural and urban areas in the places where there are remnants of the past, where the spatial organization has been maintained as it was prior to the economic boom. These are locations where the land-use structure has not yet changed too much and where urban land speculation has not yet prevailed. Some are residential quarters which can be discerned at first sight by their low density.

Respect for social customs and religious attitudes helps maintain tradition in certain parts of Thai settlements. The study of villages can serve as a guide, and can aid in understanding the complex structures of the urban fabric.

REFERENCE NOTES

I wish to thank Brian Brace Taylor who patiently read and corrected the English translation of this text.

1. Pierre Sylvain Dore assumes that this move could have taken place as early as the eighth or ninth century. "Contribution ethno-historique a la connaissance de la culture Louang Phrabanaise" (Doctorat d'Etat thesis, Paris V, 1987).
2. Cf. S. and P. Clement, Shin Yong-hak, *Architecture du Paysage en Extreme-Orient* (Paris: Ecole Nationale Superieure des Beaux-Arts, 1987).
3. For further information on Laotian dwellings, see S. Charpentier and P. Clement, *L'habitation Lao dans les regions de Vientiane et de Louang Prabang* (Paris: Peeters/SELAF, to be published in 1989); S. Charpentier, "The Lao house: Vientiane and Luang Prabang," in *The House in East and Southeast Asia*, SIAS monograph series 30 (Curzon Press, 1982), pp. 49-61.
4. M. Bruneau, *Recherches sur l'organisation de l'espace dans le Nord de la Thailande* (Lille and Paris: Honore Champion, 1980).
5. For more detailed information on the town of Louang Prabang, see L. Mogenet, "La ville de Louang Phrabang et son milieu" (Doctorat de Troisieme Cycle thesis, Paris I, 1974).
6. L. Mogenet, *Atlas de la ville de Louang Phrabang* (Vientiane: Vithagna, 1973), p. 2.
7. For further information on the town, see S. Clement-Charpentier and Kunwadee Jintavorn, "Chiengmai, sept siecles de tradition urbaine," to be published in *Archipel* 37, 1989.
8. H. Haagensen, "Ban Mae Mai, a northern Thai village. A socio-architectural case study," in *Lampang Reports* (Copenhagen: Scandinavian Institute of Asian Studies, 1976), pp. 54-71.
9. For a detailed discussion of this issue, see S. Charpentier and P. Clement, *Elements comparatifs sur les habitations des ethnies de langues Thai* (Paris: CERA, ENSBA, 1978).
10. Lucien Bernot observed the same custom among the Marma in Pakistan: "It would be unthinkable for a Marma to build his house with the ridge-pole oriented in a direction perpendicular to this river. It would be a real crime against the Lady of the River, an invisible person but whom they know is present. This lady could be wounded by the poles being laid across her way." L. Bernot, *Les Paysans Arakanais du Pakistan Oriental* (Paris: Mouton & Co., 1967), p. 421.
11. For rules of structuring space among the Lao, see P. Clement, "The spatial organization of the Lao House," in *The House in East and Southeast Asia*, pp. 62-70.
12. L. Mogenet, "La ville de Louang Phrabang et son milieu," p. 81.

THE INTERPENETRATION OF HIGH AND FOLK TRADITIONS IN MALTA

JO TONNA

In architecture and urbanism as in other forms of cultural expression most societies tend to follow two kinds of tradition: the great, high or classic tradition, which is continuously examining itself and is handed down through schools, treatises and professional institutions, and the little, low or folk tradition, which spontaneously perpetuates itself without any apparent effort at refinement or codification. Although these two traditions are commonly analyzed separately, in practice a region's great tradition, promoted by a social, cultural or economic elite, is likely to interact with the little tradition that wells up from the lives of the ordinary people who share the same space. It thus becomes important to understand how a high tradition can be communicated to the common people and absorbed into their little tradition, and how aspects of a folk tradition can be appropriated by a high tradition. One could examine how elite groups display their values and achievements to the common people and lead the latter to emulate them, how craftsmen simultaneously work in both high and low traditions and mediate between the two, and how organizational measures initiated by the elite deflect folk traditions to new ends or in new directions.[1]

A MAN-MADE LANDSCAPE

Because they are located at the center of the Mediterranean where they have attracted a succession of hegemonic groups bent on controlling the sea lanes, the Maltese Islands are well-placed for such an investigation. The islands are characterized by a complex layering of cultures, underpinned by an autochthonous culture whose major expression is to be found in a language that has a Semitic structure overlayed with a Romance vocabulary. This phenomenon has its parallels in the island's built form. Another important characteristic of the islands is the soft-grained, easily-quarried limestone which is almost the only natural resource. This material has been intensely exploited to sustain the man-made environment. In Malta, also, it is hardly possible to distinguish the natural from the man-made. "Everything one sees in Malta," noted Bowen-Jones, "is man-made and man-maintained in existence . . . man created the land on which he could live."[2] The residents of Malta accomplished this by covering stony wastes with soil transported across great distances. By some accounts, this soil was even imported from overseas.[3]

To build these artificial fields, the terrain was first cleared of loose stones and boulders, which was then used to build huts and to erect rubble walls that retained the terraced fields, defined boundaries, and sheltered crops and fruit trees from the wind. The corbelled beehive huts still to be seen in the countryside may have provided the building blocks for the first rural settlements. An early observer described these as "African huts," and noted also that peasants were just as likely to burrow into the limestone for their dwellings as to construct dwellings above ground. Natural and man-made cave complexes that included underground chapels were inhabited well into this century. The openings to some were sealed by house-fronts with doors and windows. Others were partitioned with stone walls. And sometimes entire houses were built into hillside caves so that the residual spaces around them could be stuffed with straw and animal fodder to produce perfectly insulated environments.[4]

FIGURE 1.
All-stone building
system in use in Malta
until the nineteenth
century.

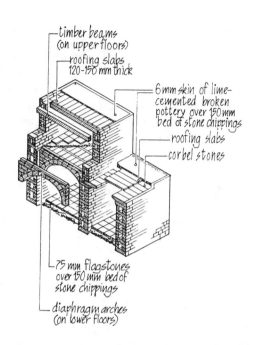

*timber beams
(on upper floors)*

*roofing slabs
120-150 mm thick*

*6 mm skin of lime-
cemented broken
pottery over 150 mm
bed of stone chippings*

roofing slabs

corbel stones

*75 mm flagstones
over 150 mm bed of
stone chippings*

*diaphragm arches
(on lower floors)*

The houses of the gentry in the cities were initially distinguished from these roughly-built rural dwellings by their dressed stonework. To produce square stone blocks, large slabs had first to be split from the quarry surface. These were then divided into units small enough to be transported to and handled on a building site. The exploitation of a quarry began by setting aside the topsoil. This was then spread back on the floor of the quarry once the good building stone was exhausted. In this way the landscape of constructed fields came to be punctuated by excavated fields that were particularly productive because of their sheltered locations.[5]

AN ALL-STONE BUILDING SYSTEM

In the absence of trees as many building components as possible had to be made from local stone (FIG. 1). The size of the elements was fixed according to what a man could carry and measure with his hand. Stone blocks were cut to a height of one *xiber*, a distance equivalent to a handspan from thumb to little finger (about 262 millimeters). Stone roofing slabs were cut as much as 150 millimeters thick and eight *xbar*, or one *qasba* (209 millimeters) long -- the maximum distance a slab could bridge without cracking. The roofing slabs could span rooms as much as three meters wide if they were supported on two corbelled courses of stonework. This roofing system generated the long narrow rooms which characterized vernacular house-types. Where longer spans were required, the roofing slabs were laid across the back of a series of diaphragm arches set about 120 centimeters apart. A 15 millimeter-thick sloping bed of stone chippings would then be laid over the roof slabs and waterproofed with a 6 millimeter-thick layer of broken pottery cemented in lime. The exterior walls were built using two leaves. These were bonded together with through-stones, and the space between them was filled with rubble. The floors were paved with square flagstones, 450 to 600 millimeters on a side and 75 millimeters thick. This overall system for constructing all-stone buildings was subjected to considerable refinement over time in response to practical and aesthetic requirements. Arch abutments were taken off the ground and into the overhead parts of the supporting walls. Roofing slabs were tailed into grooves that followed the curve of the supporting arches to produce vaults. Pointed or semicircular arches gave way to segmental or elliptical ones as the influence of the Baroque was felt. With the growth of commerce with outside countries, the diaphragm arches were partially replaced by imported timber beams -- an especially important modification for upper floors, and timber beams gave way to steel joists under the british. But stone slabs survived as a basic roofing material until the introduction of reinforced concrete in the late 1940's.[6]

FARM, HOUSE AND CHURCH

The long, narrow rooms generated by the all-stone building system were used to house people and animals as well as to store tools and farm produce. A typical farmstead consisted of several such

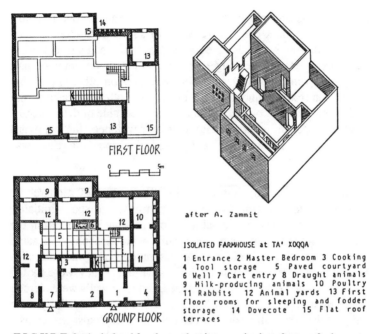

FIRST FLOOR

GROUND FLOOR

after A. Zammit

ISOLATED FARMHOUSE at TA' XOQQA
1 Entrance 2 Master Bedroom 3 Cooking
4 Tool storage 5 Paved courtyard
6 Well 7 Cart entry 8 Draught animals
9 Milk-producing animals 10 Poultry
11 Rabbits 12 Animal yards 13 First
floor rooms for sleeping and fodder
storage 14 Dovecote 15 Flat roof
terraces

F I G U R E 2. An isolated farmhouse showing organization of spaces for human and animal use.

rooms and a boundary wall that enclosed a courtyard area. The main courtyard would have a well to catch the rainwater that fell on the roofs, and it would contain an open staircase leading to an upper level of roof terraces and one or two rooms, called *ghorof*. An arched loggia, or *setah*, on one or two sides of the courtyard was a common feature of such farmsteads. Animal yards, *mandra*, were divided from the main courtyard by low walls. More elaborate farmsteads a number of animal yards and rooms, called *mqawel*, differentiated for use by poultry or rabbits, draught or milk-producing animals. The animal areas clustered around the main courtyard (FIG. 2). Herbs and sweet-smelling plants were planted here, and a vine tree, considered to be a symbol of fertility, spread overhead. Doors led into the courtyard from country lanes or fields.

Many farms and village houses had two entrances, one to admit people, the other, called a *remissa*, to admit horse-drawn carts. The smaller entrance, the one for people, could lead into either the courtyard, one of the long rooms around it or an entrance hall called an *intrata* that was flanked by rooms on other side. This transition from farmhouse to townhouse was often indicated by the addition of a suite of such rooms on the street side of the courtyard (FIG. 3). As the courtyard house-type developed, the courtyard space was sometimes tightened, and the open staircase was sometimes moved inside.

Settlements generally formed around the nucleus of a church or chapel at an important node or particularly sacred spot. Initially, these churches were not much different in scale or form from the houses around them and were built with basically the same techniques. The early churches were simple, rectangular halls with or without apses, or *tribunas*, at the east end. They were roofed with slabs laid over diaphragm arches, and their walls were pierced only by a door or perhaps a window at the west end. They were approached through a paved area, a *zuntier*, which also served as a burial ground, and was sometimes marked off by low parapet walls. As settlements grew, these churches were enlarged by aggregation. There are extant examples of twin churches sharing a common sidewall, and references exist to four or more chapels built against each other.[7]

SYMBOLIC ELEMENTS

What marked these churches as sacred spaces was their relative isolation, the paved area outside them, some limited decoration around their doors and windows, and the frescoed wall surfaces inside them. But the profane structures were not completely bereft of symbols. Cow's horns were often mounted high on buildings to ward off the evil eye. Stone niches that enclosed statues of protecting saints, or roundels that bore religious symbols, were also quite common. In addition, village houses had arched bed-alcoves called *arkova* in their master bedrooms from which husbands would withdraw through a wife's pregnancy. This made

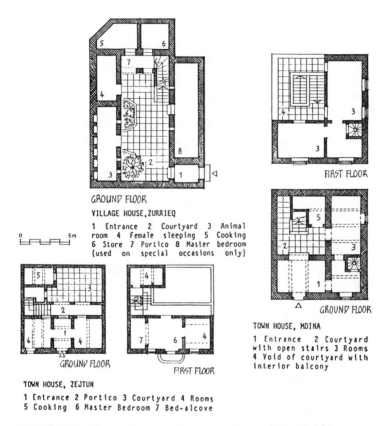

F I G U R E 3. Courtyard houses from rural and urban settlements in Malta.

the alcove the setting for childbirth and, in effect, a consecrated space which was placed under divine protection by a monogram of Christ or the Virgin carved into its keystone.[8]

As in Middle Eastern cultures these introverted houses had few openings at the street level, but the upper floor windows were used to display affluence and symbols connected with courtship and marriage. A standard feature was a stone shelf that projected into the street. The fact that a girl in the household had reached marriageable age would be announced to potential suitors by placing a pot of sweet basil on the shelf. The role of the upper-floor windows as "windows of appearances" is perpetuated by a popular saying that a plain-looking infant in the cradle would turn out to be a good-looking girl "at the window." Some sense of the significance of the ornament around the windows, which assumed different forms over time, can be gained by noting that a medieval master mason once sized up his reputation in terms of "the churches and beautiful windows" he was called upon to construct. When Malta was a Spanish fiefdom, richly decorated stonework for windows was imported ready-made from Valencia and Catalunya.[9]

SETTLEMENT PATTERNS

The progressive nucleation of rural towns around their parish churches followed three discernable patterns (FIG. 4). In about 50 percent of old Maltese villages and country towns the church is located at the head of a spine road which divides around it. In another 30 percent the church sits astride a through-street that continues to either side, and a processional street often begins perpendicular to the church facade. In the third type of village, the church occupies a node point at the confluence of four or more streets, giving the settlement a radio-concentric structure. Astride the spine streets and between bifurcations and radiating streets, urban land was progressively filled in with irregular blocks. These were articulated by roundabout streets, cut through by secondary streets and indented with dead-end lanes. Although these villages and towns developed long after the Maltese islands had passed out of Arab rule, the urban texture came to resemble that of traditional Islamic cities. An essentially Islamic typology of house and settlement pattern was realized with a Western vocabulary of forms. As mentioned earlier, this situation is similar to the development of the Maltese language. Studies of comparable cities on neighboring Sicily and the southeastern tip of the Italian peninsula have led some observers to conclude that the lessons of Islamic urbanism died hard in this part of the world.[10]

Both the islands of Malta and Gozo (the smaller island of the two Maltese islands) had fortified hill-towns to which the inhabitants

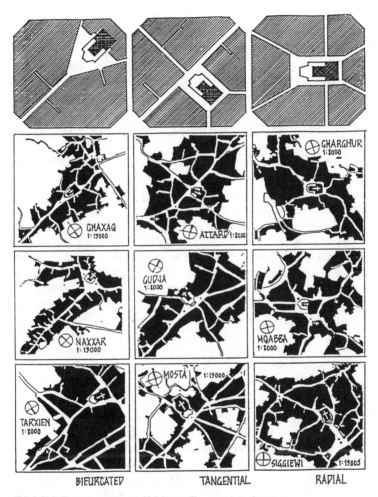

F I G U R E 4. A typology of Maltese villages and rural towns.

of outlying villages would flock for safety during major pirate incursions. The hill-town on Malta is the rump of a Roman city three times its size. Its walls were rolled back by the Arabs to create a more easily defensible Medina, by which name the hill-town is still known. Inside the Medina's walls, and in those parts of its sprawling suburb of the Rabat that are closest to it, the street pattern is suggestive of Islamic origins. Interlocking urban blocks are deeply indented with cul-de-sacs, and roundabout streets are occasionally bridged by buildings above the street level. The same can be said of Gozo's hill-town, the Cittadella. But since the Cittadella occupies an entire hilltop, it also bears an Acropolis-like relationship to its own Rabat unfolding beneath it. This suburb is even more suggestive of Arab models, with a greater concentration of dead-end streets than can be found anywhere else on the islands.

A third urban nucleus, huddling outside a fort that overlooks the entrance to Malta's major harbor, was selected as a base for the navally-oriented Knights of St. John when they took over the islands in 1530. Its texture was originally quite unlike that of the inland towns, being made up of a loose network of small blocks separated by short streets, but after the Knights had finished rebuilding it, it acquired a compact, concentric structure. The major church of Birgu, as the town was called, was located at its waterfront, not at its core. It was this settlement which bore the brunt of the Ottoman Great Siege of 1565. When the siege was raised, the Knights chose to build a planned new city across the harbor. From this point on, Maltese settlement no longer followed spontaneous and organic patterns of development -- or at least, not exclusively. The European great tradition of design came to be applied not only to individual buildings and monuments but to entire cities and complex fortifications. The new city was conceived as a closed, monumental entity. Advice was sought from the best military engineers and town planners. The layout of the city of Valetta was entrusted to Francesco Laparelli, an associate of Michelangelo, although much of the execution and detailed design devolved on Girolamo Cassar, a local architect who was prepared for the task by being sent to Florence, Rome an Naples to study the best buildings of the time. In this way, the first bridges began to be built between the local little tradition, in which Cassar was steeped, and the great tradition of the European mainstream.

The first bridges between the two traditions were consolidated by a set of town planning rules governing the building of the new city. These specified that all building stone was to be quarried from a

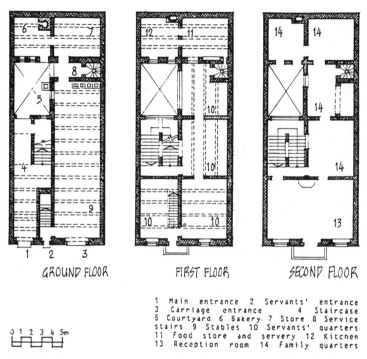

GROUND FLOOR   FIRST FLOOR   SECOND FLOOR

0 1 2 3 4 5m

1 Main entrance 2 Servants' entrance
3 Carriage entrance 4 Staircase
5 Courtyard 6 Bakery 7 Store 8 Service
stairs 9 Stables 10 Servants' quarters
11 Food store and servery 12 Kitchen
13 Reception room 14 Family quarters

F I G U R E 5. A town house from Valletta, showing clear separation of stables, servants' and owner's quarters.

site where an artificial harbor was planned. The rules also promoted social stratification by selectively assigning building sites according to "the means and status" of the developer. More importantly, they established the primacy and coherence of the urban street by prohibiting forecourts, setbacks and projecting features. Doors and street corners were singled out for mandatory ornamental treatment on all buildings. Moreover, a nominated master mason was to be engaged to design and build these elements.[11]

The building of the new city generated the need for new, more diversified house-types (FIG. 5). Unlike the courtyard houses of the older settlements, these had to fit into predetermined building plots, the result of a gridiron street pattern. They also had to cater to a highly stratified social system in which a culturally alien military elite shared the urban milieu with slaves, unskilled workers, tradesmen and an emerging class of merchants. As a result, a principle of vertical zoning emerged in the houses of the well-to-do. Stables, stores, shops and workshops were located on the ground floor, servants occupied the mezzanine floor, and household members, and their guests lived on the upper floors. These various levels were linked by spacious stairways for the guests and household members and spiral staircases for the servants.

PAROCHIALIZATION OF THE CITY

The building of a new city on this scale gave a tremendous boost to the building industry and provided the impetus for increasing specialization in the trades. The town planning rules established craftsmen who had worked their way up through the ranks as the producers, if not the arbiters, of aesthetic quality, and exposed them to the methods and ideas of the great tradition. Some craftsmen sat with the functionaries of the Knightly Order on the boards set up to oversee the building of new cities and fortification systems. The Knights had a well organized building department directed by two architect-engineers recruited abroad. These two men were assisted by twelve chartered engineer-surveyors, or *periti agrimensori*, headed by a Maltese director of works, the *capomastro delle opere*. By the eighteenth century locally trained *periti* were not only designing buildings and supervising their construction, they were involved in water supply and road construction works, land surveying and the valuation of estates.[12]

Italian and French architects and military engineers of the great tradition were still periodically brought in to design churches, public buildings and fortifications. Their projects were mostly worked out in studios overseas, often in complete ignorance of the properties and limitations of local building materials. These projects were invariably realized in stone by the local master-builders. In this way deep-rooted local building traditions were thoroughly impregnated with ideas emanating from a great tradition from abroad. Until the second half of this century unlettered craftsmen would reverently refer to a pattern book compiled by Vignola, the sixteenth-century mannerist architect, as the ultimate source of authority for moldings, proportions and rules of composition.

The recourse to local materials and expertise eventually brought about the parochialization, or vernacularization, of a city originally conceived in terms of a universal high tradition. The new building types were put together with traditional building systems, while self-consciously designed building elements like doors, windows, balconies, corbels and parapet walls were grafted onto building fronts with a vernacular disregard for compositional order. These elements were often inserted where they were functionally needed, not where they were called for by an abstract ordering system. The result was a subtle blending of folk and classic traditions, as monumentally-designed churches, palaces and public buildings were integrated into continuous street facades by a connective tissue of informally-designed buildings (FIG. 6).

THE GREAT TRADITION IN THE VILLAGES

A reverse phenomenon soon began to take root in rural towns, which began to prosper as a result of the wealth and security generated by the building of the new city: the penetration of high design into the villages. In the traditional village, the parish church was the only public building of any consequence. It provided the field for public displays of collective piety, wealth, identity and solidarity. The original parish churches began to be enlarged, rebuilt or refurbished in an ongoing process in which the entire village participated by donating funds and labor. A new generation of parish churches adapted available building techniques to the exigencies of larger scales and high design ideas (FIG. 7). The diaphragm arch and roof-slab system was refined to accomodate the barrel vaults and domes called for by the more complex spatial types of the classical tradition. These new churches appear to be massively built, but they are actually roofed

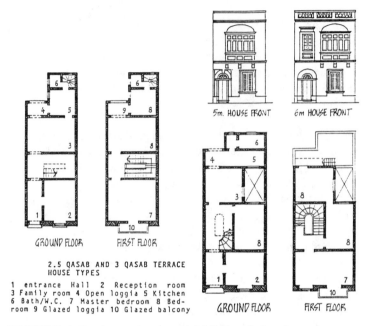

2.5 QASAB AND 3 QASAB TERRACE HOUSE TYPES

1 entrance Hall 2 Reception room
3 Family room 4 Open loggia 5 Kitchen
6 Bath/W.C. 7 Master bedroom 8 Bedroom 9 Glazed loggia 10 Glazed balcony

F I G U R E 6. Row house-types current in Malta from the late nineteenth century.

with surprisingly thin vaults -- no more than 150 millimeters thick in spans of up to 8 meters. The vaults were built from standardized roof slabs that followed the curve of the arches which supported them and were stabilized with rubble piled on their haunches. The same principle was applied to dome construction, where a thin hemispherical shell was encased in an octagonal drum that rose well past the springing line. The space between the shell and the drum was filled with rubble to hold the dome down and prevent it from bursting outwards. The careful husbanding of resources involved in putting waste material from building sites and quarries to structural use is very typical of the Maltese building tradition.

Within less than a century many of these first-generation parish churches were being superseded by larger and more complex ones that conformed to Baroque tastes. The highly efficient arch and roof-slab system could no longer cope with the complex geometry

FIGURE 7.
St. John Street,
Valletta.

and increased height and span of Baroque vaults. Each component
of the doubly-curved or intersecting surfaces of these vaults had to
be individually cut. The new style required a thorough grasp of
three-dimensional geometry. As a result, building techniques as
well as forms moved out of the realm of the little tradition and into
the realm of the great tradition.

Meanwhile, the planned settlements with their monumental
buildings and distinct house-types were becoming shut off from
the country by increasingly complex rings of fortifications. They
came to embody the highly polarized relationship that was
developing between town and country, military elite and peasantry.
To counteract this social split, public festivities were promoted to
divert attention and diffuse social unrest. Pageants, parades and
processions were staged for almost any excuse against a backdrop
of fireworks, illuminations and street decorations.[13]

The Baroque high style served the interests of the ruling elite by filling streets and public interiors with a profusion of signs proclaiming their power. It also made a permanent backdrop out of the city. House-fronts became grandstands from which the action could be watched (hence the profusion of balconies running across every building). More importantly, what began as an elitist high style was rapidly absorbed into an authentic folk tradition, as Baroque themes and details spilled over from the cities to the villages.

THE ORDERING OF SOCIAL SPACE

The rural town or village looked up to the city of the ruling elite as a source of prestige, and sought to assimilate its visible signs, including high design elements applied to vernacular buildings. The parish church, where this process began, embodied the memory of the community's past and ordered its social space. The church established the village square as the center of the community's religious, social, political and economic life. The streets which stretched from this center established a hierarchy of location against which the prestige of an individual family could be measured -- highest in the center, lowest on the periphery. This gradient of prestige was reinforced by the architectural sign system: Baroque monument at the center, unadorned vernacular on the periphery, and a graded palette of "decorated sheds" in between.[14]

Every year the village or rural town celebrated its collective identity with festivities to honor its patron saint. These culminated in a religious procession which originated in the church, wove its way through the secular domain of the streets, and returned to the sacred place. The procession moved to the sound of brass bands, bell ringing and noisy fireworks, against a background of beflagged, decorated and illuminated streets and buildings. It was customary to give buildings an annual facelift in anticipation of the festival. Their front rooms were opened up to display furniture, drapings, polished floors and other signs of family wealth and prestige. On this festive day, at least, Baroque perceptions of the perceptions of the street as theater triumphed over older Islamic notions of the street as the frontier between intensely private domains. The Baroque called for house-fronts designed as opera boxes loaded with signs of piety, wealth and status. As a result, the line between the great and little traditions is nowhere sharply drawn, except at the poles of the central church and the peripheral farm or house.

THE PROSCRIPTION OF BUILDING TYPES

The pace of urbanization, already quickened by the arrival of the Knights of St. John, accelerated even faster when the British took over in 1800. Valletta, the capital city, became hopelessly overcrowded, and conditions elsewhere in the country were not much better. A cholera epidemic in 1865 was blamed by a contemporary investigator on bad sanitation, overcrowding and lack of ventilation. This claim was supported by a correlation between the total number of deaths and the number of deaths in each tenement. Henceforth, the investigator's report concluded, health should be given priority over defense in deciding the form of buildings and settlements. He suggested that the offending cities should be demolished and rebuilt, "according to a healthy arrangement of blocks, houses and rooms allowing the free passage of air through streets and buildings."[15]

In 1880 the islands' first set of building by-laws came into effect. They established that no building should be higher than twice the width of its adjoining street. They also specified that every house should have a backyard three meters deep, except those on corner lots or between streets. This provision effectively eliminated the courtyard house as a viable house-type, and made the terrace house the basic cell of suburban towns that shortly mushroomed all over the islands. New streets began to be laid out according to a "key plan." Their construction and surfacing was financed by contributions levied from the owners of developed sites in proportion to building frontage. This encouraged development in deep, narrow plots.[16]

As speculative measures began to make their mark, terrace house-types were codified according to frontage. One could opt for a two and one-half, three or four *qasab* (five, six or eight meter) frontage. With their overall shape and dimensions thus predetermined, terrace houses lacked the morphological flexibility of the courtyard houses they began to replace. Their external appearance was also codified into a limited number of basic types, to which local variations could be made by the choice and disposition of building elements.

One could choose, for instance, between a "shell" door, *bieb arzella*, or an "English" door, *bieb la Ngliza* -- the former being set in a concave niche-like recess, the latter in a flat rectangular panel. One could have windows on one or both sides according to the frontage available, and one could have another arched recess on top, designed to give extra depth to a projecting balcony. This balcony was sometimes open, but more often it was covered and glass-enclosed to provide an extension of the upper floor into the street. These covered balconies came to provide one of the most insistent motifs of the Maltese urban landscape (FIG. 8). Originally framed in timber, they were eventually reproduced in stone, concrete or metal and were built in versions reflecting sensuous Baroque, opulent art nouveau, brutal concrete, slick aluminum or exuberant folk art styles. Most commonly found as dominant centerpieces on single family houses, they can also be rhythmically repeated across the face of tall apartment buildings, sometimes merging into a curtain wall of glass and wood suspended outside the heavy masonry.

SEMI-PERMANENT ELEMENTS

The wood, metal and glass that went into the door and window fixtures and the glass-enclosed balcony, or *gallarija*, had symbolic values of their own. House entrances traditionally had a set of double doors: a heavy, panelled door on the outside, backed up by a lighter, glazed door, or *antiporta*, on the inside. The outer doors were left open during the day and closed during the night. One flap of the exterior door was kept closed as a sign of mourning

FIGURE 8.
Covered balcony,
Valletta.

when a death occurred in the neighborhood; if the death had occurred in the house, the knockers on the door would be taken off for the duration of the mourning period. Dwarf iron gates outside this outer door marked the space between the outer and the inner doors as a private space and discouraged outsiders from sitting on the doorstep. Windows had an elaborate set of fixtures to provide privacy, security, shade and ventilation. The window frame itself, the *tieqa*, was backed up by solid wood shutters, or *kontraporti*, on the inside and protected by an independent set of louvered shutters on the outside. This added up to a finely calibrated system for controlling how much air and sunlight were allowed into the building, and how much people could see in and out of it.

These semi-permanent elements lent themselves to constant renewal and replacement, which in turn gave the house owner the opportunity to display his or her wealth, taste and status through the choice of design, material and quality of workmanship. All these decisions could be made within the framework of a permanent stone structure which was rarely altered. Shaped as they were by speculative pressures and abstract planning principles, the town and suburbs of the nineteenth and early twentieth centuries may have lacked the spontaneity and diversity of the earlier settlements, but they had their saving graces; they not only offered improved sanitation, lighting and ventilation but, they gave order and coherence through the use of common building materials and a shared architectural language. These last two factors helped bring about a measure of continuity between settlements of different periods that differed in house and street typology.

THE RELEVANCE OF TRADITION

In the final analysis the use of local stone may well be the only continuous thread in the Maltese built environment. It weaves its way through field walls and Baroque monuments, stone-age temples and modern buildings. But there is much to learn from other, less durable continuities, such as building types and street patterns, and the way these changed in response to external stimuli. The Maltese experience demonstrates the potency of organizational policies in uprooting old continuities and implanting new ones. It also illustrates the complex and sometimes unpredictable ways in which a great tradition originating outside a culture can interact with the little tradition that springs up inside it. All this has implications for environmental designers concerned with the issues of contextuality and continuity. By definition, these designers operate within the framework of a professional great tradition, but such a background only makes it more important that they tune in the little traditions that may be at work in the particular contexts in which they become involved. The problem of continuity in environmental design may well hinge on the ability of designers to abstract useful lessons from traditional architecture and urbanism. These could then be usefully incorporated into new buildings and settlements to anchor them to a cultural tradition without closing the gates to meaningful innovation.

REFERENCE NOTES

1. For a lucid exposition of the nature of great and little traditions and their interaction, see R. Redfield, *Peasant Society and Culture* (Chicago: University Press, 1960), pp. 27-58.
2. H. Bowen-Jones, "An Assessment of the Cultural Landscape," in *Malta: Background to Development* (Durham: University of Durham, 1960), p. 349.

3. E. Brown, *Travels and Adventures* (London, 1739), p. 185.

4. J. Quintin d'Autun, *The Earliest Description of Malta*, H.C.R. Vella, trans. (Malta: Debono, 1982; first published Lyons, 1536), pp. 31-49. "There are troglodytes in Malta: they dig caves, and these are their houses." Also P. Cassar, *The Meaning of the Maltese Countryisde* (Malta: Progress Press, 1960), p. 11.

5. G. Galea, *Xoghol u Snajja' tal-Imghoddi* (Malta: D.O.I., 1969), pp. 168-173.

6. For a nineteenth century documentation of the system, see H.D. Jones, *Memoranda and Details of the Mode of Building in the Island of Malta* (Dublin, 1840), pp. 197-199. The system closely resembles that of the treeless but limestone-producing Hauran region of Syria in classical times, as described in M. De Vogue, *Syrie Centrale: Architecture Civile et Religieuse du Ier au VIIe Siecle* (Paris: Baudry, 1877), pp. 7-47. Diaphragm arch construction occurs also in the popular architecture of Jordan and the Yemen.

7. M. Buhagiar, "Medieval Malta: Its Hypogea, Cave Churches and Ecclesiastical Buildings," in *Architecture in Malta* (Malta: SACES, 1986), pp. 39-49.

8. P. Cassar, "Pregnancy and Birth in Maltese Tradition," in *The Chestpiece* (Malta, April 1976).

9. Verbal communication with G. Wettinger on an unpublished medieval document; A.T. Luttrell, "Approaches to Medieval Malta," in *Medieval Malta* (London: British School at Rome, 1975), p. 61.

10. E. Guidoni, *La Citta Europea* (Milan: Electa Editrice, 1978), pp. 83-91.

11. S.R. Borg-Cardona, "The Officio delle Case and the Housing Laws of the Earlier Grandmasters," *The Law Journal* Vol. III no. 1 (Malta, 1951), pp. 39-69.

12. D. De Lucca, "The Maltese Perit in History," *Melita Historica* Vol. VI no. 4 (Malta, 1975), pp. 431-435.

13. G. Cassar-Pullicino, *Studies in Maltese Folklore* (Malta: University of Malta, 1976), pp. 40-42.

14. J. Boissevain, *Hal Farrug: a Village in Malta* (New York: Holt, Rhinehart & Winston, 1969), pp. 60-76.

15. C. Sutherland, *Report on the Sanitary Conditions of Malta and Gozo with reference to the epidemic of Cholera in the year 1865* (London, 1867), pp. 13-31.

16. J.G. Huntingford, "Town Planning Law," *The Architectural Review* Vol. CXLVI no. 869 (July 1969), p. 80.

THE PLACE OF NO-THINGNESS THE JAPANESE HOUSE AND THE ORIENTAL WORLD VIEWS OF THE JAPANESE

BOTOND BOGNAR

It is often noted that, beginning in the medieval period, the ideas of "emptiness" and "nothingness" in Buddhist doctrine came to exert great influence over the Japanese . . . . The Japanese of the time appear to have accepted these ideas literally. The shogun and poet Minamoto no Sanetomo questioned the existence of the world in a poem included in the *Kinkaishu*: "The world is a shadow reflected in a mirror; it neither is nor is not." And in a poem included in the *Shakushin hoshishu*, emptiness is seen as a basic attribute of the natural world: "Should we ever reach the sky, we would find the clouds and mist vanished." -- Mitsuo Inoue: *Space in Japanese Architecture.*[1]

The most precious thing in life is its uncertainty. -- Kenko Yoshida (1283-1350): *Essays in Idleness* (Tsurezureguza)[2]

When modern architects such as Bruno Taut, Walter Gropius and many others came to Japan, they discovered traditional Japanese architecture for not only the West but, in many respects, also for the Japanese. By the 1930s the Modern Movement had gained relatively firm ground in European architecture, while in Japan, which was in the process of rapid modernization, a small but growing group of architects was ready to promote the new functionalist and rational architecture.

The principles and forms of modern international style, however, encountered strong resistance in Japan from the official circles of the government and the ruling class which, moving toward militarization and the ideology of fascism, favored nationalism and nationalistic architecture. Paradoxically, this reactionary political trend prompted -- when it did not force -- the conditions for re-establishing contacts with traditional architecture that a Westernizing Japan was about to forget in the name of progress. Obviously, tradition was interpreted along different lines depending on the ideology it was called on to support.

Proponents of a nationalistic architecture favored a formalist approach to tradition, re-using the formal elements of Japanese architecture in an explicitly imitative manner. This trend resulted in the so-called *teikan yōshiki*, or imperial roof style, in the 1930s. The modernists also saw tradition as of strategic importance in attempting to establish and legitimize their own design concepts. In these efforts visiting Western architects provided significant initial incentives.

Bruno Taut, who devoted himself to the investigation of traditional architecture during his stay in Japan in 1933-34, understood the typical Japanese house, or *sukiya-zukuri*, as a predecessor and early representative of those ideas the Modern Movement was determined to forward, among which were rationalization of construction and function, simplicity and straightforwardness of form, and transparency and openness of spatial disposition. In *Dwellings and Lifestyles in Japan*, Taut wrote with respect to the Katsura Villa in Kyoto: "I asked this question of two of my colleagues [Shimomura Shotaro and Ueno Isaburo] here, 'How would one express this kind of style in terms of modern architecture?' In the end, they agreed that it could be said to be functional architecture. Taking the Katsura palace as a whole, no matter from what point you view it, the accommodation and integration of all the parts is so striking."[3]

More than two decades later, Gropius, another pioneer of modern design, still voiced similar opinions about the Katsura: "The old . . . Japanese house had already all the essential features demanded today for a modern prefabricated house; namely, modular coordination . . . and movable wall panels."[4] For the Japanese followers of modern architecture, including such later prominent architects as Sutemi Horiguchi and Kenzo Tange, traditional residential architecture could serve as a model in their attempts to bridge the gap between nationalism and modernism while trying to avoid the trap of literary traditionalism.[5]

Yet as Arata Isozaki has pointed out, these architects in their functional analysis and aesthetic interpretation of the Katsura and the Japanese house slowly developed a unified position that elevated the actual *sukiya* architecture into the realms of myth.[6] This modernist and largely West-inspired myth has survived to a significant extent and is still effective today. In pursuit of rational purity, modern architects often saw what they wanted to see, or rather what their cultural patterns of perception let them see. They not only purposely neglected a wide range of details and dismissed the existence of ornamentation as disturbing heterogeneity, but they also failed to recognize such not immediately obvious, yet significantly unique features as symbolism, perceptual qualities of space and the complexity of the whole design. Together with the attitude that shaped them, these features are all intimately related to the Oriental world views of the Japanese and to the Japanese way of life.[7]

THE EVOLUTION OF THE JAPANESE HOUSE

What is today generally known as the Japanese house went through a long process of evolution before reaching its maturity during the Edo Period (1603-1868). By this period residential architecture encompassed a multiplicity of building types and their numerous variations, all derivatives of previous models. Despite significant differences, these types shared much in common especially when compared to their Western and other foreign counterparts. These commonly shared characteristics are what justify the collective term Japanese house and reflect the most important traditions embodied in residential architecture. These traditions are the focus of this present investigation.

FIGURE 1.
Shinden type
residence as
represented by the
reconstructed Imperial
Palace (Gosho) in
Kyoto -- View of the
main building or
Shishinden
(mid-19th c).

In prehistoric times Japanese dwellings were constructed over small, shallow, usually circular pits dug in the ground. The rather simple wooden framework, which served partly as the structure of the wall and partly as the structure of the roof, was finished with grass and leaves. As agriculture, mainly rice cultivation, took root in Japanese soil, the consequent need to store and protect the crop caused a new type of storehouse structure, now elevated above the ground, to be developed. Soon residences followed the storehouse pattern. Applying a more advanced construction technique, the new house featured plank walls, thatched roof and a wooden platform over posts. This style of residence, through further development and, more importantly, after being influenced by imported Chinese architectural models, slowly gave way from the beginning of the sixth century to the first major type of aristocratic residence, the *shinden-zukuri*.[8] Shelters of commoners and other lower-class citizens continued to be built with the simplest methods and cheapest materials.

During the Heian Period (794-1185), the time when Kyoto was established as the seat of the Imperial court and the capital of Japan, the *shinden-zukuri* grew into an extensive complex of buildings and pavilions connected by covered corridors and centering around a main hall or *shinden*, literally "hall for sleeping." The symmetrically arranged compound faced a garden around a small pond to the south, and the whole assemblage was surrounded by thick earth walls pounded between wooden planks (FIG. 1).

Within the *shinden* style buildings cylindrical columns supported the elevated wooden floors and the large thatched roofs. The interior was a relatively unified, geometric space delimited by both fixed and mobile walls, while the more important structures were surrounded by additional hurdle verandas with decorative railings under the protruding eaves. Mobile walls, when outside, were built either as horizontally hinged swinging doors (at the end of the building) or as sliding panels (toward the verandas) and were complemented by curtains and blinds of bamboo or other material. In the interior beyond the few built-in partitions, space division was established occasionally by sliding panels and, more frequently, by such things as portable folding screens, curtain stands and drapes. For sitting and reclining, thick but movable mats of woven straw with silk borders -- predecessors of the *tatami* -- were used.

After a period of stagnation, around the end of the twelfth and the beginning of the thirteenth century the influence of Chinese culture once again intensified, introducing a new trend, Zen Buddhism. During the following medieval or Muromachi (1333-1568) and Momoyama (1568-1603) Periods, parallel with the spreading of Zen teachings, *shinden* architecture began to change, yielding in time to the *shoin-zukuri* that became the typical residence style of the ruling class -- feudal warlords, high ranking warriors or *samurai*, and monks of certain Buddhist sects.[9]

Shoin style buildings featured more extensive interior spatial division than their predecessors with more built-in yet mobile sliding screens applied as internal partitions (*fusuma*), exterior wall panels (*shōji*), and protective rain shutters (*amadō*). The raised floor area of most premises was now permanently and fully covered by *tatami*, the delicately finished thick rush matting, each approximately six feet by three feet in size. All of these elements followed a well elaborated modular system (*kiwarijutsu*) that was derived from the coordinated structural span (*ken*) between square posts. Most importantly, however, the layout of the intricately interconnected complex of wooden structures became expressly asymmetrical and almost always diagonally staggered (*suji-chigai*) (FIG. 2).

FIGURE 2.
Shoin type residence
-- The Nino-maru
Palace (1626) of Nijō
Castle (1603)
in Kyoto.

Although asymmetrical, the otherwise strictly formal, modular and codified design of the *shoin* residence was less suitable to the liking and everyday life of the aristocracy and the social elite. Borrowing extensively from the increasingly popular architecture of the rustic and humble tea house (*chashitsu*), the *shoin* was first paralleled then slowly replaced by one of its more relaxed yet elegant variations, the so-called *sukiya* style residence. The detached, or *soan*, type tea house developed by Zen Buddhist monks was directly influenced by the hermitages of medieval scholar-recluses and the simple yet refined homes of the Kyoto aristocrats of the early middle ages, and it was indirectly influenced by the vernacular of the peasant huts. As a result the *sukiya-zukuri* evolved as the unique blending of a variety of previous styles in residential architecture (FIG. 3).

The most successful examples of *sukiya* residences combine the elegance of the more formal *shoin* style with the informal mood of the tea house style, reflecting the artistic idiosyncrasies of an owner deemed characteristic of men of taste. Accordingly, each representative of the *sukiya* architecture manifests particular and individual features within a commonly shared model. Some of the general characteristics of this model were irregularity, lack of a formal canon, free and ambiguous spatial disposition, airy and elusive atmosphere, sophisticated understatement and rusticity. The characteristics applied to both buildings and their indispensable gardens or courtyards (FIG. 4).

FIGURE 3.
Tea house in the
garden of Saihōji Zen
temple (14th c) in
Kyoto.

FIGURE 4.
One of the best
examples of the
Sukiya type
residences, the
Katsura Imperial Villa
(17th c) in Kyoto.

By the second half of the Edo Period (1603-1868) the general
stock of Japanese houses can be classified within two major
groups. The first included the feudal estates of the aristocrats and
the urban or suburban mansions of the upper military class
(*yashiki*). The second was comprised of the commoners' dwell-

FIGURE 5.
Machiya, or urban
residences, in the
Gion district
of Kyoto.

ings (*minka*): the urban residences of merchants, craftsmen and the like (*machiya*); the row houses or tenements of artisans, workers and servants (*nagaya*); and the farmhouses of the rural population. Within both groups, the types and individual buildings -- with regard to such features as size, quality of design, materials, structures and spatial composition -- varied widely depending on geographic location and their owner's wealth and social status (FIG. 5).

Obviously the *yashiki* maintained the closest relationship with the *sukiya-zukuri*, having retained also the landscape or stroll garden within its extensive compound. Nevertheless, the residences of the middle and lower classes also began to gradually adapt several elements of the *sukiya*. The *tatami* floor, for example, already widely used in the homes of the higher social strata by the end of the fifteenth century, became increasingly common in the houses of the general population around the late seventeenth century. Similarly, the sliding screens of *shōji* and *fusuma* were to be utilized in every house.

In this way the vernacular architecture of the *minka*, which by way of the rustic tea hut had significantly influenced the refined poverty of the *sukiya-zukuri*, eventually acquired some of the features and qualities of the very architecture it had helped to bring about.   Beyond closing the gap between vernacular and representational architectures to a remarkable extent, this cross reference among different styles of residential building completed the evolution of the Japanese house. The result was the free style of the *sukiya* architecture which, with its flexibility, was able to express the art and life of the common people as well. As David Stewart remarked, "the evolution of the Japanese house, with its unique system of 'internal fusion' [both] reflects the traditional family system and, in turn, has helped to shape the Japanese way of life."[10]

The preceding discussion illustrates how the significance of the tradition of the Japanese house points beyond the immediately obvious, factual and formal. That significance is deeply rooted in the sensibility, mentality and collective subconsciousness with which the Japanese both conceive and perceive their architecture and their world. It is this invisible realm of tradition that needs careful attention and explication.

THE ANATOMY AND PHILOSOPHY OF A TRADITION

The most significant trend in the development of the Japanese house, similar to the course of the whole culture, is an increasing deviation from imported Chinese ordering principles, a movement away from a highly structured and rather rigid geometrical system, which initially had an impact on Japanese art, architecture and urbanism. The Japanese by nature had an aversion to such a system; after the first encounter with it they began to modify it, moving toward a more sensitively flexible "sophisticated order" that could be best described as *topological*.[11]

In the layout of architectural compounds, asymmetry became a preferred feature, as such designs responded better to the qualities and topographical conditions of the site and better satisfied the Japanese mentality and way of life. These first steps indicate a more conscious attempt by the Japanese to blend their man-made environment with the natural world. They also reveal the influence of the indigenous Shinto religion which centers around the worship of nature and the appreciation of the land. Since the Japanese understood themselves as being part of nature, their homes assumed a mediating role in order to achieve unity between human life and the world at large.

With no sharp difference perceived between natural and man-made things, traditional Japanese residential architecture beautifully expresses a mediation between the building and its surrounding landscape as converted into gardens. The understanding of house and garden as an inseparable entity is expressed by the term *katei*, a Japanese word for household, home and family that combines the words for house (*ka*) and garden (*tei*). The intimate relationship is accomplished through a variety of intermediary zones brought about by the unique spatial definition and disposition of both the house and the garden.

The non load-bearing and, more often than not, mobile walls in the building -- supported solely by the wooden structural skeleton -- could freely establish direct fusion among spaces inside and out. The veranda (*engawa*) around the house exemplifies this well. Depending upon the actual position of the *shōji* and *amadō*, this buffer zone can be adjoined to either the exterior or the interior or, more importantly, to both of them at the same time. Nevertheless, a similar possibility exists among the spaces inside the house.

The interior features other systems of thin, sliding screens (*fusuma*) which layer the space in a multiple way. In this system an outer zone always seems to envelop another inside. By opening, closing or even removing the screens, any unit can be connected to adjacent volumes creating not only smaller or larger entities at will, but also changing the whole spatial configuration. Consequently, beyond the veranda any layer of space can be interpreted as an in-between *(en)* space. This circumstantial or vague definition of boundaries and space therefore corresponds directly with the multi-functional nature of the *tatami* rooms and, indirectly, with the situational character of the Japanese (FIG. 6).

If the thin, paper-covered, translucent mobile screens could take on the roles of window, door or wall, the *tatami* could serve as a kind of multipurpose furniture. People, with footwear removed, would customarily sit, sleep and perform many activities on it, which is one of the reasons why the traditional house was sparsely furnished and empty-looking. In a similar manner, rooms with

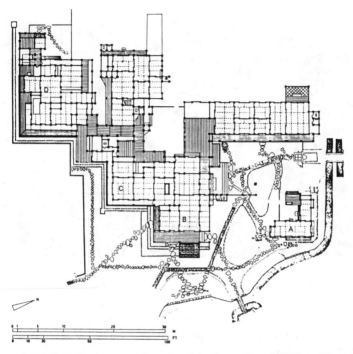

F I G U R E 6. The layout and floor plan of the Katsura Imperial Villa and the Gepparo tea house in Kyoto (17th c).

tatami flooring usually have no specific function and can be used equally easily as parlor, study, dining or bedroom with the simple rearrangement of the few accessories each use requires.[12]

In addition, within the Japanese house, as in traditional architecture in general, there is no clear distinction between spaces of spiritual purity and ordinary use -- that is, between sacred and profane (*sei* and *zoku*). A specific space or room, and even the whole residence, can be converted into a sacred domain with the performance of certain ceremonies and the temporary display of religious signs or symbols such as a small, usually portable Shinto and Buddhist altar (*Kami-dana* and *Butsu-dan*) or the sacred rope (*shimenawa*) above the entrance to the house.[13] By removing these symbols after the special event, the space or building reverts to its everyday use.

F I G U R E 7. The interior of the Japanese house is predicated by softly filtered light gradually fading to shadows and darkness (*yami*) -- Interior of the Yoshijima house in Takayama (19th c).

Often it is the ritual performance of some routine action rather than the actual enclosure that guides the understanding of a given locality in the home, as in the case of the *genkan*, or anteroom, for example. A visitor on the lower level of the *genkan* is not regarded as being inside the house even if the area, as in all modern homes, is behind the entrance door. To enter means to remove one's shoes and step up. Thus, to invite a person in, the host asks the guest to *agatte kudasai*, "please step up," equivalent to the Western notion of "stepping in."[14]

The flexibility of the multi-functional, multi-layered, porous space allows the exterior realm to penetrate into the interior step by step, generating a *centripetal* space structure (FIG. 7). Such a non-Western pattern, where spaces are brought about not as three-dimensional form by solid and fixed enclosures but as two-dimensional layers by thin, mobile membranes in variable configuration, always suggests an innermost core, or *oku*. The progression from openness to depth, outside to inside, and from light to darkness points to an elusive destination, a psychological realm where space together with the softly filtered light appear to converge to zero (FIG. 7).[15]

Since this progression depends upon both the actual, momentary disposition of the mobile screens and other signs, plus the relative position of the observer, *oku* can only be intuitively sensed and understood phenomenologically. The *oku* cannot be approached with the rationality of mind; it eludes any attempt to get to it by opening the layers wrapping around it. By virtue of the concept of *oku* -- signifying innermost, far back, deep, least visible and accessible -- the Japanese have been able to give an illusion of depth to spatial compositions regardless of their usually small and shallow dimensions. The *oku*, writes Fumihiko Maki, "is the original point (mental touchstone) in the minds of the people who observe or create it, and hence becomes the invisible center; or more precisely, it is a convenience devised by a spirit and climate which deny absolute objects or symbols such as the notion of center. The *oku* is a center which those who relate to the object can set it freely, for it does not need to be made explicit to others."[16]

This spatial quality of the Japanese house shows again signs of ritualistic modes of perception with a strong affinity with Shinto belief. According to Shinto, every phenomenon is inhabited by a *kami* spirit, and the more unique the phenomenon the stronger the spirituality. The least visible locations -- remote and misty mountains, deep valleys, thick forests or trees, various islands or rocks and cliffs that are impenetrable to the eye and unattainable physically -- were attributed such spiritual quality. In keeping with this analogy, space for the Japanese did not exist *a priori*. As Isozaki pointed out, "space was perceived as identical with the events or phenomena [natural or other] occurring in it; that is [it] was recognized only in its relation to time-flow." Space was *heterogeneous*, with increasing density around places where it would be the least spatial in the traditionally rational Western understanding.[17]

In the *sukiya* style residence, where the placement of columns is relatively free of restrictions, there are no appointed axes, symmetry, and -- because the *oku* does not signify an absolute geometrical center -- there are no centrally arranged spaces and plans.[18] Hence, the absence of a well defined center and the ambiguous spatial quality of the Japanese house are predicated on both the lack of a ruling order and the layered, indefinite boundaries that together can only define imperfect entities. These qualities, even though they generate or signify space, in a curious manner break space down or prevent it from coming fully into being. (FIG. 8).

What is experienced in such a system is a heterogeneous fabric of in-between realms, called *ma* in Buddhist terminology, that leaves everything -- forms, entities, together with their meanings -- continuously open-ended or unfinished; here nothing can assume the coherence of absolute certainty. Iwanami's *Dictionary of Ancient Times* describes *ma* as "the natural distance between two or more things existing in continuity," or "the natural pause or interval between two or more phenomena occurring continuously."[19]

Like the built Japanese environment in general, the *sukiya* type residence and its garden were designed and grew piecemeal, in an additive and sequential way, always from parts toward a collage-like larger entity. The Katsura Imperial Villa of the seventeenth century, for example, was constructed by many different builders over almost a century, with its several owners adding new sections to the previous complex. The result was again the typical zig-zag pattern, something like the formation of flying geese (*ganko-haichi*) that at the end looked almost incidental.[20] The avoidance of unified totalities in appearance thus was both an instinctive and conscious act at the same time (FIGS. 6, 9).

The house and the surrounding garden, lacking an all-encompassing clear, geometrical order, became a labyrinthine assemblage, an additive of heterogeneous elements, references and vistas, wherein the irregular network of small focal points and subtle episodes were alternatively hidden and revealed (*mie-gakure*) with the power of unexpected incident. The Japanese have

FIGURE 8.
The ambiguous
spatial disposition of
the *Sukiya* type house
-- Interior of the
Katsura Imperial Villa
in Kyoto (17th c).

FIGURE 9.
The diagonally
staggered plan is
indicative of both the
aesthetics of
"fragmentation" and
the incremental
growth of the
Japanese house --
Katsura Imperial Villa
in Kyoto (17th c).

been able to heighten the awareness of certain events by isolation
and often opposition. In such a sequence of events the building is

not a major attraction; it is carefully concealed by hillocks, trees and other elements so that the strolling person catches only partial glimpses of it. Accordingly, the approaching paths are oblique rather than focused straight and perpendicular onto the house. Mark Treib explains: "The historic house . . . within its . . . setting was not itself the subject of the view . . . . It was not an architectural entity to be approached and confronted in the tradition of formal Western architecture. The objects of contemplation, instead, were the incidents within the space: the folded screen, the transom carving, the ceramic vessel, or flower arrangement -- and, after time, the garden" (FIG. 10).21

Indeed, the history of Japanese house and architecture shows a gradual process of disintegration of geometric space and organization, while witnessing the evolution of movement or *topological* space in which a coordinate relationship among buildings and spaces hardly matters, and in which one's position relative to a

FIGURE 10.
In the irregular
network of the garden
with small focal
points, the house is
not the main attraction
-- Detail of the
Katsura Villa in
Kyoto (17th c).

FIGURE 11.
The unity of the tiny space and "microcosmic world" of the tea house is broken up by an irregular central post (*naka-bashira*), and the wooden partition (*sode-kabe*). Interior of the Shokintei Tea House in Kyoto (17th c).

larger whole cannot be positively discerned. Fragmentation, also as an aesthetic trend, went as far as, or rather came from, the miniscule interior of the tea house. Here a small wooden plank (*sode-kabe*) with its supporting irregular post (*naka-bashira*) always covered a part or one corner of the room, purposely breaking the unity of its space (FIG. 11). The Japanese devotion to intricately obstructing the line of vision robbed both the house and its garden of undisturbed, open vistas; thus, in the whole compound everything is suggested, hinted at, rather than stated or introduced in a clear-cut manner.

In the world of the Japanese house and garden, spaces and spatial systems that are easy to comprehend at one glance from certain well constructed vantage points do not exist. As opposed to modernist interpretations, *sukiya* architecture reveals a spatial disposition which could be called *opaque* rather than transparent. It defies the rules of linear or angular perspective, the mode of Western perception which, since the Renaissance, has become the expression of man as ruler of the world. A predominant reliance on vision in the West tends to objectify and instill a feeling of mastery over the environment, as the eye sets everything at a distance and establishes and consolidates an explicit, clear order.

In the Japanese environment only fragments -- often in the form of heterogeneous layers of signs and symbols -- are encountered, and these fail to provide an objective perspective of a definite, overall spatial pattern. The interwoven yet discontinuous fabric of gardens and architectural complexes can unfold in a more subtle way. Experiencing such environments necessitates active mental involvement and physical participation, and compels one to move through them. In Inoue's words, "observation . . . is always postulated on the viewer's movement whether actual or intellectual."[22] The paths, however. are never straightforward; they lead along alternating turns (*oremagari*), modulating velocity and the field of attention, heightening expectation yet also pre-empting the certainty of final arrival at an ultimate goal. Along this *indirect approximation* of something that is implied yet never really expressed, the route is as important as -- if not more so than -- the destination. Thus, the twisting, turning paths and movement in architecture and gardens have a strong affinity with the idea of mutability (*mujōkan*). In the house nothing exemplifies this better than the ritual of the long and eventful entrance sequence.

Since totality is never presented visually in the state of completeness and perfection, the whole remains elusive to be conjured up in the memory and imagination. This demands that the observer acquire a multi-focal perspective and understanding, which not only ties the interpreting person into the world by a multitude of invisible threads, but also undermines the individual identity of things. In such an engagement objects cannot obtain a fully objective character, while subjects are prevented from gaining total subjectivity. Here neither the created world nor human consciousness can claim self-contained and delimited autonomy; these are brought together in a unique metaphysical order, an integration without synthesis where neither opposition nor reconciliation occurs.[23]

It is obvious that this understanding and conduct were extensively guided by Buddhist, especially Zen Buddhist, world views, although in conjunction with Shintoism, and that the understanding thus encompassed all things as constituents of a living reality. Buddhist thought regards the world as a chain of fluid phenomena with no constancy (*samsara*). In the continuous process of transformation and change, nothing is permanent, or, conversely, every momentary stage of development is equally viable and complete. In this world everything is in a perpetually temporary state of in-between (*ma*) where becoming and fading away, growth and decay, presence and absence, reality and fiction take place simultaneously, or perhaps are one and the same thing. This sameness of different things is the domain of no-thingness, or *nirvana*, toward which Buddhist conduct leads and which is accessible through reflective learning, intuitive awareness, meditative action and life, and the eventual enlightenment (*satori*).

In such a transitory view of life, as Inoue wrote, "the present that we inhabit is nothing more than an instant wedge in eternal nothingness [*mu*]."[24] Buddhism emphasizes the evanescence and insubstantiality of all things. Universal and immutable laws did not appeal to the Japanese, and they remained equally uninterested in defining the world in dichotomies. The nature and order of things for them thus could not, and did not, reside in the logic of pure identity; Japanese things were not subject to a one-way process of individuation and objectification. The Japanese were more interested in circumstantial relationships and the concreteness of interface between things, without being much concerned about the consistency of a well defined, abstract system of wholes. They apprehended things as events rather than as substance. This outlook on the world of things has given Japanese mentality and life a highly intuitive, situational and paradoxical character. It developed slowly and reached its epitome during the Edo Period (1603-1868), but it has also been preserved to a remarkable extent as one of the most important aspects of tradition even after coming face to face with the West.[25]

This mentality and spirit were first introduced in the *soan* tea house architecture (*chashitsu*) developed and designed by Zen Buddhist monks such as Murata Shukō (1422-1502), Takenō Joō (1502-55), Sen-no-Rikyū (1522-91), and Kobori Enshū (1579-1647), all of whom were philosophers, artists and architects as well. The ritual of the tea ceremony, previously only an occasion for social gathering, was gradually transformed by these people into a form of mediation, a vehicle toward attaining enlightenment. Following the monks, aristocrats and then members of the military class came to practice the tea ceremony, and eventually it gained popularity among the commoners as well; it is still a widely accepted form of art and an integral part of Japanese life today. It is no exaggeration to say that the cult of tea played a central role in shaping Japan's cultural history, including its architecture.

Parallel with these developments, the tea house and the tea room within were progressively reduced in size. Some like the ones by Rikyu were as small as two or even one and one-half *tatami* in floor area. The tea room became a place of spiritual refuge for people wanting to escape the pressures of continuous warfare and the confines of feudal life; the ceremony provided a highly focused world of repose concentrating on the smallest details of the performance -- cultivating the senses yet controlling the self of those few who participated.

The way of tea (*chadō* or *chanoyū*) and its architecture brought about an array of aesthetic principles which were all derivatives of, or otherwise related to, Zen teachings. The carefully selected materials and elements were left in their naturally imperfect, or impoverished state, and became highly appreciated as they aged. The processes of transition, withering away and even decay informed the human senses, and sharpened the sensibilities and awareness of the Japanese; *sabi* came to connote patina, age, loneliness, resignation, while *wabi* expressed refined poverty, beauty in simplicity and understatement.[26] The ritual and setting of tea became an attempt to enact the Zen tenet, "man originally possesses nothing."

In the tea room the displayed signs and symbols, limited in number yet profound in effect, all alluded to the ephemeral, mutable nature of being. The flower arrangement (*ikebana*), the incense and its holder, and the calligraphic scroll in the *tokonoma* alcove had to be regularly replaced in response to changes in season, and the mood and taste of the host and, more importantly, the guest(s). The flickering shadows induced by the filtered light in the subdued and rather dark space provided further reminders of the passing of time and the melancholy of things (*mono-no-aware*).

With the spread of Zen and the popularity of the tea ceremony, tea architecture began to exert a profound influence on residential architecture, introducing not only many of the composing elements in the tea house but also its spirit and mentality. Human dwellings were to be regarded as temporary shelters and as such an inseparable part of the floating world of the Japanese. This fostered, as in the case of the tea house itself, a mode of symbolic building wherein nothing was symbolized, or, more precisely, where void, emptiness or no-thingness (*mu*) was symbolized. In reference to the traditional house, Chris Fawcett has remarked that "the essence of its space is a *mythos* of thinglessness, furniture-lessness, colorlessness, [and] substancelessness."27

Indeed, the history of the Japanese house and architecture is permeated by a spatial logic that is really nothing more than a hidden system, a capacity for aesthetically evaluating the nonexistent. "This architecture reminds us of the poignancy of things on the verge of disappearing or, conversely, at the moment of emerging."28 Experiencing it is a process of suspending architecture in a continuous state of in-between; its ambiguity, according to David Stewart, "embraces the 'emptiness of signs' as the essential manifestation of a reality, that is 'unknowable' and yet is able to be felt in a most concrete way."29 The perceptual immateriality of the Japanese house thus evokes *mu-no-basho*, or the place of true no-thingness.

THE CONTEMPORARY CONDITION: INTERPRETATIONS OF A PHILOSOPHY AND MENTALITY

Today modernism and its rigid Western rationality do not remain unchallenged. Post-modernism, though a composite of multifarious and often opposing trends, questions most of the reductionist, exclusionist tenets and the functionalist dogma of modern architecture and departs from modernism's categorical rejection of history. Younger Japanese architects now find it difficult to accept the usual modernist and Western interpretations -- like those of Taut, Gropius and even Tange -- that assert that their traditional architecture consists of mechanically flexible and transparent structures of space, or a precisely determined system of self-evident elements within a strict functionalism conceived of as a product of the super-rational devotion of the Japanese to the objective in the environment.[30]

Unfortunately, by embracing historic architecture, post-modernism too often succumbs to an indiscriminate re-use of the past, a stylistic revival that, in an uncritical manner, ultimately serves the exploitive interest of the present, increasingly consumerist architecture. There is, however, another approach to tradition that might appear at first anti-traditionalist. This approach does not deny the numerous achievements of modern culture, and it also intends to face the given conditions and reality of our present age. Architects, skeptical about a sentimental return to a pre-industrial past, and yet equally critical of a naive faith in the myth of technological progress, are more inclined to accept the way that the Japanese seem to have followed during most of their history. According to this way, argues Nyozekan Hasegawa, the importance of tradition "lies not so much in the preservation of the cultural properties of the past in their original form as in giving shape to contemporary culture; not in the retention of things as they were, but in the way certain . . . qualities inherent in them live on in the contemporary culture."[31] The Japanese are comfortable with the idea of change.

In the works of Japanese avant-garde architects there seems to be a re-interpretation of the philosophy of nothingness by way of establishing "new relations between the space and person."[32] There is a strong intention, especially in residential architecture, to open up the closed, deterministic and reductionist circuits of modern Western representation by challenging our normative perceptions within indefinite spatial dispositions. This signals a return to the graphic and calligraphic quality that always characterized Japanese design and building, and to a heightened sensibility to materials, details and the poetically elusive nature of things, concerns which critique the instrumentality of the representational sign.

Tadao Ando, for example, in his minimalist architecture of unfinished walls, reintroduces nature by way of carefully focused openings and sensitive modulation of light and shadow, and manages to de-materialize the structures and surfaces of the concrete and imbue space with an ephemeral quality (FIG. 12). Kazuo Shinohara describes his recent architecture of small houses as a "zero-degree machine" (FIG. 13); Kazunari Sakamoto's buildings are intended to be "environments" rather than "objects."[33] Sakamoto explains, "'building as object' depicts a building which has a dominant form . . . whose meaning . . . exists in a formal visual composition; . . . 'building as environment' refers to a building with which we or something can relate on . . . different levels."[34]

While several architects like Hiromi Fujii, for instance (FIG. 14), employ layered and fragmented concrete walls and orthogonal framework to "suspend form," other designers turn to industrially mass-produced, light-weight elements to create membraneous boundaries and collage-like ambiguous enclosures with an

F I G U R E 12.
Ando, by way of carefully designed openings and sensitive modulation of light and shadow, imbues space with an ephemeral quality -- Interior of the Koshino Residence (Ashiya, 1982).

FIGURE 13.
The "zero-degree
machine" of
Shinohara -- Interior
of the House on a
Curved Road
(Tokyo 1975).

intended "superficiality."[35] Not only is this architecture able to achieve lightness and insubstantiality, but it does this in a way that reinterprets tradition and bypasses any nostalgic use of a formal past. These architects manage to apply materials and products of industry while simultaneously expressing opposition to industrial and consumer society. The surfaceness of the intricately assembled, thin, semi-transparent layers alludes again to an invisible depth, an intangibility, an unexplainable void that frustrates rationality and causes knowledge or the subject to vacillate. Fumihiko Maki has characterized his current designs as aggregates of active, heterogeneous parts that, in generating wholes, never conform to a formula.[36]

Toyo Ito with his own residence, the "Silver Hut," goes further in de-structuring form, decomposing it into a fluid entity. Laid out

F I G U R E 14. The layered surfaces of Fujii's buildings are intended to fragment space and "suspend form." Instead of maintaining a formal unity along a contextual approach, Fujii chose to "deconstruct" the existing old storehouse in his Ushimado International Arts Festival Center of 1985 by way of a series of transformations and repetitions, rendering forms and spaces as *traces* of their originals. As Fujii wrote, "The meanings that the forms and spaces possessed before their transformation is neither retained nor entirely eliminated in these traces . . . [which] exist in an intermediate domain . . . ; they neither blend, nor contrast . . . ."

F I G U R E 15. "Waved" by the wind and penetrated by light, Ito's own residence, the "Silver Hut," attains amazing lightness (Tokyo 1984).

along a system of concrete columns in the traditional pattern, the house is defined by thin, punched-aluminum screens, diamond-shaped lattice-work vaults of various sizes, and colored fabric; waved by the wind and penetrated by light, the house attains surprising lightness (FIG. 15). Lynn Breslin has said: "Ito's dismantling of type, dematerialization of form, and deconstruction of style extends with each new building and its capacity to comment on the past."[37]

Today in our increasingly prosaic world of instrumental rationality, where the inevitable tendency is to try to reduce reality to scientifically measurable and exploitable certainty, the most significant legacies of the unique tradition of the Japanese house arise from awareness of the invisible yet poetically sensible world from which it evolved, not from its visible but often senseless formalist attributes. If history and tradition are not objectified and disconnected from the present and future by the way in which contemporary society operates, but rather are maintained as a continuity by way of *critical re-interpretation*, it will be unnecessary and impossible *pro forma* to return to them, though this often was, and still is, attempted. Nostalgia prevents us from going beyond the appearance of the past, and at the same time reveals our inability to come to terms with the present. Shinohara came to the point when he said, "tradition can be the starting point for creativity, but it must not be the point to which it returns."[38] The only viable way to establish a meaningful relationship with the past is to challenge it.[39]

REFERENCE NOTES

The place of nothingness (*mu-no-basho*) was one of the central issues in the philosophy of Kitarō Nishida (1870-1945), which was strongly influenced by Zen-Buddhist thought. See, for example, K. Nishida, *Intelligibility and the Philosophy of No-thingness*, R. Schizinger, trans. (Tokyo: Maruzen, 1958).

1. M. Inoue, *Space in Japanese Architecture*, H. Watanabe, trans. (New York: Weatherhill, 1985), p. 136.

2. K. Yoshida, as quoted in H. Paul Varley, *Japanese Culture* (Tokyo: Tuttle, 1973), p. 77.
3. B. Taut, *Dwellings and Lifestyles in Japan*, Hideo Shinoda, trans. (Tokyo: Iwanami Shoten, 1966).
4. W. Gropius, "Architecture in Japan," *Perspecta: The Yale Architectural Journal* 3 (1955), p. 9.
5. S. Horiguchi and Itagaki Takaho, *Kenchiku Yashiki Ronso* (Essays on Architectural Style) (Tokyo: Rokubunkan, 1931); *Kenchiku Ronso* (Essays on Architecture) (Tokyo: Kashima Shuppankai, 1932); K. Tange, photographs by Y. Ishimoto, *Katsura -- Tradition and Creation in Japanese Architecture*, Charles Terry, trans. (New Haven: Yale University Press, 1960).
6. A. Isozaki, "Katsura Villa -- The Ambiguity of Its Space," in A. Isozaki, photographs by Y. Ishimoto, *Katsura Villa -- Space and Form* (New York: Rizzoli, 1987).
7. In his Preface to K. Tange, *Katsura*, p. 10, Gropius wrote: "Though its intimate spaces, its pavements, and its plantings are of enchanting beauty, the overemphasis on playful details sometimes impairs the continuity and coherence of the spatial conception as a whole."
8. Together with Buddhism, much of Chinese culture and civilization was imported to Japan in the mid sixth century.
9. Many outstanding examples of *shoin* architecture are found within Buddhist monasteries, including the residences of the abbots. This is one reason for the rather strong affinity between religious and secular residential architecture. Temples and shrines in Japan, unlike in the West, were not radically different from other kinds of architecture.
10. D.B. Stewart, "Japonisme to Japonesque: Post-Modernism before and after the Letter," *GA Houses* 14, Special Issue: Residential Architecture -- Japan, Part II (1983), p. 16.
11. The term "sophisticated order" was coined by Günter Nitschke in his seminal essay, "Ma -- the Japanese Sense of Place," *AD, Architectural Design* (March 1966), p. 118.
The evolution of topological space is outlined in M. Inoue, *Space in Japanese Architecture*, pp. 137-171.
12. In larger homes, however, some "rooms" customarily have an appointed use.
13. Most Japanese, even today, simultaneously follow both Shintoism and Buddhism. One of the occasions when *shimenawa* is displayed is *oshōgatsu*, the ceremony welcoming the advent of the New Year.
14. In fact, the higher the elevation of a room or place, the further inside it is regarded to be and the higher in esteem it is kept. For further details, see B. Bognar, *Contemporary Japanese Architecture -- Its Development and Challenge* (New York: VNR, 1985), p. 60.
15. The Japanese have a profound appreciation for darkness (*yami*). One of the most eloquent descriptions is in Jun'ichiro Tanizaki, *In Praise of Shadows* (Tokyo: Tuttle, 1977; first published in 1932).
16. F. Maki, "Japanese City Spaces and the Concept of OKU," *JA, The Japan Architect* (May, 1979), p. 59.
17. A. Isozaki, "Space-Time in Japan -- MA," in *MA: Space-Time in Japan*, catalog for the exhibit in the Cooper-Hewitt Museum during the Japan Today Festival (New York, 1978), p. 13; B. Bognar, *Contemporary Japanese Architecture -- Its Development and Challenge*, pp. 50-51.
18. Though still within a rectangular arrangement, the disposition of wooden

columns in the *sukiya* does not follow the more systematic or rigid modular system (*kiwarijutsu*) or formal canon of *shoin*-type architecture. Also, beyond the fact that there are a number of standard *tatami* sizes, the tailoring of *tatami* to adjust the layout to the available floor area is not uncommon in the Japanese house.

19. The meanings of *ma* as given in *Dictionary of Ancient Times* (Tokyo: Iwanami Shoten).

20. The diagonally staggered flying geese pattern is similar to the diagonal and oblique layout (*suji-chigai*) of many elements in the garden favored by such designers as Furuta Oribe (1544-1615) and Kobori Enshū (1579-1647).

21. M. Treib, "The Dichotomies of Dwelling: Edo/Tokyo," in M. Friedman, ed., *Tokyo: Form and Spirit* (Minneapolis: Walker Art Center; and New York: H.N. Abrams, 1986), p. 113. Beyond the stroll gardens (*kayushiki-niwa*) which were influenced by the tea garden (*roji*), Zen gardens, or rock gargens, were such objects of contemplation. Most were developed as part of Zen-Buddhist monasteries such as the Ryoan-ji of late fifteenth century Kyoto.

22. M. Inoue, *Space in Japanese Architecture*, p. 147.

23. In this order of things, man is emphatically *not* the center or measure of everything, and the subject is *not* an *individuum* in the sense of Descartes' "*cogito ergo sum.*" For further details, see B. Bognar, "The Japanese Order of Things -- Notes on Humanism and the Man-Environment Relationship in Japan," *Form, Being, Absence -- Pratt Journal of Architecture* 2 (1988), p. 148.

24. M. Inoue, *Space in Japanese Architecture*, p. 171.

25. For further details, see B. Bognar, "The Japanese Order of Things."

26. Sen-no-Rikyu, for example, likened the spirit of *wabi* to the flower that blooms on a withered tree or a piece of grass growing in the snow. Tea-house architecture, and its derivative *sukiya* style, reflected freedom from the exercise of power or expressed opposition to the fancy and extravagance whereby those in authority sought to display power.

27. C. Fawcett, "The Place of Nothingness -- The Ushimado International Arts Festival Center," *JA, The Japan Architect* (September 1985), p. 23.

28. B. Bognar, "An Architecture of Fragmentation: The Japanese Example," *Reflections -- Architecture Journal of the University of Illinois* (Urbana-Champaign) (1988), p.54.

29. D.B. Stewart, "Japonisme to Japonesque," p. 21.

30. B. Bognar, *Contemporary Japanese Architecture*, p. 236.

31. N. Hasegawa, *The Japanese Character*, John Bestor, trans. (Tokyo: Kodansha International, 1965), pp. 101-102.

32. Tadao Ando, "New Relations Between the Space and Person," in *JA, The Japan Architect* (October-November 1977), p. 44.

33. K. Shinohara, "Towards Architecture," in *Kazuo Shinohara -- IAUS Catalog 17* (New York: Rizzoli, 1982), p. 15.

34. K. Sakamoto, "From Architecture as an Object to Space as an Environment," *JA, The Japan Architect* (November-December 1986), p. 64.

35. Fujii writes about "architecture as suspended form" in "Existential Architecture and the Role of Geometry," in K. Frampton, ed., *A New Wave of Japanese Architecture -- IAUS Catalog 10* (New York: Rizzoli, 1978), p. 29.

36. F. Maki, "Modernism at the Crossroad," *JA, The Japan Architect* (March 1983), p. 22.

37. L. Breslin, "Ito and Ecriture," *SD, Space Design*, Special Issue on Toyo Ito (September 1986), p. 149.

38. K. Shinohara, "A Theory of Residential Architecture," *JA, The Japan Architect* (April 1964).
39. For a detailed and eloquent discussion of these issues, see Francesco dal Co, "On History and Architecture," *Perspecta: The Yale Architectural Journal* 23 (1987), pp. 6-24.

All photos are by the author unless otherwise indicated..

CENTER AND DUALITY
IN THE JAVANESE DWELLING

GUNAWAN TJAHJONO

Javanese conceive family, community and the environment to be a totality from which the essential parts of a belief system and world view are derived.[1] This chapter explores how aspects of the Javanese world view, especially those having to do with the configuration of social reality, relate to the design and use of traditional Javanese dwellings.

The ideas of center and duality are the most important aspects of the Javanese world view for traditional design. Center is a uniting force that links the expression of dual characters. Dualities can either contrast or complement each other; for example, lord and servant, male and female and sky and earth form into pairs. The ideas of center and duality apply in both the seen and the unseen worlds that make up the Javanese experience of reality. The need to respond to this reality governs the form of the traditional Javanese dwelling, which in turn expresses the core of Javanese culture.

The heartland of Javanese culture is the south-central part of Java, especially in the ancient principalities of Jogjakarta and Surakarta.[2] This discussion concerns itself primarily with the southeastern part of Jogjakarta, and particularly with Kota Gede, a town where many dwellings were constructed a century and a half ago.[3] Kota Gede is a good representation of the culture of south-central Java because it incorporates both urban and rural areas. It is also a place where many traditional values are maintained and ritual practices observed. Dwellings will be categorized according to the typology of a Javanese master architect.[4] The concepts embodied in them will be presented and analyzed in brief.

THE SHAPE OF JAVANESE BUILDINGS

Javanese do not classify buildings according to plan or facade but according to five distinct roof shapes: *panggang pe*, *kampung*, *limasan*, *joglo* and *tajug*. The first four may be used for dwelling structures. The last, *tajug*, can only be used in a religious setting.

Panggang pe, literally "dry bake," serves only as a temporary structure.[5] It is used as a shelter for drying agricultural products and can be built quickly by attaching a roof sheet to two beams that connect the tops of two pairs of posts. These pairs of posts are of different heights, define a rectangular plan and are braced together by a ring of beams at the level of the top of the lower posts. A variety of shapes can be derived from this basic formula (FIG. 1).

Kampung, from *katepung* -- "to join," is considered the simplest dwelling structure.[6] It is composed of four posts of equal height, braced by a double ring of beams. Two posts rise from the center of one of the pairs of beams to support a ridge beam. Two roof sheets fall away on either side of this beam. A roof formed in this way can be extended in one or, more favorably, two directions. Variants can be evolved from this basic principle (FIG. 2).

Limasan, from *liman* -- "double frame," can be considered an elaborate *kampung*.[7] It usually consists of eight main posts which support a roof of trapezoidal shape. The ridge beam of a *limasan* is supported by posts that rise from beams that span the interior space between the middle posts. The main roof is usually extended evenly in four directions (FIG. 3). A conceptual center begins to emerge in the *limasan*. The inhabitants of the *limasan*

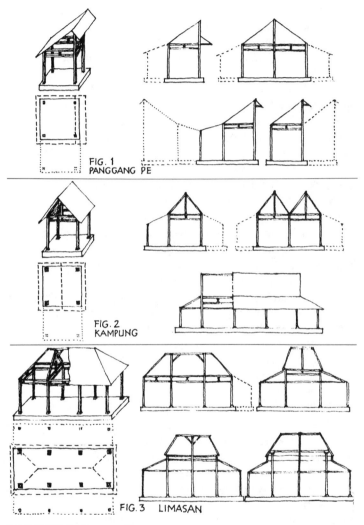

FIG. 1
PANGGANG PE

FIG. 2
KAMPUNG

FIG. 3 LIMASAN

FIGURE 1. *Panggang Pe*
FIGURE 2. *Kampung*
FIGURE 3. *Limasan*

are usually of higher social or economic status than those of the *kampung*. As status improves, however, the *kampung* dweller normally tries to remodel his dwelling into a *limasan*.

The *joglo* looks like an elaborate *limasan*, but it has several distinguishing characteristics. First, the *joglo* has a steep upper roof which resembles a pyramid that comes to two points. Second, it employs four main interior posts to support this upper roof. These determine the position of the secondary posts that support the lower roof, which rises gradually in four directions to join the upper roof. Finally, the main interior posts of the *joglo* are topped by layers of wooden blocks which step back in several directions. The outer layers of blocks support the roof; the inner layers, the *tumpang sari*, literally "essential piling up," divide into two inverted pyramidal ceilings. These resemble the ceiling of the Javanese temple, the *candi* (FIG. 4). This layering of wooden blocks can also be found in a royal *limasan*.

Joglo signifies nobility. It is considered a perfect dwelling shape for human beings and was once the privilege of aristocrats and high officials. Dutch architect Maclaine Pont suggests that it was not until the last century that common wealthy people were allowed to employ this shape.[8] Today convention dictates that those who can afford to build such a dwelling avoid precise emulation of the royal *joglo*. In a *joglo* a center can be identified as that point toward which all lines orient themselves. A *joglo's* shape is so integrated it affords fewer possibilities for variation than the other forms.

The final roof form, *tajug*, is considered the perfect shape. Its square, raised floor is covered by layers of roofs. Four main posts support the upper roof which comes to a single point (FIG. 5). It is believed that this roof shape inspired the *joglo*, since the word *joglo* derives from *tajug*, "jewel," and *loro*, "two."[9] If this is true, then the *joglo* is an integration of two *tajug* shapes. The modification of a one-point shape to one with two points is an attempt to translate the divine shape into a form that can be used by human beings.

These shape distinctions usually represent differences in socioeconomic status. Dwellings that approximate the *tajug* are more expensive, reflecting the wealth and/or higher status of the owners.

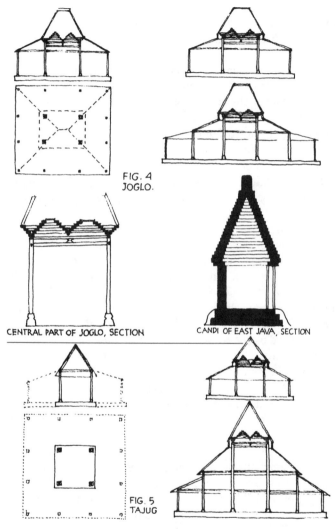

FIG. 4
JOGLO.

CENTRAL PART OF JOGLO, SECTION

CANDI OF EAST JAVA, SECTION

FIG. 5
TAJUG

FIGURE 4. *Joglo*
FIGURE 5. *Tajug*

THE PLAN OF JAVANESE DWELLINGS

The key elements of a basic Javanese dwelling are a veranda, two storage units and a sanctuary. Spatial patterns clearly demarcate inside from outside and establish a hierarchy of places along a north-south axis.

The basic dwelling unit is called an *omah*. It is usually square in plan and divided into inner and outer parts. The outer part, the veranda, can be blocked off by movable panels to become an enclosed room. On its east stands an *amben*, a big bamboo bed, mainly used by male family members; on its west is the guest reception area. The veranda is connected to the inner part of the dwelling by a door in the middle of the wall between them. In Kota Gede this front door always faces south, the direction of the former palace and of the South Sea Goddess who holds the key to the earth.

The inner part of the *omah* is often called the *dalem*. It is divided into two (front-rear) or three (front-middle-rear) sections (FIGS. 6, 7). The front section can be further divided into three zones that are defined by the roof frames. The east zone is designated for family activities such as eating and sewing. The west zone is reserved for sleeping and usually contains another *amben*. This *amben* is used by the whole family except those children who have reached puberty. After puberty, male family members move to the *amben* on the veranda, or elsewhere. In such cases the *dalem* becomes primarily a female domain. The central zone remains empty. This zone in a three-section *dalem* becomes the main hall. One proceeds from it to the house center located in the middle section.

There are some spatial differences between a two-section *dalem* and a three-section *dalem*. The main roof of the former, usually a *kampung* or *limasan*, covers the whole front section, while the rear and veranda are sheltered by roof extensions. The main roof of the latter, usually a *joglo*, covers the central zone of the middle section (the house center), while the other areas are sheltered by a secondary roof. Both types of *dalem* reserve a ritual center where incense is burned once a week in honor of the rice goddess Sri. This goddess also has a permanent place of reverence at the center of the rear section.[10]

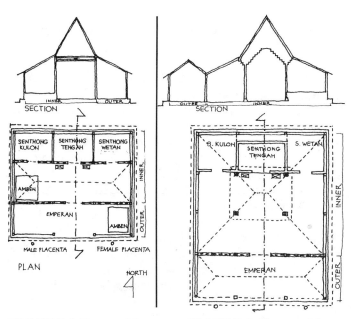

FIGURE 6. Two-part *dalem*   **FIGURE 7.** Three-part *dalem*

The rear section of the *dalem* consists of three *senthongs*, or enclosed rooms. Each *senthong* has a curtained, south-facing door. The west *senthong* is for storage of agricultural products and equipment; the east is for storing sewing tools or weapons. These two rooms are sometimes connected through the rear of the middle *senthong*, the *senthong tengah*. This room, whose floor is usually raised, contains a decorated bed on which are positioned male and female dolls, women's garments, family heirlooms and sometimes the sacred weapon, the *keris*. On both sides of the front door to the *senthong tengah* are cupboards. The bed in the *senthong tengah* is the place for Sri, the rice goddess, who also transforms into the South Sea Goddess, *Nyai Loro Kidul*, the holder of the key to the earth. Wedding ceremonies take place in front of this goddess to ensure good fortune and fertility. Only during the wedding ritual can the *senthong tengah* be opened to the public; it is the house sanctuary, and without it a building cannot be an *omah*. Most of the time it is screened with curtains to remain in darkness. In the *senthong tengah* one recalls the most ancient living environment, the cave. This womb-like milieu mysteriously reveals reproductive power.

The kitchen, the *pawon*, is often placed outside the *omah*. It is mainly a female domain and is also a place of social activity. The root of the word *pawon* is *awu*, which means "ash." Ash is the residue of cooking fires and the cleaning material for kitchen utensils. Since cooking and cleaning need water, the kitchen is normally located close by the well at the back of the *omah*. As the source of life, the well is the first structure to be established in a dwelling complex. In Kota Gede a well is usually located at the northeast or the southwest corner of the *omah*.

The space in front of the *omah* is reserved for burying the placentas of newborn childen. The placenta is considered to be the newborn's brother. It is buried in a jar or a pot which also contains offerings symbolizing the infant's future properties. The placenta is interned on the right, or east side, of the front door if the newborn is a boy, and on the left, or west side, if the newborn is a girl. The baby's spirit is thus guaranteed a place in the dwelling.

Although the design of the *omah* fulfills a family's practical and spiritual needs, a family will ideally complete the dwelling compound by adding other buildings. Additional construction might be the result of an increase in the size of the household or in family status. Ideally, a dwelling compound consists of two main buildings, an *omah* and a *pendopo*. These two are often connected by a third building, a *peringgitan*. All three buildings line up on a north-south axis.

The *pendopo* is an open structure. Its size, roof shape and pole positioning are often identical to that of the *omah*. It is a place for gathering during such ritual events as weddings, circumcisions, shadow play performances, communal meetings and informal entertainments. It is mainly a male domain, and a family's status is often associated with its shape (FIG. 8).

The *peringgitan*, a *kampung-* or *limasan*-roofed open structure, is an extension of the veranda. It acts as mediator between the *pendopo* and the *omah* or *dalem*. The *wayang*, or puppet shadow play (*ringgit* in Old Javanese) is usually performed during a ritual feast in a *peringgitan* (FIG. 9). The shadow puppet play is a central feature of Javanese ritual life. It conveys the essence of Javanese thought as it has been structured by centuries of experience. Shadow is the result of light cast over an object and, hence, reflects both the essence of light and of the essence of the object. Spectators at a *wayang* are challenged to discover the real meanings of ancient plays as they are performed by the *dalang*, the puppeteer. Javanese regard the *wayang* as didactic entertainment as well as religious ritual. The position of the *peringgitan* between

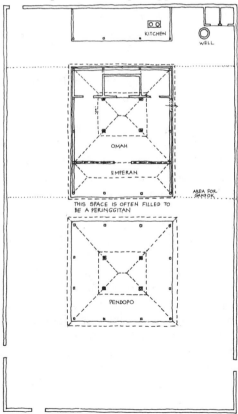

FIGURE 8.
Ideal house.

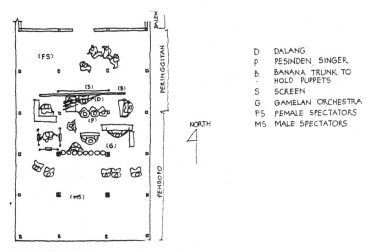

F I G U R E 9. Viewers' positions during a *wayang* performance.

the two most significant structures of the dwelling might not be a coincidence; it probably signifies the central position of the *wayang* in Javanese life.

The performance of the shadow play reveals a significant distinction between the use of the *pendopo* and the use of the *omah*. The screen, which spreads across the middle of the *peringgitan*, divides the audience into a male group in the *pendopo* and a female group in the *omah*. Since the puppeteer sits facing the *omah*, only females have the honor of watching the shadow, while males must watch the puppets (FIG. 9). The *peringgitan* is a link between two worlds during the dramatic ritual performance.

As the size and wealth of a family grow, the *omah* is first expanded to the east and then to the west to maintain symmetry. Each annex has a complete roof. The east house, the *omah wetan*, is used for daily family activities; the west, the *omah kulon*, becomes the female domain. For those who can afford to build all the components of the ideal dwelling compound, the original *omah* is left empty as a pure spiritual center. As mentioned above, the *omah wetan* becomes the focus of daily events, while an additional structure behind the *omah* accommodates such activities as

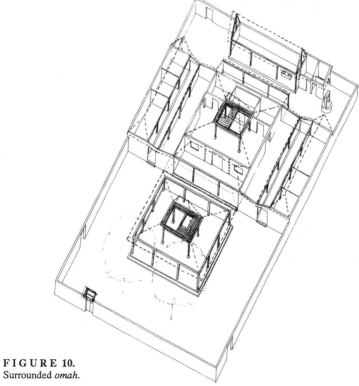

FIGURE 10.
Surrounded *omah.*

cooking, washing and bathing.   This completely encloses the original *omah*, making it the center of the complex (FIG. 10).

Since most male activities take place outside it, the *omah* (and especially its *dalem*) is mainly a female domain.   This seems to demonstrate the significant role of the mother in Javanese life. The arrangement may also reflect the Javanese belief that the father should determine policy while the mother should manage family life.[11]

This discussion demonstrates that the plan of the traditional Javanese dwelling follows a prescribed pattern reflecting indigenous beliefs and ritual practices. This pattern is true to some extent for the various social strata.

MODULAR GRID AND CONSTRUCTION RITUAL

The dwelling accommodates the actual and the ritual, the known and the unknown, the factual and the spiritual. Since one is born in it, grows with it and weds and dies in it, the dwelling shelters all stages of life. This is celebrated in the *slametan*, the ritual feast for the dead, and the *syukuran*, the ritual feast for the living.[12] Most rituals are social events that reveal spatial patterns reflecting social order. The wedding is the pre-eminent celebration. It makes use of the entire dwelling (FIG. 11). The requirements of seating and serving meals have led to the formulation of a pattern based on a four-fold system, or *rampatan*, a modular grid for determining the distance between posts.   This distance is usually about 2.5 meters,[13] about the width of two floor mats, items which the Javanese have produced for a long time.[14]

The construction of a house is both a family matter and a community event.   After a site has been selected according to certain rules, a dweller plants two different kinds of *pisang*, or banana trees, at the middle of the site. If the *pisang raja*, or king banana, grows faster than the *pisang mas*, the gold banana, the *omah* may be built at the location. If the reverse happens, the spot is reserved for a *pendopo*, and construction may be started at some

FIGURE 11.
Setting of a wedding.

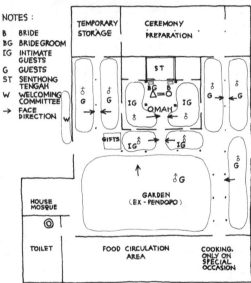

point on an axis behind it. The *dalem* is always the first structure to be built after a well has been dug.

The construction proceeds with volunteers usually organized from the community by a hired carpenter and his initial team. This team first sets building components on the site. Then, after all the main posts have been set, the dweller conducts the initial rite. The dweller digs a hole right at the center between the main posts and buries some offerings. In so doing, the dweller can feel secure that

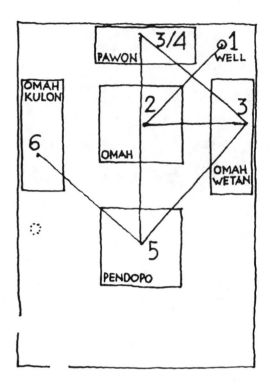

FIGURE 12.
Sequence of
construction.

earth and sky have been connected and the center of the world has been confirmed. After the ceremony all laborers must stay awake all night. The next day the roof, pre-set into a large sheet of bamboo sticks or small wooden blocks, is attached. All upper construction blocks, including the beams, should be in a horizontal position, signifying a person lying down and facing up to honor the divine being.

After the *omah* is constructed, additions may be made as needed to its east, north and west. The overall construction process normally follows a standard sequence: well, *dalem*, east *omah* or kitchen, *pendopo*, west *omah*, fence (FIG. 12). The idea of determining a center is practiced even in the construction process.

Most volunteers are familiar with traditional construction techniques. These techniques barely survive today because of

attempts by the Dutch colonial government to modernize construction practices, and because of a shortage of traditional
building materials, especially teak wood. Teak forests have been
felled at a rapid rate in order to provide agricultural land for a
rapidly expanding population.

CLASSIFICATION: CENTER AND DUALITY

Nature and community are key ideas in the Javanese understanding
of the environment. Nature is the process and force that governs
and produces the material world. Community involves a group of
people who share common ideas and live together in a mutual
relationship. A Javanese learns about community through his or
her family. His or her position is defined by well-established
relationships with other family members. Seniority, sex and social
status determine the role each member plays. A sense of security
is developed in such an environment where emphasis is placed on
tolerance, mutual aid and respect. By maintaining such traditional
attitudes, the family and the community can survive challenges
from both nature and culture.[15]

Through community the Javanese learn how to deal with nature,
which they see as a source of danger as well as blessing. The
principle of duality dominates the cycle of day and night, the
alternation of dry and wet seasons, the dissimilarity between sea
and mountains, and the contrast between sky and earth. Such
powerful dualities are seen to control human life, and are beyond
alteration by human society. In this way the rhythm of nature
becomes the rhythm of the Javanese village, and the identity of the
community becomes the identity of the individual. Unity exists
between the untouchable supreme power, the world of agriculture
and the village community.

The experience of duality in the contrasting elements of life, is the
basis of a classification system which developed into the
mancapat, the four-five classification. The real meaning of *manca*
is unclear. Dutch lawyer-ethnologist Ossenbruggen has suggested
that *manca* means "different," or "five." Historian Pigeaud, on the

other hand, has argued that it means "companion."[16] In *mancapat*, the four cardinal directions -- east, west, south and north -- are coordinated by a center. Each direction is assigned a character associated with a god, a color, and a date based on the five market days of the Javanese calendar. Each contrasting pair, such as east (representing the beginning or source), and west (representing retirement or exhaustion), or south (representing the mountain, the ancestral abode), and north (representing the sea, the outside influence), are resolved through the center. The center becomes the key to coordinating and resolving the contrasting pairs (FIG. 13). The locations of villages that have strong relations, and markets that have five-day cycles, are coordinated by the *mancapat* principle. The four walls of an *omah* are assigned values derived from *mancapat* according to the Javanese treatise *Kawruh Kalang*.[17]

The position of man in the world is foremost, for his attitude in an environment is dependent upon his position in it. The Javanese consider the navel, *puser*, as the center. The navel is the center of the human body. Nutrients are transferred to the embryo through it. It is also a point to be protected. The world accordingly has a navel as its center. This is Mt. Tidal, the navel of Java and, therefore, the world. This associative act reveals a process by which the actual is translated into the conceptual and then experienced as reality. The geometrical center, which is seldom precise, often merges with the spiritual center. The center of dwelling should be identified and then celebrated with ritual before being used. The center establishes, balances, unites and directs all contradictory energies.

The ideas of center and duality reveal a concept of unity between lord and servant by which a transcendent state of being is achieved. The lord's position is in opposition to the servant's. The lord is the center of universe, but he is meaningless without the support of his servants. In this regard duality is indispensable to life, and should be dealt with not by separately defining each extreme, but by pairing them to arrive at congenial resolution through the uniting force of the center.

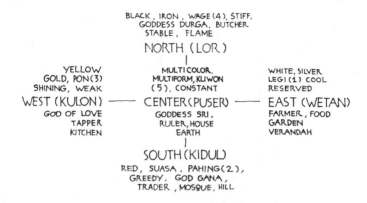

F I G U R E 13. Values assigned to cardinal directions.

THE IDEA OF CENTER AND DUALITY IN DWELLINGS

The unity of dwelling is expressed in the coordination of center and duality. The *omah* can be interpreted as a microcosm, coordinated by a spiritual center, the *senthong tengah*, and an actual center, the space defined by the four main posts in front of it. The *senthong tengah* connects the right and left *senthongs*, which are cross-associated with the gender domains of the *dalem*, the veranda, and the spot reserved for the burial of the placenta. A north-south axis is established through the *senthong tengah* to unite the series of structures with the dual domains -- male in the east and female in the west. The setting of a sacred zone such as the *senthong tengah* in such a worldly, profane realm as the *dalem* reveals the Javanese resolution of duality in unity. The *senthong tengah* is basically the transformed earth-mother, joined to the sky-father through the space defined by the four main posts that lead to the roof. Ritual acts such as burning incense to produce smoke complete this union and secure life (FIG. 14).

The *pendopo* represents the total male zone. Through its openness and/or verticality in the *joglo*, the astral forces connected through the roof encounter the earthly forces of the *dalem*. To balance this duality, the *peringgitan* is needed to reorient forces on an east-west axis.[18] In this regard the *peringgitan* becomes the horizontal center.

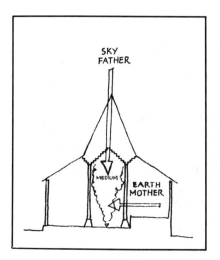

FIGURE 14.
Conceptual scheme of
the weekly ritual
initiation.

The *dalem* represents the secret, mystical side of life. Its dark interior has no windows (no such term exists in Javanese). This milieu contradicts that of the *pendopo* which represents the light, clear, sensible side of life. Both sides reflect indispensable reality. Acceptance of this dual, equal division is intensified when the roof shapes of the two buildings are identical (FIG. 15).

The ideas of center and duality are not only revealed in the plan and arrangement of the dwelling but in its construction as well. This is especially true for the *joglo*. As the most refined shape that a non-religious building can take, the *joglo* manifests itself vertically. Inside, the two inverted pyramidical ceilings made of stepped wooden blocks also imply the unity of worlds shared by male and female (FIG. 16).

This concept of center and duality extends to the religious structure, the mosque. The *tajug*-shaped Javanese mosque always has a *limasan*-shaped annex called a *serambi* at its front (FIG. 17). The mosque is entirely for prayer, while the *serambi* is used for daily events such as *Qur'an* readings and divorce court. The Javanese regard the mosque as a totally sacred domain, and hence need to attach a balancing structure to it to accommodate worldly affairs. The shape of a mosque suggests verticality, while the shape of a *serambi* expresses horizontality.

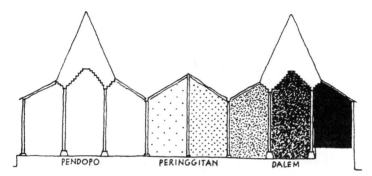

F I G U R E 15. Dual character of the house.

Maclaine Pont saw this mosque-*serambi* relationship as similar to that between the *omah* and the *peringgitan*.[19] Yet the relationship can also been seen as a union of *omah* and *pendopo*. But Maclaine Pont may have been right when he concluded that the idea of dwelling affected the mosque, rather than the mosque affecting the idea of dwelling.

The location of a cemetery, especially that of a ruler, is normally on the *qibla* side of the mosque, the direction of Mecca. This

F I G U R E 16. Mosque in Yogyakarta.

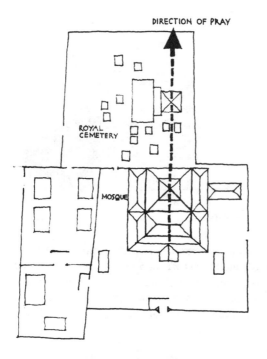

FIGURE 17.
Mosque and royal
cemetery in
Kota Gede.

FIGURE 18.
Ceiling of the center
of a house.

suggests the ambiguous nature of prayer in Javanese culture. Prayers are directed both horizontally toward the cemetery, as if the spirit of the ancestors is being venerated, and vertically toward God (FIG. 18).[20]   In this relation, the mosque becomes a center, bracing the upper- and under-worlds. Expression of the idea of center and duality in the mosque may be traced back to pre-Islamic times, when the temple was both a memorial to the ruler and a place in which to worship the divine.

RULER, PEOPLE AND TRADITION

The idea of center was historically manifested in the ruler, who represented the state which in turn symbolized the cosmos. The cosmic power was oriented to, stored in, and radiated from the ruler. The ruler became an ideal to be followed, and his dwelling set a standard to be pursued. The *joglo*, for example, might have been established in a court, then widely copied by the elites, until finally becoming generally popularized. The genesis of the *joglo* remains unclear, since no evidence of it has been discovered in the reliefs of any extant Hindu-Javanese temple.[21] Possibly the *joglo* was developed and popularized in Java during the spread of Islam.

During the period of European colonialism, the central Javanese kingdom had to consolidate its power to overcome incursions by the Dutch. Inward-looking attitudes developed, such as the desire to search for God through the inner self. The performing arts of the court, which originated in rural areas, also became fully refined. The traditions of the Javanese dwelling evolved and reached their peak under these circumstances, resulting in the widespread diffusion of the *joglo* about a century ago. The more a house resembled this elite shape, the more it manifested the ideas of center and duality. The remains of foundations belonging to royal compounds of the Hindu-Javanese era indicate that these royal dwellings were less compact than those of the present royal compound which strongly manifests the ideas of center and duality.[22] Unfortunately, almost no traces have been found of common people's dwellings of the earlier era.

Tradition developed as circumstances changed, but the underlying principles of duality and center to some extent have endured.[23] Tradition has not been handed down as an inheritance, but has been obtained through interaction between people and ruler. Shapes that prevailed in the rural areas were refined in the court, then handed back down to the people. The key position of the elite should not be ignored in this process. The creative forces that grew in the rural areas have slowly faded away, due to the rise of new construction methods introduced by the Dutch. It is now difficult to revive the old, because a population of skilled workers has little room to grow.[24]

Recognition of the long-standing abandonment of traditional dwelling forms in favor of modern living has caused an over-reaction in the opposite direction in other towns in central Java. This can be seen in the return to traditional shapes without consideration for accompanying belief and ritual practice. Attention to external form now proceeds with little regard for symbolic importance.

CONCLUDING REMARKS

The ideas of center and duality are among the factors that have shaped the traditional Javanese dwelling. They have been the product of various interactions encompassing responses to socio-economic, politico-religious and environmental issues. These ideas developed further into a classification system by which the Javanese were able to organize the world and position themselves in it. The basic concepts have survived various challenges from the outside and have retained various levels of traditionalism.

Traditional dwellings reveal underlying concepts and the structured order of the society they are associated with. Traditional Javanese dwellings strongly express the ideas of center and duality through architectural forms and spatial arrangements. Unity through opposition emerges in the division of space into opposing realms such as inner and outer domains, and it also emerges in the fashioning of complementary shapes such as the *omah* and the *pendopo*. Yet such duality is neutralized and unified by a center. Although building shapes roughly express these ideas, their importance can only be fully apprehended through rituals, for the ideas of center and duality are enfolded in a comprehensive belief system that guides social conduct.

Traditional dwellings are not a mere commodity; they reflect the actual and the spiritual, the factual and the conceptual aspects of the life cycle. In light of the rapid social and cultural change now occurring in central Java, studies oriented toward understanding the social and cultural foundation of traditional dwellings are as important as technical analysis of dwellings.

REFERENCE NOTES

1. "Javanese" generally refers to those people who speak Javanese. They make up two-thirds of Java's population and mostly live in the central and eastern parts of Java. It is commonly accepted that Javanese culture was characterized by two orientations, one toward trading and the coast, the other toward agriculture and the interior. Land forms also characterized Javanese culture. In this paper, "Javanese" refers to the people of south-central inland Java.
2. Jogjakarta and Surakarta used to be the capitals of Islamic Javanese kingdoms where the inland Javanese traditions were exemplified.
3. Kota Gede used to be the capital of the biggest inland Islamic kingdom, which existed in the sixteenth century. The rulers of Jogjakarta and Surakarta descended from this kingdom's founder.
4. Mr. Mintoboedoyo, the *empu* (master), summarizes dwelling types according to roof shape.
5. See S. Prawiroatmojo, *Bausastra Jawa-Indonesia* (Jakarta: Gunung Agung, 1985).
6. See *Kawruh Kalang*, R. Slamet Soeparno Kridosasono, trans. (Surakarta, undated). Another meaning of *kampung* is "compound," which usually is associated with a cluster of folk housing in a rural area.
7. *Kawruh Kalang*, Slamet Soeparno Kridosasono, trans.
8. For further discussion of the popularization of *joglo*, see Henri Maclaine Pont, "Javaansche Architectuur," *Djawa* 3 (1923), pp. 112-127, and *Djawa* 4 (1924), pp. 44-73.
9. See *Kawruh Kalang*, Slamet Soeparno Kridosasono, trans.
10. The main crop of Java is rice. The rice goddess Sri plays one of the most important roles in Javanese mythology. She expresses various characters. The South Sea Goddess is also associated with her. See W.H. Rassers, *Panji, the Culture Hero* (The Hague: Martinus Nijhof, 1959).
11. Compare, for example, Hildred Geertz, *The Javanese Family: A Study of Kinship and Socialization* (New York: Free Press, 1961), pp. 46-51.
12. Clifford Geertz classifies all of these rituals as *slametan*. In Kota Gede, however, rituals for the living are mostly called *syukuran*. *Slametan* is used to refer

to the dead. Compare C. Geertz, *The Religion of Java* (Chicago: University of Chicago Press, 1960), pp. 11-15.

13. Here Sri is the sum of total numbers divided by five, with one added to it.

14. See Maclaine Pont, "Javaansche Architectuur."

15. See, for example, Franz Magnis-Suseno, *Etika Jawa: Sebuah Analisa Falsafi Tentang Kebijaksanaan Hidup Jawa* (Jakarta: Gramedia, 1984), pp. 82-94.

16. For further information on the meaning of *mancapat*, see F.D.E. Van Ossenbruggen, "Java's Manca-Pat: Origin of a Primitive Classification System" and T.J. Pigeaud, "Javanese Divination and Classification," in de Josselin de Jong, ed., *Structural Anthropology in the Netherlands, a Reader* (The Hague: Martinus Nijhoff, 1977), pp. 30-60, 61-82. For a discussion of the four elements of nature and their representation, see Clifford Geertz, *Agricultural Involution: The Process of Ecological Change in Indonesia* (Berkeley: University of California Press, 1963).

17. See *Kawruh Kalang*, Slamet Soeparno Kridosasono, trans.

18. Cf. Josef Prijotomo, *Ideas and Forms of Javanese Architecture* (Yogyakarta: UGM, 1984), pp. 39-43.

19. See Maclaine Pont, "Javaansche Architectuur"; H.J. de Graaf, "The Origin of the Javanese Mosque," *Journal of South-East Asian History* 4 (1963), pp. 1-3.

20. Cf. the discussion in Prijotomo, *Ideas and Forms of Javanese Architecture*, pp. 48-51.

21. The question of the mystery of *joglo* is addressed in Parmono Atmadi, "Apa Yang Terjadi Pada Arsitekur Java," an unpublished paper presented in a bi-weekly seminar on Javanology in Yogyakarta, 1984.

22. Maclaine Pont, "Javaansche Architectuur."

23. A cosmological dualism of mountain vs. sea, winged beings vs. water beings, men of the mountain vs. men of the seacoast was a particularity of Southeast Asian culture. The Javanese developed this dualism in various aspects of life, and expressed it strongly in their dwelling tradition. See Magnis-Soeseno, *Etika Jawa*, 1984).

24. Maclaine Pont, "Javaansche Architectuur."

All photos are by the author unless otherwise indicated.

THE DESIGN OF
THE GREAT CHIEF'S HOUSE
IN SOUTH NIAS, INDONESIA

JEROME A. FELDMAN

Some of the most impressive wooden buildings in Southeast Asia are the chief's houses found on the southern portion of the island of Nias. In their finest form the houses may stand twenty meters high and be supported by approximately one hundred pillars, each a nearly perfect, polished cylinder as much as one meter thick. All of the parts of the house interlock and are precisely made of hard and exotic woods.

This house is understood by the village population in a number of different ways. Symbolically, every house is a microcosm of the universe; there is an upperworld embodied in the roof structure and an underworld symbolized in the pillars. Between these is the dwelling area, rich in carvings depicting the wild plants and animals of the living world.[1] The house represents the fertile land of the ancestors and embodies the historical reference to the ruler who conceived it and received a set of cosmic titles for his efforts. The master house-builder incorporates in his work the history of the styles and craftsmanship of South Nias architecture. In its design and decoration, the house recalls earlier houses, their histories and, consequently, the important events in the lives of the villagers.

Nias is located approximately seventy-five miles west of Sumatra. It is about eighty-five miles long and forty miles wide at its widest point. The island is subject to many earthquakes and has a formidable, hilly terrain with numerous streams that are often swollen by heavy rainfall.

The people of Nias call their land Tanö Niha, "The Land of People," and identify themselves as Ono Niha, "The Children of People." The language of the Ono Niha is surprisingly different from that of their Batak neighbors in Sumatra, with whom they are often compared. Although a branch of the Austronesian family, the Nias language is also very distinct from other Indonesian dialects. For example, no word ends in a consonant, as is common in the rest of the archipelago. A recent linguistic study has indicated the need to re-examine historical relationships among the Austronesian languages because of the peculiarities of Nias.[2] It appears that much of the vocabulary is closer to Polynesian than is the case with other Indonesian languages. Three somewhat divergent dialects of Nias language are spoken in three areas of the island.

The linguistic situation parallels all other societal traits, resulting in three culture areas with architectural, artistic, linguistic and legal distinctions. From the Nias point of view the differences go much deeper than the three areas. Each sector is subdivided into groups of villages according to the name of a common founding ancestor. To the Ono Niha significant differences begin on the village level. Each village has its own variation of the customs of its district. These customary laws, böwö or hada in South Nias, are interpreted by local village councils in terms of the dictates set forth by the ancestors.

The most magnificent buildings are the chief's houses in South Nias. These structures are commonly referred to as omo sebua, or "big houses," a very apt term by the standards of any society. The largest and most artistically impressive of the four that remain today is found in the village of Bawömataluo. It has been called "one of the finest bits of architecture ever made by a primitive people."[3]

THE HISTORICAL CONTEXT OF THE CHIEF'S HOUSE

This building is now over one hundred years old and represents the last great feat of the most powerful chiefs of Bawömataluo. *Omo sebua* can no longer be constructed because the nobility can not command the necessary labor and resources to construct them and no adequate ritual substitute has been found for the human heads used to consecrate them. Smaller, symbolically incomplete versions called *omo hada* are still constructed.[4]

The *omo sebua* at Bawömataluo is a copy of an even larger building which was destroyed by a Dutch punitive expedition in 1863. By making reference to the earlier structure, the villagers pay homage to the ancestors who built the first house and defied the Dutch. The first house was in the village of Orahili, on the same site as a new village of the same name located at the foot of the hill on which Bawömataluo is today.

In the first half of the nineteenth century the Dutch made a number of military efforts to subdue the power of certain South Nias chiefs, and until 1863 they met with failure. The 1863 offensive succeeded because the Netherlanders made an alliance with the rulers of the village of Fadoro, now called Hilisimaetanö, who were traditional deadly rivals of the rulers of Orahili. The objectives of this third expedition under the command of Major Fritzen were specifically to destroy the village of Orahili and the villages of its allies and to depose the ruling chiefs, especially Laowo of Orahili and his charismatic son Saonigeho. The culmination of many years of fighting was the destruction of the villages of Hiliböbö, Bötöhösi and Orahili.

The Orahili villagers never surrendered, nor were their rulers deposed, but they were forced to live for fourteen or fifteen years in a temporary settlement to the north of their previous locale, called Baruyosifaedo.[5] Construction of a permanent settlement must have begun immediately after the expulsion, because the new village of Bawömataluo was open and essentially complete with its *omo sebua* by 1878.[6] A new Orahili village was reconstructed on the old site after a dispute over succession to chieftainship in Bawömataluo.[7] The new Orahili is small and lacks a chief's house.

Each of the three villages destroyed by the Dutch had gigantic chief's houses. The largest and most memorable to the Nias people was at Bötöhösi, but unfortunately its design and details were never recorded. The next largest, at Orahili, was destroyed by a fire set by the Dutch after they had captured and looted the village.[8] Some artifacts, drawings and accounts preserve certain details of the old *omo sebua* so that a partial reconstruction is possible.

THE ARCHITECTURAL PRECEDENT AT ORAHILI VILLAGE

Since the design of the new *omo sebua* was based upon the old, the record of the previous house makes an interesting comparison. The house at Orahili was distinguished by its size, artistic form and beautiful workmanship.[9] Bawömataluo informants insist that it was wider than the present structure and the roof was never completed. This may explain why drawings of the house show either a truncated or atypical pyramidal roof (FIG. 1).

Other aspects of these depictions of the *omo sebua* at Orahili appear inaccurate. Figure 1 shows elaborate facades on at least two sides of the building, and it seems likely that the artist thought three or four sides of the building had this appearance. Nias houses always have only one front facade. There are shields on the corners and at the center of the front facade where carvings of composite monsters would normally be located. The monsters, called *lasara*, are necessary for the symbolic protection of all *omo sebua* but would only be installed after the house is complete. Since the roof was never finished, the *lasara* were never installed, and perhaps the shields were temporary protective devices.

Another drawing done by M. Helmkampf, a doctor with the Dutch military forces, shows some similarities and differences from Figure 1.[10] There are also shields on the facade, but the roof now

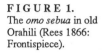
FIGURE 1.
The *omo sebua* in old
Orahili (Rees 1866:
Frontispiece).

has a dissimilar, although still truncated shape. Two recesses at
the side of the facade are undoubtedly structures called
mbarombaro, attached houses serving as homes for the sons of the
ruler. It is interesting that in the accounts of the burning of Orahili
the Dutch claim to have set fire to the council house and the "three
palaces of the raja."[11] This must refer to the *omo sebua* and two
mbarombaro. A curved stone wall is depicted behind the house;
remnants of that wall can be seen today in back of the remaining
paving stones of the house.

Although there are no documented descriptions of the interior of
the Orahili house, Nieuwenhuisen and van Rosenberg give a
general description of chief's houses before the Dutch invasions
which matches the one at Bawömataluo. It is likely that the men
had visited the house at Orahili. On the first crossbeam across the
front part of the communal room (at the front of a South Nias
house) a great amount of ceramic and glassware was hung,
including more than three hundred Chinese plates in vertical rattan

bundles. On the next crossbeam there was a row of male and female figures, the former armed with spears and the latter in dancing positions. Male figures were also suspended outside of the lattice window along the facade of the house. Other animal, bird and plant motifs were carved in relief on the walls and beams.[12]

No plan of the old chief's house was ever published; only some meager booty remains as testimonial to the house and its tragic end. A large number of Orahili weapons are presently in the Rijksmuseum in Leiden.[13] The collection of these armaments can be seen in M. Helmkampf's drawing. Two images from the house were sent to the Royal Batavian Society Museum, the Jakarta Museum, by Mr. van der Bossche of Padang in 1863.[14] One object does shed some light on the plan of the house. This is a brass ring used as a door lock to the sleeping quarters of the highest chief in Orahili.[15] The ring itself is uninteresting, but it indicates that there was a private room for the ruler, called *nifosali* in Bawömataluo. This would normally be located in the back portion of the house.

THE CONSTRUCTION OF THE NEW CHIEF'S HOUSE AT BAWÖMATALUO

The last ruler of old Orahili, Laowo, was also the first ruler of Bawömataluo. It was he who ordered and provided the feasting and funds for the construction of the old and new chief's houses. The master carpenter Olito Föna was selected to oversee construction and do the finishing touches at Bawömataluo.

Skilled house builders, *tuka sonekhenekhe*, are greatly valued in Nias society. Their work is admired on a daily basis, and the ability of a ruler to command their labor is a sign of greatness. At the South Nias village of Hilimondregeraya, the late nineteenth-century monarch Siwalowalani so jealously guarded his master builder that he had him sacrificed after the *omo sebua* was constructed so that he could never build a finer example for another chief.[16] This action was greeted with horror in

Bawömataluo as it was inhumane and jeopardized the system of royal patronage.

The construction of a new *omo sebua* represents the culmination of a series of feasts a ruler is expected to give during his lifetime. Only after all other distributions of wealth have taken place can the specific sequence of events surrounding the construction of a chief's house begin. The cost of the actual construction of the building is in addition to the cost of the feasts. In return, the ruler receives prestige and titles which liken him to the entire cosmos. In Bawömataluo Laowo was called Tuha Famaedoluo, Tuha Famaedodane -- "The Lord Who is Like the Sun, The Lord Who Resembles the Earth." There are no higher titles attainable by human beings. The titles are a reflection of the symbolism of the house and are intended to represent the totality of human existence. To this day every important song, chant or festival includes mention of Laowo's highest titles.[17]

Since Laowo had already completed the prerequisite feasts in Orahili, it was possible for him to expeditiously plan the construction of the new *omo sebua*. Such plans would be conducted in the fashion of formal oratory called *orahu*. The *orahu* perhaps more than any other social convention expresses the South Nias cultural requirement for oppositions. The two social classes must be represented and participate. These are the *si'ulu*, the upper class, and the *sato*, the commoners. The respected male elders of the *sato*, called *si'ila*, speak for the commoners in alternation with the concerned *si'ulu*. All speakers sit opposite a set of chosen respondents, *sanema li gorahua*, who do not speak a word but make sounds such as "*eeeh*" (an affirmation), *ya'ia* ("it is so"), or *aaah* ("it is not so"). If it is a large formal oratory, pigs will also be slaughtered, laid out between and perpendicular to the two rows of speakers and respondents to be divided front and back, left and right for subsequent feasting. Dualism is an essential part of the South Nias definition of culture, as it is opposed to the chaos of nature. Wherever possible, dual structures form a core for the organization of art, architecture, music and other forms of social order.[18]

FABRICATION OF THE HOUSE

The process of constructing an *omo sebua* is necessarily complicated and costly. It begins with headhunting raids into the Central
Nias district of Aramo. Four human heads must be placed beneath
the corner foundation stones as offerings to the deity of the
underworld, Lature Danö. This custom only applies to the construction of *omo sebua*. Hence another term for an *omo sebua* is
omo nifobinu, "the house that requires heads."

There are two types of foundation stones, *batu gehomo* and *batu
ndriwa*. The first is used to support vertical pillars, *ehomo*, while
the second holds oblique pillars, *driwa*. The stones are laid out in
a fixed pattern corresponding to the pattern of pillars above.[19] The
paving stones isolate the massive pillars from wood rot and
termites. Since the house is not attached to the ground, it can also
shift as a unit during earthquakes.

The substructure of the *omo sebua* consists of an elaborate interwoven pattern of heavy pillars. All South Nias *omo sebua* are six
ehomo wide. The one at Bawömataluo is eleven deep, resulting in
sixty-six vertical pillars. Along the sides of the building, every
second vertical pillar is double the height of the others. These
ehomo sodrau lagolago carry much of the weight of the ceiling
beams. There are twenty-two transverse *driwa* and twenty-four
longitudinal *driwa*, all of which meet to form a "V" shape. Both
sets of oblique pillars intersect to form a woven pattern (FIG. 2).

FIGURE 2.
Omo sebua at
Bawömataluo, the
driwa and *ehomo*.

The *batu driwa* supports the point of the "V." This makes a total of one hundred and twenty-four pillars, each approximately a meter thick.[20] The trees for these enormous pillars are only found in Central Nias and must be dragged from there. Replacement trees were planted in an area between Orahili and Bawömataluo at the time the house was constructed, however the trees were later cut down for a plantation.

The pillars are divided into two groups. The front set is six *ehomo* deep and the rear set is five. The division of each level of the house into two sets is a necessary part of the dualistic form of cultural manifestations.

A bridge, *ete*, runs the length of the house over the apices of the transverse *driwa*. The construction of the *ete* also requires the placement of one more human head below the bridge. Head offerings always impart a new name for the object of the offering, hence another term for the *omo sebua* is *omo nitoro aro*, "the house with the walkway below." One enters the *omo sebua* from the front over the front *driwa* and onto the bridge. At about the center of the house one turns right and up a flight of stairs to the front communal room. All other customary houses, *omo hada*, are entered from doors at the side.

The center or dwelling level of the house is its most complex area. Its interior must be free of all supporting pillars, and therefore loads must be transferred to the side walls. Construction of this level begins with the placement of two horizontal beams that run the length of the house and are socketed into the *ehomo* on each side of the building. These beams are called *sikhöli* and must extend beyond the facade of the house in an upward curving form resembling a horned animal, presumably a deer (FIG. 3). At the rear of the house they terminate in a curling tail.[21] The flooring is then added, and work can begin on the walls, *towa*.

The side walls consist of enormous panels called *ina laso*, "mother panels," and socketed narrow panels called *ono laso*, "child panels" (FIG. 4). The result is very strong walls which do not sag and yet can give during earthquakes. These fit together vertically

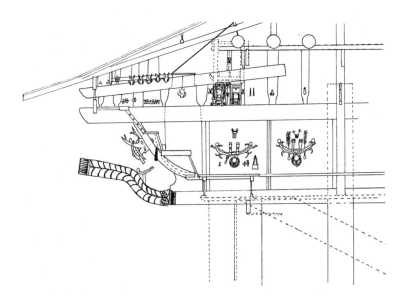

F I G U R E 3. Right wall at the front of the house (standing in the front room facing front), *omo sebua*, Bawömataluo.

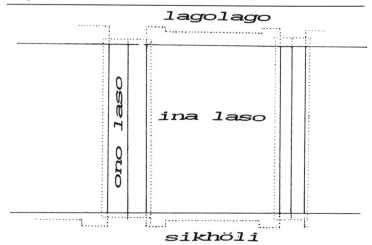

F I G U R E 4. Wall structure showing *ina laso* and *ono laso*.

and socket into the *sikhöli*. Some of the mother panels at the front of the house are show pieces, made of immense slabs of dense black wood called *kafini*. They are a sign of wealth since the rare wood must be imported from Pulau Pini in the Batu Islands to the south at great expense. The presence of *kafini* in other parts of the front section of the *omo sebua* at Bawömataluo is considered by the villagers to be extraordinary. The *kafini ina laso* are made of especially thick slabs because they also have high relief carvings, *laso so hagu*, depicting golden head ornaments. According to customary law, one cannot carve *laso so hagu* unless they actually own the ornaments and have provided village feasts for their creation.

One set of the mother panels on both sides of the front room are very special to the master builder. These are called the *laso sebua*, "big panels." Like other panels, they socket into the *sikhöli*, but they must also socket through the next horizontal beam, *lagolago*, which, like the *sikhöli*, runs the entire length of the house into a second level of mother and child panels and into a slanting horizontal beam called the *ete de'u* (FIG. 3). The installation of the *laso sebua* is watched by the entire village, as it is considered to be the test of a great carpenter. If all of the fittings can be done in the first try, it is regarded as extraordinary.

The horizontal beams in the dwelling level lock the wall system together. The *lagolago* runs the entire length of the house parallel to the *sikholi* and caps the row of large wall panels. The tall pillars, *ehomo sodrau lagolago*, socket on the exterior into the *lagolago*, adding crucial support to the heavy ceiling structure. The *ete de'u* are diagonal beams at the front and back of the building. The word means "mouse bridge" because it connects the area of the ancestor altar with the ceiling structure. Rice offerings left for the ancestors are eaten by mice, who are in turn consumed by cats after they scurry into the ceiling. The ancestral altar at Bawömataluo has the form of two chairs carved in relief on one of the upper *ina laso*. This extraordinary sculpture is also carved by the master house-builders.[22]

FIGURE 5. *Khölökhölö*, front room, with *ni'otelaugazi.*

The masterpiece of the house is the carving of the four pillars, *khölökhölö*, two in the front and two in the back of the house. These are decorative elements intended as a display of the carver's art.[23] The second pillar from the front (FIG. 5) is the supreme achievement of the master carver Dumogodanö. The disk, called *ni'o telau gazi*, has a complex design of geometric forms in a circular array, all without the slightest mistake or correction. This carving and its post, made out of a single piece of hard wood, is intended to astound the visitor. The same could be said for the entire building.

The plan of the dwelling area reflects a very complicated series of oppositions.[24] These include a public front room, *tawolo*, and a private rear room, *föröma*. At the center of the building are two hearths for each division, as well as two toilets. At the front and rear of the building elevated floor levels serve as sleeping areas, seats and storage chests (FIG. 6). Although they are not symmet-

F I G U R E 6. View of the front room (*tawolo*), *omo sebua*, Bawömataluo,
showing levels at the front beneath the trellis window. The *sikhöli* are at the
intersection of the side walls and the floor. The *lagolago* are the wide horizontal
beams above the *sikhöli*. Between the two beams there are a series of mother and
child panels. The two on either side with high relief carvings are the *laso sohagu*.
The chairs serving as the ancestral altar are visible at the right side above the
lagolago. Above this on the right and left side are the slanting horizontal wall
beams called *ete de' u.* The large panels to the front of the front *laso sohagu* are the
laso sebua. These socket from the *sikhöli* through the *lagolago* and *ete de' u.* In the
center is the *khölökhölö* of Figure 5. Figure 3 is drawn from the right corner.

rical front to back, the levels must be parallel to each other. This
condition is called *wafa sifaboro* and is essential in an *omo sebua*.
In a customary house, *omo hada*, these are also perpendicular to
each other as an indication the family did not give sufficient feasts
to qualify for the opposition. In Bawömataluo only five houses are
wafa sifaboro.

Feasts, including those for the construction of the house, are
commemorated in the front room by various displays. Thousands
of pig's jaws hang from the ceiling and from an elaborately carved
bracket running across the front. Chinese and Dutch plates also
hang from the bracket in rattan holders exactly as they were
described in the house at Orahili.[25] Carved dancing female figures

and armed male figures hang outside the trellis window, another similarity to the old house in Orahili.[26] Various carvings refer to nature in the form of wild plants and animals. These contribute to the expression of the house as a miniature cosmos, complete with its own artificial forms of life.

At the rear of the *tawolo* and near the ceiling, there is a miniature house as a place for royal women to view the public ceremonies in the front room.[27] This bower, called *malige*, is a traditional house in every detail and is entered by a stairway from the back room. In Nias society it is a position of honor to be placed high and in the center of a structure. Even if the women are not direct participants, they do enjoy such ceremonial status.

In the private quarters, *foroma*, of the house there is a special room for the ruler called the *nifosali*. The woods used here are especially smooth and hard; there is also fine detailing and carving, including coiled ferns, human hands that represent the ruler's command of labor, and treasure chests that are symbolic of wealth.[28]

In the dwelling area of the *omo sebua* there is an unexplained element. There are four side doors, two in the front room and two in the rear, leading nowhere but to a fall of nearly fifteen feet to the ground. In the smaller customary houses, *omo hada*, these doors serve as entrances and exits where ladders lead to the ground or to an adjoining house.[29] The side doors in the *omo sebua*, although serving as poorly conceived emergency exits, appear to be vestigial architectural elements, emphasizing that the *omo sebua* is a giant version of the *omo hada*.

Fully two-thirds of the height of the *omo sebua* is the roof. Nothing is stored in this area. Aside from shedding rain and dissipating heat and smoke from the hearths, it encloses entirely symbolic space. The ceiling structure is patterned after the substructure. The tallest vertical beams are called *ehomo mbumbu*, recalling the *ehomo* pillars. Oblique beams are called *driwa bato*, however, unlike the substructure *driwa*, these do not form a "V" but cross to form an "X" (FIGS. 7,8). Front and rear sections in the

FIGURE 7.
Side view, cross
section, *omo sebua*,
Bawömataluo.[30]

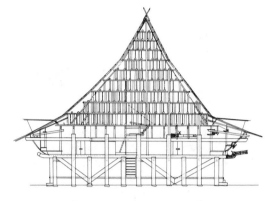

FIGURE 8.
Transverse section of
the *omo sebua* at
Bawömataluo.[31]

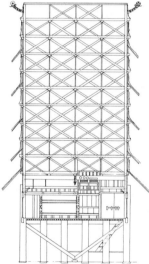

upper structure of the house are created by the insertion of a partition, *fanötö*.

Heads are a necessary offering for the superstructure. A large number are hung from the highest beam, the *bule* or *mbumbu*, and are dedicated to the deity of the upperworld, Lowalani.[32] This cements the symbolism of the house as a cosmic model with a symbolic upperworld and underworld and the dwelling area replete with representations of the wild plants and animals that live in between. There are nine levels to the ceiling. These are numbered, starting with the "navel level" and proceeding to level one,

FIGURE 9.
Logs being rolled
into place, Hilisi-
maetanö village.
(Abbot Collection,
Smithsonian Institu-
tion, Neg. No. 52.3.)

sagoto bato, level two, *duagoto bato* -- to level nine, *siwanaoto bato*. This corresponds to the nine levels of the upperworld mentioned in priests' litanies. The chants, recorded in the Batu Islands, mention the *siwa ewali*, "nine streets," and *siwa banua*, "nine villages" or "nine heavens."[33] The roof structure is also divided into front and back sections by a thin wall called *fanoto*.

The construction of the superstructure is the most astonishing of all parts of the house. There are enormous transverse logs, *ladihkowo bato*, which must be lifted as high as twenty meters. To do this a ramp must be constructed in front of the house (FIG. 9). At Bawömataluo the ramp was as long as the entire village street. Figure 9 shows such a ramp on a much smaller house, but it gives some idea of the complexity of the task.

CEREMONIAL COMPLETION OF THE HOUSE

The final act in the construction of the *omo sebua* is the sacrifice of a pig. The animal, *bawi nigulu*, is released from the ridge pole and rolled off the roof onto the pavement.

The first person to occupy the house is the master house-builder. He lives in it for a week and wears a special white kerchief called *mbombobu*, "danger" or "caution band." The *omo sebua* is so

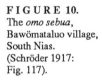

F I G U R E 10.
The *omo sebua*,
Bawömataluo village,
South Nias.
(Schröder 1917:
Fig. 117).

enormous that should the structure not hold, it would mean certain death as the heavy roof beams crash down. In Nias all transition periods in life are considered dangerous, requiring special precautions for the safety of the individual. In this case it is the ruler who must be certain that there is no danger. After the week a huge banquet is held to which fourteen villages are invited and after which the *omo sebua* is ready to be occupied by the royal family.

The completed house is indeed impressive (FIG. 10). The small attached house, *mbarombaro*, belongs to the first-born son of the ruler and is reminiscent of the two *mbarombaro* at the old house in Orahili. Unfortunately, Laowo, the ruler who achieved the cosmic title Tuha Famaedo Dane, Tuha Famaedo Luo, lived only a few years in his impressive new house. He died shortly after the *omo sebua* was completed, as evidenced by the presence of his horizontal megalith in 1881. Such stones called *owoowo*, "ships," or *darodaro*, "seats," are part of the last rites for a great ruler. It was reputed to have cost 1,500 pigs in payment to those who had to drag the stones from a river bed far below Orahili.[34]

Laowo's charismatic first son, Saonigeho, became the last traditional ruler of Bawömataluo. He moved from the *mbarombaro* to the *omo sebua* upon Laowo's death. Saonigeho managed to restrain Dutch political influence until 1908 when he was captured and detained for a ransom of gold by Dutch police. He was only released five years before his death in 1914.[35]

The *omo sebua* stands now as the largest and finest surviving monument to the architectural heritage of South Nias. The builders will be long remembered for their reconstruction of the old palace at Orahili in the new village. The structural, environmental, cultural and symbolic challenges they so eloquently mastered stand as a testimonial to the greatest era of architecture in South Nias.

REFERENCE NOTES

1. For more detailed analysis of the symbolic aspects of these houses, see Jerome Feldman, "The House as World in Bawömataluo, South Nias," in J. Becker and E. Bruner, *Art, Ritual and Society in Indonesia* (Ohio University Press, 1979), pp. 127-189; Wolfgang Marschall, *Der Berg des Herrn der Erde* (Munich: Deutscher Taschenbuch Verlag, 1976), pp. 52-53; Pietro Scarduelli, *L'Isola Degli Antenati di Pietra*, (Rome: Gius Laterza & Figli, 1986), pp. 36-44; Peter Suzuki, "The Religious System and Culture of Nias, Indonesia" (Ph.D. dissertation, Leiden University, The Hague, 1959), pp. 65-77; Alain Viaro, *Urbanisme et architecture traditionels du sud de l'ile de Nias* (UNESCO, 1980).
2. Gertrud Patsch, "Das Nias im Historischen Vergleich," *Zeitschrift für Phonetik, Sprachwissenschaft und Kommunikations-Forschung* 31 (1978), pp. 58-72.
3. F.M. Schnitger, *Forgotten Kingdoms in Sumatra* (Leiden: E.J. Brill, 1939), p. 160.
4. Although the construction of *omo sebua* is now a thing of the past, the four houses and the belief systems that created them are still alive among many of the people of Nias. For this reason the present tense is used in this paper except when discussing historical events in the past.
5. Marschall, *Der Berg*, p. 138. Marschall claims it was to the west, however informants insist it was to the north. Marschall's history of this era is taken from

informants aligned with the Dachi lineage of Hilisimaetano village. The version presented here is from the point of view of the Fau lineage of Bawömataluo and its subordinate villages. Since these villages were, and still are, adversaries, different accounts are to be expected. Construction of a permanent site must have begun immediately after the expulsion, because, on the royal lands of Hilifanayama, the new village of Bawömataluo was open and essentially complete with its *omo sebua* by 1878.

6. E.E.W.Gs. Schröder, *Nias, ethnographische en historische aanteekeningen en studiën*, 2 vols. (Leiden: E.J. Brill, 1917), p. 731.

7. *Koloniaal Verslag* (1901), p. 26.

8. "Een Nederlandsch etablishement te Lagoendi," *Tijdschrift voor Nederlandsch Indië* 1 (1860), pp. 331-349; "Nias in 1856," *Koloniale Jaarboeken* jaargang 1861-1862 (Batavia, 1862), pp. 193-219; J.F. Donleben and C.J. Berghuis, "Twee togten naar Nias en een blik op den slaven handel en den uitvoer van pandelingen aldaar," *Tijdschrift voor Nederlandsch Indië* 16 (1854), pp. 1-25; E.B. Kielstra, "Onze bemoeiingen met Nias onder generaal van Swieten," *Indisch Militair Tijdschrift* 21 (1890), pp. 125, 81-103; H.A. van Rees, *De Pionniers der beschaving in Neerlands Indië, verhall eenige Krijgstogten op de buitenbezittingen*, (Arnhem: D.A. Theime, 1866). This historical interpretation was greatly aided by my field informants who also provided the bulk of the contemporary explanations of Nias traditions. I wish to especially mention Bazanalui Fau who provided detailed information in the field and later in the mail, and who also permitted my wife and I to live in his *omo sebua* in Bawömataluo. Mendruatönöni Manau and the late Samogo Fau also provided much valuable information without which this study would be very shallow.

9. van Rees, *De Pionniers*, p. 71.

10. See Jerome Feldman, "The Architecture of Nias, Indonesia with Special Reference to Bawömataluo Village," (Ph.D. thesis, Columbia University, 1977), fig. 39.

11. van Rees, *De Pionniers*, p. 77.

12. J.T. Nieuwenhuisen and H.C.B. van Rosenberg, "Verslag omtrent het eilnd Nias en deszelfsbewoners," *Verhandelingen van het Bataviaasch Genootschap van Kunsten en Wetenschappen* 30 (1863), pp. 33-34.

13. H.W. Fischer, "Nias," in *Catalogus van 'sRijks Ethnographisch Museum* 4 (Leiden: E.J Brill, 1909), series 1239.

14. Lembaga Kebudayaan Indonesia (Koninklijk Bataviaasch Genootschap), *Notulen van het Bataviaasch Genootschap van Kunsten en Wetenschappen* 1 (1864), pp. 33-34. Unfortunately, the museum did not number its images until many years later when these became mixed with later collections. It is now impossible to be certain which images came from Orahili.

15. Fischer, "Nias," No. 1239/316.

16. T. Thomsen, "Hili Mondregeraja og dens Hovdingshus," *Fra Nationalmuseets Arbejdsmark*, (Copenhagen, 1929), pp. 56-57. This created quite a sensation in Nias and is still remembered by field informants.

17. The nature of these feasts and their sequence are discussed in Feldman, "Architecture of Nias"; "The House as World." Feasts in other South Nias villages have been treated by Marschall, *Der Berg*; Scarduelli, *L'Isola*; P. Suzuki, "Feasts Among the Niasans of the Batu Islands, Indonesia," *Anthropos* 68 no. 3/4 (1973), pp. 587-603; Y. Yamamoto, "A Sense of Tradition -- An Ethnographic Approach to Nias Material Culture" (Ph.D. thesis, Cornell University, 1986).

18. The importance of oppositions in Nias society was first extensively reported by Suzuki, "Religious System." This library thesis is, however, flawed by the arbitrary mixture of cultural information from all regions of Nias.

19. See Feldman, "The House as World," fig. 12.7.

20. The most complete and detailed description of the technology of South Nias house construction was published by Viaro, *Urbanisme et architecture*. This work is based primarily on the customary house, *omo hada*, a simplified miniature of the *omo sebua*. Although the terminology for common parts is the same, the details of the present essay pertain to certain aspects unique to the *omo sebua*.

21. "Tail" is my own descriptive term. In Bawömataluo, spirals are usually called *ni'owöliwöli*, a type of coiled fern. For a historical interpretation of the deer and tail as it appears on South Nias chiefs houses, see Jerome Feldman, "The Seat of the Ancestors in the Homeland of the Nias People," in D. Newton and J.P. Barbier, *Islands and Ancestors: Indigenous Styles of Southeast Asia* (The Metropolitan Museum of Art, Munich: Prestel Verlag, 1988), pp. 34-49.

22. See Jerome Feldman, "Ancestral Manifestations in the Art of Nias Island," in Jerome Feldman, ed. *The Eloquent Dead*, (Los Angeles: UCLA Museum of Cultural History, 1985), fig. 46.

23. See Feldman, "The Architecture of Nias," figs. 130, 131, 139, 140.

24. The symbolic aspects of the various carvings have been covered elsewhere. See Feldman, "The Architecture of Nias"; "The House as World"; "Ancestral Manifestations," pp. 60-76.

25. Schröder, *Nias*, figs. 144, 147, 150. This description is written in the present tense because it represents the way the house was originally furnished. Much, including all but four plates, has been sold or stolen. All figural sculpture is gone, and nearly all of the pig's jaws are missing.,

26. F. von Brenner-Felsach, "Reise durch die unabhängigen Batak-Lande und auf der Insel Nias," *Mittheilungen der Kaiserlichen und königlischen Geographischen Gesellschaft in Wien* 33 (1890), p. 301; Feldman, "Ancestral Manifestations."

27. See Feldman, "The House as World," fig. 15.4.

28. See Feldman, "The Architecture of Nias," figs. 141-143.

29. *Omo hada* are nearly always grouped in pairs.

30. D.W.N. de Boer, "Het Niassche Huis," *Mededeelingen van het encyclopaedisch bureau betreffende de buitengewetsen* Batavia, 25 (1920), fig. 4.

31. D.W.N. de "Niassche Huis," fig. 4.

32. As mentioned earlier, this is an important reason why true *omo sebua* can no longer be constructed.

33. W.L. Steinhart, "Niassche Priesterlitanieen," *Verhandelingen van het Bataviaasch Genootschap van Kunsten en Wetenschappen* 74 (1938), p. 21 lines 349-350 p. 22. The Batu Islands lie to the south of Nias and have a version of South Nias culture. Unfortunately, no such litanies could be found in the literature or among present day South Nias informants.

34. J.W. Thomas, J.W. and A. Fehr, "Thomas und Fehrs Reise im südlichen Nias," *Mitteilungen der geographischer Gesellschaft zu Jena* 1 (1882), p. 94

35. A. Kruisheer, "Uit de pioniertijd. De vestiging van het Nederlandsche Bestuur in Zuid Nias," *Orgaan der Nederlandsche-Indische Officiersvereeniging* pp. 226, 319, 364-366, 411, 413; Schroder, *Nias*, pp.282-283.

All photos and drawings are by the author unless otherwise indicated.

THE MEANING OF RESIDENCE IN TRADITIONAL HINDU SOCIETY

ISMET KHAMBATTA

The characteristic that distinguishes a traditional society is order, the sense of coherence in every aspect of life. This order or coherence derives from a shared knowledge of origins and gives validity to every event. In a traditional society the creation myth normally serves as the basis for the organization of society, territory, dwelling and family. The myth embodies a metaphysical doctrine and inspires every act and every artifact. This study is an attempt to understand the metaphysical doctrine that inspires, or gives life to, the physical structure of the dwelling in traditional Hindu society.

I will first lay out the central metaphysical ideas frequently referred to as the primary source of, and ultimate justification for, every institution in the Hindu great tradition. I will then try to see how these ideas are expressed through the rituals of building and the form of the traditional dwelling. This chapter will look at rituals that are practiced today and the prescriptions and practices from which they are derived. And it will trace the etymological roots of terms used to refer to various parts of the building and determine if inferences can be drawn from the use of certain ornamental motifs. Rituals and practices in a traditional society express a certain world view and serve to establish the position of the building, or any artifact, within the larger order of the universe.

This embodies a fundamental way of thinking about man-made things and their relationship with ultimate reality.

METAPHYSICAL CONSTRUCT:
THE MEANING OF RESIDENCE

One encounters the image of the human being as a microcosm of the macrocosmic universe repeatedly in the art and architecture of various cultures at various periods in their history. These images express the idea of a supreme unifying order in the universe which is embodied in man. It is this order that man has tried to grasp and imbibe in his works. The Hindu conception of the relationship between macrocosm and microcosm is not only that man is the image of the universe and vice versa, but that he is the universe.[1]

As mentioned earlier, the creation myth of a traditional society inspires and, in a sense, legitimizes every human act. The *Veda*, the set of hymns which constitute the earliest source of information about Hindu rituals and practices, describes the creation of the universe as occurring through a sacrifice in which the offering made by the gods was *Puruṣa*, cosmic man, or *Prajāpati*, the progenitor (FIG. 1). It was through this sacrifice that the world and its order were established. Every ritual in the Hindu tradition has its roots in this primordial act, and the performance of each such ritual marks a renewal and regeneration of the order of the universe. Gradually this elaborate ritual which involved several actors came to be internalized to the extent that the patron for whom the sacrifice was performed came to be identified with *Puruṣa* or *Prajāpati*, and he was seen as both the sacrificer and the offering.[2]

In the description of the cosmic sacrifice the dismembered body of *Prajāpati*, "spent in the act of creation," was restored by the gods through a sacrifice. The part left over in the cosmic ritual, the residue, was considered the immanent cause of all that exists. This residue was known as *vāstu*, from *vas*, "to assume a form." *Vāstu* also signifies residence, since *vas* can also mean, "to abide in a given condition." The part left over from the sacrifice signifies all

FIGURE 1.
Puruṣa, cosmic man.
A circular mandala of
Surya (*Agni-
Prajāpati*) with the
fertilizing power of
the fish and the lotus
ablaze his loins.
(S o u r c e : Pupul
Jayakar, *The Earthen
Drum: An Introduc-
tion to the Ritual Arts
of India*, New Delhi:
National Museum).

individual existence within which Unity or the Supreme Principle
is said to reside.   Thus every existing thing *vāstu* (*vāstu* is a
commonly used to mean "thing" or "object") is a residence in the
true sense.   It is with this understanding that the *Prāsāda*, the
Hindu temple, is seen as the body of the divinity residing within.
The human body is the visible outer casement of the invisible
Purusa.   The word *Puruṣa* derives from *pṛ*, "to fill."[3]

The realization that every existing thing is a residence is critical to
the understanding of traditional Hindu architecture.   This architecture, which often makes analogical references to the human being

and to the universe, is neither anthropocentric nor cosmocentric, but aims at imitating the divine archetype, the Supreme Principle, which is reflected in man and the universe. This purely intuitive knowledge of Unity is gained through introspection and can only be expressed through analogy; thus both man and the universe are explained reciprocally, one in terms of the other. The attempt here is to see how this knowledge of ultimate form or purpose is reflected in the dwelling itself.

The clearest evidence of the knowledge of correspondence between man, universe and building, and of each of these as a residence in the true sense, is preserved today in building rituals. *Bhumi Pujan*, performed before the building is built, and *Vāstu Sānti*, performed after it is completed, both make very clear references to the *Vedic* sacrifice which re-enacts the creation of the universe. The rituals described in various texts vary greatly in detail, but the purpose here is to draw from them the common thread of a deeper knowledge.

RITUAL DIAGRAM:
THE VĀSTUPURUṢAMANDALA

Traditionally every stage in the development of a building is regulated by astrological consultations. The regents of the stars and planets have their locations on a diagram, the *vāstumandala*, which represents the universe and is a forecast of the building. The *vāstumandala* is a *yantra*, a geometrical contrivance by which any aspect of the Supreme Principle may be bound to any spot for the purpose of concentration. "The manifest form of the Supreme Principle, or *Brahman*, is *Puruṣa*."[4]

The *Vāstupuruṣa* is always identified with the square diagram of the *vāstumandala* and is represented as lying diagonally within the square, face downward with his head in the northeast corner (FIG. 2). Though this ritual diagram is neither the ground plan of the building nor of the site, it regulates them nonetheless. The square form of the *vāstupuruṣamandala*, as also the form of the *Vedic* fire altar, derives from the image of the earth as square when ruled

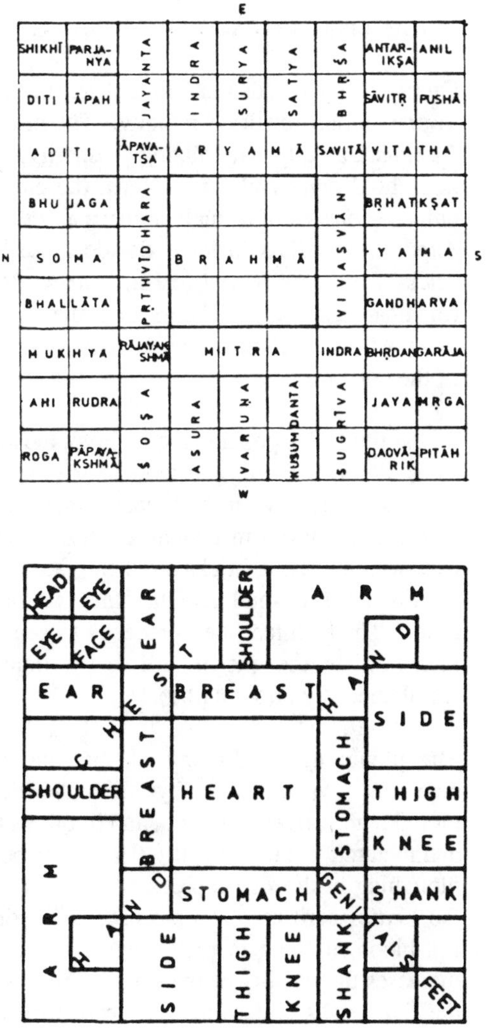

FIGURE 2.
The diagram of the
Vāstupuruṣamandala
showing the location
of the regents of the
stars and planets and
the position of the
body of the *Vāstu-
puruṣa* within the
same diagram.
(Source: Stella
Kramrisch, *The Hindu
Temple*, Delhi:
Motilal Banarsidas,
1976).

over by the heavenly order. The story of the descent of the
Vāstupuruṣa out of a nameless, formless state is again one of
creation from a primordial sacrifice. There is a clear identification
of *Vāstupuruṣa* with *Prajāpati*. In the rituals of construction the
householder is identified with *Vāstupuruṣa-Prajāpati*.[5]

THE BUILDING RITUALS: BHUMI PUJAN AND VĀSTU ŚĀNTI

On the auspicious day and time determined by a priest a pit is dug in preparation for the ceremony. The priest establishes to his left *Gaṇapati*, a deity symbolizing prosperity, and his two consorts, the household deity and *Vāstu Deva*, the embryo of the house. The embryo consists of a small copper jar with an image of the serpent *Anant* the Endless inside. Beside these he places five unbaked bricks which are *Bhumi* (earth), *Kurma* (tortoise), *Anant, Varaha* (the boar) and *Vāstu*. The tortoise, the serpent and the boar are all images from myth that have to do with the creation and sustenance of the universe.[6]

At the time of depositing the embryo, the architect, who is referred to as *Visvakarma*, the all-worker or creator, and the householder holding the embryo in both hands enter the pit. The householder places the embryo in a small depression at the bottom of the pit over which the five bricks are then placed in order -- the first three running north to south and the other two running east to west over them. The architect then proceeds to cement the bricks in place, after which the pit is filled by pouring water and earth simultaneously into it (FIG. 3).

The ploughing or digging of the site in preparation for this ceremony is prescribed by all authorities. In some cases a ploughman performs the rite, and in others the patron or the patron and the architect perform it.[7] This corresponds very closely to the ploughing of the site in preparation for setting up the fire altar for the *Vedic* sacrifice. The presence of a young woman with a red full-bloomed lotus is prescribed in some cases. Her presence increases the fertility of the earth. The placing of the embryo and the five bricks is described somewhat differently, but the images and their significance remain. The *Tantrasamuchhaya*, a ritual text, prescribes, ". . . place a *Nidhikumbha* [the embryo] made of copper or stone . . . over this place a lotus, above this a tortoise made of stone."[7] This corresponds to the setting up of the layers of the *Vedic* fire altar: "He then puts down a lotus-leaf, the lotus leaf is a womb . . . . He then puts a gold plate thereon . . . he then lays

F I G U R E 3. *Bhumi Pujan*: the architect and the householder deposit the embryo at the bottom of the pit, after which the bricks are cemented into place over it.

the gold man thereon -- he is *Prajāpati*, he is *Agni*, he is the sacrificer . . . it is a man for *Prajāpati* is the Man . . . . He then puts down a [living] tortoise . . . that lower shell of it is this [terrestrial] world . . . And that upper shell of it is yonder sky . . . and what is between is the air . . . that [tortoise] thus is these worlds; it is these worlds he thus lays down . . . ."[8] The act of digging or ploughing in these rituals has direct sexual significance. In cases where the driving in of a stake or pin is prescribed at the commencement of building operations, the association is the same -- the Earth is being fertilized and the building is being born.[9]

Within the completed building a fire altar is set up in the central room (FIG. 4). This is the domestic hearth, which usually also signifies a new marriage. The ceremony is performed by the householder and his wife, instructed by a priest. After the customary chanting of hymns and invocations to the gods, the couple are instructed to take the small copper vessel and together deposit it in a small pit already dug inside the house to the right side of the

F I G U R E 4. *Vāstu Śānti:* the fire altar is built in the central room of the house, corresponding to the domestic hearth.

entrance. The pit in this case is within the plinth of the house. The husband and wife, both holding the embryo in their hands, lower it into the pit after which it is covered as before. The priest then pours offerings of *ghee*, clarified butter, and rice into the fire, blessing the couple with prosperity and progeny.[10]

Once again the ritual sacrifice is performed in which the householder is *Prajāpati* the progenitor. The fire altar is the domestic hearth or womb. "Our allusion is, in fact, to the metaphysical identification of woman with the household fire, and the act of insemination with a ritual offering in this fire."[11] The ritual, besides being the re-enactment of an event, constitutes also a virtual return to the instant before creation began. The creative act is the creation of the universe anew -- cosmogony. The building then is a likeness of the universe.

THE DWELLING: VASTU

Further evidence of this common understanding of the deep structure of the building is to be found in terms referring to different parts of the dwelling, which were once in regular usage and may be found in descriptive literature or prescriptive architectural texts. Since it was the rule that only timber and other impermanent materials could be used for human dwellings, since stone could only be used for temples and other permanent structures, we have no real physical evidence of the houses described in these texts, except for those represented in narrative paintings or sculptures.[12]

Making a broad classification, one can differentiate between two types of houses as described in literary works and texts. The first were those with an open quadrangle or court as the essential element. The second were those categorized by the number of storys.

The śālā house essentially consisted of rooms arranged around a quadrangle. Its principle components were the śālā, or rooms; ālinda, the verandah and front yard; the garbhagraha, literally "womb-of-the-house"; and the entrance and the porch. "The Garbhagraha, the interior chamber, though the sacred-most in a temple, was the central compound with vāpi or pushkarini -- the reservoir of water -- laid with a cover over it in the residential house."[13] The main entrance or gate of the house was a structure which resembled the gateways of fortified towns, though much smaller. Across it lay a stone threshold or dehli (FIG. 5).[14]

A special characteristic of houses used to be that every roof of every room was provided with a hole, called uluka. This term has also been rendered uloka, an abridged form of ava-loka or uru-loka, meaning the free open or intermediate space that made up either the universe or any division of it, especially the sky or heaven. This description corresponds closely to the images of the Brahmarandhra (cranial foramen) or Sun Door or the occulus of the dome that serves as the threshold for transmigration from a particular to an unparticular state. This feature is coincident with

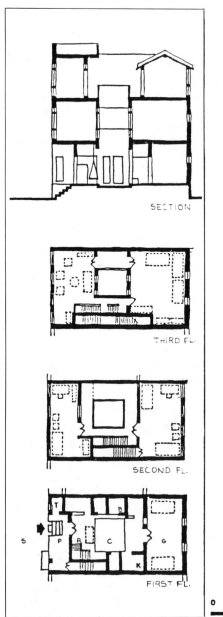

SECTION

THIRD FL.

SECOND FL.

FIRST FL.

FIGURE 5.
Floor plans and
section of a typical
courtyard house
showing the internal
organization of spaces
with respect to the
street and the central
courtyard. S) street,
P) plinth or verandah,
T) toilet, B) bath,
C) courtyard,
K) kitchen,
G) store room,
R) room.

0   5   10 M

the axis of the universe. Images of transmigration are also evident in the climbing rites during a sacrifice and in funerary rituals when the skull is broken.[15]

The second type of house form is described by Gupta:

> The *Prasada* [a seven storied mansion likened to the universe with its seven worlds] was conceived in the form of a human body with its limbs or components called after the human limbs, such as *pada* [foot] signifying foundation, *bāhus* [arms] the upper parts of the mansion, *prakoṣtha* [forearm] a room near the gate of a palace, *skandhakuta* [shoulders] the walls, . . . *nāsika* [nose] the balcony, *akṣis* [eyes] the windows, *lalāta* [forehead] the terrace, and *siras* [head] the topmost part of the edifice.[16]

The topmost part of the edifice was crowned by the pinnacle known as *stupika*, from *stupa* meaning a top knot of hair, and marked the point at which the cosmic axis pierced through the superstructure. The axis which links all the worlds and is the means of passage between them is often seen as a ladder, post, bridge or sometimes a ship or a chariot. "Just as, formally considered, there is a correspondence between the human body, human building and the whole world, so there is also a teleological correspondence: all these constructions have as their practical function to shelter individual principles on their way from one state of being to another -- to provide in other words, a field of experience in which they can become what they are."[17]

COMMON MOTIFS: PLINTH, COURTYARD AND THRESHOLD

As with the rituals that one can observe even today, the houses in many Indian cities attempt to imitate the same fundamental order described above. A case study of the houses of the old city of Ahmedabad, which are from one hundred to five hundred years old, serves here to bring out this common understanding of what the dwelling is, by studying particular motifs and elements which occur in every instance (FIG. 6).

The plinth of the house is most often ornamented with an edge of lotus leaves (FIG. 7). *Padma Pitha* is the term used for the pedestal

FIGURE 6.
Traditional courtyard
houses along a street,
Jada-bhagat-ni pol,
Ahmedabad.

or base of an image or throne, or for the plinth of the temple or *Prāsāda*. Before constructing the *Vedic* fire altar, the precursor of the base of the temple and the house, the sacrificer first lays down a lotus leaf. "The lotus means the waters and this earth is a leaf thereof: even as the lotus-leaf here lies spread on the water, so this earth lies spread on the waters."[18] The waters are the waters of chaos above which the earth is raised and forms a support for the superstructure to be raised.

The central courtyard, the most dominant feature of the house, is the womb of the house through which passes the cosmic axis (FIG. 7). A pattern in the flooring, or a diagram, marks the center and is most often octagonal or circular (FIG. 8). The axis of the universe according to the texts is usually cylindrical or four- or eight-

FIGURE 7.
The central courtyard
with an underground
reservoir for water
and the edge of lotus
leaves on the plinth of
the house.

FIGURE 8.
A diagram in the
flooring pattern
marking the center of
the courtyard.

angled. Early Indian pillars were usually either cylindrical or
eight-angled. This pattern in principle also marks the location of
the foundation stone. The earth and the entire manifest world is
said to be supported on the head of the serpent *Ananta* (the
endless) or *Sesa* (the remainder). The ritual performed at the start
of building often prescribes that the head of the serpent must be
pegged down to stabilize the site and ensure the longevity of the
building. A foundation stone with an eight-petalled lotus carved
on it is set in mortar above this peg. The laying of the foundation
stone is followed by the setting up of the central column or post,
coincident with the navel of the earth and the axis of the universe.
As described in the *Matsya Puranam*, ". . . then that pillar is to be
bathed with all medicinal plants by the Brahmans . . . then that
pillar is to be fixed by the artisans after putting round it clothes and

ornaments . . . ."[19] This description apparently alludes to the body of *Prajāpati*, "which upholds the falling heaven and earth."

In the earliest houses constructed over and around a central support -- actually the trunk of a tree -- the central post did serve as the main stay of the entire structure; but in later structures, "the importance of the axis, in principle, is no more necessarily represented by an actual pillar within the building, than it would be possible to demonstrate the empirical existence of an Axis of the Universe, which Axis is indeed always spoken of as a purely spiritual or pneumatic essence."[20] It is at this point, in the middle of the central room of the house, that a fire altar is subsequently set up during the *Vāstu Śānti* ceremony. This altar is the domestic hearth, the navel of the world from which the pillar of smoke rises to escape through the eye in the roof.

The house has usually only one entrance from the street. It is the entrance into the womb of the house with its sun door the opening above (FIGS. 9, 10). The motif of the *Purna Kalasa*, the brimming vessel, enclosed on three sides by three levels is carved on the lintel over the entrance. The *Purna Kalasa*, known commonly as an auspicious symbol, also signifies fertility and is analogous to the womb, or in some cases to a woman. The lotus, the brimming vessel and the goddess *Laxmi* are all used to connote fertility. The figure enclosing the *Kalasa* is analogous to the three layers of the domestic hearth and to the three self-perforated bricks of the *Vedic* altar that signify the three worlds -- *Bhu* (the terrestrial world), *Bhuvar* (intermediate space) and *Svar* (the celestial world). "It can be said with respect to any of the three houses (man, building and cosmos) . . . that one enters into the provided environment at its lowest level (at birth) and departs from it at its highest level (at death) or in other words, that ingress is horizontal, egress vertical."[21]

CONCLUSION: RE-COGNITION

A metaphysical doctrine has been traced as it has been expressed through prescription, records of earlier practice and observation of

FIGURE 9.
The main entrance to
a house with the motif
of the *Purna Kalasa*,
"brimming vessel," on
the lintel.

FIGURE 10.
The doorway of
egress. The central
shaft through which
passes the axis of the
universe.

building remains. Thus the building, $v\bar{a}stu$ is seen as originating
in the residue of the sacrifice within which the Supreme Principle
resides until it is restored to Unity through sacrifice. This central
idea is constantly reinforced by rituals, language and the building
itself. The forms and metaphors used served as mnemonic devices

that remind one of the primordial event from which all order was generated. In repeating them, that event is generated anew. This constant renewal and regeneration is the essence of tradition.

The use of these forms in the modern house may have been reduced to little more than a symbol painted over a doorway, but the rituals still form an essential part of any building activity. Their function, however, has become one of legitimization.

REFERENCE NOTES

1. This idea can be said to have been expressed at its most literal level by cultures like the Dogon of Mali and at its most abstract in medieval Christian philosophy or in Hindu philosophy. See Geoffrey Parrinder, *African Mythology* (London: Paul Hamlyn, 1969); A.K. Coomaraswamy, *Christian and Oriental Philosophy of Art* (New York: Dover Publications, 1956).
2. See Julius Eggling's introduction to Satapatha Brahmana, *Sacred Books of the East*, Vol. IX-XIII, Max Muller, ed. (Oxford: Clarendon Press, 1882).
3. Ref. Raj Bahadur Sirsa Chandar Vidyarnava, *Chandogya Upanishad*, the Panini Office Bhuvaneswari. See also Stella Kramrisch, *The Hindu Temple I* (Delhi: Motilal Banarasidas, 1976), pp. 21-27.
4. Thus in the arts we have the following: in poetry, *Sabdabrahman* and the *Kavyapurusa*; in music, *Nadabrahman* and the *Prabandhapurusa*; and in architecture, *Vāstubrahman* and the *vāstupuruṣa*. See Bettina Baumer, "Purusa and the Origin of Form," in Bettina Baumer, ed., *Rupa Pratirupa: Alice Boner Commemoration volume* (New Delhi: Biblia Impex, 1982), p. 33.
5. Kramrisch, *The Hindu Temple I*, pp. 22-39. Cf. the *Vedic* sacrifice where the circular fire altar represents this terrestrial world, and the square fire altar represents the celestial world. For the story of the *vāstupuruṣa*, see Manmath Nath Dutt Sastri, ed., *Agni Puranam* (Varanasi: Chowkambha Publishers, 1967), ch. XL, p. 149. See also Jamna Das Akhtar, ed., *Matsya Puranam* (Delhi: Oriental Publishers, 1972), ch. CLLII.
6. Kramrisch, *The Hindu Temple I*, pp. 62-63. "A great serpent (naga) moves encircling every site by its movement in the course of a year . . . it is a manifestation of *Ananta* or *Sesa*, the Endless, the Remainder, which encircles in the perpetuity of its movement and also supports on its head, the earth and the entire manifest world."
7. Goudriaan, *Kasyapa Jnanakandah: A Ritual Handbook of the Vaikhanasas* (The Hague: Mouton and Co., 1965), p. 18. See also Kramrisch, *The Hindu Temple I*, pp. 15-17.
8. Satapatha Brahmana, *Sacred Books of the East*, Vol. IX-XIII, Muller, ed. (Oxford: Clarendon Press, 1921).
9. Coomaraswamy, *Yaksas I and II* (Delhi: Munshiram Manoharlal, 1971), p. 44. ". . . it is suggested that linga, langala, and langula all having amongst other meanings that of membrum verile, and the second meaning also more usually

'plough' are derived from a common non-Aryan root having the general sense of, 'to push in, to make a hole'." See also Coomaraswamy, *Rg Veda as Land-Nama-Bok* (London: Luzac and Co., 1935). ". . . the use of 'Krsti' (literally that which is ploughed up) to mean man, parallels the notion of the sexual act as a ploughing, implied in the notion of woman as a field." See also Margaret Sinclair Stevenson, *The Rites of the Twice Born* (London, 1920), p. 354; Coomaraswamy, *Traditional Art and Symbolism*, Roger Lipsey, ed. (Princeton: Princeton University Press, 1977), p. 430.

10. Kramrisch, *The Hindu Temple I*, p. 12. In the building of a temple, the height at which the embryo is deposited varies with the caste of the patron and indicates the level from which the ascent towards the highest point, the apex, is undertaken. For the *Brahmans* it is highest, at the level of the topmost molding of the plinth. It is correspondingly lower for the other castes, but above ground level for all.

11. Coomaraswamy, *Traditional Art and Symbolism*, p. 425.

12. Kramrisch, *The Hindu Temple I*, pp. 62-63. The head of the serpent, on which the earth is supported, moves by one degree every day, and with it the *Vāstupuruṣa* is also said to move. This rotating *vāstu* is called *caravāstu* and is distinguished from the *sthiravāstu* whose position is fixed with its head in the northeast. For all permanent work like the building of a temple the *sthiravāstu* is worshipped, and for all impermanent work like the dwellings of men the *caravāstu* is worshipped. For drawings of domestic architecture reconstructed from descriptions, paintings and sculpture, see K. Krishnamurthy, *Early Indian Secular Architecture* (New Delhi: Sundeep Prakashan, 1987).

13. D.N. Shukla, *Vāstu Sastra: The Hindu Science of Architecture, Vol. I* (Lucknow: Shukla Printing Press, 1961), p. 310.

14. This description of the house closely resembles the houses that will be used in the latter part of this study to discuss the motifs and elements used in the houses of the old city of Ahmedabad.

15. Coomaraswamy, *Traditional Art and Symbolism*, pp. 415-450. Every building, city or country is seen as having its location above the hypothesized center of the universe. The cosmic axis passing through this central point has its image in the pillaring apart of heaven and earth or the rising of the primordial mound from the waters -- a separation of order from chaos. See also John Irwin, "The Stupa and The Cosmic Axis: The Archaeological Evidence," *South Asian Archaeology*, 1977.

16. Dharmendra Kumar Gupta, *Society and Culture in the Time of Dandin* (Delhi: Meharchand Lachmandas, 1972), p. 406.

17. Coomaraswamy, *Traditional Art and Symbolism*, p. 424.

18. Satapatha Brahmana, *Sacred Books of the East*, Muller, ed., VII, 4, 1, 8.

19. Jamna Das Akhtar, ed., *Matsya Puranam*.

20. Coomaraswamy, *Traditional Art and Symbolism*, pp. 425-428.

21. *Ibid.*, pp. 425-428.

SACRED SPACE, RITUAL AND THE TRADITIONAL GREEK HOUSE

ELEFTHERIOS PAVLIDES
JANA E. HESSER

Religion can be one of the most conservative institutions, and religious practices can be some of the most resistant to change. Religion may serve as a repository for traditional cultural elements in times of profound social change. When a new religion takes hold, elements of an old religion may be preserved through syncretism. Sacred aspects of a dwelling are those elements of architectural form and function that are subject to the strong traditional influences of religion.

Domestic space provides the stage for an extraordinarily complex range of activities including religious rituals. In their formative years some religions were exclusively practiced in domestic environments. Even in traditional societies which have specialized religious buildings, dwellings maintain significant sacred features and functions. Permanent features of the house as well as various movable of perishable objects serve specific religious purposes. Consecration rituals similar to those for socialized religious buildings are also performed for the construction of houses.

This chapter examines religious rituals associated with the construction and use of domestic space in Greece. It is based on fieldwork done in Eressos, a traditional village of 1,200 inhabitants on the island of Lesbos far from urban influences, and in

Epidaurus, a transitional village of 1,500 inhabitants located close to Athens.[1] Systematic visual documentation of houses was combined with participant observation and ethnographic interviews to construct a comparative view if these two settlements. In Eressos information spanned the last one hundred and fifty years; in Epidaurus information spanned the time since its more recent settlement eighty years ago. The ethnographic works of du Boulay, Campbell, Friedl, and Dubisch were also surveyed for information about sacred aspects of dwelling in Greece.

In addition to describing these practices and their importance in the Greek communities, some comparison is drawn with dwelling-related religious practices of other cultures. Raglan may be one of the few scholars who has attempted to look at the sacred aspects of dwelling on a cross-cultural level, and his work provides a wealth of information which reveals how the sacred is essential to the act of dwelling in many traditional cultures.[2]

Raglan's work makes it possible to identify similarities across cultures in rituals expressing the sacred nature of dwellings. Obviously, similar ritual forms or activities may have different meanings or social significances in different cultural contexts, and more detailed information is needed to extend these comparisons. However, Raglan's work has provided a primary source for making comparisons between the sacred aspects of the Greek house and the sacred aspects of houses in other parts of the world.

In both Eressos and Epidaurus sacred rituals are performed during house construction, before moving into a house, as well as on a daily, weekly and annual basis, and during major life events. The house entrance and the *iconostassi*, or icon place, are the two major locations for religious activities in the house. The *iconostassi*, a major focus for prayer, also serves as a repository for objects brought from or to be taken to the church. In this sense it acts as an umbilical cord connecting the house to the religious and moral life of the community. Rituals performed at the house entrance mark the threshold between the sanctuary of the home and the dangers of the external world.

Knowledge of sacred practices and the features necessary to accommodate them can provide designers with opportunities to include them as programmatic elements. Such programmatic elements can find expression in architectural form. Such an activity also raises the general possibility of reinforcing social cohesion through architectural expression of common values within dwellings.

THEORETICAL APPROACH AND METHOD

The theoretical approach for this study is provided by socio-semiotics as defined by Pavlides and inspired by socio-linguistics.[3] This approach to semiotics requires extensive fieldwork utilizing both ethnographic and art historic methodologies. A detailed documentation of visual form is followed by interviews using photographs to elicit the meaning, use and significance of various architectural features for different contextually-defined categories of inhabitants.[4]

The original intent of the studies was to identify in the broadest sense the use and meaning of domestic architecture for the inhabitants of both Eressos and Epidaurus. In the course of our study and analysis of Eressos, it became apparent that a set of significant ritual activities was associated with specific parts of the house and that a significant component of sacred meaning was associated with the house itself. As a result, a more conscious effort was made when studying Epidaurus to look for sacred aspects of dwelling on order to contrast the two villages.

In Eressos research was carried out over nine months in three phases. The first phase involved becoming familiar with the variation of architectural form and decoration of the village's eleven hundred houses, through taking photographs and making drawings. The second phase involved detailed documentation, including the making of measured drawings of forty houses. Simultaneously, participant observation and informal interviews provided in-depth understanding of the use and significance of architectural form since the 1850s. The last phase involved conducting slide interviews to learn how architectural form was interpreted by the inhabitants, and how interpretation was related to factors such as socio-economic standing, gender and age.

In Epidaurus similar work was carried out on a smaller scale during the summer of 1987 with the help of a team of students. Each student was assigned to photograph the variety of one particular environmental feature, such as windows, doors, walls, roofs or use of color. Slide interviews, intensive observation and interviews with such expert informants as old members of the community and old construction workers provided verbal information on local interpretations of the history and use of village architecture.

THE SETTING

Eressos and Epidaurus were both important cities in classical times, however Eressos has been inhabited continuously while Epidaurus was abandoned after an earthquake at the time of Christ, and it was not resettled until the nineteenth century. In the nineteenth century Eressos was a thriving community with a Christian majority living harmoniously with a Muslim minority under Ottoman rule. By 1922, when Greece and Turkey exchanged populations, Christians from Asia Minor replaced the town's Muslims.[5] The discussion which follows is based only on study of the Christian population of Eressos. In the twentieth century Eressos experienced a loss of population to distant urban centers, primarily to Athens. Conversely, Epidaurus has grown continuously over the past eighty years, since its proximity to Athens has provided an accessible market for its agricultural products.

Eressos and Epidaurus represent two ends of the spectrum of modernization in contemporary Greece. Epidaurus is a wealthy, growing community where 70 percent of the local economy is based in agricultural production and the rest in tourism. Its houses are predominantly of reinforced concrete frame construction (FIG. 1). In 1978 Eressos was almost totally dependent on a mix of

FIGURE 1.
Epidaurus house.

FIGURE 2.
Eressos house.

subsistence and commercial agriculture and shepherding, with a shrinking population and a predominantly old housing stock of rubble masonry construction reinforced with timber (FIG. 2).

The houses in Eressos were studied in great detail for their spatial arrangement and a variety of other architectural features. Their history was traced through three periods. During the earliest period, the mid-nineteenth century, a range of seven house-types existed, expressing a socio-economic stratification which was further elaborated and amplified through numerous house features including the sacred corner. During later periods, change in house form and decoration included stylistic features that expressed Greek ethnic identity, interior spaces defined by furniture, and house features that expressed socio-economic standing.

FIGURE 3.
Epidaurus
neighborhood.

FIGURE 4.
Eressos
neighborhood.

Throughout these changes the sacred aspects and uses of the house remained constant.

Architecturally, Epidaurus looks more modern than Eressos, and with its proximity to Athens, it has developed a sense of urbanity very different from Eressos (FIGS. 3,4). The variety of house-types and features of the Epidaurus houses were not studied through time as exhaustively as those of Eressos. Knowledge of the sacred features and religious uses of the Eressos houses directed a search for similarities or differences in the houses of Epidaurus. At first glance, one would expect Epidaurus to have lost many of the traditional village customs. However, the sanctity and ritual life of the house is very similar to that displayed in Eressos. Thus the descriptions and discussions which follow are applicable to both villages unless noted otherwise.

RELIGION IN GREEK VILLAGE LIFE

The following discussion of sacred aspects of traditional Greek dwelling requires a general introduction to religion in Greek village life. Juliet du Boulay provides a masterful description of this, which is as relevant to Eressos and Epidaurus as it was to the small mountain village she studied. She wrote:

> Beliefs regarding the metaphysical nature of the world and of human thought and action within that world . . . fall roughly into two categories, one derived from Christian Orthodoxy, and the other from the religious beliefs of pagan or "folk" philosophy . . . . These latter beliefs . . . are based on an understanding of the world according to which man, far from being the child of God, mediated for and protected by the sacred presences of the Orthodox hierarchy, is the object of impersonal and irrational forces . . . . It is a philosophy in which an ineluctable fate is woven around men by chthonic powers, a fate which, good or bad, is "written and cannot be unwritten.

> In spite, however, of the prevalence of this type of thinking . . . it is the Christian philosophy which forms for the villager the more coherent and explicit system, and it is in terms of this philosophy that his ritual and ceremonial life is largely organized.

> This belief is one in which according to the world, created and sustained by God, is continually being fought for by the Devil who sends out his emissaries -- the demons in all their various guises, the evil eye, the evil hour, the nereids, and so on -- to torment and corrupt mankind. Man is thus seen as being in a central position between God and the Devil in a world where these two powers strive endlessly for mastery.[6]

The role of ritual in this system of belief is both to ward off the ever-present forces of evil and to evoke the presence and protection of God. Humans must continuously take steps to re-establish and perpetuate a relationship within which the power of God can operate.[7] The rituals we identified in house construction and inhabitation reflect these beliefs and help encode the built environment with social meaning.

RITUAL AND HOUSE CONSTRUCTION

The act of constructing a house goes beyond simply providing protection against the elements. It also requires assuring spiritual protection for those who will live in the house. Supernatural powers are focused on a site in advance of any actual construction as well as upon the completed building. In both Eressos and Epidaurus the presence of God is invoked during a ceremony held within the foundation trenches for a new house. A priest uses basil to sprinkle water sanctified for the ceremony on the foundation and on those present -- owners, construction workers and friends. During the ceremony the blood of a freshly slaughtered rooster is sprinkled over the open trenches.[8] Sanctifying a building's foundations is said to serve many purposes. It ensures the stability and longevity of the building, it protects the construction workers against injury, and it invokes divine help for the owner in completing this most difficult undertaking.

Protection of the foundation of a building through the use of holy water or animal blood is encountered in many cultures. Sprinkling the foundation with holy water is similar in form to the Buddhist practice of sprinkling holy water on eight round stones and burying them around the site where a temple will be built. Animal sacrifices made around the foundation of a house or other building have been widely reported. The killing of a goat, hen, rooster, sheep or boar on the foundation has been reported in Kenya, Palestine, Syria, the New Hebrides and many other places. Even human sacrifice has been alluded to; in Greece there is a famous medieval song about the bridge of Arta where the master craftsman built his own wife into the foundation. Similar legends exist in Denmark, Serbia, Japan and Wales. In England, Lord Leigh was actually accused in 1881 of having built an obnoxious person into the foundation of a bridge.[9]

In both Eressos and Epidaurus precautions against the evil eye are taken throughout the construction process. A cross placed on top of the walls as they are being raised, or over an incomplete roof, provides assurance that the construction will be completed with no

F I G U R E 5. The Blessing of the house at Epiphany.

complications and that the building will stand for many generations.

The completed building is blessed in a ceremony similar to the one performed in the foundation trenches. After a priest has completed the ritual of prayers and blessing, holy water is sprinkled on the newly constructed rooms to make them appropriate for inhabitation, and then those present drink some holy water. Every year on Epiphany (Jan. 6) all houses are blessed anew, as the priest visits each to sprinkle it and its inhabitants with holy water (FIG. 5). Rituals, sometimes involving animal sacrifice, performed after a building is finished and before it is occupied are reported from many other cultures.[10]

Once occupied, houses in Eressos and Epidaurus become the setting for many religious rituals. Religious rituals are performed on a daily, weekly and yearly basis, as well as on special occasions. The primary locations for the rituals in the house are the *iconostassi*, or sacred corner, and the house entrance.

THE *ICONOSTASSI*

The *iconostassi* is a small shrine; translated literally, the word means "the place for the sacred icons." An *iconostassi* signifies that God is present within a house and marks a house as suitable for human habitation. The shrine varies from being a simple wooden shelf or hanging icon to being an elaborate decorative plaster construction. Some have small curtains to protect the icons inside from dust and light (FIG. 6). The size and elaborateness of an *iconostassi* is one of several indicators of status in a house. A cross is the most common decoration, though angels and an eagle were also found (FIG. 7).

In Eressos and Epidaurus, *iconostassi* were found most often on the ceiling near the east wall or on the eastern edge of the north wall. These locations are common in many villages in Greece, including Mystra, a Byzantine town built in the thirteenth century.[11] In recent years, as interior space has been redefined by the introduction of furniture, villagers have come to place *iconostassi* on a table or in a window whose exterior shutters have been permanently closed.[12] The *iconostassi* has been found in rooms furnished as bedrooms, living rooms and dining rooms, but it is always located on the east side of the room. Churches in Greece always have their apses, which contain their altars, on the east.

In addition to icons, a number of other sacred objects and implements are kept at the *iconostassi* for use in various ritual activities. These include objects brought from the church such as dried flowers or laurel leaves, and marital wreaths which were worn during the church wedding. The marital wreath is often stored in a special, protective, decorative display case. Holy water brought from the church is kept in little bottles. The holy water protects the house and its occupants and is used for a variety of purposes. For instance, when a member of the family leaves for a long trip, some of this holy water is poured into another small bottle and placed in the traveller's suitcase to ensure a safe return.

FIGURE 6.
Iconostassi.

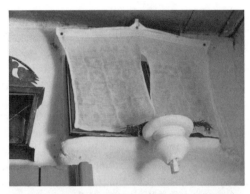

FIGURE 7.
Iconostassi.

A number of small implements for ritual activities are kept at the *iconostassi*. These include a votive oil lamp, a wooden stamp with religious designs around the monogram of Jesus Christ, an incense burner and candles brought from church. The votive light is supposed to burn olive oil night and day in front of the holy icons. This is considered a form of sacrifice, an offering to Christ, Mary or the saint depicted on the icon. The concept of the sacred fire in domestic worship was also present in ancient Greece.[13]   In modernized houses a small electric light has replaced the oil lamp. The wood stamp is used to imprint a religious design on bread which is baked at home and brought to church. Such breads are called *prosforo*, or "offering", and are brought to church on holidays or on those occasions when the family holds a special service to God, for example to heal a family member. The *prosforo* is blessed by the priest along with wine and is turned into sacrament. Small pieces are then given to the parishioners after the liturgy. Incense if burned every day or every Saturday, and just before sunset on those days preceding important holidays. The bible and liturgy books are also considered to be sacred objects. (On certain occasions they are kissed in the same way that one kisses the holy icons.) They too are stored at the *iconostassi*. These books are used in church during the liturgy.

The *iconostassi* is one house feature not found in the Turkish houses of Eressos or in other communities where Greeks and Turks lived together. Muslim houses had no special shrine; the Koran was stored on the mantel over the fireplace, which was sometimes elaborately decorated with sculpted plaster. Christian houses had equally elaborate mantels, but these were usually used for displaying secular objects. On rare occasions the highly ceremonial form of the mantel was exploited for religious displays (FIG. 8).

The presence of a sacred corner or space in the house is found in many cultures. The yard of every ancient Greek or Roman house had an altar where sacrifices were offered to the gods. Altars or shrines are reported in the houses of the Purum along the Indo-Chinese border, the Anang of Nigeria and the Baila of Rhodesia, as well as in Hindu and Muslim houses in several parts of India.[14] The presence of an ever-burning light at the house altar is a widespread practice, as for example among the Chinese.[15]

F I G U R E 8.
Fireplace mounted
with icons.

In function, the *iconostassi* resembles a miniature chapel. It replicates the main features of the Orthodox church -- the holy icons, the perpetually lit oil lamp, the burning incense. As a focus for prayer in the house, and as a repository for objects taken to or brought from the church, it acts as an umbilicus connecting the house with the village church. The house, as a primary domain for individual and family worship, is thus linked with the religious life of the larger community. In fact, a single member of a household can represent the whole family at church, a clear reflection of the place of the house-family unit in village social organization and the importance of the *iconostassi* in the religious life of the family. "The house . . . is a place where the demons are already defeated, and where the victory of Christ over the Devil -- already in the eschatological sense a reality and seen recurrently in the festival of Easter -- is in the human and social world also achieved. Here is the area where man may physically and spiritually relax, lapped in

FIGURE 9.
Smudged cross under
the lintel.

peace and surrounded by order," du Boulay has written.[16] After
the midnight service on Easter a candle lit in church is carefully
carried home to light the votive oil lamp at the *iconostassi*. Thus
the spirit of the resurrected Christ fills the house anew each year.

THE HOUSE ENTRANCE

The house entrance is the second area where ritual activity is
focused. Unlike the *iconostassi* which is physically decorated as a
sacred corner, there are few visual indications that the entrance is a
ritual location. A smudged cross under the lintel (FIG. 9) and a
wreath of dried flowers hanging next to the door for part of the
year are the only evidence that ritual activities take place here.

Following the weekly and sometimes daily offering of incense to
the icons, the incense is placed in front of the door to finish
burning. The vertical column of smoke is though to block any evil
from entering the house. Thus the entrance and the house interior
are provided constant spiritual protection.

There are several rituals that occur annually at the house entrance.
On New Year's day the house is blessed with a ritual in which a
pomegranate blessed at church is smashed on the threshold.
Wishes are made for riches and fertility for the entire year that will
be as numerous as the pomegranate seeds. Another ritual involves
dropping a feather in the doorway accompanied with wishes that

worries and unhappiness in the coming year will be as light as the feather.

After the Easter midnight service smoke from the candle that brings the sacred flame to the *iconostassi* is used to create a cross under the door lintel or metal overhang. This cross protects the house against all misfortune, including the evil eye.

On the first of May a flower wreath is constructed and hung by the door for luck and protection and is left there for several months. In Eressos villagers used to make bonfires in the streets on the evening of St. George's day in July. The May wreaths were ceremonially burned while children and young adults jumped over the flames.

In addition to daily and seasonal ritual activities, there are other occasions when rituals are enacted at the house entrance. When a household member leaves for a long journey, a special farewell to ensure return involves pouring water over the traveller's shoe and giving him or her a small bouquet of flowers and basil. A pot of basil is kept by the entrance because it is considered beneficial, and a branch of basil is often used to sprinkle holy water; basil is also believed to ward off snakes. A plate is smashed outside the door when a corpse is removed from the house to prevent death from returning.

As creation of a sacred corner in a house occurs in many cultures, so does the placing of objects on or near doors to bring spiritual protection. Chinese houses have paper door-gods pasted on the doors. In ancient Babylonia and Assyria figures of deities on the door brought protection to the house. The same practice is currently followed in Central America. Among Orthodox Jews touching the *mezuzah* attached to the door, which contains a ribbon with God's name on it, brings protection. The sacred significance of the threshold and various rituals associated with it is discussed extensively in Raglan's *The Temple and the House*.[17]

In Greece, the entranceway to the house marks the boundary between the sanctity and protection of the family sheltered within, and the world outside which is always seen as potentially hostile. Du Boulay writes ". . . the tightest group of society is . . . in the members of a house, for outside that house lies the outside world, and the outside world represents always different loyalties and opposing interests."18

THE EVIL EYE

A variety of objects are displayed in the house and in the yard against the ever-present danger of the evil eye. Belief in the evil eye is widespread throughout the Mediterranean world, extends northward into Europe and eastward into Asia, and has persisted for four thousand years or more. The harmful effects of the evil eye may occur by intent, through the beholder's envy, or unintentionally through the beholder's admiration. The evil eye is believed to cause physical or psychological harm and is believed to have the power to hurt or damage an animal, plant or physical object.19

Concern about the evil eye was found in both Eressos and Epidaurus. An effort to protect against it is made by placing one or more of a variety of objects in the house and/or in the yard. Such objects include an empty eggshell, a sea urchin, snake skin, a sea star (FIG. 10), a blue bead, a string of garlic heads or one of many other objects that can be hung on trees, walls or above doors. These objects protect the house's inhabitants, the house itself or the specific object to which it is attached. Personal protection against the evil eye is also achieved by wearing such things as blue glass beads or tiny wood crosses, or through a ritual involving the flame or oil from the votive lamp of the *iconostassi*. Such practices are found all over Greece.20

RELIGIOUS SPACES IN THE MODERN HOUSE

Extensive ritual functions of the house were identified through fieldwork in both Eressos and Epidaurus. There are four broad areas where the house is related to the spiritual life of the people.

F I G U R E 10.
Sea star in house
interior to protect
against evil eye.

First, the process of construction is heavily influenced by ritual activity to ensure the safety of both the construction workers and the future occupants. Second and third, there are two major focii of religious ritual in the house -- the *iconostassi*, and the entrance door. Finally, protection against the evil eye requires a variety of objects to be placed in the house and yard. In Eressos and Epidaurus the sanctity and ritual life of the house were found to persist even in the face of modernizations that have dramatically changed the materials used, the size and number of rooms, interior furnishings and the house facade.

These observations raise two major questions for the practice of architecture today. Neither the training of future designers nor the work performed by designers of housing today considers the ritual use of houses. The religious affiliation of the user is not considered as relevant to the design process and is not used in the development of programmatic requirements and design criteria. In some populations, ignoring the religious function of a house can hamper its acceptability to prospective inhabitants. The literature is full of examples where development projects have been left abandoned in favor of self-built houses. The causes of these failures are not always understood, but some have been related to the failure of designers to accommodate religious beliefs and practices.

Of course, the inhabitants of a house or apartment built with no knowledge of its possible religious function can modify it or use it despite its lack of specific religious features. In modern apartments in Athens, urbanized villagers continue many of their traditional religious rituals. However, opportunities to generate architectural form may be lost by designers who are ignorant of such activities. Full knowledge of the ritual life of the people who will occupy a certain building will provide opportunities to celebrate that ritual life through architectural articulation.

A second issue raised here has to do with the houses in our secular society. In Greece, the traditional house and household is strongly tied to a central religious institution, reinforcing community cohesion. In secular society, where individualism is a dominant ideology, the house is an island. Does discarding sacred ritual and its associated elements from the domestic environment reflect the dissolution of social and communal bonds? Is the loss of ritual a necessary concomitant of secularization, or are there secular activities with qualities similar to rituals in traditional societies? What are the major events in the turn of the seasons or in our daily or weekly lives, and how are these expressed in our houses? What activities do we share with others which generate a sense of community? Are we living in a period when new traditions are being formulated? Today we seldom make explicit the underpinnings of our secular lives. Rituals that structure life for individuals and provide social identity and social cohesion are only implicitly and incompletely expressed in our architecture. Knowledge and awareness of the richness of traditional ritual and the sacred aspects of dwellings and their architectural expression can provide a glimpse of what might be.

REFERENCE NOTES

1. The research in Eressos, located on the island of Lesbos in the eastern Aegean, was carried out in 1977-1979 and 1981 by the authors, an architect and an anthropologist. The study in Epidaurus, a coastal village in the Argolid, was carried out by the authors with the help of students in architecture and anthropology field courses during the summer of 1987.

2. Lord Raglan, *The Temple and the House* (New York: W.W. Norton & Co., 1964), pp. 1-7. However, his thesis that the very origin of the house is the temple does not seem plausible.

3. E. Pavlides and J. Hesser, "Vernacular Architecture in its Social Context," in Setha Low and Erve J. Chambers, eds., *Current Perspectives on Housing and Culture* (Philadelphia: University of Pennsylvania Press, 1989); E. Pavlides, "Vernacular Architecture in its Social Context. A Case Study of Eressos, Greece" (Architecture Ph.D. thesis, University of Pennsylvania) (Ann Arbor: University Microfilms, 1985).

4. E. Pavlides, "Architectural Change in a Vernacular Environment. A Case Study of Eressos, Greece," in *Environmental Change/Social Change* EDRA 16 (1985), pp. 57-65; E. Pavlides and J. Hesser, "The Influence of Women's Roles on House Form and Decoration in Eressos, Greece," in Jill Dubisch, ed., *Women in Greece: New Perspectives on Traditional and Gender and Power in Rural Greece* (Princeton: Princeton University Press, 1986).

5. It is interesting that religious affiliation took precedence over language in determining ethnic identity. Turkish speaking Christians were considered to be Greek, and vice versa.

6. J. du Boulay, *Portrait of a Greek Mountain Village* (Oxford: Clarendon Press, 1974), pp. 51-52.

7. Boulay, *Portrait*, p. 102.

8. Animal sacrifice at the foundation of a house may have pre-Christian origins. On the island of Lesbos, at a location still called by its pre-Christian name "Taurus" (Bull), a bull is sacrificed annually in a ceremony which involves the sprinkling of its blood and the giving of a blessing by a Christian priest. The pre-Christian nameplace of the location suggests that this ceremony is also pre-Christian.

9. Raglan, *The Temple and the House*, pp. 17-21.

10. *Ibid.*, pp. 23, 24.

11. The *iconostassi* at Mystra are the oldest surviving in Greece. The *iconostassi* at Mystra were little edicules with an arch and a triangular pediment above the arch supported by two columns. A. Orlandos, "Mystras," in *Arheion Byzantinon Mnimion Ellados* 3 (1937), p. 114.

12. Pavlides, "Vernacular Architecture."

13. Raglan, *The Temple and the House*, pp. 10, 79.

14. *Ibid.*, pp. 11, 78.

15. *Ibid.*, p. 10.

16. du Boulay, *Portrait*, p. 54.

17. Raglan, *The Temple and the House*, pp. 9-10.

18. du Boulay, *Portrait*, p. 18.

19. E. and R. Blum, *Health and Healing in Rural Greece* (Stanford: Stanford University Press, 1965), p. 131.

20. *Ibid.*, p. 68.

All photos are by the author unless otherwise indicated.

SITING AND GENERAL ORGANIZATION OF TRADITIONAL KOREAN SETTLEMENTS

SANG HAE LEE

This chapter investigates traditional settlements and dwellings found in contemporary but traditional rural areas of Korea. The siting and general organization of these dwellings and settlements will be examined from the point of view of the presiding ideas and guiding principles of traditional Korean domestic architecture. The study concerns the way in which Koreans have developed traditional ideas of how to site and organize their settlements, and how a socio-cultural symbolism reflecting societal norms and cultural entities has accumulated over many generations.

The aim is to demonstrate that the siting and organization of traditional Korean settlements are symbolic, and that they exhibit characteristics of order, place-definition, location and structure. These qualities contribute to the idea of settlement control as a form of cultural setting, and result in the identification of the villagers with the village and the house in such a way that they refer to them as "ours" and "home," respectively.

The chapter consists of two parts. The first deals with some aspects of the siting and organization of Korean settlements at the village level. The second discusses the same aspects at the level of the individual dwelling -- that is, at the level of the inner structure of the settlement. This chapter does not involve a detailed study of

F I G U R E 1. An example of a traditional farming village in Korea.

variations among settlements or dwellings in different regions of Korea.

RURAL FARMING VILLAGES IN KOREA

Mountains may well be the dominant element of the Korean landscape, and farming villages in rural areas are mostly located at the foot of sloping hills or in mountain valleys.[1] The villages nestle midway between open rice paddies and sloping tracts of dry fields, with mountains or hills in the background. Usually a well sited village faces south, is surrounded by two projecting branches of the mountain behind it, and is served by a watercourse gently flowing in front of it. In between the village and a small mound, which usually lies beyond the watercourse, lie broad fields of rice through which the watercourse runs. Access to the village is usually possible by way of winding paths through the fields. A village with such features is described as being well protected by mountain ridges and provided with a watercourse nearby (FIG. 1).

Such siting and organization reveal certain self-regulating characteristics. The village, like the basic ideas of the Korean world view, is imbued with the belief that man cannot be thought of apart from nature. In essence, the siting embodies a feeling for harmony with nature considered by the villagers to be appropriate and propitious for dwelling. The particular siting of a village is also intimately related to siting principles which have been espoused through history. The siting is the result of collective necessities that reflect larger societal and cultural collaboration.

VILLAGE SITING AND *FENG-SHUI*

Among the better-known ancient principles for siting and organizing a village is the traditional architectural theory termed *feng-shui*. Literally "wind and water," this term is generally translated into English as "geomancy." *Feng-shui* is a traditional art and science which deals with the formation of the landscape and the evaluation and selection of sites for settlements and dwellings for the living and the dead. It is also a traditional theory of architecture.[2] It was developed in China, and it first diffused to Korea around the middle or the end of the Silla Dynasty (57 B.C.-A.D. 935).[3]

The theoretical basis for *feng-shui* is that man is under the control of *ch'i*, the cosmic vital breath prevalent in the heavens and on earth.[4] Traditionally it is believed that the current of *ch'i* and its presence in certain places on earth are visibly linked to the geographical features of the landscape. For this reason, *feng-shui* mainly concerns how to find a site for villages or dwellings where the *ch'i* is substantial, and how to properly treat the *ch'i* in establishing a village or dwelling. If these things are not done properly, it is believed that the destiny of man in relation to the site will be adversely affected.

The proper application of *feng-shui* is thought to be achieved when the village site is surrounded by mountain ridges on three sides in a graceful curve so that the ends of mountain ridges gently turn to face each other with a watercourse nearby.[5] If a site satisfies these conditions, it is considered auspicious. The most important concerns in *feng-shui* are the geographical features and orientation of the site, and the layout of important architectural elements on it. At the village level, *feng-shui* involves relating the organization of the village to the nearby hills, streams and fields.

For the most part *feng-shui* was widely accepted in Korea and remained unchallenged until modern times. A geographical book entitled *Taengni-ji*, written by Yi Chung-hwan (1690-1752), demonstrates this fact. In this book Yi gives an account of four important factors governing the selection of a favorable village site:

> In general, for the selection of a site for human settlement, the feng-shui condition of the site should be considered first, then its economic condition, followed by the traits of the people's minds, and finally its natural scenery. If the site defects one of these important factors, it will not be a favorable one.[6]

Among these factors, the *feng-shui* condition is especially important. Yi further describes it as follows:

> How should the feng-shui condition of a site be examined? First, observe the mouth of the watercourse, then the features of the field, the forms of the mountains, the color of the earth, the availability of water, and finally the facing mountain and watercourse.[7]

The above description is associated with certain practical concerns. The *feng-shui* of a site is related to climate control and spatial effect. The extent to which the climate can be controlled and spatial effects achieved depends on the size if the site, which is directly related to the "features of the field." The third and sixth points of consideration, the forms of the surrounding mountains and the facing mountain and the facing watercourse, are associated with scenery. Finally, the color of the earth and the availability of water are associated with ecological aspects related to good harvest and irrigation (FIG. 2).

When it is located at the foot of a hill or mountain, a village does not occupy good farmland, but it does have good water supply and natural drainage, and it is protected from the reach of floods. In

F I G U R E 2.
Schematic representation of the
traditional Korean farming
village.
A) trees, B) vegetable gardens,
C) village settlements,
D) public space and entrance
to a village, E) rice paddies;
1) main mountain,
2) facing mountain,
3) mountain on the left,
4) mountain on the right,
5) outer facing mountain,
6) watercourse,
7) watermouth,
8) outer watermouth,
9) path; a) devil posts and
entrances to a village domain,
b) spirit tree,
c) totem pole,
d) village shrine.

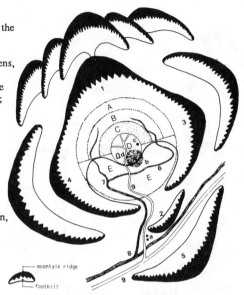

addition, the hill behind the village provides a grove of trees for
shade and firewood. On a slope above the watercourse are dry
fields for vegetable cultivation, and at the edges of the valley, in
the field in front of the village, and beyond the watercourse are
rice paddies which need to be irrigated. Thus it can be said that on
a practical level the basic structure of a Korean village sited
according to *feng-shui* embodies a distinct system of peasant
farming.

Since the village is sited at the foot of a hill, its temperature during
the summer is relatively cool due to the shade of trees and cool
winds that blow from the lower valley to the summit of the hill.
Conversely, during the winter the village is sheltered from the
chilly north wind by the mountain behind it, and the houses enjoy
good sunshine because they face south. The aspects of village
siting show the ecological soundness of *feng-shui*.[8] A village that
is thus sited within a well-ordered ecological system assures that
its inhabitants will be able to take full advantage of the natural
landscape.

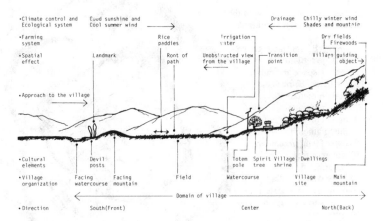

F I G U R E 3. Schematic representation of various aspects of village space alignment.

ORGANIZATION OF VILLAGE SPACE AND CULTURAL LANDSCAPE

In addition to examining how village siting and organization is related to the *feng-shui* principle, it is of great significance to examine architectural elements within the village. An understanding of the relation of these elements to traditional culture and values can provide a better understanding of the attitude toward the organization of village space. Along with various local conventions, these traditional elements constitute the village as a unit of life and give villagers a sense of belonging, intimacy and unity. For discussion of this aspect this chapter will examine several important architectural objects or landmarks found in many traditional villages (FIG. 3).[9]

In general at the outer approach to a village there is a pair of male and female shamanistic devil posts called *changseung*. These are thought to guard villagers against evil spirits. As a tutelary landmark of the village, the posts implicitly indicate its boundary. Beyond this boundary access to the village is usually by way of a winding path. At the very entrance to the village there is almost always a towering spirit tree. Beneath this tree villagers meet to talk and gossip. This is, in a sense, the village *agora*. Here, and at a pavilion nearby, people enjoy their leisure time, talking over communal affairs and watching the comings and goings of others.[10] Although there are variations among villages, the village annual ritual is usually performed under or in the vicinity of this tree in the first month of the lunar calendar. This ritual protects the villagers and their domestic animals from disasters and insures a bountiful harvest for the coming year. Near this area there is a village shrine called the *dangjip* where the villagers perform a ritual for the well-being of their village. Enshrined here is the tablet of the earth god, the guardian deity of the village, who governs the fertility of the soil. In some cases near the village shrine stands a totem pole called the *sotdae* around which villagers perform rituals and dance. These religious objects and landscape elements, as well as the rituals performed by the villagers, are the means by which the villagers promote friendship among themselves and create a sense of oneness. This in turn cultivates a strong sense of solidarity.[11]

Awareness of the association of cultural landscape elements with the sense of solidarity allows a better understanding of spatial organization in the village. To an outsider the majority of rural farming villages in Korea may look disordered and featureless. Nonetheless, when the siting principles of *feng-shui* and the cultural landscape on which they are formed are understood, the villages reveal a persistent and enduring organization. From this organization as it appears in many variations can be generalized an ideal norm for the organization of villages.

From a village's boundary, marked by the devil posts, many levels of spatial progression and transition are present. The symbolic transformation of cultural landmarks into architectural objects also occurs within a village. In other words, the landscape and the environment of the village, associated with *feng-shui* and cultural landmarks, provide comprehensive cues for understanding a village's spatial organization. The basic structure of the village domain has four stages of rhythmic progression: first, the introduction to the village; second, the development and elucidation of the spatial system; third, the climactic transition point that includes pre- and post-climax stages; and fourth, the conclusion and summing up of the progress, and the beginning of the next stage of progression from the inside of the village to the inside of the house, where the same four levels are repeated. The levels of progression constitute a spiritual experience for the villagers.[12]

The layout of the village domain is itself the visual world. Physically, there are no village boundaries or edges. At the entrance to the village, there is simply a pair of village posts to greet the oncomer. More than anything, these posts mark the point of entrance to the village. Once through the entrance, one feels a sense of enclosure. But the sense of space and the view beyond the entrance is merely a mental image prompted by the awareness of having passed an indication of entrance. This description points out the richness of the sense of introduction to the village domain. After passing the entrance, one follows a meandering path which seems relatively long, and the fact that the village itself is not within one's range of vision makes one feel tired. This draws attention to the notion that one's passage involves a process of spatial development up to a transition point where the whole village scene suddenly comes into view. At this point the sense of tiredness melts away.

Through the stages of passage to the village one experiences several spatial intervals (FIG. 4). These intervals provide a sense of the differentiation of space in the village domain as well as the sequence of space from one interval to the next, from one place to another. This sequence of space is heightened at the place where the towering spirit tree and village shrine are located. Here the village spatial system is clarified, and the whole aspect of village organization is grasped. This sequential effect provided by the village space can be ascribed to a well-defined landscape, physical and cultural. This is dictated by the principles of *feng-shui* and by the placement of cultural landmarks at the transitional places. Thus it can be said that cultural landmarks play a role in the organization of the village domain.

F I G U R E 4. An example of a pair of devil posts as the entrance to a village domain.

SYMBOLISM IN VILLAGE SITING AND ORGANIZATION

It is next important to briefly outline ways village organization can be symbolically analyzed. The cultural landmarks included in the layout of the village convey the idea of hierarchical organization. In other words, the cultural landmarks derive from their relationship to each other a total symbolic import which needs to be examined within the wider context of the village landscape.

The characteristics of sequence result from the practice of *feng-shui* and village rituals. The cultural landmarks nearer the center of the village are more strongly related to the important rituals of the villagers. Like the ritual aspect of village organization, village space is experienced progressively from the outside to the inside. Placement of ritual elements at the transitional points increases the awareness of the village's spatial qualities. Thus the cultural landmarks and landscape features encountered during the passage give a sense of place at the micro-level, of the village. At the macro-level the peak of the mountain behind the village acts as a spatializing, guiding object for those outside the village.

In summary, the sequential spatial alignment of the village includes direction, route of path, landmarks, sense of place and landscape features. The landscape of the village is not simply an object which happens to be there for the enjoyment of the villagers. Familiar landmarks allow villagers to identify with the content of the village; that is, they allow villagers to know they are in it and of it. This demonstrates a progression from the functional to the symbolic or cultural, and leads to a matter-of-fact perception of the environment and landscape. In a sense, it can be maintained that the cultural or non-material aspects of village life are partially associated with the physical appearance of the village. In other words, the ecological perspective and spatial organization of the village, related to *feng-shui*, are juxtaposed with the cultural landscape of the village. Within the context of the village, dwellings are deliberately placed.

DWELLING ORGANIZATION AND *FENG-SHUI*

The selection of an appropriate site for a dwelling and the location of dwelling elements are also mostly based on the principles of *feng-shui*. First, if the landforms and objects around the house site satisfy *feng-shui*, then the directional conditions of the site are verified. After that, the sitting and facing direction of the dwelling within the site is determined. The *feng-shui* in association with the sitting and facing direction is believed to create harmony and balance with the surrounding landscape. After deciding the proper sitting and facing direction, the house size and building layout are determined. Thereafter, locations of the important house elements are decided. This process must include consideration of the householder's *feng-shui* -- a matter of fate-determination according to his birth year. It also entails a description of the type of dwelling as well as the location of the dwelling site best suited to the individual concerned.

The *feng-shui* of the dwelling places utmost importance on the location of the main entrance gate. For this reason the first thing to be decided is the direction and location of this gate. According to *feng-shui* belief, the auspicious *ch'i* in the air flows into the house only through the gate doorway. Thus, the gate needs to be located so as to maximize the reception of *ch'i* and to accommodate the fate-determination factor of the householder. For example, if the householder was born in the year 1988, then a gate located in the southeast would be favorable. Thereafter, locations of the other house elements are decided in relation to the gate direction.

In particular the facing directions of the principle room and the fire hole of the kitchen range are determined in relation to the gate direction. This consideration, in fact, involves arranging house elements into two categories. East, southeast, south and north make one category, while northeast, northwest, west and southwest make another.[13] If the gate direction is assigned to the southeast, then the directions of the principle room and the fire hole should be either east, south or north to be of the same category, hence auspicious. This method of determining the location, orientation and arrangements of important house elements implies a certain ritualistic attitude.

In actuality the classification into two categories is a method of controlling the various *feng-shui* dimensions. Different locations of gates, principle rooms and kitchens distinguish one house from another so that each house can have its own significance. Thus, the location of the gate, principle room or kitchen is meaningful only in relation to the whole structure of the house, providing a holistic orientation to the entire house configuration. Furthermore, a holistic house configuration gives house elements a sense of belonging and expresses the idea of location control. Hierarchically different levels of elements are ordered into a whole, and the house configuration is felt as harmonious oneness.

HOUSE ORGANIZATION AND SOCIAL NORMS

From the moment the dwelling-type is settled upon by consideration of *feng-shui*, the dwelling begins to distinguish itself from nature. As soon as the dwelling structure is conceptually acceptable, the dwelling begins to occupy itself with mundane matters such as the governing social norms of family regulation and the teachings of Confucianism. The *feng-shui* principle, and its expression in the planning of a dwelling, will bring about a completed whole system through the control of Confucian ethics.

By building social norms into the plan of a dwelling and adjusting them to the *feng-shui* principle of the house, the dwelling becomes more meaningful and understandable. Together *feng-shui* and Confucianism establish certain underlying rules of architectural formation that reflect a way of domestic life. Some aspects of these notions will now be examined based on typical examples of house plans in the southern part of the Korean peninsula.

The traditional dwellings of Korea are usually composed of a couple of buildings around courtyards.[14] The size and number of the buildings depend on the social status and wealth of the householder. The buildings consist of the inner house (or main building) for women, the side quarters in front of it for children, the outer house (or annex) which is the living space for the householder and the reception quarters for male guests, and the servants' quarters. These pieces may be either connected to or detached from each other. Within the enclosure of these buildings and the walls connecting them are courtyards which serve different purposes and functions.

The servants' quarters are usually located at the outer part of the house complex, with the main gate to the house attached to them. The courtyard in front of the servants' quarters is called the *haenglang madang*, or courtyard for the servants, and access to the house is possible through this courtyard. Next to the servants' quarters stands the outer house. It's size and form are indications of the householder's social status and wealth. The courtyard in front of it is called the *sarang madang*, or courtyard for the master of the house. Next to it, in the innermost section of the grounds, is the inner house. The courtyard in front of it is called the *anmadang*, or inner courtyard. Visitors, excluding females and relatives, are not permitted to enter this space.

Variations in the layout of buildings and courtyard spaces are made according to the content of family life, which is mostly subject to the rigid regulations of Confucian ethics. Family members in rural farming villages of Korea are generally grouped hierarchically, the head householder at the top, followed by his spouse and children, the spouse of their eldest son, their children, and finally dead ancestors. The ethics of Confucianism hold that the segregation of men and women, the hierarchy of old and young, and ancestor worship are the most important aspects of family life. The importance placed on adhering to these regulations is reflected in the planning and arrangement of the house complex. Confucian regulations have greatly influenced traditional spatial use of the house.

In accordance with the regulation governing segregation of men and women, the inner chambers are mostly for females, while the areas near the outer house are for males and servants. Thus the arrangement of rooms as well as the overall house plan are related to social regularities of Confucianism within the context of the house *feng-shui*.[15] From the outside of the house through the outer courtyard to the inner courtyard and the women's quarters, the room arrangement takes into account the occupants and the use to which the space will be put, providing a diagram for a way of life.[16]

In addition, as required for ancestor worship, a building for the ancestral shrine is located at the most sacred place within the house grounds: the innermost section of the house site. One reason for this is that enshrinement is carried out by male descendants of the family, and traditionally the shrine has been located in the householder's quarters directly opposite them. For example, if the householder's quarters are in the southeast corner of the complex -- that is, near the gate -- the shrine is placed in the northeast corner of the house grounds.

Within this frame of social norm, the inner structure of the dwelling is planned. In this method of arrangement Confucian ethics are coordinated with the house *feng-shui*. For example, if the sitting location of a house is to the north of the site and its facing direction is south, then the northernmost part of the dwelling will be the inner chambers for women so as to satisfy the above-mentioned Confucian regulation. The proper location for the principle room of the house is selected from one of the northern directions according to the house *feng-shui*.

All these aspects can be shown in diagrams of typical dwelling arrangements (FIG. 5). Among the different arrangements, even the organization of a single-building dwelling complies with these aspects. For example, the first drawing in Figure 5 shows a house with two bedrooms, a living room with a wooden floor called *maru*,[17] and a kitchen. It is used and arranged in accordance with the ethics of Confucianism and the house *feng-shui*. After establishing a gate direction, one of the two bedrooms is designated the principle room. Once the direction of this room is decided, the kitchen and the living space are attached to the sides of it and the location of the remaining room is assigned. Thus a principle room for women and another room for men and male guests are established that satisfy the Confucian regulation governing segregation of sexes in the house.

As seen above, the projection or transformation of Confucian ethics and house *feng-shui* into the organization of the house determines basic structural relationships even for the simplest structure of the dwelling. In particular it can be found that the regulation of Confucian ethics and the principles of house *feng-shui* are increasingly well consolidated and ordered as one progresses up the social scale from the basic structure of the commoner to the complex house of a person from the upper reaches of society (FIGS. 6,7).

HOUSE DEITIES WITHIN DOMESTIC SPACE

The dwelling space itself is considered a sacred place, thought to be guarded by deities. The house deities are related to objects of home faith. Representatives of these guardian deities are Songju-nim, T'oju-taegam, Chowang-shin and Sam-shin.[18]

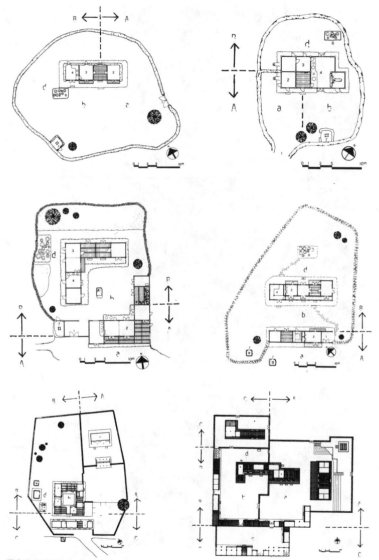

F I G U R E 5. Examples of typical traditional house plans in Korea. A) male quarters, B) female quarters, C) servants' quarters; 1) entrance gate, 2) outer chamber (house), 3) inner chamber (house), 4) kitchen, 5) ancestor shrine, 6) soy-jar terrace, 7) privy; a) outer courtyard, b) inner courtyard, c) courtyard for servants, d) back yard.

FIGURE 6.
An example of a
commoner's house
with a thatched roof.

FIGURE 7.
An example of the
inner quarters from a
house belonging to a
person from the upper
reaches of society.

Songju-nim is a guardian deity of the house, family, and especially the head of the family (FIG. 8). He is treated as the family deity of health and peace, and thus is also called Ant'aek-shin, the deity

FIGURE 8.
An example of
Songju-nim.

who brings peace to the house. He is considered the highest deity of the traditional dwelling, therefore the altar where Songju-nim is enshrined is located on the ridge beam across the ceiling of the living space, *maru,* of the house. Since the main hall belongs to men, especially to the house master, the Songju-nim is dedicated to it.

T'oju-taegam is the protector and overseer of the building grounds (FIG. 9). This deity is thought to bestow wealth and prosperity on the home, and for this reason T'oju-taegam is thought to occupy the foundation of the home and is often identified as the deity of the housewife.[19] It is deified in the inner courtyard or in the backyard near the soy-jar terrace and the kitchen. The shrine is enclosed by a straw-covered hut about two or three feet in height. Inside the enclosure is a small jar containing new crops.

Chowang-shin is the guardian deity of the kitchen and fire. This deity is thought to control the life and safety of the family. Since the fortune of a family is considered to be symbolically related to the fire flame, the kitchen is regarded as the place where Chowang-shin is enshrined. This particular deity is dedicated in a small bowl filled with water located in the indentation of the wall of the kitchen range. Every morning before sunrise the housewife replaces the water in the bowl with rightly drawn water.

Sam-shin is the female deity of procreation and the protector of children. Since the inner chamber of the house belongs to women

F I G U R E 9. An example of T'oju-taegam near the soy-jar terrace.

and children, it is here that Sam-shin is dedicated. She is enshrined in a paper bag or cloth pouch often hung on the wall. Inside the bag is money or rice, and the bag is often covered with a triangular-shaped hat called a *kokkal*.

As seen above, the deities residing in the dwelling are related to the fundamental use of dwelling space. This fact reveals that the main hall, the inner chamber, the outer space around the inner chamber, and the kitchen are essential in the traditional Korean house. Furthermore, it demonstrates that the traditional belief system of Korea and the Confucian regulation of house life complement each other, together forming a unique organizational system within the dwelling. These are adjusted within the larger context of the house *feng-shui*.

SUMMARY AND INTERPRETATION

Certain points concerning the siting and organization of traditional Korean settlements have been made. First, favorable siting of the village is attained in accordance with *feng-shui* principles.

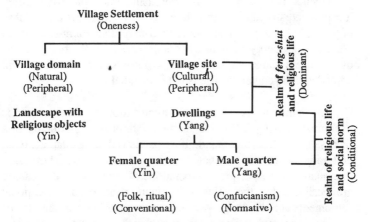

F I G U R E 10. Diagram of the ideas behind the organization of traditional Korean settlements.

Second, the site with good *feng-shui* corresponds well to the peasant farming system and ecological aspects of village organization. Third, the religious elements related to village community life constitute an important cultural landscape within the village domain. Fourth, the demarcation of the village site with *feng-shui* features and ritual objects creates a sense of territory and place. Fifth, the cultural landmarks of the village domain are ordered so as to create hierarchical progress of space from the outer world to the village. Sixth, the selection of the house site, its orientation and the location of important house elements are mostly decided by house *feng-shui*. Seventh, the selection of the house category and the location of the house elements reinforce the domestic order and provide the internal organization of the dwelling. Eighth, the planning of the dwelling is further determined by certain social regularities such as Confucian ethics. Ninth, traditional belief systems related to domestic life are incorporated into the use of domestic space. Finally, the notions of *feng-shui*, religion and social norm are incorporated into the symbolic meaning of the traditional settlement and conceptually integrate the settlement as an organic whole (FIG. 10).

In brief, the siting and organization of traditional Korean settlements manifest ideas of symbolism, order, place-definition, location and structure. The difference between the presiding ideas of *feng-shui*, religion and Confucianism is that *Feng-shui* as an architectural theory regulates and substantializes the organization of settlement plans, while the notions of religion and Confucianism adjust how the content of life is to be included.

On one hand, if the siting and organization of a settlement is examined as a physical object, it is configurated by a principle or a theory. On the other hand, if it is viewed as a man-centered cultural context, it is dominated by symbolic meaning. This means that shared and structured associations of principle and meaning are designed for the siting and organization of the traditional settlements and dwellings.[20] This aspect contributes to the idea of settlement control, which makes it culturally acceptable, and result in villagers being able to consider their villages and houses as "ours" and "home," respectively.

It can be maintained that the ideas and certain key elements behind the settlement organization, and the way inhabitants are believed to express this organization, cause the product of traditional Korean settlements to be a form of cultural setting. They provide the process of dwelling at certain locations on the earth and in the house, and hence embody symbols of meaning and conventional understandings. Thus, this interpretation of the siting and general organization of traditional Korean settlements offers an inside view, one which is relevant to Korean traditional architecture.

REFERENCE NOTES

The research and field survey of the villages for this paper were made possible by a grant from the Korean Science and Engineering Foundation (KSEF). The author gratefully acknowledges the KSEF support. The author is also grateful to Mr. Hwang Heonman for his permission to use photographs of FIGURES 1, 4, 6, 9, 10 and 11. Other photographs and drawings are by the author.

1. For an introductory reference work on Korea written in English, see Patricia M. Bartz, *South Korea* (Oxford: Clarence Press, 1972).
2. The whole perspective of *feng-shui* is complex. In theory it rests on the natural philosophy and cosmology of China and Korea. *Feng-shui* is the Chinese word. The Korean word is *pungsu*. For an in-depth explanation, see Sang Hae Lee, "*Feng-shui*: Its Context and Meaning" (Ph.D. dissertation, Cornell University, 1986).
3. The historical development of *feng-shui* in Korea is discussed in Hong-key Yoon, *Geomantic Relationship Between Culture and Nature in Korea* (Taipei: The Orient Cultural Service, 1976), pp. 257-275.
4. It is difficult to find an equivalent English word for *ch'i*. *Ch'i* is usually translated as cosmic breath, ether, matter-energy, vital force, and so on.
5. These geographical features of *feng-shui* are analogically represented by the four numinous superbeings: the azure dragon on the left, the white tiger on the right, the red bird in the front and the black tortoise in the back.
6. Yi Chung-hwan, *Taengni-ji*, *pokgo* section. It is believed that the book was finished around 1750.
7. *Ibid.*
8. The ecological aspect of the *feng-shui* system is examined in E.N. and Marja L. Anderson, *Mountains and Water: Essays on the Cultural Ecology of South Coastal China* (Taipei: The Orient Cultural Service, 1973), pp. 41-55, 127-146.
9. Many aspects of village life in Korea are cited in Internal Cultural Foundation, ed., *Korean Society* (Seoul: The Sisayoungosa Pub., 1982). For a more detailed discussion, see *A Report of Comprehensive Survey on Korean Folklore* (*Han'guk Minsok Chonghap Chosa Pogoso*), Series I-XVII (Seoul: The Bureau of Cultural Properties, 1969-1987).
10. The existence of these elements in traditional villages of Korea has already been noted by Homer B. Hulbert, *The Passing Korea* (first edition, 1906; reprinted edition, Seoul: Yonsei University Press, 1969), pp. 249-250.
11. For a discussion of village rituals and customs in Korea, see T'aek-gyu Kim, "History of Village Customs in Korea" ("Han'guk Purak Kwanseupsa"), in *An Outline of Korean Cultural History* (*Han'guk Munhwasa Taegye*), Vol. IV (Seoul: Korea University, National Cultural Research Institute, 1971), pp. 637-766.
12. It is interesting to note that a similar progression of four levels forms the foundation of a classical Korean poetic form known as the *sijo*.
13. The theory of house categorization can be explained by the *yin-yang* theory. For a detailed explanation, see Sang Hae Lee, "Feng-shui: Its Context and Meaning," pp. 302-319.
14. For an understanding of traditional Korean domestic architecture, see Shin Yung Hoon, *The Traditional House in Korea* (*Han'guk ui Sallimjip*) (Seoul: Yulhwadang, 1986); Chu Nam-ch'ul, *The Korean Residential Architecture* (*Han'guk Chut'aek Konch'uk*) (Seoul: Iljisa, 1985).
15. The consideration of *feng-shui* topography is also applied analogically to the house structure. For example, the side quarters on the left and right of the courtyard are considered the azure dragon and the white tiger respectively. The front quarters, located in front of the house complex, are considered the red bird, while the main quarters to the back are the black tortoise.
16. For the social status of women in the traditional society of Korea, see *Woman of the Yi Dynasty, Studies on Korean Women's Series I* (Seoul: Sookmyung Women's University, Research Center for Asian Women, 1986). The seclusion of

women from the outer world in traditional society of Korea had been observed by Isabella Bird Bishop, *Korea and Her Neighbours* (first edition, 1897; reprinted edition, Seoul: Yonsei University Press, 1983), p. 340.

17. There are two kinds of floors in traditional Korean architecture, *maru* and *ondol*. *Maru* is a wooden floor, where one side of the room is usually open to the air. *Ondol* is a floor finished by oil paper. It is heated through underground flues from a fire hole in the kitchen cooking stove.

18. For a discussion of house deities of Korea, see Yi Cong-yong, "Shamanistic Thought and Traditional Korean Homes," in *Korean Folklore*, Korean National Commission for UNESCO, ed. (Seoul: The Sisayongosa Pub., 1983), pp. 193-210. For a more detailed study on Korean folklore written in Korean, see Kim Kwangon, *Traditional House Styles in Korea (Han'guk ui Chugo Minsokji)* (Seoul: Minumsa, 1988).

19. The assignment of Songju-nim to the householder and T'ojutaegam to the housewife may be related to the *yin-yang* concept in Korea. *Yin* represents the earth that is related to the female, and its counterpart *yang* represents the heaven related to the male.

20. This idea is borrowed from Amos Rapoport, "Images, Symbol and Popular Design," in *Ekistics* 232 (March, 1975), p. 166.

SPEAKING TO AND TALKING ABOUT: MAORI ARCHITECTURE

MICHAEL LINZEY

When a New Zealand Maori orator, standing to speak on a *marae*, addresses the meeting house in the breath in which he addresses the assembled people, this may be taken as representative of a surprising comportment towards architecture by a traditional society. The Maori intuition that the *whare whakairo*, the carved house, is a living presence is richer than mere simile; it is beyond the idea of metaphor or representation in a European-educated sense. For the Maori, the house is not *like* an ancestor, it *is* the ancestor. In European-educated terms this may appear peculiar, nevertheless it constitutes a legitimate subject for phenomenological attention.

The Maori comportment of *speaking to* architecture is alien to European-educated ways of thinking. Europeans are permitted to speak to one another, but they may only *talk about* architecture. The respective linguistic comportments, speaking to and talking about, are evidence of distinctly different ways of seeing and understanding architecture.

This chapter tries to contradict the common racist myth that the architectural comportment of the Maori is more primitive, while the European-educated perception of objective profanity is more advanced. It argues, on the contrary, that Europeans are excluded by prejudice and linguistic prohibition from a potent world of architectural meaning. To gain access to some of the nourishing possibilities of indigenous architecture, it is necessary to confront impeding myths within the European-educated outlook, certain philosophical attitudes which prevent us from addressing architecture in its imaginative fullness.

PAPER TALK

This paper talks about a peculiar aspect of the New Zealand Maori dwelling experience: that Maori people directly address and include the carved house, the *whare whakairo*, in the rhetoric of tribal occasions and public gatherings, thus showing that a work of architecture is a living presence in their hearts. In ceremonial greeting, for example, when one group of people visit another on their traditional land, an orator will do several things. He will extend greetings to the land, the *marae*, lying before him; he will greet the house as an ancestoral presence standing on the land; he will acknowledge the ever-present mythical-spiritual world of Papa and Rangi, earth and sky; and only then will he address the people gathered together.

We cannot talk about this traditional phenomenon, remarkable as it is, without also acknowledging a certain tensioning and quickening of interest within the European-educated consciousness. The Maori comportment has survived within the predominantly European ambience of New Zealand life. It has survived despite the fact that nothing Maori do in modern New Zealand is isolated from the European majority culture, just as nothing European is isolated from the Maori presence. (Much as some New Zealanders might resist acknowledging it, New Zealand is bi-cultural.) Europeans, however, in the new world as in the old, do not speak to their houses or to architecture. Europeans are permitted to speak to one another, and some Europeans speak to God; but there is a tacit prohibition (it is not extreme to say, in Maori terms, that it is a *tapu*) against Europeans speaking to mere things for fear of looking ridiculous. (Dr. Dolittle was considered eccentric and amusing because he spoke to animals.)

European-educated interest in the Maori comportment of emotion and appreciativeness towards architecture is tensioned by a spirit of lamentation. We lament the loss of meaning in European architecture; some go so far as to say our architecture is dead. There is reason to suspect that this absence of meaning, this reduction in the living value of modern European architecture, stems from a prohibition that derives from the European-educated tradition itself.

While this chapter talks about a peculiarly Maori phenomenon, it also speaks to an anonymous international readership. (Is it not strange that in the European-educated world it is unacceptable to speak to architecture, yet it is completely appropriate for a mere text to speak to an invisible, possibly nonexistent audience?) Whatever the case, I presume that readers of this chapter are European-educated and that they are aware of how this sense of loss and lamentation has been brought to a fashionable pitch in the post-modern condition of intellectual and theoretical life. Lyotard, for example, portrays traditional societies as dominated by "grand narratives" -- traditional mythical legendary narratives that combine descriptive, normative and aesthetic elements, that legitimize social institutions and that serve as models for the inclusion of individuals into those institutions.[1] The European-educated tradition, on the other hand -- in particular the tradition of modern science -- purports to be purely descriptive, to have cut itself free from ethical, aesthetical and religious connotations. The purely descriptive language games of modern science generally set out to de-legitimize traditional narrative forms.

Specifically in relation to architecture, Perez-Gomez has traced the slow demise of "mytho-poetic" dimensions in European architecture as related to the crisis of modern science.[2] The principle of functionality can no longer be seen as a positive and sufficient attribute of modern architecture; it must be felt instead as an absence or lamentable loss, a setting aside of traditional mytho-poetic dimensions.

The richly carved and decorated elements of Maori architecture make many direct references to traditions, poems and myths, and must ultimately be comprehended in terms of the mytho-poetic dimensions of traditional life. This chapter will touch on some of these dimensions, by no means exhaustively. In particular, it will address Maori architecture in terms of the comportment of the orator, in terms of the peculiar image of an orator standing on the *marae* and speaking to the carved house.

This chapter attempts also to turn our observations onto ourselves. As we explore the mytho-poetical foundations of a Maori behavior, we must bear in mind those European-educated narratives that seem to underpin our own architectural behaviors. In this way we may gain understanding of our own cultural inhibition, our prohibition against speaking to architecture.

HUMAN METAPHOR IN ARCHITECTURE

The *whare whakairo* is often profusely decorated with human figures, both realistic and abstract. The carved house is in a sense designed to be spoken to. There is usually a carved headpiece, a *koruru*, at the apex of the gable to which speech is directed. And inside the house are carved *poupou*, or sideposts, and rafters painted with traditional patterns. The central line of posts supporting the ridge beam, and the ridge beam itself, are also carved with human and mythological forms. All this carved timber is no mere ornament added to the architecture, as it might be interpreted to be in a European sense. Usually the house itself is named for a specific ancestor and is, in its whole construction, the actual embodiment of that man or woman. The ridge beam is the ancestor's spine, the rafters are the ribs, the interior space is the belly, and the outstretched bargeboards, the *raparapa*, are the arms with fingers extended in greeting.

Te Tokanganui-a-noho is a *whare whakairo* standing at Te Kuiti in the central North Island (FIGS. 1,2). Perhaps the oldest, fully-carved meeting house in New Zealand not to be found in a museum, Te Tokanganui was built in 1874 and has since been relocated and partially rebuilt several times. The original architect was Te Kooti Rikirangi, an outstanding military and religious leader of the late

FIGURE 1. Te Tokanganui-a-noho, opened in 1874, stands today in the town of Te Kuiti. (S o u r c e : Anthropology Department, Auckland University.)

nineteenth century who was born on the East Coast and was forced for a time to seek asylum with the Maniapoto people. According to Phillipps, the house was presented to the Ngati Maniapoto in recognition of the hospitality they extended to Te Kooti during his enforced sojourn among them.[3] The house was originally named Rawaho-o-te-Rangi after an important tribal ancestor.

On the East Coast of New Zealand there is a story about Rua-te-pupuke, the man who first acquired the art of carving from Tangaroa, the god of the wild ocean. Tangaroa had kidnapped Rua's son, carried him away to his land under the sea, and there transfixed him upon the gable of his house. After a long search, Rua came to the house beneath the sea. He recognized his son in the carving and angrily set fire to the house, removing his son and several other carvings from its outside. There were carved figures inside the house as well, and they had the power to speak, but all of them were destroyed in the blaze. It is said that because Rua only took carvings from the outside of the house, carvings now cannot speak.

This founding narrative of the *whakairo* provides insight into how the Maori think, for to tell a story about why carvings do not speak seems to suggest that carvings might once have spoken. Anybody who has had the experience of sleeping a night "in the belly of an ancestor," surrounded by richly carved *poupou* and other fine works of Maori art will readily acknowledge the power this possibility presents to the imagination.

European architectural tradition also ascribes human character to houses in a number of ways. Le Corbusier, for example, clearly imprinted the stamp of his personality on his work. The Maison La Roche in Paris, an early work, contains his trademarks -- pilotis, ramps, roof gardens. Moreover, the controlled and measured spaces, in particular the picture gallery and the main entranceway, speak to us of him. Entering the house today, one almost feels his ghost stalking the empty spaces. But it is not exactly the experience of a haunted place that we describe when we use the word ghost; and it is not the presence of ghosts or phantoms, nor mere egotistical trademarks, that mark good architecture in the European tradition. We do not advocate that architects impose their private egos on their work as mere contrivance and idiosyncrasy. A building may genuinely haunt us and somehow persist in our imagination, so that many years later we may spontaneously and vividly recall its characteristic shape, detail or ambience. This remembrance comes upon us in the same way that we might fondly recall a much-loved or strongly-delineated person who has dwelled in our imagination and memory. When architecture becomes a person in this way, we also see the creative authority of the architect shining through like a family resemblance. Such architecture has human scale; it speaks to us at a number of levels simultaneously with some of the same richness as lively human dialogue.

European architecture's license to speak to us is strictly proscribed by certain rules of metaphor. Architecture speaks to us, but it can only do so metaphorically. (And we may not speak in turn to architecture, either metaphorically or in any other way.) Geoffrey Scott described architecture, particularly that of the Renaissance, in terms of "the universal metaphor of the human body." He

FIGURE 2.
Detail of a side
post, *amo*. The
predominant carving
style is Ngati Awa.
The carvers were
visitors to Te Kuiti
from tribal areas
further to the East.

wrote: "The tendency to project the image of our functions into concrete forms is the basis, for architecture, of creative design. The tendency to recognize, in concrete forms, the image of those functions is the true basis, in its turn, of critical appreciation."[4]

However, there is nothing in this very European-educated analysis of architectural humanism that would sanction speaking to architecture. Scott's project is rigorously proscribed by two typically European-educated barriers or fences -- one between metaphor and reality, the other between body and mind. The human functions spoken of by Scott are strictly confined to the bodily functions, and architecture is the transcription of the body's forms into forms of building. Architecture speaks to our body memory through the physical articulation of line, space and massing.

CAVES AND SHADOWS

Certain mytho-poetic imagery of the Maori will now be compared with similar or related figures in the tradition of European education so that we may perhaps draw closer to comprehending the apparently radical difference in the permitted comportments of Maori and European-educated people towards their respective architectures. This course is in line with that strand of post-modern thinking which redirects attention to the myths and metaphors, the grand narratives upon which all theories and philosophies appear to have been founded. The shaping power of grand narrative as primal image is as significant for European-educated conditions of thought as it is for Maori.

This attention to the mytho-poetic underpinning of a culture is by no means exclusively post-modern. Sir George Grey, Governor of New Zealand in 1845, wrote: ". . . I found that these chiefs, either in their speeches to me or in their letters, frequently quoted in explanation of their views and intentions fragments of ancient poems or proverbs, or made allusions which rested on an ancient system of mythology . . . ."[5] Grey soon perceived that he could neither successfully govern nor hope to effect conciliations with the Maori without first coming to terms with these myths and narratives, the paradigms of Maori social existence. Sir George may perhaps not have been quite as ready to acknowledge that similar primal imagery also underpins and informs European-educated views and intentions.

For example, our views about education are molded by Plato's well-known story of the cave. The peculiar affection we have for notions of transcendence, our readiness to adopt a two-world view about subjects as diverse as education, divinity and metaphysics, can be shown to presume upon this simple but evocative tale from the *Republic*, in which ordinary people lie enchained in a cave, and ordinary phenomena are somehow represented to them as shadows on a curtain. Education, according to Plato, draws people up out of this cave into the light of the sun. The sun, transcending the shadowy world of transitory and expedient appearances, symbolizes the form of the good; it is also *logos*, the second person of the Christian Trinity, reason, rationality and many other things.

Plato forced onto European education a predilection for a radically other world a two-world image of the cave wherein all is shadow and illusion, and the educated world that is animated by light and form. In doing so, he set up a massive disturbance within the course of European philosophy.[6]

In New Zealand there is another cave narrative altogether, which presents us with an opposite image of the place and aspirations of man. It is the story of Maui, the trickster, the thief of fire, the inventor of rope. It is, among other things, the story of how that invaluable commodity, rope, was first discovered. Maui is presented as already being outside the cave, already in the world of light, and, instead, it is the sun that is ensconced in a cave. Maui travelled with his brothers to the mouth of a cave on the eastern edge of the world out of which the sun would shortly set forth to take its daily course across the sky. The story goes that the sun had been misbehaving by travelling far too quickly across the sky, and that Maui set about to teach it a lesson. But first he had to show his brothers how to make rope. They learned how to plait flax fiber into stout, square-shaped ropes, *tuamaka*, how to plait flat ropes,*paharahara*, and how to spin round ropes.[7] With these they snared the sun, held it down and beat it severely so that it was subjugated to the will of man.

It is interesting to compare these two myths. As European-educated people, we believe we may only speak to transcendent entities, to other souls and to God. It offends our common sense to speak to architecture because architecture is not a sun-like thing. At different times in European history it would have been considered unreasonable, irrational, unenlightened or even unchristian to speak to an inanimate thing. The prohibition may be traced to the mythology of sun-worship, the myth of transcendence, the primal image of Plato's cave. In New Zealand Maori culture, whose grand narratives are altogether different, there is not this same prohibition against speaking to inanimate things.

The focus of the Maori on the primal image of Maui's invention and clever use of rope disturbs the traditional European-educated tendency to believe, or somehow accept the notion without really believing, in discrete categories of existence -- even to the extent of forcing a chasm of unknowing between forms and appearances. The Maori narrative attends instead to the reality of tension between categories; the Maori image attends to the weave and structure of rope itself.

Maui once tricked his brothers to take him fishing. With a hook made from an ancestors jaw-bone, and with a strong fishing line made, of course, from rope of his own invention, Maui managed to snare the door-sill of the house of Tonga-nui. He pulled upon his line and fished up the whole North Island of New Zealand, which is known to this day, poetically, as Te Ika a Maui, or Maui's fish.

It can be difficult for us to appreciate how powerful this primal image of Maui's rope may have been in neolithic everyday life.[8] In the days before there were reliable metals, there were only compressive, earth-bound structures in the Maori world. The exception were the tensile, fibrous kinds of things like ropes, woven mats, cloaks, fishing nets, eel traps and crayfish pots. Houses themselves in pre-European times derived structural identity from ropes called *tua whenua*. These were slung across the back of portal frames formed by pairs of *poupou* and *heke*, posts and rafters, and then tensioned with large wooden levers against the massive *tahuhu*, or ridge beam (FIG. 3). "The creaking of timbers was heard under the strain."[9]   The *tahuhu* and *pou tahuhu* must be massive in Maori house construction, because they must sustain the tension forces induced by the *tua whenua*. In the European colonial tradition of the light timber frame construction, and the Chicago balloon frame, the ridge board carries no con-

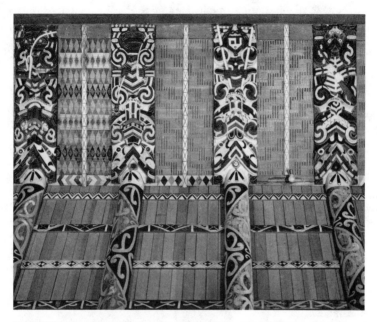

F I G U R E 3. An interior view of part of the side wall of the *whare* shows carved posts *(poupou)* alternating with panels of woven *tukutuku.* The second *poupou* from the right shows the mytho-poetic figure Maui holding two ropes, with one of which he has snared a Europeanized depiction of the sun god, Te Ra. The style of the carving, painting and weaving combines pre-European forms and Ringatu, or Christian, symbolism in a way that is characteristic of Te Huringa, the turning, or early European contact period. (S o u r c e : Anthropology Department, Auckland University.)

structional load whatsoever, and is present only to form the line of the roof. Structural integrity is achieved with steel nails instead of rope. It is instructive to recall how highly valued were metal nails as trade items in the first European contacts.

In the beginning of European imperial history, Alexander the Great announced his colonial intentions in a way that appears bizarre today, but which may have been more significant in his own time: he took up his bronze sword and cut the *gordios* knot. We note that Alexander was educated in the spirit of Platonic enlightenment by Aristotle himself.

In New Zealand, European-educated missionaries were not slow to class the Maori as benighted savages. The New Zealand mythos seems from our European point of view almost to have gone out of its way to *devalue* enlightenment. Maui and his brothers subjugated the sun when it misbehaved, travelling too quickly across the sky. And the New Zealand Maori version of the creation myth, when earth and sky were separated, differs subtly from that told in most places in eastern Polynesia. In most of the island groups, the primal father is called Atea, Expanse of Light, but in New Zealand he is known as Rangi, which simply and matter-of-factly means Sky.

We may also note that the Polynesian word *mana*, which means the power or virtue that a person acquires in the social weave and tension of family and kin group, does not translate exactly as "charisma" or "aura" just as the word rope does not translate as "an instrument of transcendence." The unique meaning of this Polynesian word, *mana*, is reflected in the considerable currency it has already achieved in European languages, certainly within New Zealand.

PHENOMENOLOGY OF DIALOGUE

The philosophical project to deconstruct Plato's two-world image of education, to debunk the cave metaphor, was begun by Aristotle.[10] It has been well in train since Galileo in the whole corpus of modern science. Phenomenology of dialogue directs attention in this regard to the constituting power of language and thought, and in particular it raises the issue of the constitutional difference between the linguistic comportments of speaking to and talking about. We proceed by the Husserlian method of *epoche*. We temporarily suspend whatever metaphysical presuppositions we might hold about the animacy or inanimacy, the transcendence or lack of transcendence of the other, and direct our attention instead to the linguistic structure of dialogue itself, the mode of address, the comportment by which the other is confronted. Martin Buber's radical observation sets the stage here: "if one deliberately sets out to talk about the other, then the other naturally takes on attributes of it-ness."[11] But when one sets out to speak to the other, then its "you-ness" is naturally disclosed. The comportment -- the way of seeing, addressing and understanding things -- is also the way things are constituted. These alternative comportments, speaking to and talking about, are not an irrevocable dichotomy, not an ontological chasm in the place of the old split between appearance and reality, light and shadow. The difference between speaking to and talking about is not a radical difference in the constitution of the vocalizing subject; nor is it a property inherent in the predicated object. It is a difference precisely and only in comportment, a property not of any particular person or thing but of the linguistic realm between two such people or things. They are different modes of address, poles of possible and actual meaning. Buber calls them "basic words."

Buber's basic words, "I-It" and "I-You," are linguistic comportments. But language cannot be divorced from thought and imagination. For in terms of the surface grammar of language alone, the words you and it are merely pronouns, equal in valence. But to talk about something is to see and comprehend it as an it, as a mere thing. To speak to something is to see and comprehend it as a person or as something personified. The constituting meaning of the pronouns, and in particular the significant difference in meaning between them, only appears after the pronouns are understood and experienced, when consciousness fleshes out the potent linguistic forms in active intuition.

One cannot experience the full weight of the comportment of speaking to unless one is prepared to listen to the other, to admit that something other demands to be recognized, and then to let oneself be told something by it.[12] Gadamer describes how the full value of speaking to is undercut by speaking down or up to someone. He emphasizes that speaking to is a comportment of equality. It can not be fully achieved when the other is treated as a means to a selfish end, as a tool that can be known and used, or when the dialectic of the relationship is used to "reflect oneself out," as for example when one claims to understand the other better than the other understands himself. The other then loses the immediacy with which he would otherwise make his claim.

Without this immediacy and equality, unless one is prepared also to listen, there cannot be a fully human relationship.

Theunissen identifies three formal features by which the comportment of talking about may be contrasted with speaking to.[13] Spatially, talking about is "perspectively ordered." The subject, I, is the midpoint of a constituted world; "it," "the other," is the sphere of having, centered on the subject. But speaking to is not centered spatially on the I, nor on the You; it is symmetrical and equal. A conversation is carried out precisely in the realm between two people, in a dimension that is equally accessible to both of them. Secondly, in social terms, talking about "secures for the human being the mastery of his essence." The other is determined; I determine. It is a product; I am the producer. It is the slave; I am the master. But speaking to, by contrast, is a relation of mutuality. There is no connotation of superordinacy or subordinacy. Theunissen identifies a third distinction, that to talk about something is to ensnare it in a "world project." The thing is mediated by a horizontal space with which a person surrounds objects in their objectification, a " . . . conceptuality that fixes beings with a determinate sense and orders them into the system of unified signs." But the comportment of speaking to is not constrained by this semiotic model, because although the I is separated from the other, they are not separated *"through the barrier of the meaning-instituted project."* You are not in general the signified term in speaking to.

This last point also reflects a difference in the way we denominate the third-person pronoun, as opposed to the second-person pronoun. "It" or "he" or "she" must in necessity stand in the place of the name of something; but "you" can remain unnamed. For a person to say "I love her," is to talk about someone. But who precisely is being talked about? We immediately demand to know. Who do I love? Name her! The sentence, "I love her," is almost meaningless without a name; the project is blatantly incomplete. But if instead a person says, "I love you," then the loved one's name becomes almost superfluous. To use the name in speaking to serves only to make the sentiment slightly more formal. However, not to use the name in talking about, to refuse to nominate what is being talked about, is deliberately to mystify a situation.

When a person talks about something, the name of that thing has to be readily and explicitly available to their consciousness. It is the that-ness of reference by which representation is achieved. They cannot honestly and legitimately talk about something; they must be immediately prepared to name it. But when they speak to someone, that person's name is submerged, interiorized, only tacitly beheld. Regardless of whether a person knows what another person's name is, they will hardly ever be forced to use it in speaking to them directly. Consequently, namelessness is no impediment in the comportment of speaking to, although it is in talking about.

There are many kinds of things -- strange things, unborn things, beautiful things, numinous things -- that we experience difficulty talking about, because talking about them requires us to name them, to fix them in the system of unified signs. In attempting to name them we may find that their very meaning dissolves or shifts awkwardly. In these situations it may be wrong to talk about a thing, for to do so requires us either to pretend to know its name or to misname it when it may be intrinsically unnameable. It is also highly inappropriate to blandly ignore these things, to turn our backs on them. A more appropriate and respectful comportment towards nameless things is to address them directly, to draw them into imaginative dialogue, to find out who they are by speaking to them. Speaking to is the one mode of address that does not demand an explicit name.

Speaking to, using the second person pronoun rather than the third, enables us to address a subject directly even though it may be nameless, even if it is unnameable by nature. Speaking to is a linguistic structure that is appropriate for an encounter with the Living Presence, because gods are also often unnameable. This is not to say that the other has to be nameless in order to be spoken to; speaking to may simply create the appropriate degree of respect and openness. The Maori meeting house bears the name of a tribal ancestor, and in ceremonial and other situations it may indeed be addressed by this name.   It is held in the deepest respect, veneration, affection, but it is not worshipped as a God.   When Maori people speak to their house, the house takes on a corresponding numinous quality -- the quality of the living presence of the ancestor, not the awful, unnameable, numinous quality of the Living Presence of God.

Of course a Maori also is free to talk about the meeting house. The peculiarly Maori comportment of speaking to architecture (which we are suggesting is only peculiar in the respect that it is not European-educated, not prohibited by the effaced mythology of sun-worship), does not preclude the Maori from talking about architecture in other circumstances.   (One might note that the quality of respect and the general tone of voice is different when a Maori talks about a *whare whakairo* than when he talks about European buildings. For example, a Maori elder at a *marae* work committee meeting might say that the meeting house needs a new coat of paint on the roof, or perhaps that "he would like" to be repainted.)

"This often-referred-to 'symbolism' [of the meeting house] is quite literal," wrote Austin. "But Maori attempts to explain 'in *pakeha* terms' their feeling for the *marae* . . . come out as either obscure expressions such as 'a symbol of *maoritanga* [Maoriness],' or 'being a Maori,' 'where I met my ancestors,' or apparent trivilities such as 'the food,' 'the people,' 'sleeping alongside my kin,' and so on."[14] But this apparent incompetence to talk about what is the central dimension of their own architecture is by no means peculiar to the Maori; it is not a cultural deficiency somehow concomitant with their demonstrated competence to speak to architecture. European-educated people too prove incompetent in this respect. The main cultural difference seems to be that European-educated people are also incompetent to speak to architecture.

Speaking to is a natural and a sensitive comportment with which we may address certain aspects of the human environment. It is a comportment that Maori use in everyday life in contemporary New Zealand to show respect for their architecture.   But in the European-educated view it appears very peculiar to speak directly to a building which we understand to be inanimate and unenlightened. We have suggested a possible explanation for this: Europeans are inhibited by a kind of intellectual *tapu* which stems from a founding myth of European education itself. It may or may not prove to be possible or even desirable for us to deconstruct this linguistic impediment, to lift the *tapu*, thus perhaps to enhance the European-educated comportment towards European architecture. But in contemporary New Zealand society such a program of philosophical deconstruction would be more than an academic exercise or a contribution to architectural theory. It might also prove a positive and necessary step towards forming a healthy pluralistic society.

REFERENCE NOTES

1. J.-F. Lyotard, *The Postmodern Condition* (Minneapolis: University of Minnesota Press, 1984).
2. A. Perez-Gomez, *Architecture and the Crisis of Modern Science* (Cambridge: The MIT Press, 1983).
3. W.J. Phillipps, "The Te Kuiti House," *Art in New Zealand* 10: 1 (1938), pp. 82-9.
4. G. Scott, *The Architecture of Humanism* (London: Methuen & Co., 1961), p. 213.
5. G. Grey, *Polynesian Mythology* (Christchurch: Whitcoulls, 1974).
6. "Presence disappearing in its own radiance, the hidden source of light, of truth, and of meaning, the erasure of the visage of Being -- such must be the insistent return of that which subjects metaphysics to metaphor. . . . The sensory sun, which rises in the East, becomes interiorized, in the evening of its journey, in the eye and the heart of the Westerner. He summarizes, assumes, and achieves the essence of man, 'illuminated by the true light'." J. Derrida, "White Mythology," in *Margins of Philosophy*, A. Bass, trans. (Brighton: The Harvester Press, 1982), p. 268.
7. Grey, *Polynesian Mythology*.
8. The Maori word for rope, *kaha*, also means strength, persistence, the line of hills and the boundary line of land, umbilical cord, line of ancestry, and various other things having to do with divination. See H.W. Williams, *A Dictionary of the Maori Language*, 7th Ed. (Wellington: New Zealand Government Printer, 1985).
9. Makereti, *The Oldtime Maori* (London: Victor Golancz, 1938).
10. "In opposition to the privileged ontological status that Plato accords to the idea, Aristotle emphatically asserts that the primary reality is the particular individual . . . but even so he remains within the framework of Plato's orientation towards the logoi." H.-G. Gadamer, *The Idea of the Good in Platonic-Aristotelian Philosophy*, P.C. Smith, trans. (New Haven and London: Yale University Press, 1986).

11. M. Buber, *I and Thou*, W. Kaufmann, trans. (Edinburgh: T. & T. Clark, 1970).
12. H.G. Gadamer, *Truth and Method*, 2nd Ed., G. Barden and J. Cummings, trans. (New York: Continuum Publishing Company, 1975), pp. xxiii, 321-2.
13. M. Theunissen, *The Other*, C. Macann, trans. (Cambridge, MA: The MIT Press, 1984), p. 275.
14. M.R. Austin, "A description of the Maori marae," in A. Rapoport, ed., *The Mutual Interaction of People and their Built Environment*, (The Hague: Mouton, 1976), pp. 229-241.

MORAL ARCHITECTURE: BEAUTY AND ETHICS IN BATAMMALIBA BUILDING DESIGN

SUZANNE PRESTON BLIER

"Art is a means of keeping and communicating values, that is, it makes values become common." -- Christian Norberg-Schulz[1]

"The beautiful is the symbol of the morally good." -- Immanuel Kant

Every field is identified with a seminal work that has served both to focus scholarly and popular attention and to stimulate new research. In the field of vernacular architecture[2] that work is Bernard Rudofsky's *Architecture Without Architects*, a catalogue written in conjunction with an exhibition Rudofsky curated at the Museum of Modern Art in 1964. Rudofsky described his concerns in the catalogue preface:

> Architectural history, as written and taught in the Western world, has never been concerned with more than a few select cultures. In terms of space it comprises a small part of the globe - Europe, stretches of Egypt and Anatolia . . . . Moreover, the evolution of architecture is usually dealt with only in its late phases . . . . Architectural history as we know it . . . amounts to little more than a who's who of architects who commemorated power and wealth; an anthology of buildings of, by, and for the priviledged . . . . *Architecture Without Architects* attempts to break down our narrow concepts of the art of building . . . .[3]

Scholarship in the field of African aesthetics can be traced to another seminal work, Harris Memel-Fote's "The Perception of Beauty in Negro African Culture," a paper presented at the First World Colloquium on Negro Arts in Dakar in 1966. Memel-Fote noted in this paper that,

> there was a time when to search for the perception of beauty in Negro-African culture, worse than [illegitimate] . . . and senseless, would have been forbidden . . . . Whether we look for beauty in an art which is disinterested, not involved in everyday life, or whether we look upon it as the emanation of a service art, it is always and everywhere possible to fit African aesthetics into it.[4]

Today looking back at these works, we might note how Rudofsky's interests in vernacular architecture dovetailed with the dominant social and political issues of the 1960s, a period which saw both an expansion outward from Europe as the *sine qua non* of architectural form and an exploration inward to investigate the social and political dynamics at play in various types of artistic expression. It is also clear as we look at Rudofsky's survey that some of the ideas taken up by him derived from the same Eurocentric grounding that he so deplored. Today scholars no longer assume -- as Rudofsky did -- that indigenous architecture is timeless, unchanging and inherently "traditional," or that it necessarily represents a beginning point of architecture.[5]   In addition, current scholars no longer share Rudofsky's view that these buildings are important primarily because of the insights and impetus they can provide to architects of the West.

From this perspective, we might also note that Memel-Fote's article displayed many of the concerns of other Negritude writers of the 1960s. It presented a survey of African forms of aesthetic expression that assumed both a general similitude among African cultures and a predominant emphasis on action, as opposed to thought, in African philosophies and art. Memel-Fote's overview also rarely went beneath the surface to treat the complexities and unique qualities of African ideas of beauty. More recent scholars concerned with African aesthetics have generally stressed both the variability of aesthetic expression in Africa and its identity with local systems of thought.

The fact that the orientation of scholars of vernacular architecture and African aesthetics today is different from the concerns of Rudofsky and Memel-Fote should not distract us from the importance of their respective writings. More than anything else, the studies of Rudofsky and Memel-Fote encouraged scholars to travel to Africa or to write from within Africa in order to examine the associated works *in situ*. As a result the number of studies that have been undertaken both on African architecture and on African aesthetics has increased substantially since the time when Rudofsky and Memel-Fote first published their texts.

Interestingly, although Memel-Fote's article encouraged new scholarship and debate on aesthetics in African sculptural traditions, there did not follow a concomitant scholarly interest in the aesthetics of African architecture. Similarly, while scholars writing after Rudofsky have looked at vernacular building traditions from a wide variety of perspectives -- environmental, functional, symbolic and historic, among them -- relatively little attention has been given to the nature of aesthetics in vernacular architectural form or the ways in which aesthetics are defined and delimited by local architects, builders or residents. That is striking both in view of the scholarly importance of aesthetics in recent writing about architecture[6] and in view of the significance which aesthetics has been seen to play in complementary sculptural contexts in Africa and elsewhere. This chapter combines an analysis of African aesthetics with an exploration of related features of architectural symbolism. It examines below the aesthetic criteria and terminologies identified with building traditions of the Batammaliba (Tamberma or "Somba") people of northern Togo and Benin, and it investigates how these aesthetic canons offer insight into Batammaliba society and the architectural forms it has created.

Rudofsky saw architectural beauty as a natural corollary of the practical aims of built form. "The beauty of this architecture has long been dismissed as accidental," he wrote, "but today we should be able to recognize it as the result of rare good sense in the handling of practical problems."[7] Memel-Fote's view of artistic beauty was also closely linked to pragmatic concerns:

> . . . the relationship of beauty to the idea of good, in its most immediate, its most concrete, its widest sense, indeed takes on an aspect of the pragmatic. It is commonly acknowledged that Negro Art is an art that is integrated into everyday life, it is a social art, a service art . . . . This means also and above all that beauty . . . is required to aid, it is called upon to participate and is a participant to the . . . [efficacy] of the object, to the realization of its function. This means, if you will, that beauty has its own . . . [efficacy]. The more beautiful the object, the better it accomplishes its effectively desired, imaginatively dreamed, technically hoped for effect.[8]

The interrelationship between architectural aesthetics and practical aims and functional efficacy suggests in turn an important connection between social values and beauty. That this is the case in Africa is clear. Memel-Fote provides a brief analysis of African terms for beautiful, ugly, good and bad.[9] In this overview he shows how ideas of beauty relate to the notion of good, and how ugliness is linked to the idea of evil. Among the Adjukru, for example, *akpl* and *mamn* mean both beautiful and good, while *uw* and *lugnn* designate at once ugly and bad. Similarly, among the Attie, *leudja* means beautiful and *leu* means good, while *gnigna* signifies both ugly and bad. A similar correlation between beautiful and good on the one hand and ugliness and evil on the other has also been found in traditions of African sculpture by Messenger and Vogel.[10] Taking an example among the Igbo, masks with beautiful features are identified with positive values and individuals of good character, whereas masks with ugly or horrific features make reference to negative qualities and antisocial behavior.[11] It will be argued here that the concept of beauty in Batammaliba buildings also assume an active role in defining how these social mores are delimited and expressed.

CONCERN WITH AESTHETIC AND ETHICAL VALUES
IN BATAMMALIBA ARCHITECTURE

Architecture among the Batammaliba, as I have shown else-where,[12] is associated with a multiplicity of roles and identities in conjunction with its diverse functions as home, fortress, temple, *imago mundi*, paradise exemplar, psychological model and theater, among others (FIGS. 1-4). These divergent roles together play a part in determining the shape each building will assume, the actions that are structured within it, and the meanings it conveys. Aesthetics also constitutes an important part of architectural meaning. What makes Batammaliba buildings beautiful? As foreign observers, what may strike us most in these fortress-like structures is their symmetry and rhythmic composition of circles, curves and ovals. Two-story in height, Batammaliba earthen domiciles also stand out for the monumentality of their form and the cohesiveness of their parts. Oppositions are clearly defined in them as well. With single west-facing portals and darkened ground floor interiors, they both invite approach and discourage penetration. At once sky-reaching and earth-hugging, balanced and dynamic, curving and rigid, austere and lively, these structures are among the most visually interesting of West Africa's architectural forms. But how is their beauty defined locally? Are the aesthetic values that we as outsiders discern the same as those that are appreciated by their builders and inhabitants? In what ways does an understanding of their aesthetic grounding help us to know more about the nature of the society and the meanings of its architecture?

It is perhaps best to begin with the last question, for as will be argued here, an important part of Batammaliba architectural meaning is grounded in local ethical canons and social mores. In part for this reason each house is oriented toward the west to face the abode of Kuiye, the deity charged with, among other things, ethics, morality, life and death. From the western sky Kuiye is able to observe all that goes on inside the house and community. In addition, each house is positioned when possible on the foundation of an ancient house, and thus it incorporates within its ground plan and walls the corporate identity of the past family and community members. As such, each house is associated with the power of moral proscription. This power is at once symbolic and real. "The house will leave a person who, through sorcery, becomes a menace to society," explained Tchanfa Atchana.[13] Since the Batammaliba employ the same word (*takienta*) to mean both house and family, an implicit link is made between the two. If the house is strong, then at least in linguistic terms so too is the family. Conversely, if the family is weak, then the house shares this weakness.

Turning to the first question, it is clear that architectural beauty is important in this society. "I want my house to be beautiful," explained the elder Aita of Kousankikou at the foundation-laying of his new house.[14] "It is easy to tell if a building is beautiful," asserted Tchakwe Takwete, a senior architect from Koufitoukou.[15] "All of us, when we walk around and see a house well built, we recognize its beauty," noted Tchanfa Atchana another architect from that same village.[16] Architectural criticism, in turn, is a central part of the design and building process. Each house is constructed by an individual male architect, called *otammali*, "one who creates, or builds, well with earth." Each such architect-builder undergoes a lengthy apprenticeship alongside someone who is experienced in design and construction. In turn, master architects -- generally those who have built more than ten structures -- oversee the design of the ground plan of every new structure in the community. They assure that structural and aesthetic standards are maintained. It is these masters who then will critique every new structure that is built. Where it is deemed necessary, they can insist that a particular building part be redone, as was the case with the early works of Tchakwe Takwete, whose entrances were judged to be too tall and had to lowered.

GENERAL AESTHETIC TERMINOLOGIES :
YOUTHFULNESS AND DURABILITY

Although technique is important in architectural evaluation, beauty is appraised and appreciated separately. Ibenekuaku Falifa noted in this light, "some architects know how to build well, but cannot construct a beautiful house."[17] At the same time in Batammaliba aesthetic terminology there is a clear linkage made between ideas of strength and ideals of beauty. Two words, *teleceta* and *kuiyenku*, are employed interchangeably to express the idea of beauty. *Teleceta* also means "youthful," describing that period of life associated with optimum beauty, strength and potential. In part because of the stress on youthfulness in architectural beauty, houses are often rebuilt at important occasions or transitions in life, such as adolescence (initiation), marriage (birth), and approaching eldership (death) so that the house will be at its most beautiful when these changes are ceremonially marked. Each year a new plaster surface and stain are also usually applied to the outer walls of the house to give it the appearance of newness and youth. Interestingly, this quality of youthfulness or ephebism is also something which is highly appreciated in African sculptural traditions. In African art, works portraying elders generally show them with the physical features of much younger persons. As Robert Farris Thompson points out, for the Yoruba it is important that one portray a person at the time of optimum physical beauty.[18]

At the same time that youthfulness and newness are ideals that are strongly valued in aesthetics, the opposite qualities of degeneration and decline have sharply negative connotations. Thus when a cow broke a Batammaliba house shrine figure, a special ceremony was held to replace the sculpture with a new one so that the associated powers would remain efficacious. Batammaliba buildings which are delapidated or show signs of age similarly are replaced by new structures as soon as feasible. There is an important moral component of this practice. The image of an unkempt, uncared-for or broken house is identified with ideas of disorder and disequilibrium. As such, unkempt or dilapidated houses are frequent metaphors for death, disease, or other problems affecting the family. As one elder inquired sadly in the course of a geomancy session:

> Has the house fallen on us? You should know. If the house falls and kills all the people inside would one be happy? Is it my house that has fallen? Is it my crosspieces that have fallen? Has my house fallen and my crosspieces been burnt? . . . There where I built should I leave there?[19]

Old house foundations similarly are associated with death and the social disequilibrium that accompanies it.

The second word that is employed by the Batammaliba to mean beauty is *kuiyenku* (*layeni*), a term which means at the same time "durable" and "solid." This word derives from the root *yene*, "to dry in the sun," an action which promotes durability, longevity and strength whether one is speaking of harvested grains, pottery or earthen buildings. This term not only suggests the importance of strength in architectural evaluation, but it reinforces the role of Kuiye, the solar deity, in architectural structure, beauty and meaning. It is Kuiye, generally, who is identified as the first architect, the deity who not only built the Earth in the model of a house terrace, but also constructed the first domicile here for himself and his first sons. Drying something in the sun thus imparts to it both the force of this solar deity and his power as architect. Kuiye's role as moral arbiter is also important. A building which is made durable and strong through the heat of the sun is beautiful not only because it is better able to fulfill its function as a house but because it encourages one to see in oneself those qualities given by Kuiye, qualities which are essential both to one's well-being and the well-being of society.

In these two terms, *teleceta* and *kuiyenku*, qualities of good and beauty clearly are interrelated. To be youthful and strong is to be beautiful -- to be full of potential and a source of support for the family and community. As Susan Vogel notes for Baule sculptors, "their praise of youthful features and their disapproval of anything old looking is linked with their praise of fertility, health, strength, and the ability to work hard."[20] Accordingly, the Baule praise in their sculptures those features of beauty which are indicative of hard work -- a strong neck, well muscled calves and firm buttocks. A closer look at the individual aesthetic criteria valued in Batammaliba architecture suggests that these qualities of beauty and goodness also interrelate with each other in an ongoing way. The individual aesthetic canons not only offer insight into the finer points of architectural criticism, but they also provide insight into the social and ethical dynamics that underlie architectural expression. As we will see, these aesthetic values -- evenness and balance (*yala*), straightness and smoothness (*kunanku*), and unity and containedness (*tamkumutabe*) -- underscore the close linkage between beauty, structural soundness and social mores in Batammaliba society.

F I G U R E 1. House of Ibenekuaku Kousanti. Architect: Ibenekuaku Kousanti.
Village of Koufitoukou. Jan. 1978.

CONCERN FOR EVENNESS IN ARCHITECTURE AND LIFE

Evenness (*yala*) constitutes one of the most important of the aesthetic values that architects look for in appraising the beauty of individual houses (FIGS. 1, 2). In a beautiful house, Tchanfa Atchana explains, the walls, the granary supports and the entrance must be even (*yala*). Tchakwe Takwete noted in turn that "in all beautiful houses, what distinguishes them is their evenness (equality). The reason this house is beautiful is that everything in it is even."[21] Batchamu Bunanka observed similarly that when an architect "knows how to build well, he will build and his levels will be even . . . . When he finishes building, everything will be

F I G U R E 2. House of N'sati Tafanata. Architect: Okweta Tayanta. Village of Koufitoukou. Jan. 1978.

even. All his levels will be equal. They will be alike and it will be good."[22] Interestingly, evenness and balance (symmetry) are also strongly valued in certain African sculptural traditions such as those of the Fang, Yoruba, Chokwe and Baule.[23]

In Batammaliba architecture, as suggested above, the quality of evenness is defined in several ways. Most importantly, it can be seen in the even positioning of building levels and in the even placement of rooms, walls and other building parts (FIG. 4). This factor of evenness also is defined architecturally in the proportionality of house features. A beautiful house is one that is evenly proportioned, one which is neither too tall nor too short, neither too wide nor too narrow. "When it is short but not too short, and tall but not too tall, it is good," explained Tchanfa Atchana.[24] Ibenekuaku Falifa, another architect-builder, expanded on this idea: "If the house is too tall, it will not be beautiful. If it is too low, it will not be beautiful. It has to be in the middle. If it

F I G U R E 3. House of Nkete. Architect: N'weta Bayamu. Village of
Koufitoukou. Jan. 1978.

is in the middle, we will say it is beautiful."[25]   This emphasis on
moderation similarly is found in African sculpture.   In Baule
aesthetic evaluation, according to Philip Ravenhill,

> . . . a given physical attribute should ideally be 'just so' . . . being neither
> too pronounced nor too diminutive . . . a neck should not be too long
> ('like a camel') nor too short ('like a cricket') nor too thick . . . it should
> approach the *ideal* of [an] elegant or beautiful . . . neck.[26]

Criticism of Batammaliba buildings also stresses the importance of
evenness in aesthetic evaluation.   Accordingly, buildings which
display opposing aesthetic values (FIG. 3) are strongly condemned.
One of the qualities most highly denigrated in architecture is *pie*,
the state of being out of line, unequal, uneven or at an angle.

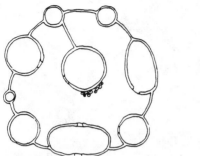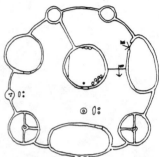

F I G U R E 4. House ground plan.

Tchanfa Atchana's comments on a newly constructed house in Koufitoukou are of interest in this regard. "The house parts are all unequal; it is uneven. If you go inside, you will hit the granary support and you will not have a place to pass."[27] Evenness clearly is an important concern not only for building aesthetics but also for effective building use. Rooms that are correctly positioned allow for the best use of space. Evenness is also necessary for structural soundness. Construction levels and other building parts that are even can more effectively carry and distribute the weight of the upper walls, floors and roofs. In turn when the accepted and time-tested width to height proportions are maintained, buildings are more likely to have the requisite strength and durability.

The term *yala* and its identity with evenness also has real significance within the Batammaliba architectural sign system as an expression of ideals of political power. Village control is not a matter of chiefly hierarchy, but rather the elders of major lineages meet and come to an agreement whenever important village decisions are to be made. What characterizes this political system is its strong concern with egalitarianism. Like each of the various walls and support chambers, each family unit in the village must evenly carry its own political and religious weight. Evenness also is important in terms of social well-being. Here too a fundamental link is made between the beauty of buildings and ideals of social harmony. Evenness -- whether in architecture or in life -- is a sign that things are in order, that they are what they should be. Many building parts, accordingly, are paired. Most Batammaliba houses incorporate two earthen horns above the door. These horns represent many things among them the marital couple who reside in the house. When only one such horn is present (i.e. when the number of horns is no longer even), it is a sign that the male owner of the house is deceased and the family is in a state of disunity and disequilibrium. Three horns conveys the fact that the original house owner is dead, but a son or grandson has rebuilt the house, and it has become a ritual center for the extended family, lineage or clan. So too each house ordinarily includes two raised front granaries, one for male crops and the other for female crops. When a house is without one of these granaries as occasionally occurs (FIG. 3), it is a sign that the family residing within is either very young, and thus not complete or impoverished or missing one of its important members through death or divorce.

STRAIGHTNESS IN AESTHETICS AND ETHICAL VALUES

Straightness (*kunanku*, from *nanta*, "to grind") is another important value that is frequently emphasized in architectural beauty. In the words of Ibenekuaku Falifa, "you will know that a building is really beautiful when the builder brings up the walls to be really straight."[28] Tchanfa Atchana remarked about a new building that "the entrance is well done, and it is straight. If everything in the house was like that, it would be fine."[29] Batchamu Bunanka, praising the works of another architect, noted that "the walls did not come out or go in; they were straight and correct."[30] Criticism of buildings is of equal interest. In appraising another building, Batchamu Bunanka noted,

> When he finished the house it was not beautiful. The walls turned this way and that. When he made one level it is on the outside and the next level is on the inside. This presents a problem for the crosspieces. One level goes well with the wood and the next level is inside. In addition, sometimes the middle of a wall is so thin that the sides almost meet. Then the next level will flare out again.[31]

The ideal of straightness also finds expression in the smoothness of exterior wall surfaces. "The beautiful house," Ibenekuaku Falifa suggested, "is one which is smoothly plastered. It is so clean [smooth, straight], that from far away you will not see the demarcations from the various levels."[32]   Similarly Batchamu Bunanka praised one architect's work this way: "If you saw his building, you would think that it was plastered with clay -- but it was not yet plastered."[33] Although straightness and smoothness of walls are the responsibility of the architect, the plastering of the exterior wall surface is done by women. Both men and women thus contribute to the beauty of each building. Straightness and smoothness, like many of the other aesthetic values that have been discussed here, also are strongly valued in African sculpture. "His nose is as straight as though it were sculpted," the Baule will say.[34] Smoothness and straightness also are highly praised in Yoruba sculptural traditions.[35]

Straightness and smoothness, like the qualities of evenness explored above, have considerable impact on the structural soundness of a building. In this architectural tradition where walls are elevated to a two-story height it is essential that they are made straight and smooth. If there are recesses, thin areas or wall sections which are angled the wrong way, the building will lack essential solidity. Surface smoothness and straightness are also important in keeping the earthen core of the walls watertight. Walls which have pockets, cracks or other surface irregularities offer little protection from the damaging rain.

Like the aesthetic qualities of evenness and balance, straightness and smoothness have important moral and ethical significance as well. In both everyday speech and prayer the idea of straightness is closely identified with correctness. "May it go straight [well] for him," the deceased elders are implored in one prayer.[36] "She should give birth, and it will be straight [without problems for her]," another prayer noted.[37] Straightness, whether in architecture, wall decoration or speech implies a situation in which there is order. If something is straight and smooth, it is without difficulties, deviations or other problems.

Psychological soundness is also tied into this idea. Each person is believed to have an independent spirit-entity or soul (*liyuani*), a miniature of oneself, that is placed directly in front of each person's body to provide guidance and protection in life. The idea of straightness here too is critical, for it is said that when one's protective spirit-entity is out of line with the body, one will suffer from disorientation, illness and in some cases even death.[38] In architecture this is expressed most poignantly in the building of miniature earthen soul-mounds for family members directly in front of the house in line with the door. Like the soul which generally remains aligned with the body and protects it from harm, the soul-mound is positioned directly in front of the door. These mounds also, by their very straightness, visually reaffirm for the individual and his or her family the fact that order prevails and that difficulty in life will be surmounted. According to both Batammaliba psychological perspectives and architectural aesthetics, when things are not straight, when they are slanted to the side, disequilibrium rather than order and harmony may follow.

IMPORTANCE OF UNITY

Unity (*tamkumutabe*) the third aesthetic value which is important for architectural beauty, is closely identified with the ideas of harmony and integration. For a building to be considered beautiful, each structural part must fit within the whole; it must contribute to the unity (FIG. 4). In such a house none of the parts should extend beyond the pre-established integrated plan. As Tchakwe Takwete explains, "if the house is totally united, everything will go together."[39] According to Tchanfa Atchana, in a beautiful house "the building parts must go together, like companions or friends."[40] The entrance should not extend too far in front, the kitchen and storage rooms should not protrude too far to the side or back, the granaries and portal horns should not rise too high above the house. Ibenekuaku Falifa noted in this light that "the granary that is well set into the facade is the one that is beautiful; the granary that extends too far into the air is not . . . . Similarly short [portal] horns are more beautiful than tall ones, for they are on the same level as the entrance."[41] There is considerable criticism of buildings which display discontinuity between individual parts, or parts vis-a-vis the whole. Here too structural strength is important. Buildings with unified building parts have an inherent structural solidity that structures which do not share these characteristics do not have.

The concern with unity and containedness in architectural form also has important parallels in moral and social valuation. Unity is essential for family and community well-being. In the decidedly non-hierarchical political structure of Batammaliba communities, there is an ongoing stress on group harmony. In many respects, each building stands as an attestation to this ideal. In the same way that cohesiveness is vital to architectural solidity and beauty, so too a completely integrated and unified village grouping is essential to the long-term vitality of both the family and the community. "Humans come together to aid each other while animals do not," it was explained vis-a-vis the differences between humans and animals.[42] The strength of humans, in other words, is based on their ability to come together to make decisions and take action for the benefit of the group as a whole.

In burial traditions this same idea is expressed. Those who are viewed as malevolent and who demonstrate this behavior through anti-social deeds are buried outside the communal cemetery. Thus, because they took action in their lives against the group, after death they remain isolated from the community. Departure from the ideal of unity in this way represents a break from the values of harmony and cohesion that are necessary for the vitality of one family and village. Detachment, whether in architecture or in life, represents the potential malevolence that accompanies anything that lies apart. Something that is detached in turn signifies values or powers that potentially can weaken the group.

AESTHETIC VALUES WITH RESPECT TO ARCHITECTURAL AREAS

The ideal of social unity is expressed in architectural form in another way as well. This value is found in the structural division of each house into front and back areas with their respective positive and negative moral associations. The front of the house is identified in many ways with one's public position in the community. Family position, history, religious affiliation, medical rights, and political ties can all be read in the various signs that are incorporated into building facades. House fronts thus reinforce the contributions that individual families and individuals make to the community.

The back of the house, in contrast, is identified with anti-social values and related ideas of disorder, malevolence and death. Accordingly, neither doors nor windows give access to this part of the structure. Ritual action reinforces the identity of the rear of the house with danger and death.[43] In anatomy the back is similarly identified with death and potential danger. Those who are dead are thought to pass things to one from behind their backs. Sorcerers are believed to have a second pair of eyes hidden in the backs of their heads, which allow them to do things that ordinary people cannot do.[44] Complementary traditions link the back with ideas of moral turpitude. Turning one's back on someone needing aid is a serious moral offense (*cala*), a crime which the solar God, Kuiye, can punish with death.[45] To talk behind someone's back or to do something in back of a friend or a family member is also a serious *cala*.

While front and back suggest contrasting values of opposition and support, selfishness and selflessness, interior and exterior building parts make reference to other individual or group orientations. Interior light and shade are particularly important. Darkness and light of course vary inside each house as different sections are illuminated and cast into shade in the course of the sun's daily passage. What is described as being the most beautiful feature of house interiors is the interplay between these dark and light areas.[46] Some sections of the interior always should remain relatively dark, it is explained. "A man should not see all the dark corners of another's house," a Batammaliba proverb recounts. Thus while much of the house and the village are open to the gaze of all, there remains for each house and each person those dark corners, those secrets, which are an important part of each individual and family identity. Far from being negative, these secrets often are an important part of one's inner strength. If the facade of a building represents the projection of each person in the community, then the interior is identified with one's inner self.

Concerns with the family as opposed to the village are also raised in various elements of architectural setting. For the house to be beautiful, one architect explained, "we say that it is the placement [*baconcome*: siting, position] which is important."[47] Accordingly, careful consideration is given to selecting village sites in which each house will be clearly distinct. A house is rarely placed in such a way that it will block the view of another. Historically, most houses were built along the steep slopes and ridges of the Atacora mountains from where one could easily observe travelers passing along the plains below. From below, in turn, each house retains its individual identity. Today more and more people build their houses on the plains rather than on the slopes or mountain heights. Even here, however, house placement is important, reinforcing an ideal of individual identity for each family.

CONCLUDING NOTE

In art as in life, to paraphrase Immanuel Kant, the beautiful often serves to symbolize the morally good. Bernard Rudofsky and Harris Memel-Fote each have noted that on a primary level aesthetic valuation reflects critical moral and social canons of pragmatic efficacy and usefulness. This is also true of Batammaliba architecture. But more than being a mere reflection of these values, Batammaliba buildings serve as forceful proponents of a moral code that reaches broadly into the society and that has an impact on and in turn is grounded in local politics, psychology, religion and individual expression. Architecture, in assuming this active role through the spaces it shapes and the actions it delimits, requires each of its residents to live out on a physical plane the ideals and values of the society. Beautiful houses, because they are seen to be at once strong (*teleceta*) and youthful (*kuiyenku*), extend these same ideals to their inhabitants and builders, encouraging in them a high valuation of youthful energy and hard work. Beautiful buildings with their combined qualities of evenness (*yala*), straightness (*kunanku*), and unity (*tamkubutabe*) encourage these same values in each architect and member who resides within.

Serving in much the same way as a motto or creed, Batammaliba architecture continually promotes values which are critical to the society's identity and well-being. The counterposed values of disequilibrium and disunity by the same means continually are condemned within the ongoing practice of architectural construction and criticism. The distinctions that are made symbolically between house facades and backs on the one hand and house interiors and exteriors on the other bring up the opposing values of selfish and selfless orientations and individual and community identity. House placement underscores similarly juxtaposed concerns of family and village. Buildings that are beautiful and buildings that are well situated serve thus as powerful emblems of community codes of behavior. Each beautiful building visually reaffirms the social mores and ethical values that help to bind the community together. It is clear that for the Batammaliba, the central tenets of the society are expressed through the forms and meanings of their buildings.

REFERENCE NOTES

Research for this article was carried out in the Republic of Togo from December 1976 to January 1978 with the support of a Fulbright-Hays Dissertation Research Fellowship, which I gratefully acknowledge.

1. Immanuel Kant, *Critique of Judgment*, J.H. Bernard, trans. (Hafner, 1951), p. 199; Christian Norberg-Schulz, *Intentions in Architecture* (Cambridge, MA, 1965), p. 68.
2. There are clearly numerous problems with the term vernacular as a classificatory label for African or other architectural forms which lie outside the standard Western European architectural history repertory because of its primary association with slavery and/or rural settings.
3. Bernard Rudofsky, *Architecture Without Architects: A Short Introduction to Non-Pedigreed Architecture* (Garden City, NY, 1964), p. i.
4. Harris Memel-Fote, "The Function and Significance of Negro Art in the Life of the Peoples of Black Africa," in *Colloquium: Function and Significance of African Negro Art in the Life of the People and For the People* (Dakar: 1st World Festival

of Negro Arts, April 1-24, 1966). Unfortunately, the English edition of the conference proceedings is marred by sloppy editing and numerous misspellings.
5. For a discussion of historical changes that have occurred in the Batammaliba architecture, see Suzanne Preston Blier, "Toward a History of Tamberma Two-Story Architecture: Origins, Impetus, and Factors of Change," in Christopher D. Roy, ed., *Iowa Studies in African Art*, Vol. I (Iowa City, 1984). Scholars of African sculpture are beginning to think that whereas in the past these arts were assumed to be timeless relics of a period long past and strongly traditional in their aims and orientations, in fact many traditions of African sculpture seem to have witnessed striking changes in the course of time.
6. Norberg-Schulz, *Intentions in Architecture*; Roger Scruton, *The Aesthetics of Architecture* (Princeton, NJ, 1979).
7. Bernard Rudofsky, *Architecture Without Architects*, p. [4].
8. Memel-Fote, "The Function and Significance of Negro Art," p. 57.
9. *Ibid.*, p. 56.
10. John C. Messenger, "The Role of the Carver in Anang Society," in Warren L. d'Azevedo, ed., *The Traditional Artist in African Societies* (Bloomington, IN, 1973), p. 121; Susan M. Vogel, *Beauty in the Eyes of the Baule: Aesthetics and Cultural Values* (Philadelphia: Institute for the Study of Human Issues, 1980); *African Aesthetics: The Carlo Monzino Collection* (Venice, 1985). The link between beauty and efficaciousness is of course not unique to Africa either in linguistic terminologies or in actual practice. As Claude Roy has noted (in Memel-Fote, "The Function and Significance of Negro Art," pp. 47-48): "Just as the African dialects have, for the most part, only one adjective to mean beautiful and good, so any Greek dictionary will remind us that *aghatos* meant, at the same time, beautiful, good, brave at war. To assimilate beauty and goodness does not mean denying the former."
11. Herbert M. Cole, "Art as a Verb in Iboland," *African Arts/Arts d'Afrique Noire*, Vol. 3 no. 1, pp. 38-41; Suzanne Preston Blier, *Beauty and the Beast: A Study in Contrasts* (New York, 1976).
12. Suzanne Preston Blier, *The Anatomy of Architecture: Ontology and Metaphor in Batammaliba Architectural Expression* (New York, 1987); "Solar Plexis/Spatial Nexus: Architectural Dimensions of the Soul," *Daidalos: Architektur, Kunst, Kultur*, 1988.
13. Interview of July 24, 1977 in Koufitoukou.
14. Interview of Nov. 12, 1977 in Kousankikou.
15. Interview of Dec. 19, 1977 in Koufitoukou.
16. Interview of Nov. 18, 1977 in Koufitoukou. Rarely, however, will a builder praise his own works. When I asked him how he would evaluate the buildings he had worked on, the young Koufitoukou architect Ibenekuaku Falifa explained in an interview of Nov. 11, 1977: "I cannot give myself praise. Others will have to judge and determine if it is beautiful or not."
17. Interview of Nov. 11, 1977 in Koufitoukou.
18. Robert Farris Thompson, "Yoruba Artistic Criticism," in d'Azevedo, ed., *The Traditional Artist in African Societies*, pp. 56-68.
19. From a geomancy session recorded in Lissani on Apr. 14, 1977, as reported in Rudolph Blier, "Health Care and Community: A Study in the Sociology of Batammaliba Medicine" (Ph.D. dissertation, Northwestern University, 1987).
20. Vogel, *Beauty in the Eyes of the Baule*, p. 13.
21. Interview of Dec. 19, 1977 in Koufitoukou.
22. Interview of Nov. 17, 1977 in Kouatie.

23.   James W. Fernandez, "Principles of Opposition and Vitality in Fang Aesthetics," *The Journal of Aesthetics and Art Criticism*, 25, 1, (1966) pp. 53-64; Thompson, "Yoruba Artistic Criticism," p. 55; Daniel J. Crowley, "Aesthetic Value and Professionalism in African Art: Three Cases from the Katangaa Chokwe," in d'Azevedo, ed., *The Traditional Artist in African Societies*, pp. 246-7; Vogel, *African Aesthetics*, p. xii.

24.   Interview of Nov. 18, 1977 in Koufitoukou.

25.   Interview of Nov. 11, 1977.

26.   Philip L. Ravenhill, *Baule Statuary Art: Meaning and Modernization* (Philadelphia, Institute for the Study of Human Issues, 1980), p. 7.

27.   Interview of Nov. 12, 1977 in Kousankikou.

28.   Interview of Nov. 11, 1977.

29.   Interview of Nov. 12, 1977 in Kousankikou.

30.   Interview of July 24, 1977 in Koufitoukou.

31.   Interview of July 24, 1977 in Koufitoukou.

32.   Interview of Nov. 11, 1977 in Koufitoukou.

33.   Interview of Nov. 17, 1977 in Kouatie. It is important to note that some elements do not affect the beauty of the house. Ibenekuaku Falifa suggests (interview of Nov. 11, 1977), for example, that the wooden beam ends, "are beautiful regardless of whether they extend out a good distance, or are kept close to the facade." The size of the house's earthen levels also does not affect its beauty. "It depends on the architect, if he builds large levels it will be beautiful, [and if he] builds small levels, it will also be beautiful." These diverse factors, while not being seen as important in architectural beauty, are frequently essential determinants of architectural style.

34.   Ravenhill, *Baule Statuary Art*, p. 9.

35.   Thompson, "Yoruba Artistic Criticism," p. 53.

36.   Recorded during a ceremony on June 2, 1977.

37.   Recorded during a ceremony on July 16, 1977.

38.   See R. Blier, "Health Care and Community," p.133.

39.   Interview of Dec. 19, 1977 in Koufitoukou.

40.   Interview of Nov. 18, 1977 in Koufitoukou.

41.   Interview of Nov. 11, 1977 in Koufitoukou.

42.   Interview with N'tcha Lalie in Lissani on July 25, 1977.

43.   The cords of a dead woman are thrown behind the house before burial.

44.   Interview with Batchamou Bunanka on Aug. 15, 1977 in Kouatie.

45.   Interview with Batchamou Bunanka on Dec. 16, 1977 in Kouatie.

46.   Interview of Dec. 19, 1977 in Koufitoukou.

47.   Interview of Nov. 18, 1977 in Koufitoukou.

THE OASIS OF FARAFRA
IN THE EYES OF ITS INHABITANTS

AMR ABDEL KAWI

Professionals in architecture are inclined to study so-called traditional settlements with an attitude not very different from that adopted by various other disciplines. The subjects of their studies are usually objectified to allow for easy classification into neat intellectual taxonomies. Although there have been considerable contributions made by research in this field, most of it remains one-dimensional in that it relays only one story; that of the professional. Seldom is the story of the people concerned heard, at least not in the manner in which they would tell it. Furthermore, the labels we place upon these people, primitive, vernacular or traditional, reflect the expert-like, even parternalistic, attitude professionals often adopt when they make it their business to study these communities.

In this chapter I attempt to question such a professional attitude by re-telling the story of Farafra, an isolated oasis in the western desert of Egypt, as it was told to me by several of its inhabitants.[1] Through photographs these people took of their village, they attempted to tell me how they saw their world and what they believed was important in it. While talking about those photographs, they exposed a story that was strikingly different from the one I was inclined to tell as a professional architect.

The differences between these two world views are very hard to ignore. They not only highlight the wide gap that exists between professional and non-professional perceptions of the built environment, but they call into question the labelling of such communities that fall outside professional realms. They force us to "problematize"[2] our professional inclination to objectify the physical environment and reduce it to a world of objects divested of meanings. The people of Farafra, the Farfaronis, helped underline the importance of seeing the physical world as the embodiment of a complex system of social and environmental relationships, not simply as an expression of those relationships. To understand the physical world of others, or any other aspect of that world, we have to understand the meanings those others embed in it.

ONE VIEW OF THE VILLAGE

This exercise, part of a two-year project in the village, was instrumental in bringing about a confrontation with otherness; a process of seeing our all-too-familiar world through different eyes, of questioning what we take for granted, of learning through the possibility of difference.

To best illustrate the differences in world views that emerged from this experience, I shall begin by giving a verbal image from my field notes. It is of my perceptions of Farafra before I had any interaction with its inhabitants:

> The sight of the village all clustered up on the slope of a low hill in the faint orange and purple shades of the setting sun was all that I needed to forget the frustrations and agonies of the last six hours of the trip. The hill stood alone as the only highland in this vast expanse of desertscape in which I was engulfed all the way from Cairo. At this moment, the hill appeared to be flickering into life, as single light bulbs scattered on the walls of most houses suddenly glowed. The houses at the road level, where I slowed down to relish this sight, appeared to be rising on each others' shoulders as my eyes followed them up the small hill. The village stood as one shadowy mass that grew out, in no ordered fashion, from the gentle slope of the hill.

> With the image of Farafra rising on that hill filling up my senses, I was slowly drawn towards it. The road ahead cut through the mass of houses

that seemed to spill down the hill like a mud slide flowing onto the flat lands with no apparent limits to where it might go at its own powers. The mud walls of the village embracing the contours of the hill were very distinct and strong, forming a seemingly formidable protective shell around the village. Several one-story, contemporary-looking structures littered the flat expanse between the road and the hill. They could not get any closer. They did not belong there. Moving ahead, the road made a kink from which an offshoot emerged and ran straight up the hill and through the mud mass, pushing it wide open as it got closer. I followed that road, in its upward climb eager to take in a quick taste of this dream-like setting before darkness swallowed it.

As the asphalt road broke through the mud mass in its trip to the top of the hill, it began tearing at the two sides of the wound gradually pushing them farther and farther apart, until it ended in a large shapeless bubble-like space where everything seemed to flow. The mud mass was in control again. The scale of the buildings and streets around that space returned to where the car was a very obvious intruder. The central guardian of that space was, as one might have expected, the mosque. It was surrounded by what I presumed to be civic buildings.

People did not stop as they passed a curious look upon that strange car roaming the streets of their world. I too paid no heed and continued through it as if in a trance pulled by the power of the walls that stretched, then turned, and turned once more to bring me back to where I started from. The open streets I was sucked into seemed to be surprisingly rectilinear. In years past I had read about the oases and seen pictures of them; all of these images were now racing through my mind attempting to form a reconcilliation with the world I was actually seeing. Orange mud surrounded me on all sides except above me where a predominantly orange sky closed in the sphere. As a result I felt everything blending into each other; nothing stood out on its own. The people in the streets all around me were not there, except as floating images that completed the scene. The place was not real yet.

A tone of romanticism definitely emerges from these words. But this is understandable considering my educational background which presented architecture to me as only the structures designed and built by architects. Anything that stood outside this realm was given different names and thus made to fit under different categories. Primitive dwellings, traditional buildings, vernacular architecture, architecture without architects -- all these are terms that have been coined to classify structures beyond the realms of the professional field of architecture. In the past two and one-half decades various movements have surfaced voicing questions, doubts and misgivings about aspects of our modernized, industrialized, urbanized world. These movements have called for world peace, a return to nature, a nuclear-free world; all concerns that in one form or another express a dissatisfaction with the impersonality of the modern age. With the emergence of such doubts and questions, the isolated and increasingly romanticized world of the peasant, the isolated bedouin, the African tribesman, all those societies that have been until now the special domain of anthropologists, have become the interest of a mass of parties, among them architects.

Architects began searching these worlds for clues to what made them work so well in the hope that they might give clues to how we, as professionals, could improve the services we provide to society. Naturally, this view was not widely shared in the profession, but it eventually became accepted enough to have its own publications and scholarly conferences. This was not anthropology; it was not social studies; it was architecture. It may have been rebellious in some ways, especially in seeking answers in the future in the primitive and the pre-industrial. However, the trend to study traditional settlements eventually built a strong enough argument to overcome most opposition and justify incorporation into the professional world.

FOUR DIFFERENT VIEWS OF THE VILLAGE

When I approached Farafra I belonged to the rebellious faction of the profession. I had my reservations, doubts and questions about my adopted attitude, but I was definitely an architect. The images of that different world portrayed in my field notes were exactly what I expected in terms of uniformity, cohesion and simplicity. Immediately on entering the village I began trying to capture it. I drew general plans and plans of various buildings; I asked inhabitants about building techniques and design decisions, hoping to tie physical elements to environmental, social and religious factors. My camera was also busy. I photographed houses inside and out. I paid particular attention to construction and decorative details, and composed photographs of streets and collections of houses to portray the atmosphere. At first, it did not really matter if those photographs included people; if they did, that was fine since people added life and a sense of scale. But sometimes I made attempts to exclude people because they hid important features I wanted to capture. There was no question about it -- my initial object was to document the physical elements of this world before it was engulfed by the indiscriminate monster of urbanization. Only as my stay in the village continued, and my understanding of the people developed, did I participate in an exercise that revolutionized my perceptions. One day I asked four village residents I had been working with to use my camera to take photographs that were important and telling to them. The photographs I had taken were not much different from those other architects have taken in similar contexts. They told, more or less, the same stories that have been told in numerous books and publications. But the photographs the Farfaronis took were far from my expectations; they told distinctly different stories. What follows is a presentation of a few of these photographs. Let us listen to what those individuals who took them had to say.

MABROUK

Mabrouk was a man in his late fifties who placed a strong emphasis on social relations and social cohesion in the village. He was very conscious of the complex patterns of social relations and the responsibilities and duties they entailed. In this he was not very different from most Farfaronis. He worked at the village health clinic, and he tended to his various plots of land, since agriculture is the major basis of the village's economy. When he chose to capture the most important and telling features of Farafra, all the photographs he took, except for one, were of people who represented various social institutions to him. "They are all equally important, all the ones I photographed," he said. "The *Sheikh* [village saint] is a man of *baraka* [blessings], and all people believe in God and in him, and the *wehda* [health clinic] has its business, and the co-op has its business, and the school has its business, and the *maglis* [village council] has its business, and the *omda* [social head of the village] also has his business. But each has his work to do. I mean, we can't do without any of them . . . all of us, we can't do without any one of them, not one.

FIGURE 1.
Tomb of *Sheikh*
Marzouk.

FIGURE 2.
The *wehda*.

"Of course I took one of *Sheikh* Marzouk (FIG. 1). This is one of God's saints, who feared their God rightly, and God placed in him *baraka*. So all the people believe in God and in him because he is a man of *baraka*. All the people, of course, visit him and celebrate him on the *Eid* [feast] and the *Big Eid* . . . and still, every day. Yes, his importance is in that he chose that his tomb be built in the center of the village. He chose that his mausoleum be here, to be built in the center of the village. This way he is close to all the people. All people seek him, for if someone makes him a vow [*nadr*] he fulfils it.

"Then, of course, those are the employees of the *wehda* and its workers (FIG. 2). They are my colleagues. At the same time, I chose to photograph it because it is very important in the village. It has great importance . . . the students, the strangers, the companies, all of them get transferred to the *wehda* night and day. The village suffered a lot before 1967. Before '67 there was no *wehda* and there was only a nurse and minor things like that. But since the *wehda* was built here, there is a doctor and improved health care in the village.

FIGURE 3.
The Agriculrural
Cooperative
Society.

FIGURE 4.
The School.

"Then there is the co-op which is very important in the village because it provides all the food provisions (FIG. 3) . . . so it is important. It sells cheaper than the small shops, at the same prices presently found in Cairo or in all of the governorate. It is a public service not only for the people in the village but also for the companies in the village. It brings flour, sugar and tea, subsidised and at free market prices as well . . . also different cans like luncheon meat, cocoa and what have you . . . yes, everything is there.

"This is the school (FIG. 4). I took this picture because the school is very important in Farafra. It educates children from first primary until sixth primary, and it has three intermediate level classes: first, second and third. And as of this year, '86 - '87, the intermediate school has become independent with its own headmaster and its own teachers."

Mabrouk also took pictures of the *omda* who has been the social head of the village since 1940, and of the village council, or rather, the workers in the village council. When I inquired why he talked about institutions, while choosing to photograph people only not the buildings or places they were using, he replied, "of course, the place without the people cannot do. Assume the co-op is now closed and has no people, how will the people outside benefit from it? Who will sell to them? Who will buy from it or sell to them and benefit from it? It's the people who sell. They are more important than the land and the buildings. I mean, the people . . . the men, they are more important than the land and the building. Because people give and take together, but the building doesn't move. I went and found the co-op closed with no people in it; now who will give me what I need? Of course, nobody will give me. The same goes for the *wehda* and the *omda*. So I can't do without any one of those. As for the *Sheikh*, he too . . . we can't do without him, because this is a person whom God gave *baraka*. So we ask God through his pious soul . . . we ask him to ask God to help me with my request, because he is accepted with God more than I and the rest of the people."

HASSAN

For Hassan, another participant in the exercise, the most important aspects of the world of Farafra were the ever-increasing work opportunities brought about by the new well and the government's large scale land-reclamation projects in the region. Hassan was one of a rising group of entrepreneurs who were very concerned with bettering the quality of life in the village through the exploitation of these opportunities. However, his zeal for work and improvement did not diminish the protectiveness and jealousy he felt toward the village. He did not see that change and a better standard of living should entail a degradation in moral values and ethical standards. Like Mabrouk, he chose to represent those ideas in photographs of individuals. It was only in the case of the two companies, which he saw as pivotal in Farafra's economic development, that he photographed objects -- in this case their billboard signs. "What places here could be photographed?" he explained. "As you can see it is all a bunch of buildings and some walls with some people sitting and working. It is not the most important thing . . . at least not to me.

F I G U R E 5.
Amm Muftah, the carpenter.

F I G U R E 6.
A peasant.

"Here in the next two, everyone is struggling in his own way. This one is holding his saw and working hard (FIG. 5). Yes, that's *amm* Muftah who comes four hundred kilometers to get a *hassana* [charity]. He rides from Dakhla, from Gharb el Mawhoub, on any car that is heading this way. There isn't anyone who does this work here. You won't find anyone who would accept to work at this job . . . just so. They don't consider it a job that would make a living.

"That other man has the *leif* [netting from palm trees] and is working making rope so as to make himself fifty piasters, ten piasters, a pound (FIG. 6). He sells this rope as a means of making ends meet, to bring in bread. Or he uses it for his cows or animals, instead of going to buy it and sitting in the sun -- no, he keeps busy with the rope. He is a man who is struggling, of course. There are others who are sitting, playing *siga* [a local game like checkers] or football or those who are sitting not benefiting the village in any manner whatsoever. In all of these people are struggling, everyone in their own way. Before the road, the whole village . . . we all had to work at those jobs with our own hands."

FAWZYA

In the case of the only woman participant, Fawzya, the outcome was not much different. It was very hard to find a woman who would agree to participate in such an exercise, since in this community women did not go out of their houses during the day. Even now, when things are changing, those who go out still restrict themselves to the small side streets. Fawzya was one of the few women, if not the only one, who could help me in such a task. She was a rebel in many ways since she chose not to conform to many of the local habits that restricted the freedom of women. Fawzya owed much of that attitude to the long period she spent in Cairo before returning to settle in Farafra. This knowledge of the outside world afforded her the unique position of being able to look critically at her own culture without having to accept all aspects of it. She was both an insider and an outsider to her own culture.

Friday, during the prayers, when all the men were in the mosque, women could go out to socialize and visit with each other freely. With their freedom of movement restricted all week, the women naturally saw Friday more as a day of feasting than as a simple holiday. And this was what Fawzya chose to capture in her photographs, the happiness and joy that were usually associated with this occasion. All five of her photographs were of smiling women and happy girls holding flowers. Of course, the choice was partially affected by the fact that Friday was the only day she could actually go out to carry out such a task.

"This woman had a *nadr* [vow] at the *Sheikh's* up there (FIG. 7). But even if she did not have that *nadr* I would have gone up anyway. Because it is beautiful . . . one feels at rest there. When you go up there you feel you are rested like that . . . the spot itself is really nice. She was placing her hand on the box putting the money in.

FIGURE 7.
Women near the
Sheikh's Tomb.

FIGURE 8.
Happy children.

"Then we were coming out to go down, we found the children happy and laughing (FIG. 8) . . . they were happy with the basil they had. So I felt that when you see a happy child, you yourself feel good and glad. So I took this one when we were coming down. We were still happy, this one was laughing and that one was joking, everyone was saying something about this and that . . . we were happy."

When I questioned her more about the reasons behind that happiness, she went on to explain, "You see, for us Friday is like the day of a feast . . . It is even better than the feast. They would say Friday is coming so it is like the arrival of the feast."

"It is even like the feast in that people wear new clothes," her sister, who was sitting next to her, added. "A woman might have brought something new, she wears it on Friday to show it off . . . it's normal. This is the best day we have."

"The women themselves are happy because this is our chance. Friday is our chance, the one who doesn't see another sees her at that time,"

Fawzya went on. "We go out together . . . whoever has something says it . . . this one is unhappy . . . this one is looking at that one's dress . . . things like that . . . happy. If anyone wanted to do anything they can't do it then. I mean, if you are going to cook or do something like that you have to postpone it until after the Friday . . . after the prayers. So there is the woman who is going out laughing and that one who is saying something, and one who is passing time, and another seeing what she hasn't seen before . . . so it is a nice and happy occasion."

ISMAIL

Ismail was another person who shared with Fawzya the position of being both an insider and an outsider, also by virtue of the eleven or twelve years he had spent outside of Farafra pursuing his education. He chose to return and live in Farafra because of the strong roots he had there. And even though he felt a strong sense of belonging to it, this did not mean that he had to accept all aspects of life there without questioning. He was always caught up in the process of resolving the dichotomies of change, of which he was an agent himself. He was a teacher of art who took up photography as a hobby, which somehow seemed very appropriate since he was inclined to use his camera as his third eye, the distanced eye through which he saw his own world and was able to re-position himself. I saw his photographs as a bridge between my own impersonal photographs of objects and the others' more person-centered, object-free ones.

"I wanted to show someone like this person working some handicrafts (FIG. 9). In the old times those people never knew anything about buying wool, buying shirts for the winter or such. They used to spin sheep's wool and make it into shirts . . . some with sleeves and some without. Here also, I am photographing the four individuals too, for it represents the manner of their *kaada* also . . . the manner of sitting of Farafra. Well, this manner of sitting could be a result of how in the old days there was little work. There wasn't much water or wells and things like that, so they had free time. Now, the young ones don't sit. The ones who sit are the older ones, those who are used to sitting like that . . . there wasn't any water or land then. But most of them would work at some craft while sitting there. The most popular craft was that of the wool, particularly when they were sitting like that against the wall. He would either be spinning or weaving or something like that.

"This man, I took his picture because he is a man who represents the history of Farafra (FIG. 10). This is a man who has approximately

FIGURE 9.
Old men sitting
against wall.

FIGURE 10.
An old man.

ninety-five years. He never saw any hospitals, nor was he treated by a doctor, nor . . . nor . . . and until this day, the men like him are still working. But now it's become that every other minute someone says he needs a doctor, he has this and that. While this man probably lived for ninety-five years without going to a doctor. So how come this is so? All these things make one feel that this person is an artistic treasure in the

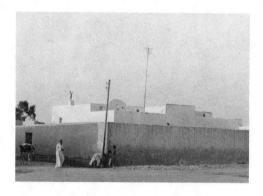

FIGURE 11.
The house of a
teacher.

village . . . from the point of view of how he looks and the effect of the
sun and weather on him and all that.

"This one . . . It is the house of one of the teachers here (FIG. 11). I was
thinking that this man used the same material but in an organized
manner and without cost. I mean, that the materials found here are the
same as in any other house you see around. He didn't bring anything
from the outside. But he used his brains in it, so that the materials are
the same while he worked on the house in a technical manner. But the
materials are the same . . . in the plastering technique the walls came out
straight; and he made the layout of the house without the help of an
architect. If you entered his house, you will find his layout with a guest
room, a kitchen, toilet, bedrooms and all this, but it is all on the basis
that he is a man who has been out and has seen, so he benefitted. But he
applied it with the same materials that we have. And this is the most
important point, because he did not use reinforced concrete or whatever .
. . it was the same wood and *garried* that we have. This is *tatawour*
[progress]. It is progress in the material . . . in the use of the material. It
is the right progress.

FIGURE 12.
The new section
of the village.

"I felt that this area represented *tatawour*, progress . . . the new part in the village (FIG. 12). Though the system of these resthouses is good, but merging the two next to each other! . . . In my opinion, if they were kept farther away from the old ones, then the old part would have been able to keep its same old character and the contemporary things would have just been farther away. If those structures had originated from the old ones it would have been good. It would have been a development in the material itself and it would have remained with the same idea and typology that we follow. But this is reinforced concrete. It changes the whole idea. Then the onlooker who comes from the outside, who might not even have that aesthetic side, or any idea of how materials are used without cost, he would look at those and see that what is behind them is zero, is ugly. Why? Because he looked at the contemporary in the midst of the old things. He cancelled the old side totally, why? Because it was those that attracted his attention. The first impression of the onlooker should be of an oasis. Yes, because I am entering an oasis. I am not entering a touristic city or whatever."

THE WORLD AS A MEANINGFUL PLACE

When reflecting upon the images presented by those individuals, we cannot help noticing the diversity of their perspectives. Mabrouk saw the village as a society of individuals constituting social institutions that contributed, each in a different manner, to the survival and well-being of the society as a whole. What he saw and talked about were the institutions, the *wehda*, the co-op, the *maglis*; what he photographed were the people. To him the institutions were the people who worked there, the particular individuals. He definitely did not see the buildings that housed these institutions as representative of them as I would have been inclined to see, as is evident from my own photographs of the same institutions. Then, when he did take a photograph of a building, the tomb of the saint, he talked about the picture as if it were of the saint himself. He said, "I took one of *Sheikh Marzouk.*" He did not say, "I took one of the tomb of *Sheikh Marzouk.*" He saw the *Sheikh* as being very much present, and that was the reason he was such a highly revered character. The tomb was only the physical sign of his presence.

Hassan saw the increasing work opportunities and work ethics as the most significant aspects of the world of Farafra. He relayed that through the photographs of individuals at work and of institutions that helped create work opportunities and thus contributed to the village's prosperity. Fawzya also saw that same world, but through the eyes of a woman who questioned the restrictions imposed upon women. These three all shared the same world, but each saw it through a slightly different lens, embedding it with different meanings. However, the manner in which they chose to reveal those meanings was clearly the same; it originated from one meaning-making system. Together they revealed to us a fairly telling image of the world of Farafra, quite a different image from the one we would expect to hear from a professional.

On a different note, Ismail's photographs and words exposed a different point of view. He had an inclination to objectify the subjects of his photographs as symbols of certain ideas and concepts. He chose to see the old man as an "artistic treasure" rather than by his name. He was able to see buildings and compositions of buildings as important elements that conveyed a message related to their owners and users, a conception of the world that was significantly different from Mabrouk's. In doing so, Ismail was reflecting the outsider part of him, the part that detached itself from the context when reflecting upon it. As the photographer and narrator, he talked about "them," "they" and "their," rather than "I," "we" and "us." Yet it was not hard to detect his attachment and belonging to this place he was talking about. The first photograph he chose to take was of the house he grew up in. The second-to-last photograph was of the house he presently lived in with his family. His photographs clearly reflected the struggle that Farafra was living through, the struggle he was an agent of. He photographed his history in the form of the old men, women and houses. He then photographed the new struggles of the present in the form of the newer section of the village, the same section he was building in. He was very concerned with reconciling the old with the new, the process of developing without discarding one's history and identity. This was a very personal dilemma for him. Ismail's photographs and words reflected an attitude that was much closer to mine than the others. He used his camera as a distancing tool. It allowed him to look in on his own world from the outside, to talk about it in objective terms.

As I listened more to these individuals, I began realizing how differently I was inclined to see their world. When I looked at their world, whether through my camera or through my eyes, I was always distancing myself. I objectified what I saw so as to fit it within a preconceived set of classifications. The other co-researchers, were more inclined to see through the superficial appearances of this world and capture its meanings. In other words, even though a formal analysis of the structure housing the *wehda* could tell us something about the nature of the environment and local building techniques, it would provide a fairly distanced view of what the *wehda* is to Mabrouk and the other Farfaronis.

Except for Ismail, there was general agreement that the world of physical objects was not of concern to them. The photographs they took were not simply of men and women they knew, but of the activities that these individuals performed. Together they represented significant parts of the world in which they saw themselves existing. This was how they preferred to see their world; this was how they gave meaning to their existence. And even though their vantage points differed, it was clearly a world that they shared. The silent physical aspects of that world were important only to the extent they were the setting in which those individuals went about their activities of making the world.

As opposed to these people, I, like other architects trained in a common professional tradition, was more inclined to see their world as a physical environment which they occupied. Capturing their world entailed capturing the physical environment as representative of it; in other words, capturing the buildings, streets, spaces, volumes, construction techniques, materials -- all the constituents of, and factors affecting, the physical world. This could also include capturing the people as representatives of some part of that world. One has only to examine the substantial literature that has been written about the subject to see how pervasive such an attitude is. Most authors are concerned with capturing the objects of a society and relating them to different aspects of a culture.   Such aspects used to be primarily environmental, though the people and their social and religious habits are now increasingly being considered. Authors differ on the emphasis they place on these various relationships. Yet in most cases the buildings and artifacts are at the center of attention, and everything else, including their makers, revolves around them. Of course, it could be argued that such an attitude is no less meaningful than that of the users and makers of the buildings and objects, since it merely establishes its own set of meanings. But the question remains: how related are these meanings to the meanings of the users and makers?   And what is it that we are studying, the world the users and makers have constructed, or our own construction of it?

A brief detour is in order here to look at another verbal image, one that would explicate what the literature has to offer. In *Shelter and Society*, Paul Oliver briefly summarized the predominant attitudes and responses of architects to vernacular shelter, as expressed in their writings and in the professional press. His list went as follows:

> a) Primitive -- supposed as the antecedent of formal architecture.
> b) Historical -- in recognition of a heritage of non-formal building which demands documentation and preservation.
> c) Functional -- in recognition of the expression of function of vernacular buildings in their form.
> d) Structural -- recognizing the forms most appropriate to the available materials used.
> e) Technological -- recognizing the limitations imposed by materials and the skillful employment of them to exploit their resources.
> f) Formal -- recognizing the use of primary forms to create mass and control spaces.
> g) Organizational -- in recognition of the disposition of parts, the separation of functions, the hierarchy of spaces in vernacular planning.
> h) Inspirational -- as a part of the visual sensory experience from which the architect may derive a stimulus to his own creativity.
> i) Derivative -- as a source of forms and treatment for their own work.4

Oliver seems to think that even though the first and the last categories might be unjustified in the terms of the present, there is still validity in each of the other approaches, and that their cummulative effect may lead eventually to a wider recognition of the value of vernacular building.

Such attitudes, be they functional, structural or formal, clearly belong to one discourse, regardless of their variations. If we contrast them with the attitude revealed by Mabrouk and Fawzya, we begin to realize the shortcomings of such intellectual taxonomies geared toward an objectified reality. Formal or structural aspects are definitely a part of that world, but alone they fail to reveal its most important aspects, the meanings that the makers of that world embed in it. How could they when the inhabitants themselves are often objectified so as to fit into the requisite set of categories! Moreover, such categories are usually quite meaningless to the inhabitants of a world, and hence rarely represent the same reality. So, if such categories are not relevant to people like Mabrouk and Fawzya, to whom are they significant? To the architects who are the only ones who understand this language?

This leads us to another significant question. Why have we chosen to use such terms as "traditional dwellings and settlements" or "vernacular architecture" to label the physical environment of these communities? Is it because they were not built by professional architects? Or is it because they do not follow our recognized formal and structural rules and norms? Would it follow then that there are two main categories of people, those who are traditional and those who are not, those who inhabit traditional dwellings and those who inhabit architecture?

Is it not also true that urbanism and modernism are simply other forms of traditions, and that when we say we are looking at traditional dwellings and settlements, we are saying no more than that we are looking at traditions that are different from ours? But who are we that we might fall under one banner like that? Clearly "we" refers not to our common cultural background but to the architect, sociologist or anthropologist in us. "We" implies the existence of a culture of professionalism that transcends other cultural boundaries. Like any culture, there is a discourse particular to this professional culture according to which the world is framed and defined. However, when this culture makes it its business to study the world of others, it becomes important to recognize that those others may have different world views.

CONFRONTING OUR DIFFERENTNESS

The experience I have just related problemizes the viability of our current professional attitude. It highlights what can be missed by an attitude that considers a building as simply an object made of certain materials, employing certain techniques, constructed by certain people, and located in a certain context. As Hassan and the others have so aptly showed us, a building is more than the sum of its parts. It only becomes a place through people's appropriation of it; and people only appropriate it by giving it meaning through their daily acts. Human beings are condemned to meaning, as Merleau-Ponty has said.[5] Everything they do and say is invested with meanings that are related to their particular view of the world. Hence, the question of studying the products of a people separate from the meanings that lie behind them becomes critical. Research on traditional dwellings has mostly avoided dealing with this subject, and has thus become another tool that adds to the museumification of culture. We have become too concerned with studying foreign settlements, in the sense that they are non-professional in origin, with the aim of preserving them before they are swallowed up indiscriminately by modern urbanization. But what customarily gets placed in the museum is the artifact and not its meanings. In this manner the artifact lends itself easily to classification, analysis and comparison.

It is legitimate to ask if it is ever possible to reach the deeper meanings of a physical environment without going to the meaning-makers as a primary source. It would not be enough for us to understand how the health clinic was built and how its form satisfied the various social and environmental factors around it; the people of Farafra showed us how one-dimensional such an understanding would be. The more I listened to Mabrouk, the more I began to understand the complexities behind such a simple word as a *wehda*. Mabrouk and the others taught me that three-dimensionality was not as I thought, the x,y, and z axes used in the construction of a drawing. A three-dimensional understanding was one that was built on the depth factor afforded by a lived reality. As long as I placed the physical object at the center of my vision, using it as a reference for everything else, my vision continued to be one-dimensional. Photographs and detailed formal analysis of the physical environment are not irrelevant; they are simply incomplete. It is only through authentic engagement with others as co-researchers and not merely subjects that we bridge the canyon of otherness and move closer to understanding the deeper meanings of the physical environment.

As professionals, we need to reevaluate our approach to the study of other traditions; this is where we could learn from the Farfaronis. Rather than seeing buildings as artifacts that express a culture and a people's way of life, we need to refocus our vision so as to see them as embodiments of a culture. The word "express" implies that buildings are representations of a way of life, which puts them on the same footing as products to be studied in a museum. Yet, they are more than that. They are manifestations of the culture. The physical environment, with its landscapes and buildings, is the spatial embodiment of the culture, just as the body is the spatial embodiment of the human being; both are inseparable and irreducible. We cannot think of the human being without the spatiality dictated by the human body, as Merleau-Ponty has explained. Likewise, we should not separate a culture from its spatiality. Even though a square room could be physically the same anywhere in the world, the meaning of a square room in Farafra is significantly different from that in Cairo, New York or Delhi. Differentiating between worlds primarily on the basis of material and formal criteria is too simplistic and one-dimensional a view of human culture. It reduces a qualitatively complex reality to a neat, abstract system of taxonomies. Paradoxes and contradictions are harmonized, and many dimensions are flattened into one. Such an approach makes the world more manageable, measurable and controllable, but does it allow us to understand the same world that people inhabit?[5]

REFERENCE NOTES

1. In writing this chapter, I have been influenced by the following written works not otherwise cited in these notes: H. Fathy, *Architecture for the Poor* (Chicago: University of Chicago Press, 1973); D. Frazer, *Village Planning in the Primitive World* (New York: George Braziller, 1968); P. Friere, *Pedagodgy of the Opressed* (New York: Continuum, 1984); C. Geertz, *The Interpretation of Cultures* (New York: Basic Books, 1973); *Local Knowledge* (New York: Basic Books, 1983); M. Heidegger, *Poetry, Language, Thought*, A. Hofstadter, trans. (New York: Harper Colophon Books, 1975); P. Oliver, *Shelter, Sign and Symbol* (New York: Overlook Press, 1977); S. Moholy-Nagy, *Native Genius in Anonymous Architecture* (New York: Horizon Press, 1957); C. Norberg-Shulz, *Genius Loci* (London: Academy Editions, 1980); A. Rapaport, *House Form and Culture* (Englewood Cliffs, NJ: Prentice Hall, 1969); E. Relph, "Place and Placelessness" (Thesis, University of Toronto, 1976); A. Saint, *The Image of the Architect* (New Haven: Yale University Press, 1985); J. Taylor, *Commonsense Architecture* (New York: W.W. Norton & Co., 1983); Y.F. Tuan, *Space and Place* (Minneapolis: University of Minnesota Press, 1977).

2. The term is used by Paulo Freire to mean a critical questioning of the taken-for-granted aspects of our world.

3. *Amm* is the Arabic word for uncle. Older men are called by this title out of respect.

4. P. Oliver, *Shelter and Society* (New York: Frederick A. Praeger, 1977), p. 25.

5. M. Merleau-Ponty, *Phenomenology of Perception* (London: Routledge & Kegan Paul, 1962).

COLONIAL COTTAGE SETTLEMENT
IN TASMANIA

JOHN C. WEBSTER

With the benefit of hindsight, European settlement in Tasmania can be examined as a colonization process on a *tabula rasa*. New building traditions evolved in Tasmania in the period 1804-1880 through the transportation of ideas from England, Scotland, Ireland and Wales. This process occurred in isolation over a relatively short period of time. Tasmania offers opportunities to examine in detail the development of a traditional dwelling and settlement style under almost laboratory conditions.

This chapter looks at the variety produced within the restraints of Georgian style, the limitations caused by the lack of an established building industry, and the process of developing designs for dwellings and settlements. This work is only in its infancy in Tasmania, and little consistent analysis has been undertaken so far.[1] However, the School of Architecture in Tasmania sees the study of early Tasmanian dwellings and settlements as a possible pointer toward development of a regional architecture that can meet current community needs. There is a perceived demand for dwellings that reflect fundamental principles of traditional architecture.[2] Such dwellings would allow for construction by an owner with or without professional help; they would embody designs that are adaptable, flexible and expandable; they would use local materials and rational construction methods; and they would respect rather than abuse the local context. These are all qualities that early settlers seem to have taken for granted.

Tasmania in the nineteenth century was six months sailing time from Europe and two weeks from Sydney. The isolation caused stylistic influences to lag behind European developments. But early environmental impacts were the product of conscious thought and deliberate action, and occurred at a time of shared values that gave direction and form. The process of settlement was also controlled by a bureaucratic, democratic military administration. Out of a series of restrictions -- military regulations and guidelines, a lack of industrial capacity, and limited knowledge of skills and construction techniques -- emerged a tradition of improvisation, adaptation and independence.

It now seems remarkable that the British Government chose such an *ad hoc* method for providing the skills and knowledge needed to build new settlements in Tasmania. Even more remarkable is that some of the environments created by the early settlers are still valued to this days and that many are still in use. The first settlers were a diverse group of emigrants: naval officers, marines, soldiers, convicts and free settlers. Many had no building experience. They drew upon remembered experiences, manuals, pattern

Australia

Tasmania ▽

FIGURE 1.
Australia and
Tasmania.

books and trial and error to produce a new Australian vernacular based on borrowed images and ideas about the old world.

In this year of the Australian Bicentenary, it is sad to reflect that the violence of European settlement in Tasmania prevented the assimilation of forty thousand years of aboriginal experience. The European settlers chose to live off the land; the aborigines were a part of it. Political decisions in Tasmania to this day are characterized by a vigorous debate over whether to conserve or exploit a rich body of natural resources.[3]

EARLY MARKS ON THE BLANK SLATE

Tasmania could well represent the Platonic ideal of an island.[4] It occupies 26,215 square miles and lies between 40 and 43.5 degrees south of the Equator. These are the same latitudes as northwestern Spain and the extreme north of California -- an area with which Tasmania has much in common climatically. Tasmania is a mountainous island with marked micro-climatic variations from north to south and east to west. It is one of the states which make up the Commonwealth of Australia.

The British established the first permanent European settlement in Australia in Sydney on Jan. 26, 1788. Fifteen years later the decision was made to form permanent settlements in Tasmania, primarily to thwart a French presence and influence in Australasia.[5] The first settlements in Tasmania were in the south of the island, at Hobart in the Derwent Valley in 1803, and in the north of the island in the Tamar Valley in 1804.

Tasmania's early settlers were all of British descent. They found a temperate climate and abundant supplies of water, wood and wild game. Arable land was quickly found and crops were planted. Breed stock was imported from the homeland. Tasmania became in the early nineteenth century a place of convict settlements and the emigration destination of second sons of more wealthy landowners in Britain. The combination of cheap convict labor

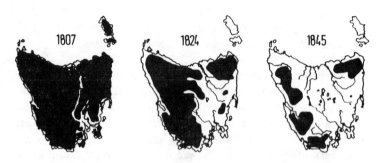

F I G U R E 2. Exploration and settlement of Tasmania, 1807-1845. Based on information in *Atlas of Tasmania*.[7]

and motivated emigrants, free settlers and ticket-of-leave persons,[6] resulted in the energy and motivation needed to produce permanent dwellings and settlements and quickly establish a tradition. Figure 2 gives an indication of the speed with which the small number of early settlers explored the difficult terrain of mountainous, thick forests. The areas unexplored by 1845 are still uninhabited.

The original community which settled in the Tamar Valley was a military party comprising a lieutenant colonel, a surgeon, a storekeeper, three officers, sixty-four soldiers, twenty women, fourteen children, a free settler, seventy-four convicts and two convicts' wives: in all one hundred and eighty-one persons.

King argues that Australia's settlement was not a traditional process but a concerted attempt by a "military dictatorship" to create a provisional England in the Antipodes.[8] If one accepts this assertion, it is remarkable that the process was so successful and that the gradual adaptation of built form to climate produced very pleasing traditional forms both in settlements and dwellings.

In the process of settlement on isolated virgin territory, what constraints, real or imagined, controlled the first decisions? What education, skill or knowledge did the early decision-makers, both in the London Colonial Office and in the Office of the Governor in Sydney, have in terms of settlement formation?   Where did the military officers actually controlling the layout of new settlements learn the craft of site planning? The fact that the first sites chosen for settlement in both the north (York Town) and the south (Risdon) were abandoned, suggests that the process was more intuitive than scientific.[9]

The settlers imported their ideas and culture to a new land. In setting up these early settlements, the requirements of access to drinking water and land for food-production competed with military considerations such as strategic location. There was no need in Australia to site towns for defensive purposes or to concentrate dwellings. Land was plentiful, and speculative land subdivision became a major factor in Tasmanian settlement formation.

The grid pattern was universally adopted as a conceptual framework for new town development. This led to the imposition of street layouts that ignored topography and natural drainage. Some resultant street designs and detailing produced memorable and interesting townscapes. The current practice of regulated subdivision design influenced by contour street planning, gravity sewerage and traffic engineering might be logical and rational, but it certainly does not produce memorable townscapes. The early land surveys were based on a grid pattern which offered many advantages to surveyors opening up new territories (FIG. 3). New boundaries could be made by extending existing survey lines, and lots formed by this grid could easily be surveyed. Denholm has developed the theme of the surveyors' influence and the straight line.[10]

Governor Darling, in regulations published in the *Sydney Gazette* in May 1829, formulated simple rules for the development of country towns in Australia. These regulations appear to have been almost universally followed from the early days.

1. The streets, wherever practicable from the nature of the grounds, are to be made rectilinear, and cross streets are to be laid down at right angles to the main street.
2. The width, to be reserved for main streets, is to be one hundred and twenty feet, consisting of a one hundred foot carriage way and a footpath, on each side of ten feet. In cross or inferior streets, width is to be eighty-four feet, that is a carriage way of sixty-six feet and a footpath

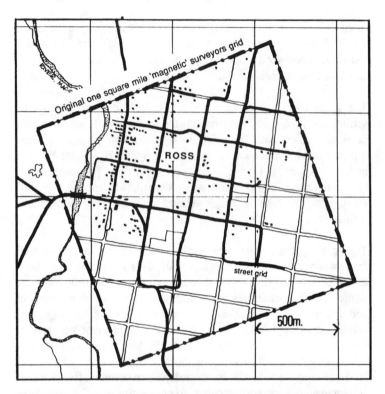

F I G U R E 3. The surveyor's grids; Ross. The sketch indicates the original surveyors' blazed square mile magnetic survey boundary, with the later and smaller square street grid related to a water course. This results in two offset grids overlaying each other, clearly reflecting settlement layout based on pure geometric considerations. The sketch is based on aerial photographs.

on each side of nine feet.
3. Within the limits above mentioned, no steps or projections of any kind will be allowed.
4. The distance from the footpath in every street, at which all persons will be required to build, will be exactly fourteen feet, and the open space thus left is to be appropriated exclusively to open verandah, or such plantation as may be desired. The distance, therefore, between the opposite houses, will be one hundred and twenty-eight feet in the main streets, and one hundred and twelve feet in the cross or inferior streets.
5. With the view of preserving general continuity of line, the above-mentioned space of fourteen feet, in front of the houses will be required to be enclosed with an open fence or where it may be desirable to have free Ingress and Egress as to shops, etc., by posts, ten feet apart.

The early settlement patterns were controlled by regulations. These regulations provided the broad framework within which the richer overlaying patterns of roads, sidewalks, gardens, fences and eventually the dwellings could be developed. The grids formed a chessboard, metaphorically and literally, upon which the games of traditional dwelling and settlement could be played.

The rules and guidelines for settlements seem to have been developed in the very early days by the lieutenant governor in Tasmania. The primary method of communicating the rules for urban settlement was by means of the early newspapers.[11] The year 1817 seems to have produced an outburst of regulations by the lieutenant governor; they appeared in the *Hobart Town Gazette* on May 17, Aug. 30, Oct. 25 and Nov. 1.[12] The primary concerns appear to have been to ensure that land was fenced and that dwellings were erected quickly. The threat of resumption of land by the crown seems to have been the method by which the regulations were enforced. Control over the design and construction of dwellings was entrusted by the governor to the deputy surveyor. In addition, surveyors were to control the layout of individual dwellings and ensure that fences and elevations con-

F I G U R E 4. Land subdivision; Zeehan.

formed to accepted standards.[13]   The relationship of buildings, sheds or outhouses to the street was of concern, as was the encroachment of buildings onto crown land. It is interesting to speculate on the reasons these regulations were promulgated. Were they the result of a military sense of order or the beginnings of local municipal improvement, or were they based on urban design ideals and the desire to make a place out of no place?

The need to mark the land and define land ownership was a strong pattern in the early landscape (FIG. 4). The regulations exhorted landowners to fence the land to define ownership. This applied to both urban and rural holdings. The issue of defensible space must have been a strong natural force in what must have seemed to Europeans a largely undifferentiated environment. In Tasmania, defensible space was reduced in some situations to the cottage garden which had to be protected from marauding native wildlife (FIG. 5). The fence pattern continued to be a significant feature in later buildings (FIG. 6).

The fence in colonial Australia was an important traditional dwelling element. A block of land with only a tent or rude shelter on it would first be fenced and defined. Then erection of a more permanent or durable dwelling could begin.[14]

TRANSPORT OF TRADITIONS

A rich history of cottage architecture was brought in the mental baggage of the early settlers. Published works describing ideas for building form and plan type were numerous in Britain, based on a romanticized view of the world.[15]   Numerous pattern books existed. They contained designs for structures from cottages to villas, accompanied by analytical and critical comments. The desire to influence the formation of the built environment is part of a long continuum of desire to develop a better sense of place by design with patterns.

F I G U R E 5.
Early rural fence;
unknown location.
(S o u r c e : The
Archives Office of
Tasmania -- F.
Smithies Collection.)

F I G U R E 6.
Arthur's Circus fence;
Hobart.

The influence of pattern books in Tasmania has not been researched adequately. No original pattern books have been found in public library collections. To the average colonist, expert architectural advice was not readily obtainable. Copy or pattern books must have been a powerful influence on the development of traditional Tasmanian building form, particularly in the more polite architecture.

According to Powell, pattern book designs were more or less influenced by picturesque ideals and social morality.[16] Their basic theme was to provide designs for model cottages that would help in matters of health, morality, style and cost. Powell outlines specific advice from a number of pattern books of this time. The patterns offered advice from correct ceiling height, to the design of "easy" stairs, to plans for tool sheds, privies and convenient water supplies. The patterns promoted dryness and health by advising that ground floors be raised above their surroundings, that buildings not be built against earthen banks, and that bedrooms not be built in attics. All these faults were common in traditional late-eighteenth-century British architecture.

A typical recommendation of these early books was that entrances should be screened and that cottages should face east or south with carefully positioned doors and windows. This advice was regularly followed in Tasmania with no allowance for the fact that the sun moves from east to west across the northern sky in the Southern Hemisphere.

The important point to note is that the Georgian patterns of the early nineteenth century were followed almost universally in Tasmania, and were based upon aesthetic, functional and technical considerations. Glassie has provided insight into the process by which a tradition is developed in new surroundings.[17]

Early settlers would have been faced with a vast range of possible settlement solutions on the *tabula rasa* that was Tasmania. Considering the magnitude of the problem, the obvious solution was to start with forms transported from home. In this way settlers could concentrate on solving a smaller number of more pragmatic problems. Glassie has concluded, ". . . greatest problems were solved when he accepted the traditional forms that were efficient summaries of problems already solved. His procedure was to keep on replicating forms -- to stay within his traditional competence -- until the form appeared wrong."

The underlying architectural pattern language consisted of Georgian proportions brought to Tasmania in the subconscious minds of military officers, prisoners and freemen. The great advantage of this was that it provided a shared common direction for legislators, owners, builders and clients, and the potential to create a *genius loci*.[18] The Georgian culture that these early settlers brought provided a model upon which decisions could be made according to a set of rules. These rules promoted symmetry, balance, order and regularity -- a geometrical discipline of the person, the house, the garden, the street frontage, and the farm based on the idea of the straight line.

Denholm argues that these geometric patterns based on straight lines resulted from two traditions: the orthodox military and the purely aesthetic.[19] These two traditions often complemented each other, frequently merging in the middle ground between real problems and aesthetics. This happy marriage helps account for the widespread use of a geometrical dwelling and settlement tradition inspired by Graeco-Roman forms.

In his argument for a return to a Georgian aesthetic in dwelling design, Terry has recently outlined what he believes to be the seven points of a classic approach.[20] These are as follows: the plan is symmetrical, albeit with slight variations; the front door is in the middle; the windows are about right in size and shape and come in the right place; the roof is pitched and simple; the materials are traditional; the walls that you see are solid and load-bearing, carrying the roof and walls; the proportions of the house are expressed by one of the classical orders; and the proportion of the ground floor is often expressed in small order around the front door.

The Georgian model was adopted for practical reasons as well as for considerations of aesthetics and familiarity, and it evolved over time. It was simple and concise, easy to build and capable of numerous variations. This is shown by evidence that the Georgian style was adopted for all levels of building endeavor, from rude timber huts in the bush to the politely-mannered, architect-designed stone mansions of the wealthy (FIG 8).

DURABLE DWELLINGS

In most cottage pattern books the largest number of rooms was four, which seems to have been at or above cost limitations. Designs for smaller cottages were put forward down to one-room size. These were built well into the twentieth century, using

F I G U R E 7. The simple Georgian cottage (rectangular plan). (S o u r c e : Mr. E. Bezzant, The Archives Office of Tasmania.)

F I G U R E 8. Settlers' dwelling in a clearing in a typical Tasmanian eucalyptus forest known locally as the bush. Note the fencing, slab construction, raised floor and outbuilding with chimney, presumably the kitchen. (S o u r c e : The Archives Office of Tasmania.)

methods of rude timber construction based on the Georgian model for plan form and window placement.[21]

It is interesting to note the similarity of the historical development of dwellings in Australia and America, where, according to Morrison, an evolution from rude to more polite cottages took place.[22] The Australian gold rush produced a strong link with California in the mid-nineteenth century, and the migration of building ideas from this source has not been fully researched in Tasmania.

The predominant form for a dwelling was that of a small wooden, brick or stone cottage of one or two rooms with a central door and a window on either side of it. This basic unit was adopted throughout the nineteenth century. Most early dwellings were made from variations of this basic unit according to simple rules of addition. Figure 9 shows typical generic cottage plans.

Salmond has classified possible arrangements of the basic "Georgian box cottage" by the combination of simple elements. The possibilities included the following: the addition of another box unit, the variation of roof form solutions to similar plans, the addition of a verandah, and the addition of a lean-to or skillion.[23] These simple formal possibilities produce as many as 216 combinations without taking into account ornamentation, orientation, window shape or the use of dormers. Figures 10 and 11 illustrate basic cottage forms based on the repetition of simple basic units. Figures 12, 13 and 14 illustrate actual cottages.

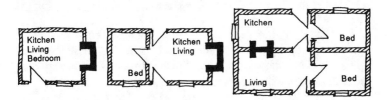

F I G U R E 9. Typical cottage plans.

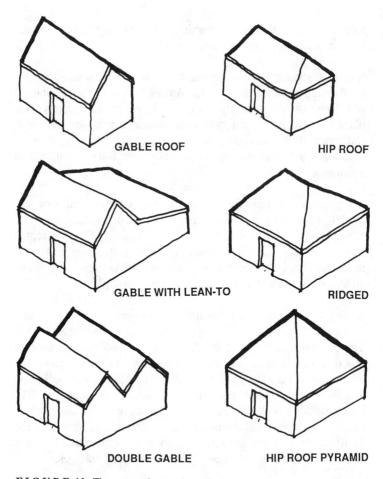

GABLE ROOF

HIP ROOF

GABLE WITH LEAN-TO

RIDGED

DOUBLE GABLE

HIP ROOF PYRAMID

FIGURE 10. The rectangular or square plan cottage.

A successful design feature of these simple forms was their flexibility, especially when built in timber. It was possible to put up the shell of a house, and then finish it inside when money and time allowed. The enlargement of dwellings by addition was easily accommodated. Many were designed so extensions could be added without disruption to the original form. Rapoport has said: "Another characteristic of vernacular is its additive quality, its specialized, open-ended nature, so different from the closed,

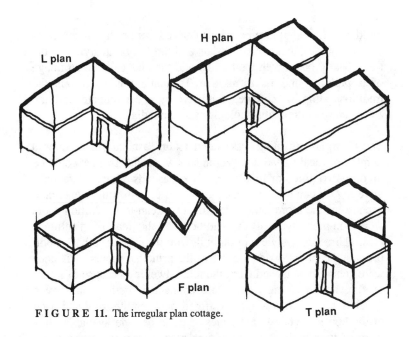

F I G U R E 11. The irregular plan cottage.

final form typical of most high style design. It is this quality that enables vernacular buildings to accept changes and additions which would visually and conceptually destroy a high style design."[24]

William Hodges, a landscape painter who accompanied Captain Cook on his first voyage to the South Pacific in 1768, stated that buildings would have to be adapted as a result of climate conditions. He also presented an important precedent, which could be applied to architecture of the late eighteenth and early nineteenth century in Australia, when he wrote: "When emigrations to foreign climates take place, their prototype will follow the colonist, and, by its own rules, genius will, and may at last stretch and improve it to the highest degree of perfection."[25]

Because the early settlers came from a variety of areas within the United Kingdom, the regional influences of any particular county or district is not found in Tasmania, as it is for example in the German settlements in Hahndorf in South Australia.[26] The early buildings were simple expressions derived from minimal construction techniques, available materials and the Georgian style. In the traditional process both the builder and the client shared an image of a building and its form. In Tasmania this form was the traditional English cottage, tempered by local climate and the architecture of the British colonies such as India.

The Georgian dwelling was added to in Tasmania to produce a number of local variations. Verandahs were added which could be on one, two, three or four sides of the basic dwelling. Verandahs were not as common in Tasmania as on the Australian mainland because of the more temperate climate. Lean-to or skillion roofs were common, typically as additions at the rear of dwellings. Central breezeways were often built from front door to back door, providing central corridor access to the principal rooms. Kitchens were generally detached from the main dwelling because of a fear of fire, and in some cases were connected to the house by a covered way. Window types differed between the front and back of the house. When larger panes of glass became available, they were of very high cost, and sliding sashes were more expensive than the established smaller six-, eight- or twelve-paned casement windows. The more expensive windows appeared on the public front of dwellings, with the older and cheaper windows installed in the rear. Wall thicknesses were recommended in the pattern books at 16 inches for stone and 13 1/2 inches for brick.

The wide availability of building materials in Tasmania gave rise to only minor regional variations. All areas had access to timber, however sandstone was of better quality and easier to obtain in the south. The availability of convict labor made dressed-stone construction feasible in the early days of settlement. Dressed stone was used in combination with all other materials: brick, timber, dolerite and sandstone rubble (FIG. 15).

Bricks were used from the earliest days of settlement and many local kilns were built. The quality of the bricks varied greatly, but they were generally soft, being fired in timber kilns. Handmade convict bricks are a feature of Tasmanian building heritage,

FIGURE 12.
Hip roof pyramid;
Richmond.

FIGURE 13.
Ridge roof;
Tunbridge.

FIGURE 14.
Verandah; Perth.

bearing distinctive thumbprint and government arrowhead marks impressed into them.

The ready availability of large-section timber made the use of wood-frame construction widespread. Tasmanian timbers are exceptionally hard, particularly when seasoned, and they were

FIGURE 15.
Dressed sandstone
and brick cottage;
Oatlands.
(S o u r c e : The
Archives Office of
Tasmania.)

difficult to work with hand tools. Tasmanian eucalyptus, which was exploited by the early settlers, could be split cleanly, and a tradition of using rough weather-boards, palings and shingles developed (FIG 16). The timber was also used in round sapling form, particularly for roof construction. Timber was worked in its green state as well as when dry and seasoned, and sawing and nailing were often next to impossible. Shrinkage was a problem, and construction detailing often had to allow for as much as 20 percent shrinkage.

The use of bark, palings or shingles for roofing was widespread until the mass production and importation of corrugated iron.[27] This material was identified in Loudon's pattern book in 1833:

> Corrugated iron roofs are composed of sheet iron, impressed so as to present a surface of semi-circular ridges, with intervening furrows, lengthwise of the sheet. By this means the sheet, from a plain flat surface having no strength but from its tenacity, becomes a series of continued arches, abutting against each other; and the metal by its new position, acquires strength also from its hardness. To give an idea of the strength acquired, it is observed by Walker, the inventor of this mode of preparing sheet iron, that a single sheet of iron so thin it will not continue in a perpendicular position, will, after undergoing the process of corrugation, bear upwards of 700lbs weight, without bending in the least degree.[28]

The use of corrugated iron roofs is perhaps the most singularly enduring tradition in Tasmania. Corrugated steel is still used widely in Australian domestic architecture in both traditional and non-traditional ways. The material has endured and been adapted

F I G U R E 16. Shingle cottage; Middlesex Plains. (S o u r c e : The Archives Office of Tasmania.)

to use in dwellings for more than one hundred and fifty years.[29] Because of the relatively high amount of rainfall, early roofs using shingles had to have a steeply-pitched form, often 45 degrees. This roof form continued after corrugated iron came into widespread use, even though the pitch, and consequently the amount of material, could have been reduced. The practice of laying corrugated iron directly over existing shingles could have contributed to the development of this tradition. Laying corrugated iron over shingles had the added advantage of providing thermal and sound insulation. The tradition of a steeply-pitched roof over the main building, with a less steeply-pitched lean-to or verandah appended to it, is central to the Tasmanian vernacular (FIG 17).[30]

THE FUTURE ISN'T WHAT IT USED TO BE

Three architectural authors, Boyd, Cox and Rapoport, have all independently reached conclusions which focus on the central issue in the decline of traditional dwellings today.

FIGURE 17.
Gable roof
with lean-to.

In 1969 Boyd described the problem as a desire for "featurism."[31] He identified this as, ". . . the evasion of the bold, realistic, self-evident, straight-forward, honest answer to all questions of design and appearance in man's artificial environment."

Cox believed that the decline was related to that of excessive choice. "In any art or architectural exercise, the limitation and economy of materials is an essential ingredient of that art. Today there are too many alternatives, which cause the breakdown of craft, art and tradition. Our architecture generally shows an assorted array of new materials, each competing for dominance with the architectural framework."[32]

Rapoport concluded that three reasons accounted for the demise of the traditional as a regulator in the built environment: the greater number of building types required today, the loss of a commonly shared value system, and the premium our culture puts on originality. "In most traditional cultures, novelty is not only not sought after, but is regarded as undesirable," he wrote.[33]

A traditional style evolved in Tasmania because of the need to adapt to place as well as to attend to social, economic and aesthetic needs. The important links with the motherland in house style fulfilled an important psychological need. The use of familiar forms also had many other practical advantages.

The development of dwellings and settlements was successful in conditions far less favorable than today. The *tabula rasa* experiment seems to have worked and a tradition seems to have been established. It would be interesting to consider what the outcome of a similar experiment would be today.

Today new dwellings and settlements are still largely generated by speculative subdivision of land. However, the form of buildings no longer reflects a common community ideal and purpose. Rational construction methods and optimization of dwelling form are no longer priorities. Little or no thought is given to the long-term public costs of speculative subdivision and development. The cost the community will continue to pay for this lack of leadership is sad, economically, visually and spiritually.

A return to the simple repetitive box cottage unit, with all its possibilities for addition, adaptation and simplicity, could be a more attractive and attainable model for future building. For the under-employed, the concept of owner-building or sweat equity could be very attractive. This suggests that we might look to the ideas of the past and search for a new attainable vernacular. As fundamental changes occur in the structure of society, a new direction and leadership may have to be adopted that may once again create a community approach to settlements and dwellings.

We can all learn from the past. The lessons from the Tasmanian *tabula rasa* experiment may be relevant to our emerging needs for the provision of dwellings and settlements in the late twentieth century.

REFERENCE NOTES

1. For details of the 43 unrelated studies covering 3,468 heritage sites undertaken up to 1985, see C.B. Tassell and M. Morris-Nunn, *Tasmanian Heritage Assessment: A Study* (Australian Heritage Commission and the Queen Victoria Museum and Art Gallery, 1985).
2. This demand is seen in a small depressed island economy as issues emerge as to future lifestyles, and as fundamental questions are raised about settlement formation and conservation.

3. The confrontations between supporters and opponents of the proposed dam on the Franklin River, located within a World Heritage National Estate, drew local, national and international news coverage and divided the community between the "greenies" and the "exploiters." An on-going debate surrounds the issues of sustainable futures and exploitation of natural resources. The current concern (October 1988) is a $1 billion chemical pulp mill.

4. M. Roe, *The Heritage of Australia -- The Illustrated Register of the National Estate* (Melbourne: Macmillan Company, 1981), 7/1. "Its shape of triangle or heart stands clear, its beauty is rich and varied. Island-ness is the central fact of Tasmanian life affecting economic growth, social attitudes, personal experiences."

5. Until 1856 Tasmania was called Van Diemen's Land. The name "Anthony Van Diemenslandt" was originally given to the island by the Dutch explorer, Abel Janszoon Tasman, who discovered the island in 1642. The island's name was changed in 1856 to remove the stigma which had come to be associated with the original name because of the transportation of convicts to the island and the harsh penal settlements on it.

6. A ticket of leave was a document which entitled a convict to freedom of occupation and lodging within a given district or colony until the original sentence expired or until he obtained a pardon.

8. A.D. King, *The Bungalow* (London: Routedge and Kegan Paul, 1984). In chapter 4 the author develops the theme of the influences that appear to have shaped Australia's colonial urban environment.

9. The Dec. 8, 1987, issue of *The Bulletin* argues that the military background of the early governors and lieutenant governors, navy and army, had a marked influence on the early land subdivisions.

10. D. Denholm, *The Colonial Australians* (Melbourne: Allen Lane, 1979). Chapter 4, "Men Drawing Straight Lines," p. 57, contains the following description: ". . . a relentless pattern of military precision, square, upon square endlessly repeated with minimum regard to terrain whether hill, valley or cliff, every last square mile of grid oriented to magnetic north."

11. The first edition of the *Hobart Town Gazette* appeared in 1816. The *Tasmanian and Port Dalrymple Advertiser* was established in 1825. The role of the printed word in the development of traditional buildings and settlements in Tasmania is important and warrants further study.

12. Typical regulation from the Oct. 25, 1817, *Hobart Town Gazette*:
    "The Public are required to take notice that no Buildings in this township are to be erected but in a Regular line of the Streets; and in future the plans of those dwellings intended to be built must be submitted to the Inspection of the Deputy Surveyor, in order that they may be in Conformity with the Regulations fixed upon His Excellency the Governor in Chief on the subject. No Skillings are permitted; and those which have been built, being in breach of a former Order, if they be not added to with Twelve months from this Date, will be Removed. It is further directed that all persons in possession of Town Allotments, without lots of Time, make a path-way, nine feet wide, in front thereof; and it is also expected, that the paling or fence put up in a decent and regular manner, or other wise they will be removed. The intent being that those Individuals who are allowed Town allotments should immediately proceed to fence them in and to build, in any case where no steps for commencing these objects are taken within one month from the period of the Ground being taken in possession by the Deputy Surveyor, he will authorize to revoke the location, and to allow it to any other

person up the regulated terms. It is therefore proper that no person should make application for a Town allotment until quite prepared to build; but the Deputy Surveyor is instructed to state that the Lieutenant Governor will attend to Applications for such from all well conducted persons; their being Crown prisoners forming no objection. By Command of His Honour the Lieutenant Governor.
G.W. EVANS, Deputy Surveyor General."
13. *Hobart Town Gazette*, May 17, 1817: ". . . the duty of seeing that all private buildings in the Town be constructed according to the ordered Elevations and Form; has the fences of all. Town allotments be placed in the direction assigned for the streets; and that no individual be allowed to encroach upon ground not included in the space actually allotted to him . . ."
14. The regulations reinforced this pattern, as in the *Hobart Town Gazette*, Aug. 30, 1817: ". . . to all such persons that unless they immediately enclose allotments that have been measured to them, and erect suitable buildings there on within two years from the time the land was marked out for them, agreeably to the Conditions of the obligations entered into by them, the Land will revert to, and be taken possession of by the proper Officers accordingly, A. W. H. Humphery."
15. It is ironical that many early convict settlers were able to achieve a measure of this romantic and idyllic vision, whereas members of their more unfortunate peer group in Britain were feeling the depression of the Napoleonic Wars.
16. Pattern books available at this time included the following: John Loudon, *Encyclopaedia of Cottage, Farm and Villa Architecture and Furniture* (London, 1833); John Wood, *Series of Plans for Cottages or Habitations of the Labourer* (1781); Nathaniel Kent, *Hints to Gentlemen of Landed Property* (1775); Richard Elsam, *Hints for Improving the Conditions of the Peasantry*; David Laing, *Hints for Dwellings* (1801).
17. H. Glassie, *Folk Housing in Middle Virginia, A Structural Analysis of Historic Artifacts* (Knoxville: University of Tennessee Press, 1975).
18. For a detailed discussion of the concept of *genius loci*, or "spirit of place," see C. Norberg-Schulz, *Genius Loci Towards a Phenomenology of Architecture* (New York: Rizzoli, 1980).
19. Denholm, *The Colonial Australians*, p. 49.
20. T. Terry, "Genuine Classicism," in *Transactions 3*, Vol. 2 no. 1 (London: RIBA Magazines, 1982).
21. For a contemporary account of rude timber building (1840-41) with construction details, see D. Burn, *"The Colonial Magazine"* -- *A Picture of Van Diemen's Land* (Hobart: Cat & Fiddle Press, facsimile 1973).

"The mode of erecting these log-huts was extremely simple; first, four strong corner posts were sunk, then a somewhat lighter sort were upreared; into which were afterwards inserted the doors and windows. Strong wall plates are then laid along; these are, in some instances, grooved; a heavy log, with corresponding groove, being partially sunk in the earth beneath. Split gum or string bark are then inserted and hammered close together, until the wooden wall becomes complete. Where the groove is unused, the one end of the slab is nailed against the wall-plate, the other being sunk some six or eight inches into the soil; in either case one of the gables is left for a chimney, whose ample dimensions and primitive masonry fills up the entire of this space. The tie beams, connecting the wall plates, are frequently adzed; and these, being laid with boards, serve as excellent bed-chambers for juvenile branches. Thatch or shingles was the usual roof covering. The master's hut completed, another for his convicts was erected at some little distance -- this latter serving likewise as a kitchen for the family. It was rather uncommon to plaster the interior of these wooden walls some having their interstices entirely open, others being caulked, as it were, with wool, and some being plastered outside. The geniality of the climate without, and the roaring log-fires within, subjected the inmates to no hardship, and little inconvenience."

22. H. Morrison, *Early American Architecture, from the first Colonial Settlements to the National Period* (New York: Oxford University Press), p. 9.

23. J. Salmond, *Old New Zealand Houses 1800-1940* (Auckland: Reed Methuen, 1986).

24. A. Rapoport, *House Form and Culture* (Englewood Cliffs, NJ: Prentice-Hall, 1969).

25. W. Hodges, *A Dissertation on the Prototypes of Architecture* (London, 1787), pp. 2, 12-13.

26. For a concise overview of the ethnic groups that built America, see D. Upton, *America's Architectural Roots* (Washington D.C.: The Preservation Press, 1986).

27. The term corrugated or galvanized iron is widely used in Australia but is not technically correct. The material it refers to is zinc-dipped steel.

28. J. Loudon, *Encyclopaedia of Cottage, Farm and Villa Architecture and Furniture*, p. 1130.

29. For a detailed description of the contemporary use of corrugated steel in Australian Architecture, see P. Drew, *Leaves of Iron Glen Murcutt: Pioneer of an Australian Architectural Form* (Sydney: The Law Book Company, 1986).

30. For a full description of hot-climate cottages in Australia, see P. Bell, *Timber and Iron Houses in North Queensland Mining Settlements, 1861-1920* (Brisbane: University of Queensland Press, 1984).

31. R. Boyd, *The Australian Ugliness* (Melbourne: Cheshire, 1969), p. 26.

32. P. Cox, *The growth and decay of an Australian vernacular architecture; Man and landscape in Australia* (Canberra: AGPS, 1976), pp. 216-230.

33. Rapoport, *House Form and Culture*, pp. 6-7.

All photos are by the author unless otherwise indicated.

THE EMERGENCE OF
THE CENTRAL HALL
HOUSE-TYPE IN THE CONTEXT OF
NINETEENTH CENTURY PALESTINE

AHARON RON FUCHS
MICHAEL MEYER-BRODNITZ

The central hall house is a traditional type of dwelling that appeared in mid-nineteenth century Lebanon and Palestine, becoming by the end of the century a prominent element in the landscape. Its plan is based on a central hall flanked by rooms on either side. Characteristically the hall opens through a triple-arched opening in the center of the facade. The house is often, though not always, topped by a steep, tiled, hip roof (FIGS. 1-5).[1]

The second half of the nineteenth century was a period of dramatic change throughout the Ottoman Empire, affecting both Lebanon and Palestine, then Ottoman provinces. In many ways the emergence of the central hall house-type is an expression of the impact this period had on Lebanese and Palestinian societies. We aim to demonstrate how this occurred in the context of Palestine.

The study of vernacular architecture in traditional societies seeks to explain how certain forms emerge out of certain physical, social, technological and economic contexts. However, only rarely is it possible to trace the forces that influence the emergence of a specific house-form at a particular time. Actual historical events, their links and their sequence, can be obscure; so can be the

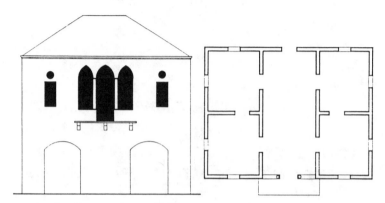

F I G U R E 1. The central hall house: schematic plan and elevation.

deliberations of contributors to the evolution of the form, and the meanings they and their contemporaries associated with it. It is, therefore, difficult to establish with any degree of certainty what the architectural origins of a vernacular house-type are. Nevertheless, when confronting such a house-type, architectural scholars must speculate about the forces involved in its birth. Evidence may be circumstantial and arguments conjectural, but without a general theoretical framework to map the relationships between a particular house-type and its evolution within as broad a context as possible, the ground is not set for more focused research. The general mapping may be regarded as a learned working hypothesis within which detailed research may take place. This discussion of the central hall residential house-type is an example of the theoretical and practical difficulties of such research. It is quite clear this house-form that became prevalent in the late nineteenth century was different from its immediate local predecessors and yet not completely new to the region. What is not clear is how it established itself. The events and circumstances of this period also mark a break with a long period of stagnation in the Levant. This chapter attempts to link architectural evolution with historical change. It is based on the general assumption that architecture is not the arbitrary whim of individuals but the selective outcome of a diffused, intricate, social preoccupation with construction. It is also based on the assumption that the types and forms that best suit the purposes they serve, the meanings they

FIGURE 2.
A central hall house
in Haifa. Built 1888.

FIGURE 3.
Yefet (Ajami) Street,
Jaffa. Central hall
houses line this street,
that follows the line
of the fortifications
dismantled in the
early 1870s.

carry, and the means used to carry them get accepted as norms and become the vernacular of their times. The study of these questions of suitability constitutes the proper course for research into the origins of vernacular form.

In 1800 Palestine was one of the most neglected provinces of the Ottoman Empire. Inhibiting tenure laws, ruthless taxation, lack of security and isolation from the West had brought centuries of stagnation. But in the nineteenth century the challenge of the West and its industrial revolution made reform inevitable. The Ottoman reform policy launched in 1839, the *Tanzimat*, gradually introduced new legislation, revised the taxation system, and abolished restrictions for Europeans and for subjects who were not Muslim. Law and order were enforced with greater determination, and as a result, the economy expanded and the population grew. In fact, all aspects of life were affected. A new age began.

FIGURE 4.
An interior of a
central hall house in
Nazareth.

FIGURE 5.
An interior of a
central hall house in
Nazareth. A loggia
with an arcade
(a *riwaq*) is seen
through the triple arch
of the central hall.

THE CENTRAL HALL HOUSE AND THE PROCESS OF URBANIZATION

A process of urbanization was one of the new developments in
many Ottoman provinces in the nineteenth century. In Palestine

some cities grew rapidly, especially Jerusalem and the coastal towns of Jaffa and Haifa. Jaffa, with 2,750 inhabitants in 1800, grew to a population of 10,000 by 1880. The population of Haifa grew six-fold in the same period, from 1,000 to 6,000 residents. In 1800 these towns still had unbuilt spaces within their walls, but during the first decades of the new century these were gradually filled in. In the 1860s, when security still required the closing of town gates at night, living outside the walls was unsafe. A turning point occurred in the 1860s and 70s when accelerated population growth and improved security caused some towns to expand beyond their ancient boundaries. Fervent building activity began. Conrad Schick, a Swiss architect resident in Jerusalem, wrote in 1880, "It may be estimated that the number of dwellings during the last 25 years has been more than doubled, probably trebled."[2]

The central hall house seems to have evolved during this period and was certainly an important part of the new Arab building activity. Proud new houses of the type started to crop up in the ancient fabric, as in Acre, or outside the walls, as in Jaffa, or in both places, as in Haifa. By the turn of the century, these new houses with their characteristic red tile roofs transformed the urban landscape. A comparison of earlier and later photographs of towns such as Haifa and Nazareth demonstrates how change took place.[3]

The new central hall houses differed considerably from houses of the older tradition. These earlier dwellings had a closed and introverted character. The rural Palestinian house was a single, poorly-lit space -- a basic type known in many parts of the Middle East. Townhouses often had an inner court, secluded from the outside.[4] In contrast, central hall houses had an extraverted character. They were not arranged around courts but often stood detached in a garden (FIG. 2). They had wide apertures and open balconies, and their exterior design reflected their interior arrangements and the wealth of their owners.

Some have already suggested that the central hall may have been a transformation of the traditional court, but the hierarchical differentiation between the two types of closed spaces, the hall and rooms, was a new concept.

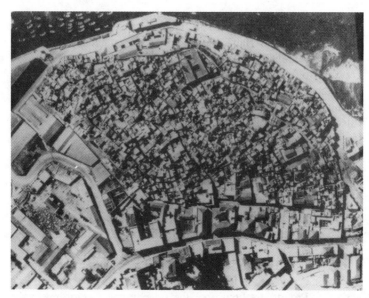

F I G U R E 6. Aerial view of Jaffa, 1936. Tile roofs of central hall houses, some of which are seen in Figure 3, contrast with the fabric of the old town.

Towns in Palestine usually conformed to the traditional Arab type. They had a dense, compact structure and were often surrounded by walls. The new central hall houses, which appeared outside the town walls, often formed a dispersed urban tissue that contrasted with the dense fabric of the traditional town. An aerial photograph of Jaffa reveals the contrast between the old and new fabrics (FIG. 6). The open character of the new manner was in part an outcome of an increased sense of security, but it may also have reflected a change in attitude toward environment and community.

SOCIAL CHANGE AND THE IMPACT OF THE WEST

An important development in Palestine in the second half of the nineteenth century was the rise of a new class of rich, educated city dwellers called *effendis*. Economic growth, trade with Europe and the import of capital offered new opportunities to amass wealth, which city notables were in the best position to exploit.

They also benefited from the growing apparatus of the local Ottoman administration in which they came to hold positions.

Some actions of the Ottoman regime indirectly helped the prosperity of this class. Tax farming passed into urban hands when the government began auctioning off the job of tax collection instead of entrusting it to rural sheiks. The new tenure law of 1858 which introduced land-registration indirectly caused the accumulation of large tracts of farm land by city notables and merchants, who thus became landlords. The villagers distrusted the intentions of the government and failed to register their land, which led eventually to loss of ownership. Attempts to collect taxes in cash, instead of in kind as previously, also allowed city moneylenders to gain control over land of indebted villagers.

Urban landowners were usually absentee landlords. They preferred speculation in land, collection of rent and moneylending to investment in agricultural intensification. Large sums could thus be spent on building luxurious houses. The central hall house was the typical dwelling of the rich urban elite. With its extravagant tile roof, reminiscent of an *effendi's* red *fez*, it became a status symbol of the new class.[5] The central hall house expresses then the class consciousness and concern for public image that was characteristic of this new class.

The nineteenth century marked the end of a long period of isolation for the Levant. Although the process of opening to the world was much slower in Palestine than in Lebanon or Egypt, it was still of great significance. The development of new transportation options made possible an ease of travel and trade that had been unknown for centuries. Steam ships, which started to arrive regularly in Jaffa in the 1850s, made the journey to European ports faster and safer. Inland transport also improved, as roads suited for coaches were built in the 1860s and a railway was constructed in the 90s.

Communication developed. European post agencies started to operate in the 1850s, telegraph communication reached Jerusalem in 1865, and newspapers and translations from European languages appeared. The presence of foreigners on the local scene began to be felt in various ways. Western merchants and tourists moved freely after the Egyptian occupation of 1831-1840, European consulates opened, and missionary organizations initiated various philanthropic enterprises.

NEW BUILDING MATERIALS

One result of the opening of the Levant was the introduction of imported, industrialized building materials. Sawed timber, roof tiles and sheet glass were the first products to appear, gradually gaining acceptance during the later half of the nineteenth century.[6] The basic forms of the central hall house probably originated without relation to the new materials. Nevertheless, their use as in tiled roofs and glazed windows quickly became an integral part of the design.

The traditional builder usually had to rely on materials found in the nearby environment. Therefore, the methods of construction varied regionally -- the availability and quality of wood being a major determining factor. Imported materials brought freedom from local resources. Sawed timber and roof tiles permitted the construction of a light roof, simpler than vaulted structures and superior to the traditional earth-packed roof. It also permitted the construction of relatively thin walls thirty centimeters in thickness, instead of the massive walls that resulted from traditional techniques.

The typical triple-arch opening belongs to a light roofed structure, as it implies a flat ceiling, made possible only by the use of timber. More massive building methods would have required the construction of relieving arches and biforic or triforic openings, as is common in traditional stone structures in Palestine. The triple arch could have originated in regions such as Mount Lebanon where enough timber existed to permit flat ceilings of a reasonable span.[7] Yet only imported timber can account for the widespread adoption of the central hall house, with its typical openings and hip roof, especially in Palestine where wood was scarce.

The earliest central hall houses seem not to have had glazed windows, but by the 1880s glass became integrated into their design. The arched openings were fitted with wooden frames and divided by decorative mullions, which were sometimes very intricate and patterned with colored glass. The glazing of the triple-arch opening allowed the hall to be enclosed, thus protecting it from the weather, and yet admitting adequate light. The hall turned from a semi-open space into a protected room that suited the standards of modern, and Western, living. After it was enclosed, the hall could be lavishly furnished and decorated.[8] European furniture -- tables, chairs, beds, cupboards -- was alien to Oriental domestic architecture, and its introduction must have caused changes in the multi-purpose way that rooms in the Orient were used. Central hall houses also lacked storage niches characteristic of Oriental houses.[9]

CULTURAL INFLUENCES

Along with new materials and products came acquaintance with Western ways and ideas. The rich urban elite was most affected by Western culture. Its members adopted Western clothes and manners, traveled to Europe, learned foreign languages and sent their sons to study in Western-style schools and universities. Nevertheless, traditional values remained rooted. Western influence was superficial, "a thin varnish" as Oliphant writing in 1884 put it.[10]

To what extent does the central hall house reflect Western influence? Writing on Lebanon, Feghali regards this type as unauthentic, a result of foreign influences, and Weulersse speaks of "la nouvelle demeure imitee de l'Occident."[11] It is true that by being a detached, independent block, arranged in pedantic symmetry, this house-type was not alien to Western norms. It can remind one of a Palladian villa or even of a Virginian Mansion. Its similarity to medieval Venetian architecture has been pointed out by many. Still, besides occasional decorative elements, it is difficult to interpret it as outrightly and definitely derivative of European models. Furthermore, the central hall house could most

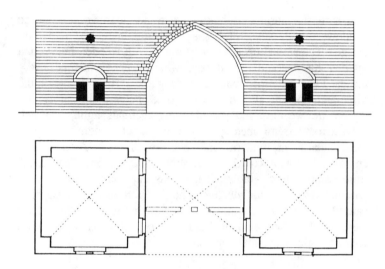

F I G U R E 7. *An Iwan*-House in Yafa, near Nazareth.

convincingly be explained as an evolution of a traditional Islamic form, the *Iwan*, or more accurately of the simple vernacular type, the *Iwan*-house (FIG. 7).[12] Such a view conforms with the idea that nineteenth-century Levantine society was basically traditional. The central hall house should be interpreted as more the outcome of a process of modernization than of Westernization. It was as different from European design as it was from traditional design. In describing Lebanese society at the end of the century, Hitti said a new "rhythm of life emerged in Lebanon, one that is neither old nor new, but a combination of the two."[13] The central hall house may be considered an expression of this new rhythm.

Another possible source of influence on the design of the central hall house could have been Turkish architecture. Turkish cultural impact in the Arab provinces was never deep, especially in daily life. Before 1908 the Ottoman regime never followed a policy of Ottomanization, and did not try to impose Turkish ways and culture on the provinces, leaving the various communities a degree of autonomy. In this atmosphere, indigenous provincial styles of architecture persisted. Paradoxically, in the nineteenth century, when the Empire was slowly disintegrating, Ottoman influence on architectural style seemed to grow. It was the independent Muhamad Ali of Egypt who added to Cairo's Mamluk skyline the prominent Ottoman silhouette of his new mosque. Istanbul, the Ottoman capital, was still a dominating political and cultural center for a large part of the Near East. Its impact on provincial daily life strengthened, as a policy of reform brought greater involvement by the regime in the provinces. More attention was paid to the Arab provinces as the Empire was losing its European possessions. Until the end of the century, when Arab nationalism developed, most subjects, particularly the urban elite, generally identified with the Ottoman system. The red *fez* was adopted as a symbol of Ottoman loyalty. Thus, in provincial towns, Istanbul must have been regarded as a model to be imitated, and with improved transportation and communication, its fashions became more accessible.[14]

To be sure, Ottoman influence, though more marked in the nineteenth century, could have been little more than superficial. Furthermore, Turkey itself was in the process of absorbing Western influences, and to a certain extent what it transmitted was second-hand Westernization. The Turkish Baroque style may be an example of this kind of influence. This combination of Ottoman and Baroque styles, which started to evolve in eighteenth-century Istanbul, spread in the nineteenth century to many provincial towns in vernacular and sometimes vulgar versions. Emigration in the nineteenth century had brought large numbers of minorities of widely varied ethnic backgrounds to many eastern Mediterranean cities such as Alexandria and Beirut. The Turkish Baroque perfectly suited the cosmopolitan atmosphere that evolved in these towns. The influence of this style has been described in Cairo and Baghdad.[15] It is also evident occasionally in central hall houses in some decorative elements such as decorated ceilings or window grills.[16]

The central hall house may have more than a stylistic affinity with Turkish architecture. Resemblance to the Turkish vernacular mansion, the *konak*, can be shown in several respects.[17] First, the *konak* often stands in a walled garden, one of the patterns common to central hall houses. Second, the placement of a *piano nobile*

F I G U R E 8. Houses in Bethlehem. A nineteenth century drawing. (S o u r c e : L. Valentine, *Palestine Past and Present*, London, F. Warne, p. 75.)

over a ground floor used for services is typical to both types. In both types the ground floor is usually built more massively. Third both types often employ tiled, hip roofs, although these are quite different in detail. Fourth, triple-arched arcades constructed of wood are common in Turkish houses as subdividing elements, often in front of the *Iwan*. Stone versions of such arcades, identical in design to the triple arch opening on the facade, often serve a similar function in central hall houses.[18] The floor of the *Iwan* thus formed may be slightly raised, as often is the case in the Turkish house. Houses in Turkey may occasionally present three-arched openings on the facade. The final similarity between the two house-types is that the plan of a *konak* consists usually of three basic elements, the *sofa* (which is a wide deck), *Iwans*, and rooms, composed in various combinations. In the latter part of the nineteenth century it became common to group rooms and *Iwans* on both sides of the *sofa* so as to create a central hall scheme.[19] Sometimes *Iwans* were placed on both sides of the *sofa*, forming a cross-like space. This variation finds a parallel among the sub-variants of the central hall house.[20]   It would be reasonable to suggest an interpretation of the central hall house as a Levantine version of the *konak*.

The central hall scheme appeared in some other vernacular traditions influenced by the Ottomans, especially those in Greece and Bulgaria. This gives rise to the suspicion that the central hall house may be part of a wider phenomenon.[21] Thus, the central hall house seems to capture the ambiguities of old and new, Orient and Occident, indigenous and cosmopolitan in nineteenth-century eastern Mediterranean culture.

THE CENTRAL HALL HOUSE IN LEBANON

The Mount of Lebanon has been suggested as the region where the central hall house evolved.[22] The abundance of central hall houses in Lebanon may imply that the focus of the phenomenon is there. Unlike Palestine, Mount Lebanon was a prosperous region in the first half of the century. This was due to its natural resources and to its autonomous position in the Ottoman Empire. Conditions in the Lebanon were thus favorable for the evolution of architecture of a higher quality. The rule of Bashir II (1800-1840) was a golden age for the Mountain, and fine palaces, especially that of Bashir in Beit ed-Din, were built. Whereas in Palestine it was difficult to find experienced masons in the first half of the century, Mount Lebanon had already developed such building traditions.

The 1860s were a turning point for Lebanon as well as for Palestine. The Organic Act of 1861 restored stability after twenty years of turmoil that reached a peak in the massacres of 1860. The processes that began in Palestine at the same time -- modernization, economic growth, the flourishing of coastal towns, and the rise of trade with Europe -- likewise occurred in Lebanon, yet even more intensely. Central hall houses also appeared at this time. Beirut, depicted in David Robert's drawings as a town of old, traditional architecture, was being transformed with central hall houses.

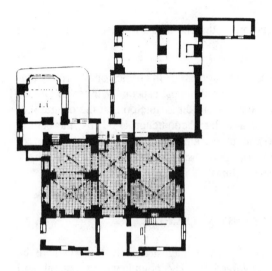

FIGURE 9.
House Ticho, off
Jaffa Road, Jerus-
alem. The older core
(dotted) is a single-
story, vaulted
structure which dates
to before 1864.
Based on D.
Kroyanker, 1985,
p. 209.

Some of the new developments in Lebanon did not have parallels
in Palestine. Unlike Palestine, where land was passing into the
hands of a few urban notables, Lebanese society included a class
of small landowners.[23] The formation of this class was the result
of the decline of the Lebanese feudal aristocracy, whose privileges
were finally eliminated in the 1861 constitution. Village families
were able to buy land from the feudal landowners with money
earned in Beirut or abroad. This was probably the initial social
background for the spread of the central hall house in Mount
Lebanon.[24]

The phenomenon of emigration is also peculiar to Lebanon. It
began in the 1870s and intensified in the 1890s. In the years 1900-
1914 Mount Lebanon lost a quarter of its population. The result,
however, was the remittance of money to family members
remaining on the Mountain. Former emigrants later returned to
retire.[25] The central hall house evolved to meet the needs of a
well-established rural population that was no longer dependent on
agriculture and was acquainted with modern comfort. These
people could afford to build spacious houses, though the houses
were more compact and bourgeois than the feudal palaces of the
old order. Most of the houses in Mount Lebanon were probably
built as a side-effect of emigration.[26]

THE PALESTINIAN ASPECT OF THE CENTRAL HALL HOUSE

The central hall houses examined by Fuchs in Palestine in 1987, mainly in Haifa, but also in Acre, Nazareth and Jaffa, do not differ significantly from those described in Lebanon. It is plausible to regard central hall houses in the coastal towns and in northern Palestine as an extension of the Lebanese phenomenon. The Palestinian coastal region is geographically similar to the coastal region of Lebanon. Beirut was more than a regional center; the towns of Palestine, including Jerusalem and Jaffa, depended on its port, and it also was a cultural center in the Arab world. It is no wonder that the Palestinian elite found Beirut a model for imitation.

There also had been some immigration of Lebanese into Palestine. Merchants, who invested there and bought land and plantations, eventually came to stay.[27] Part of the Christian population of Palestinian coastal towns may have originally come from Lebanon. Thus the Lebanese themselves could have introduced Lebanese architecture into Palestine.

F I G U R E 10. House Duzdar, Jerusalem. Between 1889-1910. (S o u r c e : D. Kroyanker, 1985, p 170 .)

In Palestine the central hall house seems to have been a predominantly urban phenomenon, whereas in Lebanon it was also a rural one -- although the distinction between town and village in these regions may be ambiguous. The difference in the social development of Lebanon and Palestine described above may explain this.

The presence of central hall houses in a Palestinian town reflects that town's prosperity in the nineteenth century. They may also have cultural significance in that they indicated the extent of the town's conservatism or openness to new ideas. This is not a wholly geographical question. Central hall houses were scarce in conservative Muslim Safed, whereas they were abundant in nearby Nazareth.

Central hall houses in their classic Lebanese form are most common in Palestinian coastal towns and in the north of Palestine. Towns in the inner parts of the region, particularly in the Judea mountains, seem to have developed central hall traditions that were distinct from the Lebanese tradition. These traditions were also based on the *Iwan* house. Bethlehem provides a good example. Schick writes that the building activity in Bethlehem was particularly intensive and conveyed "the impression of a newly built town."[28] Bethlehem also became a center for skilled masons. Old photographs and drawings of the town show a townscape dominated by houses with arched, *Iwan*-like openings at the center of their facades. These houses, some of which survive today, have not been studied. They probably had a central hall plan. Figure 8 shows an example of such a house which seems to have a central hall two rooms deep similar in plan to the house in Jerusalem shown in Figure 9. Like the typical Lebanese central hall house, this house consisted of a *piano nobile* above a ground floor. The *piano nobile*, however, had a vaulted ceiling, although Ragette says this never occurred in central hall houses.[29]

The central hall plan was very common in the new Arab houses in Jerusalem, but these deviated in detail from the Lebanese canon. In spite of the fact that imported building materials were available and often used, many houses were built with traditional techniques employing vaults, thick walls and biforic windows. The delicate triple-arch openings that do not belong naturally in such massive construction tended to take the form of three independent apertures, a door flanked by two windows (FIG. 10).[30]

Tradition was stronger in Jerusalem than in Haifa, Jaffa or Nazareth, towns that grew rapidly from mere townships. Jerusalem had a more conservative society and a more substantial architectural heritage, which may partly explain why traditional forms were adhered to there. On the other hand, the extensive building activity of European organizations in Jerusalem caused the adoption of many Western decorative motives which combined with Oriental elements to create a unique stylistic mixture.

HISTORIC CHANGE AND THE CENTRAL HALL HOUSE

Vernacular architecture is the product of a wide range of environmental, functional, social and cultural factors relevant at a given period. A vernacular house becomes the reflection of the spirit of an age by expressing the combined effect of these factors on a way of life. The study of the evolution of a vernacular type is instrumental to understanding the real significance of historical developments.

The study of the central hall house is of particular interest, as it gives an insight into a period of dramatic change -- change that rapidly affected every aspect of life, as a stagnant, medieval society underwent rapid modernization. The house-type this period produced evolved indirectly out of such processes as Ottoman reform, the Industrial Revolution, European Imperialism, and the Lebanese struggle. The emergence of the central hall house coincides with the 1860s, the period when the impact of these processes began to be most significantly felt. The changes to nineteenth-century Lebanon and Palestine did not destroy local tradition nor overwhelm it. Rather, they permitted the evolution of an architectural idiom of independent qualities, one that was neither new nor old.

The central hall house phenomenon is not restricted to Lebanon, as has been claimed. But in Palestine it had a somewhat different social background, and in the inner areas of the region, it evolved in indigenous ways. The existence of similar solutions elsewhere in the eastern Mediterranean, such as in Turkey, the Balkans and Venice, gives rise to the suspicion that it might have been an even wider phenomenon, a fact that invites further research.

REFERENCE NOTES

This paper is partially based on an M.Sc. dissertation, "The Arab Central Hall House Type in Israel," submitted in 1987 by A.-R. Fuchs to the Faculty of Architecture and Town-Planning, Technion -- Israel Institute of Technology, Haifa. It was supervised by Dr. M. Meyer-Brodnitz and Prof. A. Kashtan.

1. A detailed description of central hall houses in Lebanon, with many drawings and photographs, is given in Friedrich Ragette, *Architecture in Lebanon: The Lebanese House During the 18th and 19th Centuries* (Beirut: American University of Beirut, 1974), the most comprehensive work on the subject. An important criticism of Ragette is found in Philippe Panerai, "Geometries et Figures Domestiques," in *Cahiers de la Recherche Architecturale* 10-11 (Paris L'Equerre: SRA, 1982), pp. 126-139. Other references to Lebanese houses may be found in Jacques Weulersse, *Paysans de Syrie et du Proche-Orient* (Paris: Gallimard, 1946), pp. 262-270; Soraya Antonius, *Architecture in Lebanon*, (Beirut: Khayat's, 1965); Haroutune Kalayan, *L'Habitation au Liban* (Beirut, 1966); Fouad el-Khouri, *Domestic Architecture in Lebanon* (London: Art and Archaeology Research Papers, 1975). Detailed descriptions of Palestinian central hall houses, with plans and photographs and a typological study based mainly on fieldwork in Haifa, is included in A.-R. Fuchs, "The Arab Central Hall House Type." Little attention was given previously to this house-type in Palestine. Toufiq Canaan, *The Palestinian Arab House, Its Architecture and Folklore* (Jerusalem: Syrian Orphanage Press, 1933, also published in *Journal of the Palestine Oriental Society* 12-13, 1932-1933), dedicates five sentences to the central hall scheme. A paper on the subject is J. Koerner, "Arab Building Practice in Town," in *Bisde Hathechnika* (Tel-Aviv: The Engineers, Architects & Surveyors Union of Palestine, 1942, in Hebrew), pp. 36-38. See also David Kroyanker *Jerusalem Architecture -- Periods and Styles, Arab Buildings Outside the Old City Walls* (Jerusalem: Keter, 1985, in Hebrew), pp. 67-154.

2. C. Schick, "Progress in Palestine," in *Palestine Exploration Fund Q. St.* (1880), p. 187. For a summary of statistics on Palestinian towns in the late Ottoman period, see Yehoshua Ben-Arieh, "The Development of Twelve Major Settlements in Nineteenth Century Palestine," *Cathedra* 19 (Jerusalem: Yad Ben-Zvi, April 1981, in Hebrew), pp. 83-143. For detailed descriptions of individual towns, see Alex Carmel, *Gesichte Haifas in der turkischen Zeit 1516-1918* (Wiesbaden: Otto

Harrassowitz, 1975, Hebrew edition 1969); Ruth Kark, *Jaffa -- a City in Evolution 1799-1917* (Jerusalem: Yad Ben-Zvi, 1984, in Hebrew); Yehoshua Ben-Arieh, *Jerusalem in the 19th Century: the Old City* (New York: St. Martin Press, 1984, Hebrew edition 1977); *A City Reflected in Its Times: New Jerusalem -- the Beginnings* (Jerusalem: Yad Ben-Zvi, 1979, in Hebrew).

3. Houses employing a central hall scheme may date earlier than 1860. An example is Abdallah Pasha's summer house on Mount Carmel, built in 1827-1828 (Carmel, *Gesichte Haifas*, p. 76). Dating houses from the Ottoman period is difficult for lack of records, but Ragette succeeded in establishing approximate dates of construction of Lebanese houses as early as 1725 (*Architecture in Lebanon*, p. 129.) Mary E. Rogers, sister of the British vice-consul in Haifa, gave an early allusion to the central hall in Palestine in *Domestic Life in Palestine* (London: Bell & Daldy, 1862), p. 81. The drawings depicting Palestinian landscapes and towns made by the British painter David Roberts around 1839 show no central hall houses. Collections of old photographs, such as Ely Schiller, ed., *The First Photographs of the Holy Land* (Jerusalem: Ariel, 1979) and *The First Photographs of Jerusalem and the Holy Land* (Jerusalem: Ariel, 1980), show no central hall houses before the 1880s, if the dates of the photographs may be trusted; however, one photograph of Haifa in the 1880s in Schiller, *The First Photographs*, (1979), p. 90., shows quite a few such houses. It would not be safe to date typical houses earlier than 1855.

4. For a recent study of the Arab rural house, see Yizhar Hirschfeld, *Dwelling Houses in Roman and Byzantine Palestine* (Jerusalem: Yad Ben-Zvi, 1987, in Hebrew), pp. 54-128. Detailed studies of traditional dwellings in Palestinian towns are lacking. For recorded plans, see Hirschfeld, *Dwelling Houses*, pp. 119-128; H. Waddington, "A Note on Four Turkish Renaissance Buildings in Ramleh," *Journal of the Palestine Oriental Society* 15 (Jerusalem: 1935), pp. 1-6. Other references include Shimon Landman, "Notes on the Structure of Nineteenth Century Arab Dwellings in Jerusalem," *Cathedra* 25 (September 1982, in Hebrew), pp. 177-182; Canaan, *The Palestinian Arab House*, pp. 63-71.

5. For a short account of the changing structure of Palestinian society, see Joel S. Migdal, *Palestinian Society and Politics* (New Jersey: Princeton University Press, 1980), pp.9-17. On agrarian relations, see Gabriel Baer, *Introduction to the History of Agrarian Relations in the Middle East 1800-1970* (Hakibbutz Hameuchad, 1971, in Hebrew), pp. 7-82. On the houses of the Muslim elite in Jerusalem, see R. Kark and S. Landman, "Muslim Neighborhoods Outside the Jerusalem City Walls During the Ottoman Period," in E. Shaltiel, ed., *Jerusalem in the Modern Period* (Jerusalem: Yad Ben-Zvi, 1981, in Hebrew with English abstract), pp. 174-211. On the roof as status symbol, see Ragette, *Architecture in Lebanon*, p. 112; El-Khouri, *Domestic Architecture in Lebanon*, p. 16.

6. Timber was imported from Turkey, tiles from Marseille. Local round tiles were used very occasionally before the 1860s, as drawings and photographs indicate. The Marseille ones are flat. The first tile roofs were probably added to existing flat-roofed structures, which may partly explain the acceptance of the hip roof form and the avoidance of gables. Drawings may imply the occasional use of sheet glass by the 1840s. Titus Tobler, *Nazareth in Palastina* (Berlin: Reimer, 1868), p.31, described as fairly frequent the use of glazed windows in "Turkish houses" in Nazareth in 1868. Schick, "Progress in Palestine," p. 187, writes in 1880: "Nearly all houses have now glass windows, a rare thing 20 years ago." Iron "I" beams were already available in 1880 according to Schick, "Die Baugeschichte der Stadt Jerusalem," *Zeitschrift der Deutschen Palastina Vereins* Vol. 7 (1894/95), p. 270. Concrete floors were introduced toward the 1920s. This permitted the construction

of houses with several floors of the central hall scheme. The main features of central hall house did not begin to disintegrate until the 1930s, when reinforced concrete frame structure was introduced (Ragette, *Architecture in Lebanon*, pp. 188-191; Fuchs, "The Arab Central Hall House Type," pp. 44-45).

7. A photograph of Majdal e-Shams, near Mount Hermon, from the 1870s in Eyal Onne, *Photographic Heritage of the Holy Land 1839-1914* (Manchester Polytechnic, 1980), p. 28, shows a village with houses roofed probably in traditional packed-earth style. Many houses seem to have unglazed triple-arched arcades. These forms were most probably made possible by the availability of local wood.

8. The details of the masonry of the triple-arch openings continued to ignore the need to install window frames (Ragette, *Architecture in Lebanon*, p. 109).

9. See the detailed list of typical furniture in Michel Feghali, "Notes sur la Maison Libanaise," in *Melanges Rene Basset*, I (Paris: Leroux, 1923), pp, 164-165; Ragette *Architecture in Lebanone*, p. 115. Rogers describes the naive use of European furniture in a house in Nazareth (*Domestic Life in Palestine*, chapter 7).

10. See the chapter on "Domestic Life among the Syrians" in Laurence Oliphant, *Haifa, or Life in Modern Palestine* (London, 1887). See also Shimon Shamir, "The Impact of Western Ideas on Traditional Society in Ottoman Palestine," in Moshe Ma'oz, ed., *Studies on Palestine During the Ottoman Period* (Jerusalem: Magnes Press, 1975), pp. 507-514. On Westernization in Lebanon, see Philip K. Hitti, *Lebanon in History* (Macmillan & St. Martin's Press, 1967), pp. 470-473.

11. Feghali "Notes sur la Maison Libanaise," pp. 164, 165; Weulersse, *Paysans de Syrie et du Proche-Orient*, p. 267.

12. The *Iwan* (*Liwan*) is an architectural motive prevalent in many forms of Muslim architecture. It appears in its most basic form in the *Iwan*-house -- a vernacular type known mainly in Syria and Lebanon. For descriptions, see Richard Thoumin, *La Maison Syrienne* (Paris: Leroux, 1932); "Deux Quartiers de Damas," *Bulletin d'Etude Oriental* (1931), pp. 120-125; Ragette, *Architecture in Lebanon*, pp. 66-87. For a detailed discussion of the origins of the central hall house, see Ragette, *Architecture in Lebanon*, pp. 88, 115-119. J.-Ch. Depaule, Sawsan Noweir and others, *L'Habitation Urbain dans l'Orient Arabe -- Elements d'Architecture* (Ecole d'Architecture et d'Urbanisme de Versailles, 1984) discusses the manipulations of the *Iwan* motive in a wide array of oriental domestic traditions. It discusses the central hall house on pp. 125-131.

13. Hitti, *Lebanon in History*, p. 473.

14. On policy toward Arab provinces, see Engin D. Akarli "Abdulhamid II's Attempt to Integrate Arabs into the Ottoman System," in D. Kushner, ed., *Palestine in the Ottoman Period* (Jerusalem: Yad Ben-Zvi, 1986, and Leiden: Brill, 1986), pp. 74-89. On Ottomanization of the urban elite, see Ruth Roded, "Social Patterns Among the Urban Elite of Syria During the Late Ottoman Period," in *Palestine in the Ottoman Period*, pp. 152-160. On Turkish influence on clothing, see Shmuel Avitsur, *Daily Life in Eretz-Israel in the XIX Century* (Tel-Aviv: Am Hassefer, 1972, in Hebrew), p. 54.

15. See Janet L. Abu-Lughod, *Cairo* (Princeton: Princeton University Press, 1971), p. 94; John Warren and Ihsan Fethi, *Traditional Houses in Baghdad* (Horsham: Coach, 1982), pp. 154, 168; John Fleming "Cairo Baroque," *Architectural Review* 579 (March 1945), pp. 75-82

16. Decorated ceiling panels found in the more elegant central hall houses were often painted with geometric or floral motives and landscapes (Fuchs, "The Arab Central Hall Type," photo. 101-117; Kroyanker, *Jerusalem Architecture*, pp. 182, 196, 202, 203). These clearly belong to the similar ornamental tradition of

decorated and painted ceilings in Turkey and the Balkans. See, e.g., Godfrey Goodwin, *A History of Ottoman Architecture* (London: Thames & Hudson, 1971), pp. 484, 488; Dimitry Philippides, *Greek Traditional Architecture*, Vol. 1 (Athens: Melissa Publishing House, 1983), pp. 80, 93.

17. Descriptions of Turkish domestic architecture are numerous. See, e.g., Goodwin, *A History of Ottoman Architecture*, pp. 429-453; U. Vogt-Goknil, *Living Architecture: Ottoman* (New York: Grosset & Dunlap, 1966), pp. 139-149. The affinity of the Lebanese central hall house with Turkish examples was already been pointed out. See Panerai, "Geometries et Figures Domestiques."

18. Panerai, "Geometries et Figures Domestiques," p. 134. Ragette admitted the Turkish character of this arrangement (*Architecture in Lebanon*, p. 189). He also observed "sham arcades" in Lebanon constructed of wood (p. 54).

19. Goodwin, *A History of Ottoman Architecture*, pp. 440, 441; Vogt-Goknil *Living Architecture: Ottoman*, pp. 140, 141; Mehmet Akkaya, "Vernacular Housing in Amasya, Turkey," *Open House International* Vol.10. no. 2 (1985), p. 37. The central hall scheme is described as the usual feature of traditional houses in the Gediz-Emet provinces by Yasmin Aysan, "Houseless in 42m^2," *Open House International* Vol.12. no. 2 (1987), p. 22.

20. See, e.g., Ragette *Architecture in Lebanon*, p. 102; Fuchs, "The Arab Central Hall House Type," p. 25.

21. For examples, see A. Anastasiadis, "The Upper Town (Pano Poli) in Thesaloniki. Study of a traditional settlement part of an urban center," *Architecture in Greece* 16 (Athens: 1982), pp. 98-107; Werner Blaser, *Structural Architecture of Eastern Europe* (Basel: Zbinden, 1975), figs. 78-79, 96-99; E. Camesasca, ed., "Landliches Rokoko in Sudost-Europa," in *Das Haus* (Gutersloh: Bertelsmann, 1971), p. 244. According to Henry Minetti, *Osmanische provinziale Baukunst auf dem Balkan* (Hannover, 1923), p. 37, the central hall in the Balkans originates from the "two story high Iwan" of "Vorderasien."

22. This is implied repeatedly by Ragette, *Architecture in Lebanon*, pp. 88, 167. Weulersse, *Paysans de Syrie et du Proche-Orient*, p. 268, points out the urban character of the central hall house and places its origin in Beirut, whence it spread to the Mountain.

23. Baer, *Agrarian Relations in the Middle East*, pp. 59-65.

24. Ragette explains the evolution of the central hall house from the *Iwan*-house as an adaptation to the environment of Mount Lebanon, especially to the topography. Environmental reasons can only be a partial explanation, however. See the criticism of Panerai, "Geometries et Figures Domestiques," p. 133. The *Iwan*-house probably always has been the house of the better-off, whereas most people lived in simple closed rectangular houses. Goodwin seems to observe just this in an Anatolian village: "The better houses have arched eyvans [*Iwans*] or loggias but the humbler ones are simply crofts" (*A History of Ottoman Architecture*, p. 430). An old photograph of Hasbayya in Lebanon in Andre Geiger, *Syrie et Liban* (Grenoble: Arthaud, 1932), p. 50, shows a village of mostly simple houses with a few *Iwaned* ones. It is interesting to compare this with a later view of the village transformed with central hall houses (Ragette, *Architecture in Lebanon*, p. 164). It is possible to suggest that when Lebanese villagers became prosperous in the later half of the century, the *Iwan* was a natural starting point for an improved house. Clustering *Iwan* units around inner courts (Ragette, *Architecture in Lebanon*, pp.68-83) -- as was the case in the palaces of the feudals of the ancient regime -- was both unfeasible in a mountainous terrain and unnecessary for security and the social needs of the last decades of the century. The *Iwan* was developed as a compact

villa for the new rich.
25. Hitti, *Lebanon in History*, pp.473-477.
26. *Ibid*, pp. 474-475.
27. Kark (*Jaffa*, p. 59) quotes such an instance.
28. Schick, "Progress in Palestine," p. 187.
29. Ragette, *Architecture in Lebanon*, p. 108; Canaan (*The Palestinian Arab House*, p. 64) seems to describe central hall houses as usually vaulted. His work deals mainly with the vicinity of Jerusalem. For photographs of Bethlehem, see Schiller, *The First Photographs*, (1980), p. 168; *The First Photographs*, (1979), p. 234; Henry Kendall, *Village Development in Palestine during the British Mandate* (London: The Crown Agents from the Colonies, 1949), fig. 17.
30. References to the central hall house in the new Arab neighborhoods in Jerusalem are given in Kark & Landman, "Muslim Neighborhoods," p. 197; Kroyanker, *Jerusalem Architecture*, p.67-78. According to Schick ("Die Baugeschichte der Stadt Jerusalem," p. 270), improving the road to Jerusalem made possible the import of timber and tile after 1880. However, builders continued to prefer vaults and massive walls, because they found the traditional methods superior in stability and heat insulation. A tile roof was added over the vaults for better water isolation. According to Kark and Landman ("Muslim Neighborhoods," p. 195), traditional methods were still used after the 1890s. Kroyanker, *Jerusalem Openings* (Tel Aviv: Zmora Bitan, 1987, in Hebrew), completely ignores the triple arch.

All photos are by Aharon R. Fuchs unless otherwise indicated.

THE HYBRID METROPOLIS: WESTERN INFLUENCES IN INDIA

NORMA EVENSON

Post-modernist architectural tracts frequently include reference to the proliferation of Western modernism in the Third World, deploring its influence, and comparing it unfavorably with local traditions. In former colonies, such as India, however, the importation of European architecture long antedates the glass-walled skyscraper, and has acquired sufficient longevity to have become, in itself, a part of the local tradition. Over the years, repeated waves of foreign influence introduced a wide range of European styles accompanied by Western artistic ideology. Controversy over the impact of Westernized architecture, moreover, is by no means new; it has flourished for over a century, inspiring efforts at traditional revival as well as stylistic fusions of East and West. Although foreign influence had its origin in colonialism, it has persisted unabated since independence. A cosmopolitan architecture continues to characterize major Indian cities, reflecting a way of life that has become in many ways international.

THE COLONIAL CITY

The initial focus of Westernization in India was the colonial metropolis. The great port cities of Bombay, Madras and Calcutta were physical and social hybrids virtually from their inception. Founded as new towns by the British in the seventeenth century, and subsequently attracting sizable Indian populations, these colonial centers were neither typical British nor typical Indian settlements, although they reflected aspects of both cultures.

While in many parts of colonial India village life was to continue virtually unaffected by the British presence, the major cities became powerful instruments of change and Westernization. They embodied mixtures of population groups not found elsewhere, with unique juxtapositions of caste, religion and language. A system of Westernized education, together with a new range of occupations, opened up in the cities. The unprecedented size of the metropolis, with its rapidly-evolving fabric, promoted new building types and constant alteration of traditional building forms.

Initially, the British and Indian districts of the colonial cities stood in sharp contrast. Even though they came from a nation characterized by relatively dense terrace housing, the British showed little inclination to reproduce such dwellings in India. Generally small in numbers, the British population was generally restricted to the prosperous managerial and administrative classes. In a seeming effort to emulate the lifestyle of the landed gentry, they took advantage of the cheap land and virgin sites of the colonial settlements to create a sprawling pattern of low-density residence beyond the commercial core. By contrast, the Indian population included a wide range of social classes. The Indian districts eschewed the functional zoning of the British areas in favor of a compact mixed-use settlement. Although in many respects the Indian districts reflected regional traditions, intense growth pressures soon produced modifications in housing types.

Bombay was particularly noticeable for the height of its building. Built on an island, Bombay was characterized by high land values, prompting efforts to intensify ground coverage and facilitate high population densities. The regional vernacular dwelling was typically a one or two-story wooden-frame house with a tiled, pitched roof and a front veranda. While such houses would continue to be seen in the outlying suburbs of Bombay, they would be transformed in the central districts into buildings of five or six stories on narrow street frontages, with no open space other than small, walled yards at the rear (FIG. 1).

Dwelling patterns were also affected by the preponderance of single men in the urban work force. Most of these men considered themselves temporary residents, and were willing to tolerate the

FIGURE 1.
Borah Bazaar in Bombay, shown in 1885. (S o u r c e : *Journal of Indian Art* vol. 1, 1885.)

FIGURE 2.
Bombay *chawl*.

most minimal shelter. Housing in nineteenth century Bombay came to be dominated, not by family dwellings, but by crowded lodgings for single men. The building type that came to characterize Bombay was the *chawl*, a multi-story tenement in which one-room dwellings opened onto common balcony-corridors. (Additional stories were often added to existing houses to accommodate the demand.) A single *chawl* of five to seven stories might have between 500 and 1000 inhabitants (FIG. 2).

Calcutta, with its more expansive site, was initially spared the intensive ground coverage of Bombay. The houses of the more prosperous Indians were generally of two or three stories; they were built of brick, had flat roofs, and were designed to enclose interior courtyards. Built to the outer edges of the lot, such buildings provided the privacy demanded by the custom of *purdah*, in which women were secluded from public view. Like Bombay, Calcutta received a continual stream of immigrant working men. These men were generally accommodated in tracts of mud-and-thatch huts, called *bustees*. The urban fabric evolved as a complex interweaving of *pukka*, or permanent, and *kutcha*, or non-permanent, buildings. Although Calcutta continued to develop *bustees*, increasing congestion eventually inspired the construction of multi-story *chawls* as in Bombay. By the early years of the twentieth century, city planners were to observe that the haphazard and narrowly-spaced pattern of *bustee* huts had often provided the ground plan for the construction of tall permanent buildings.

In general, the colonial cities were not noted for architectural distinction. The consolidation of British control in India coincided with the break-up of the Moghul Empire and a period of political instability. Recurrent warfare and a decline in aristocratic patronage is often credited with fostering a widespread decline in artistic production. Assuming that the arts generally flower in conditions of prosperity and security, the colonial cities, with their thriving merchant class, might well have become centers for a revitalization of Indian traditional architecture. This, however, was not the case, and for all their wealth, the new commercial cities were often judged as devoid of aesthetic interest.

A nineteenth-century description of the Indian quarter of Calcutta judged it to consist of, "dusty brick houses, utterly devoid of architectural merit." Another observer complained that the houses, "have not a single picturesque feature," adding that, "the bazaars would be equally uninteresting . . . were it not for the dense crowds who move through them." "For beauty, regularity and ornament," one writer concluded that Calcutta was, "not to be compared with Benares and Delhi, the handsome stone cities of Upper India." As to religious architecture, a turn-of-the-century guidebook advised that, "in this city there are no Hindu temples worthy of mention . . . . What pundit in his senses would recommend the tourist, who has Benares and perhaps the stupendous temples of Southern India to visit, to waste even an hour at Kalighat? . . . Calcutta is essentially a place of English interest."[1]

Among the colonial ports, Bombay was deemed the only one that, "reproduces the character and charm of the older centres of population." A British visitor in 1830 found its streets to, "bear a far closer resemblance to those of Amritsar and Lahore than to anything in the other towns that have grown up under British rule." Except for the often-admired wooden decoration on house fronts, however, the Indian quarters were judged to have little praiseworthy building. An Indian Parsee discussing nineteenth-century Bombay declared that, "a stranger . . . will be irresistibly struck by the total absence of any kind of notable architecture in the places of religious worship of the principal communities." Although the city contained four hundred Hindu temples in addition to numerous mosques and Parsee fire temples, he maintained, "there is not one such edifice which can satisfy the artistic eye." Bombay, in his view, "is in reality an upstart, a parvenu, and cannot hold comparison beside the ancient Hindu shrines and temples in Northern and Southern India." Attributing the state of Bombay architecture to the domination of the crass commercial class, he noted that, "Bombay has been intensely shopkeeping, and that is the reason why the temples, the mosques, and other places of worship inspire neither reverence nor awe, let alone beauty and joy."[2]

Wealthy merchants, however, have been known to be both generous and enlightened art patrons. The lack of support for traditional
architecture in the colonial cities clearly derived from factors other
than the commercial economy. Well-to-do Indians sometimes
shared with the working classes a sense of uprootedness, and many
continued to return to small towns and villages for important festi-
vals and family celebrations. In spite of the material prosperity of
the colonial cities, the impetus to create a permanent architectural
heritage may have been lacking.

A major factor in eroding traditional building art was the adoption
by Indians of European architecture. The colonial city provided a
continual exposure to British design, and for many Indians, city
living involved alternating between two physical environments.
An Indian might dwell in an essentially traditional house, but if he
bought a railway ticket, mailed a letter, testified in court, attended
a university, received hospital treatment or worked in a government office, he would do so in Western surroundings. In many
ways, private life was Indian, public life was British.

HYBRIDIZATION

It was inevitable that British architecture would begin to influence
Indian building. European culture embodied prestigious associations with a ruling elite. British educational policies in India,
moreover, were directed toward forming a class favorably dispos-
ed to Western ideas. To many Indians, Western styles symbolized
cosmopolitan enlightenment. European classicism, moreover, was
deemed by its proponents to be essentially universal, the reflection
of basic principles as valid in India as in Britain. It also provided a
fashionable novelty. Just as British aristocrats had begun to adopt
Italian classicism in the sixteenth century, many Indians among the
progressive-minded avant garde began to adopt European design.

As early as the eighteenth century, some wealthy Indians were
adopting European classicism in their houses, and by the
nineteenth century, European motifs were relatively common in

the Indian mansions of Calcutta. The traditional plan of the court-yard dwelling was usually retained, however. A classical portico might face the street, and the internal courtyard be surrounded by colonnaded loggias. Some wealthy Indians also began to acquire country houses in the Western style (FIGS. 3, 4, 5).

European architectural motifs could be found in many types of Indian building, often juxtaposed with traditional styles. Just as the English, during the Renaissance, sometimes made classical additions to medieval buildings, Indians sometimes incorporated European features when repairing an old structure. Sometimes buildings were designed with a mixture of Western and Indian elements, as was the Gopalji Temple, built in Calcutta in 1845. The temple compound was designed to be entered through a classical portico, and its inner courtyard was surrounded by a Doric colonnade; but the temple's upper levels embodied tradition-al Indian forms.

The adoption of Western architectural styles among Indians was accompanied by the use of Western furnishings and, eventually, changes in living patterns. In some nineteenth-century Indian houses, the creation of a European interior was primarily a concession to foreign guests. Those Indians developing social relations with the British felt obligated to provide an environment in which Europeans would feel at ease, and the Westernized portions of a house might be used only when foreigners were being entertained. During the 1870s an English guest in an Indian house reported that, "we were ushered into a splendid drawing room, furnished in European fashion, and in the most costly manner . . . . It was touching to see the keen desire this native gentleman displayed to do all honour to European tastes by thus expensively furnishing those fine apartments, which neither himself nor his family ever occupied."[3]

Western furnishings might also differentiate the portion of the house used by men from that used by women. The long-lived *purdah* tradition required the seclusion of women from public life, and even within the household often resulted in a separation of men's and women's living quarters. While this tradition remained

FIGURE 3.
The house of Raja Manmatha
Nati Ghose, Calcutta.

FIGURE 4.
Courtyard of the house of Raja
Manmatha Nati Ghose, Calcutta.

FIGURE 5.
The Mullick house, built in 1845
in Calcutta. Although this house,
like other Indian mansions,
incorporated an interior courtyard, it also followed the British
custom of surrounding the
dwelling with a landscaped
garden. The family had an
extensive collection
of European art.

in force, only men associated with foreign guests and had occasion to use and develop a taste for Western furniture.

In Bombay, the Parsees were among the most Westernized of the Indian communities, and a visitor to one of their houses declared that, "you might well imagine yourself in the drawing room of some wealthy Englishman" (FIG. 6). Reminiscing about his youth in the 1860s, a Parsee recalled such furnishings as, "large mirrors in gilt frames, . . . all shades of chandeliers. The Bohemian or Venetian glassware was the pride of the rich, and he who hung in his hall the largest number of these decorated by the glittering prismatic drops, was esteemed a man of great riches . . . As commerce increased the richer classes imported Brussels carpets and many other knickknacks to adorn their halls."[4]

In addition to employing European styles for their own buildings, Indians often provided patronage for public institutions employing Western design. This was especially true in Bombay, where a rich and philanthropically-minded Indian community contributed extensively to the architectural image of the city. The Gothic Revival library at the University of Bombay was endowed by a Hindu businessman, Remchand Roychand, with a soaring clock tower dedicated to the memory of his mother. The University Senate Hall, similar in style, was donated by a Parsee, Sir Cowasjee Jahanghier. Although it might be regretted that wealthy Indians whose generosity might otherwise have encouraged local art forms chose to patronize an alien style, Western architecture may have seemed natural for institutions having no indigenous roots.

Although classicism had a long and pervasive influence in India, nineteenth-century colonial building reflected a wide range of European revival styles, from the Italianate to the Queen Anne Cottage. As in Britain, however, the strongest rival to classicism was the Gothic Revival. In terms of symbolism, Gothic might have been judged an unlikely style for export. While classicism had been regarded as a universal style based on rationally-apprehended principles, Gothic had associations that were peculiarly national and Christian; it was linked to the craftsmanship and intuitive artistry of a particular culture. Unlike classicism, it had originated in northern Europe, and although the crisp forms of classical design seemed aesthetically well-suited to the brilliant sun of India, some doubted the appropriateness of Gothic building. It proved, however, to be functionally adaptable to Indian conditions, and its specifically Christian associations were susceptible to symbolic dilution. Like classicism, the Gothic style could be reduced to the level of decorative motif.

By the mid-nineteenth century, architecture employing European styles reflected not only Indian patronage, but also Indian participation in design and construction. Although professional training in architecture was slow developing, many Indians were trained along Western lines as civil engineers, finding employment in government public works departments.

WESTERNIZATION CHALLENGED

Many of the British in India felt a sense of pride in the cultural transformation they were effecting. Westernization was equated with progress. Some, however, deplored the apparent decline in local architectural traditions, castigating themselves for having imposed European styles and for promoting a system of construction that displaced the traditional master builder, or mistry, in favor of the British-trained engineer. The Arts and Crafts Movement encouraged interest in craft production, and emphasized the value of art as an expression of society.

British efforts to stop the erosion of local tradition during the last half of the nineteenth century included attempts to redirect artistic education to promote traditional forms. Most art schools were located in the major metropolises, however, far from the old artistic centers, and their students, drawn from the Westernized urban classes, often felt little enthusiasm for a seemingly outmoded tradition. One of the strongest proponents of indigenous art was E.B. Havell, who headed the Government College of Art and Craft in Calcutta. His policy that, "Oriental Art will be the basis of all instruction given,"[5] provoked a vigorous student protest during which a third-year student successfully led some of his fellows to secede and form a new institution based on the teaching of Western art.

Discussing the J.J. School of Art in Bombay, an Indian writer concluded that, "when the European teachers . . . exhorted the students to study Indian manner of work, the students did not like it . . . . The impact of Western sciences, art and life was very powerful and fresh. It blinded the Indians and the art students . . . . Only a few persons who studied ancient Indian traditions suspected that the great admiration which the Europeans expressed towards Indian culture may be genuine."[6]

During the latter part of the nineteenth century, debate continued among the British as to their responsibility for the decline of Indian traditional architecture. E.B. Havell once declared that, "even the Goths and Vandals in their most ferocious iconoclasm did less injury to art than that which we have done and continue to do in the name of European civilization." A government architect argued, however, that, "if it should prove to be true that native Indian architectural art has died under our rule, I think it is very doubtful whether we should be blamed for it. Only art with little vitality could be killed by Government's letting it alone, which is all we are accused of doing."[7]

The desire to produce an architectural mode appropriate to India was eventually manifested in a hybrid style termed Indo-Saracenic. Just as the Indians had once applied classical motifs to traditional Indian forms, the British began to apply Indian motifs to Western building forms. While some critics objected to the superficiality of the style, others considered this an advantage. Opposing the contention that Indian design was unsuitable to modern requirements, a British architect pointed out that, "the style can be successfully applied to any plan whatever."[8] Indian stylistic elements were often employed without regard to building type or plan and with indifference to regional tradition. In the National Gallery of Art in Madras, for example, Northern Moghul design was applied to a building in the Hindu south (FIG. 7). While it had been hoped that Indo-Saracenic building would assist the survival

FIGURE 6.
Interior of Esplanade
House, built by a
Parsee, J.N. Tata,
in 1887.

FIGURE 7.
The National Gallery
of Art, Madras,
1906-1909.

of local craftsmanship, workers on such structures were often compelled to follow mechanical patterns fully as foreign to them as classical and Gothic designs.

Although the idea of encouraging local tradition persisted, the applicability of this tradition to the colonial metropolises was not always clear.   At the time the Victoria Memorial was being planned for Calcutta, the Viceroy, Lord Curzon, an enthusiastic admirer of Indian architecture and an ardent preservationist, insisted that Calcutta was, "a city of European origin and construction, . . . which possessed no indigenous architectural type of its own."[9] The Memorial was therefore designed to reflect European classicism. Dispute over the issue of style became particularly intense when New Delhi was planned in 1912. While some argued that the new capital should provide for a revitalization of Indian building art, the principal architect, Sir Edwin Lutyens, emphatically advocated a classical solution. The government complex became a grandly-scaled embodiment of Baroque classicism slightly embellished with Indian motifs.

New Delhi was characterized by abundant open space and low residential densities, reflecting long-standing British predilections and also a growing preference among affluent Indians.   In Bombay, for example, an outbreak of plague in 1896 had given considerable impetus to suburbanization. Although the cause of the plague was not known at the time, the disease was seen to be concentrated in the densely-built Indian quarters, while the British neighborhoods escaped entirely. The detached house came to be associated not only with the taste of a ruling class but with healthy living.

With the adoption of a common housing type among British and Indians, the segregation of these two groups within the city began to diminish. High land costs and rising population, however, rendered the single-family house increasingly difficult to obtain. Apartment buildings were observed in Bombay as early as 1906, and were common in Calcutta by the 1920s. Those contemplating residence in India in 1923 were informed that, "cities situated on the coast, such as Calcutta, Bombay, Madras, Karachi, and Delhi, the seat of the government of India, are naturally very cosmopolitan in character, and in them Europeans of different nationalities and Westernized Indians live in common residential districts . . . . The old, roomy, . . . bungalows . . . are rarely to be obtained nowadays. They are being rapidly replaced by flats or small modern houses with very limited garden space. Rents are very high, ranking with those of London and Paris"[10] (FIGS. 8,9).

Some reportedly welcomed the new way of life. An Indian architectural journal noted in 1937 that, "young people, fed on the

FIGURE 8.
Esplanade Mansions,
Calcutta. Built in
1910, this building
contained both offices
and apartments.

FIGURE 9.
Calcutta apartment
house, 1926.

international outlook day by day, by the newspaper, the cinemas and the radio, with the speed lines of the motor car and the aeroplane as familiar as were once the family bullock cart and the richly caparisoned elephant . . . are not satisfied with the old traditional family home that took generations to come to its fruition. They require a little home of their own and one that does not require an army of servants to keep tidy; the modern flat is the only possible solution, at any rate in the large cities."11

THE MODERN MOVEMENT

While some architects continued to express pious respect for local tradition, by the 1930s building in the major cities was increasingly influenced by the European modern movement. In many respects, the International Style might be deemed yet another foreign fashion to be grafted onto the local scene. To the true believer, however, modernism was not a superficial style but a rational, functional, culturally neutral, universally applicable approach to design. The visual qualities of the International Style were such, in fact, that when it was introduced in the West, many complained that it wasn't sufficiently European. (Many Europeans associated flat roofs with North Africa, and Le Corbusier's International Style housing project at Pessac was derisively dubbed, "the Moroccan district.")

Westernized architectural education had, by the 1920s, become established in Bombay, and this city would long continue to be the center of the profession in India. Indian architects quickly adopted the vocabulary of the European modern movement, together with its basic attitudes. Although India as a whole was far from the urbanized, industrialized society that the modernists idealized, the major commercial centers reflected many of the attributes of Western metropolises. Bombay, especially, became the site of modern industrial buildings, high-rise office blocks and apartment houses, moving picture theaters, restaurants and night clubs.

Among the supporters of the modern movement in India was an engineer, R.S. Despande, author of a popular series of books on house design published beginning in 1931. In his view, "the Modern Architecture seems to transcend not only the limitations of time and space, but even national traditions and bias. It is not the property or patent of any particular body of any one nation, but a universal art offering boundless scope for development." As to the aesthetic of the International Style, he judged it, "most suited to our country. In the first place, it is in keeping with our philosophical ideal, 'plain living and high thinking.'"

Despande was an advocate of Western furnishings, insisting that, "dining on tables is infinitely better than dining on floors in a squatting position." The traditional Indian kitchen he deemed, "the very embodiment of drudgery." Cooking with solid fuel at floor level created excessive smoke, while lengthy squatting caused back pain.

The modernist emphasis on health and sanitation had particular appeal to Despande. Although traditional building favored a shaded interior, Despande, like European modernists, associated darkness with tuberculosis. Discussing the high tuberculosis rates among Indian women, Despande pointed out that, "men go out into the open air at least for some part of the day, but the females of the middle classes and especially those in purdah, have to confine themselves for 24 hours in the house."[12] If women could not go outside, it was essential to get abundant sun and air inside, and many of his model house designs featured large areas of unshaded fenestration (FIG. 10).

One aspect of modern design that accorded with Indian tradition was the simplification of interior furnishings. Traditionally, Indians had employed almost no furniture. It was from Europeans that they had learned to fill their houses with heavy carved sideboards, chintz-covered sofas and assorted bric-a-brac. Now they were instructed to admire the clean lines and pure forms of tubular steel.

Some had predicted that the traditional Indian predilection for ornament would prevent them from embracing the austerity of the International Style. European modernism, however, provided an

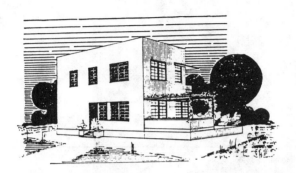

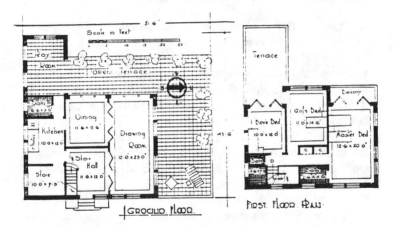

FIGURE 10. Model house from *Modern Ideal Homes for India* by R.S. Despande, 1939.

alternative in the Art Deco, and it was this sumptuous mode that dominated building of the 1930s and 1940s. Streamlining and "modernistic" decoration became particularly notable in Bombay (FIG. 11).

The introduction of the modern movement coincided, of course, with an intensification of the independence movement. Many

FIGURE 11.
Mayfair apartments,
Bombay, 1937.
The architect was
Merwanji Bana.

anticipated a future when India would become free of Western domination and be able to assert her own cultural identity. An Indian scholar mused in 1934, "have we ever imagined to ourselves an India politically and economically free, but artistically and culturally dominated by Europe, slave to the ideals of modern commercialism, dragged at the chariot wheels of the modern machine age?"[13]

The debate over modern architecture continued as independence approached. A British architect attached to the J.J. School of Architecture in Bombay concluded in 1940 that, while some of the faculty had hoped for, "a real Indian Architectural Renaissance, . . . it seems this is not to be . . . since the young Indian architect is bitten by what we know as Modern Architecture, and sees no reason why his country, alone, should revert back to medievalism."[14]

THE ARCHITECTURE OF INDEPENDENCE

The attainment of independence in 1947 did not greatly transform the cosmopolitan image of the Indian metropolis. Many architects continued to view modern design as essentially international.

Some, however, judged Western modernism symbolically inappropriate, and the architect, V.R. Talvalkar urged that, "our national and other public buildings be designed hereafter only in indigenous style." Among those seeking a return to tradition, there was little agreement as to what this might entail. Some favored the approach seen previously in the Indo-Saracenic style, in which contemporary buildings were clothed in traditional decorative motifs. A critic in Delhi, for example, reported that, "we saw modern office blocks capped with domes because that was supposed to make them look Indian." In Delhi in 1955, a large government-sponsored hotel, the Ashoka, was redesigned to provide a surface of Indianized decoration reportedly in response to bureaucratic pressure. While critics deplored the, "political decision to clothe it with its present bizarre trappings," tourists may have responded to the symbolism in the same spirit that they enjoyed the elephant rides through the grounds.[15]

Some architects concluded that the search for a national design should focus not on the revival of traditional style, but on the employment of traditional patterns of building placement. The courtyard house, with its sheltered interior, was advocated as far more suitable for India than the free-standing house. The vernacular townscape of the old provincial centers, with its pedestrian scale, spatial enclosure and short vistas came to be studied and admired. A Delhi architect, Ranjit Sabikhi, reported that, "for many of us who started work in and around Delhi in the early sixties, the traditional architecture of the Indo-Gangetic Valley has held considerable fascination . . . . The traditional cities of North India have a closely built organic structure with a clearly defined hierarchy of open spaces. They are dense and compact constructions designed to effectively counteract the intense heat to which they are exposed for the major part of the year."[16] The Brutalist aesthetic of the 1950's, moreover, suggested a compatibility between modernism and Indian tradition. The well-publicized work of Le Corbusier and Louis Kahn in India emphasized exposed brick and concrete, thick walls, restricted fenestration and sun-shading devices.

FIGURE 12.
The Asian Games
housing complex by
Raj Rewal.

FIGURE 13.
Traditional styling in
housing by Charles
Correa in New
Bombay.

Efforts to infuse modern housing with evocations of the traditional townscape appeared in Delhi in the work of Ranjeet Sabikhi, Raj Rewall and Charles Correa (FIG. 12) . The largest project was the Asian Games housing complex designed by Raj Rewall in 1981-82. In this grouping of 200 houses and 500 apartments, the architect attempted to create spatial variety through the use of squares connected by pedestrian lanes. Although most such complexes avoided the use of historicizing motifs on the buildings, an ensemble designed by Charles Correa for a new district of Bombay evoked tradition not only in site planning, but in the stylistic detailing of the houses (FIG. 13) .

While attracting critical attention, such design has tended to represent the taste of a handful of Westernized high-art architects rather than the general public. The courtyard house, for example, was long associated with the *purdah* tradition, and may have lost much of its function in a society in which women have emerged from rigid seclusion. Most middle-class clients seem content with free-standing suburban houses in which traditionalism is restricted to decorative arches and filigree (FIG. 14). Observing that, "an American . . . does not find it difficult to live in a house designed for an orthodox Indian family in any of the suburbs of New Delhi," an Indian architectural journal concluded in 1962 that, "a uniform pattern of living is unconsciously forging itself out the world over."[17]

The only Western building-type to have created any degree of controversy in Indian cities is the skyscraper. High-rise offices and luxury apartment blocks, through their conspicuous bulk and costliness, dramatize the prevailing gap between rich and poor within the city as well as the gap between the metropolis and the rest of India. An architectural journal once queried, "do our social

FIGURE 14.
Dewdrops. "Indian" decoration on a house in the Salt Lake district of Calcutta.

priorities and economic resources permit us to allow a handful of developers, in a nation of 700 million, to make fortunes and use of colossal energy resources for these skyscrapers . . . when millions of urban dwellers live in dark and dingy hovels, and ten times their number in our rural areas do not have electricity with which to run their tubwells?"[18] In Bombay, however, where restricted space

FIGURE 15.
Luxury apartment
buildings in the
Cuffe Parade landfill
district in Bombay.

FIGURE 16.
Old Delhi.

and expanding population have produced some of the highest land values in the world, tall buildings characterize most new development (FIG. 15).

In spite of the rapid and destructive changes taking place in the built environment, questions of preservation seldom arise in the major Indian cities. Pointing out that those interested in, "problems of preservation are considered eccentrics," an Indian architectural journal noted in 1962 that while many new buildings were given superficial applications of traditional motifs, genuinely old buildings were allowed to deteriorate. The well-to-do, especially, showed a consistent preference for new building, and it was observed that, "whilst in some countries the highest premium is paid for an apartment in the oldest districts of the city, for example Paris and Rome, in India the very thought is considered too funny for words."[19]

For those presently concerned with preservation issues in the major cities, it is often old British building rather than Indian building that is seen to comprise the local tradition. There is, for example, apprehension that post-independence development will alter the character of New Delhi. Anxiety has also been expressed by some critics that new high-rise offices will mar the harmony of the old British business districts in Bombay and Calcutta. The principal area of Indian building to have attracted preservationists has been Shahjehanabad (Old Delhi), the seventeenth-century capital built by Shah Jehan and now incorporated in greater Delhi. Although the built fabric of this area has been altered considerably over the years, present day planners have urged conservation of the overall townscape as an embodiment of traditional urban form (FJ) . 17).

It has been observed, however, that those most concerned with preserving Old Delhi are not those who live there. Increasing commercialization of the district has aided the attrition of old buildings, and an architectural journal reported that, "a trucking company owner who is also a prominent politician maintained that if he wished to pull down the narrow gateway to the courtyard of his ancestral haveli, no one could stop him. His new fleet of large trucks needed access to the parking area within."[20]

To some, any discussion of Indian tradition in the context of the modern metropolis would be irrelevant. The great city itself may be judged an artificial foreign implant, and in the view of one Indian urbanist, "it is high time we realized that the . . . western path of industrialization-urbanization-modernization is not the best path for us . . . . We cannot fully erase the past settlement pattern but the hangover of colonial urban development cannot last forever."[21] Much of India is still rural, and it is the village culture that many deem to be the real India. Similarly, New York is not the real America, which lies, presumably, somewhere in rural Kansas, Paris is not the real France, and London is not the real England. Real or not, however, the great cosmopolitan metropolis has become a fact of modern life. Wherever such cities occur, they are places where cultures clash and meld, and where the pace of cultural evolution is accelerated. They embody a way of life that has become, for better or worse, international.

At the same time, there is growing evidence that the giant metropolis cannot be effectively maintained technically or economically in India. Given the state of continuing crisis existing in Indian cities, it is natural that many would seek some alternative pattern of settlement. Yet the forces set in motion by colonial urbanization seem largely irreversible. Current estimates indicate that by the year 2000 half the world will live in cities, with Indian centers projected among the largest. Delhi's population at that time is anticipated to be 13.3 million, Bombay's to be 16 million and Calcutta's 16.6 million. In India, as elsewhere, there seems no way back to Arcadia.

REFERENCE NOTES

1. William Henry Adams, *India: Pictorial and Descriptive* (London: T. Nelson, 1888), p. 219; W.H. Carey, *The Good Old Days of the Honorable John Company* (Calcutta: Thacker, Spink and Co.), p. 454; Rev. W.K. Firminger, *Thacker's Guide to Calcutta* (Calcutta: Thacker, Spink and Co., 1906), p. 14.

2. Dr. Stanley Red, quoted in R.P. Karkaria, *The Charm of Bombay* (Bombay: Taraporevale, 1915), p. 360; Mrs. Elwood, *Narrative of an Overland Journey, 1830,* quoted in *The Gazetteer of Bombay City and Island* (Bombay: Times Press, 1909), p. 195; Sir D.E. Wacha, *Shells from the Sands of Bombay, 1860-75* (Bombay: Bombay Chronicle Press, 1920), pp. 314-319.

3. Norman Macleod, *Peeps at the Far East* (London: Strahan and Co., 1871), pp. 209-210.

4. Dennis Kincaid, *British Social Life in India, 1606-1937* (London: Routledge and Sons, 1938), p. 220; Wacha, *Shells from the Sands of Bombay,* pp. 179-80.

5. *Centennary - Government College of Art and Craft, Calcutta, 1864-1964* (Calcutta: Statesman Press, 1964), p. 15.

6. *Story of J.J. School of Art* (Bombay: Government Central Press, 1957), p. 53.

7. E.B. Havell, *Essays in Indian Art, Industry and Education* (Madras: Nateson and Co., 1912), p. 8; "The Indian Master Builder," in *Royal Institute of British Architects Journal* 20, 3rd series, no. 1 (Nov. 23, 1912), pp. 59-60.

8. F.O. Oertel, "Indian Architecture and Its Suitability," in *East India Association Journal,* New Series 4 (1913), p. 278.

9. Marquis Curzon of Kedleston, *British Government in India,* Vol. 1 (London: Cassel and Co., 1925), p. 189.

10. Kate Platt, *The Home and Health in India* (London: Balliere, Tindall and Cox, 1923), pp. 16-17.

11. Editorial, *Journal of the Indian Institute of Architects* 4, no. 1 (January 1937), p. 1.

12. R.S. Despande, *Modern Ideal Homes for India* (Poona: United Book Corporation, 1939), pp 55-56, 92-93.

13. Perviz N. Peerozshaw Dubash, *Hindu Art and Its Social Setting* (Madras: National Literature Publishing Co., 1934), pp. 254-255.

14. Claude Batley, "Architectural Education in India," in *Journal of the Indian Institute of Architects* 6, no. 3 (January 1940), p. 83.

15. V.R. Talvalkar, "Future of Indian Traditional Style," notes from a paper given to the Indian Institute of Architects, Aug. 28, 1947, reproduced in *Indian Institute of Architects Journal* 15, no. 1 (January 1948), p. 51; "Indianness in Artistic Expression," in *Design* 1, no. 2 (November 1957), p. 15; G.H. Franklin, "Towards an Indigenous Architecture," in *Design* 1, no. 2 (November 1957), p. 5.

16. Ranjeet Sabikhi, "Outdoor Space in the Indian Context," in *Techniques et Architecture* 3, no. 61 (August-September 1985), p. 133.

17. Editorial, *Indian Architect* 4, no. 8 (August 1962), p. 5.

18. Editorial, "A Capital of Quality," in *Design* (January-March 1984), p. 21.

19. "Time to Establish a National Trust for Historic Buildings," in *Design* 19, no. 3 (March 1975), p. 17; Editorial, *Design* 6, no. 8 (August 1962), p. 15.

20. "Saving Delhi from Becoming the Private Preserve of a Few," in *Design* 26, no. 4 (October-December 1982), p. 21.

21. Ashish Rose assisted by Jatinder Bhatia, India's Urbanization 1901-2001, (New Delhi, Tata McGraw Hill, 1978) p. 29.

SETTLEMENT AND RESETTLEMENT IN UMM QEIS: SPATIAL ORGANIZATION AND SOCIAL DYNAMICS IN A JORDANIAN VILLAGE

SETENEY SHAMI

Studies of rural architecture usually stress the technical and functional characteristics of housing. In lieu of placing house-forms in historical context, they assume that environmental factors and tradition impose continuity and regional uniformity both in terms of structure as well as use of space. However, in examining Umm Qeis, a village in north Jordan, it becomes clear that in order to understand the structure of houses as they may be frozen at a certain point in time for analytical purposes, one has to take into account the history of settlement, the changing social structure of the village, and the evolution of its spatial organization.

The analysis presented here focuses upon the village houses of Umm Qeis during the period 1880-1930. This is the period in which the inhabitants of the village first built substantial and permanent dwellings. The spatial evolution of the village and its houses reflects the role of social, economic and political factors in determining settlement patterns. The state also has played a role in this process in this particular village, where settlement and resettlement have been and continue to be intimately tied to government policies and actions.

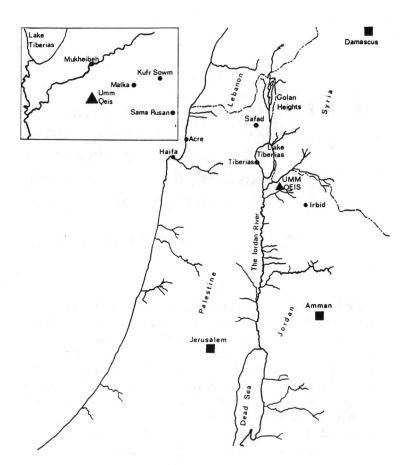

F I G U R E 1. Map of Jordan showing location of Umm Qeis. (D r a w i n g : Ali Zeiadeh.)

Through historical reconstruction, the factors that determined house-forms are identified. These include household and agricultural cycles as well as the dynamics of political power and social relations in the village. Without such a holistic and contextual approach, the study of the architectural and technical characteristics of housing contributes little to the interpretation of the relationship between material and social life.

F I G U R E 2. The Malkawi house is a fine example of one of the houses dating
to the Ottoman period. The house was reconstructed and mud-built structures were
taken down. It is now used as a headquarters for archaeological excavations.

UMM QEIS TODAY

Umm Qeis is a village of about four thousand inhabitants situated
in the northernmost tip of Jordan (FIG. 1). Its location is dramatic;
built on the top and sides of a small hill, a *tell*,[1] overlooking the
Syrian border, Israeli-occupied Palestine and the Golan Heights, it
has a magnificent view of Lake Tiberias and occupies the former
site of the ancient city of Gadara, now one of the biggest Greco-
Roman archeological sites in Jordan. Together with the town's
well-preserved stock of late Ottoman vernacular architecture (FIG.
2), this makes for a compelling setting.

Spatially, the village can be described as consisting of three
sections (FIG. 3). The first includes the houses dating to the
Ottoman period, which are located on the top and sides of the *tell*
under which extend the remains of Gadara. The second is the
eastern extension of the village, the part of the old village that
underwent the most expansion, a processs that accelerated after the
late 1960s. The third section is the new housing project at the far

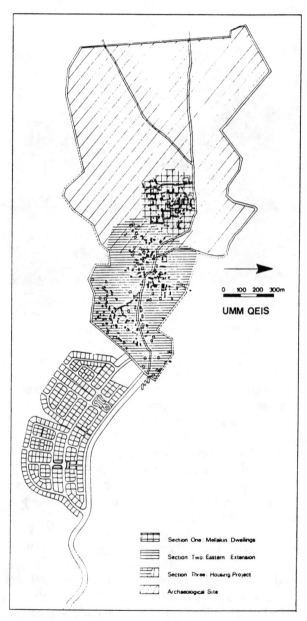

Section One: Mallakin Dwellings

Section Two: Eastern Extension

Section Three: Housing Project

Archaeological Site

UMM QEIS

0   100   200   300m

F I G U R E 3. Map of present-day Umm Qeis showing the three main sections of the village. (D r a w i n g : Ali Zeiadeh.)

F I G U R E 4. House-front showing the use of black basalt, Greco-Roman remains. These have been used for functional purposes such as strengthening the wall and as lintels, as well as to decorate a main doorway.

end of the village. The project was first planned in 1975, it was begun in 1982, and the first houses were completed in 1986.

In 1975 the Department of Antiquities, the governmental agency responsible for archeological sites and excavations in Jordan, appropriated the land on which the Ottoman houses stand in order to preserve the Greco-Roman site for archeological excavations. The inhabitants of the houses were to gradually move out, and the houses were to be left to disintegrate or be knocked down if the excavations demanded it. Since cut stone and decorative carvings from the ruins had been used in the building of the houses (FIG. 4), the utilization of such remains for display or study would have required at least the partial dismantling of the houses. In return for their property, the villagers were given monetary compensation and priority in registering for a new house in a proposed housing project at the far eastern end of the village.

This appropriation had the effect of preserving the main structures of the Ottoman village. After 1975 the owners of the houses that lay within the appropriated area were forbidden to make any changes to them, or even repair damage to them. In spite of the major changes in the economy and way of life in Umm Qeis over the past fifty years, the main features of these houses were still largely unchanged at the time of the appropriation. This shows that the changes in the economy of the village had different impacts on housing in different sections of the village.

The contemporary transformation of the economy of villages such as Umm Qeis began to be especially significant from the 1940s onwards and began to have its full effect upon rural housing in the early seventies. With increasing opportunities through education as well as through army careers, many villagers began to abandon agriculture for employment in the civil service and the military. This trend appeared in the families of both the landowners and the landless. However, the incentives for the landless were greater in the earlier periods, and for them a change in occupation often meant a total change in household economy, with subsequent changes in the dwelling structure. In the case of the major landowning families, however, the fact that some members of the household left agriculture did not mean that the family's heavy involvement in agriculture ceased. Furthermore, although land-ownership was fully privatized under Jordanian law, and property was divided and sub-divided through inheritance, most landowning families did not divide their agricultural land in ways that were detrimental to production and profits.

In terms of housing, additions in concrete to the landowners' houses began to appear in the late 1960s, however the total transformation of these dwellings had not yet begun when politics intervened in the shape of the appropriation by the Department of Antiquities. Those members of the household who no longer were involved in agriculture and those families who had grown too big for their old dwellings built modern concrete houses in the eastern section of the village. This was the part where the landless peasants had lived in the past and which did not fall within the

F I G U R E 5. Sections one and two of the present-day village. The old village is on top of the *tell* while the eastern section shows the large number of new concrete houses being built.

appropriated area. The transformation of the old houses in this part of the village, underway since the 1940s, accelerated while the transformation of the landowners' houses halted (FIG. 5).

This eastern section of the village provides good data for the study of recent transformations in village spatial organization and housing, however it is impossible to trace the relationships that existed between the houses within the area in earlier times. It is also difficult to trace the stages of transformation that these houses have gone through. Since they belonged to landless peasants, they were poorly built to begin with and were not as well preserved as the landowners' houses. Also, most of them have been partly or totally converted into concrete structures, either through the addition of rooms to an older structure or sometimes by the construction of a new house in place of an old one (FIG. 6).

The third section of the village, the housing project, is startling in its contrast to the other two parts. Laid out in neat square plots with widely spaced rows of small white-washed square concrete

FIGURE 6.
A common sight in
the eastern section,
older houses are
gradually being
replaced by concrete
structures.

FIGURE 7.
The new housing
project with its wide
streets and evenly
placed houses is in
complete contrast to
the other sections of
the village.

houses, it gives no indication of the relationships between the families who inhabit it (FIG. 7). Set apart from the rest of the village and referred to as "the housing," it is a source of constant discussion and controversy among the people of Umm Qeis. As can be seen from Figure 3, the project section has the potential of dominating the village and imposing a new form of spatial organization on it. At the moment, however, only a fraction of the proposed houses have been completed, and their inhabitants are already making additions and alterations in accordance with their needs and conceptions of domestic space.

This chapter focuses mainly on the large dwelling-complexes situated at the top of the *tell*, since the research project on Umm Qeis has until now centered upon this threatened part of the village.[2] Although the structures are still standing, the task of reconstructing their use does pose some difficulties. When the research project on Umm Qeis began in 1984, most of the houses were already partially abandoned, as nine years had passed since the appropriation of the land. Although the inhabitants of the houses had registered for units in the housing project, which was then still unfinished, many had preferred to build new houses in the eastern section while keeping the housing project unit for one of their sons. For some, the appropriation provided the final impetus to move to cities where they worked or where their sons resided. Therefore, researchers often found only the remnants of families in the houses, usually the older members biding their time until they were forced to leave. Sometimes the inhabitants were poor relatives of the original household who needed a place to live and who took care of the house in return.

In spite of these limitations, the information and insights gained provide the background for the study of the present-day village. In addition, they provide tools to help reconstruct the more ancient processes of settlement which await the results of the archeological excavations underway for the past ten years. It is clear that the history and social structure of Umm Qeis should be studied as one whole. One of the biases in previous research on this and similar areas that combine sites from antiquity with contemporary settlements has been that researchers have selected historical periods without regard to the continuity of settlement -- a bias which has led to serious historical misinterpretations.[3] The focus of this chapter on the late nineteenth and early twentieth centuries is designed to explain why and how settlement at Umm Qeis took the physical form of large and substantial buildings. These buildings document an important turning point in the history of the region.

SETTLEMENT IN THE LATE NINETEENTH CENTURY

The history of Umm Qeis is one of continuous settlement and resettlement with sometimes the economic factor, and sometimes the political, playing the determining role. Settlements like Umm Qeis came into being due to a combination of environmental and political factors. Land use in this part of Bilad ash-Sham[4] seems to have been characterized by periodic cycles of settlement and abandonment as a result of the interpenetration of agriculture and pastoralism. This shifting but continuous land-use system was well adapted to the ecological constraints of dryland farming. It also was adapted to the political reality of fluctuating state control, which varied unpredictably from the peasant's point of view between benign neglect and exploitation by military force. It appears reasonable to assume that under ecological and political conditions favorable to successful production and peasant autonomy, villages were established and re-settled, and cultivation was extended although at the level of local consumption only. When conditions worsened, however, whether in times of drought or taxation, the villagers would become transhumants or even nomadic pastoralists.[5]

The main factor that intervened in the late nineteenth century, and forced the inhabitants of the area to change from this shifting system of cultivation to a more permanent form of settlement, was political: namely, the attempts of the Ottoman government to increase grain production in the area through the establishment of permanent agricultural settlements. An analysis of agriculture during the early Islamic period, the eighth to the twelfth centuries, indicates that similar expansions of agricultural production, accompanied by an increase in village settlement, also occurred in earlier times, again as the result of strong state intervention and state interest in the development of agriculture.[6]   Since the Ottoman tax registers from the sixteenth century show a thriving village in Mkes, as it was called until recently,[7] that period also appears to have been one in which a settled peasantry, through coercion or incentive, produced a surplus that was substantially taxed.[8]

The difference between this period and the nineteenth century may have been in the degree, and certainly in the methods of coercion. This particular state effort to expand agricultural production was singular in that it entailed enforcement of a new land registration scheme. The Ottoman Land Code of 1858 stipulated that private land ownership, continuous cultivation of land and the restriction of the size of village herds would be conditions for obtaining the right to cultivate land.[9] Even if these measures could not be fully enforced by the government, the appearance of land records for these areas from the 1880s onward shows that land registration, at least, was carried out. In addition, the oral history is rich with accounts of heavy taxation enforced through various means. These changes meant that engagement in agriculture now required a larger investment by the cultivator, and that it was no longer possible to escape taxation and government coercion through the adoption of pastoralism.

At this time, therefore, settlements such as Umm Qeis acquired a more permanent character, as those who were able to afford the registration fees and other taxes and those who had connections in the Ottoman administration registered lands that they had previously cultivated only sporadically. Those who could not register land became sharecroppers and laborers. There may have also been considerable migration from villages to cities.[10]

The second major difference in the nineteenth century was the gradual incorporation of the region into the world market, which had the effect of both expanding the trade potential of small villages and determining the kinds of crops that villagers grew. The late nineteenth century saw several periods of good prices for grains, and this allowed even modest peasant-landowners such as those of Umm Qeis to make a profit. Several of them began to establish regular trade connections with merchants and middlemen in cities such as Damascus, and the ports of Palestine such as Acre and Haifa.[11] Others were not as fortunate, and found themselves forced into selling part or all of their lands to other villagers or to merchants and moneylenders from outside the village. Furthermore, the village began to attract a number of agricultural laborers from neighboring areas such as Mukheibeh in the Jordan Valley.

The spatial organization of Umm Qeis as a whole, and the houses that the peasants built, were directly related to these changes in the economy. The physical structures that are still to be seen in Umm Qeis represent the stages of settlement starting with the turn of the century. By this period agricultural production had begun to enable some peasants to invest in elaborate buildings, while others remained in simpler houses. The spatial organization, therefore, reflects the growing stratification of the community and the resulting increase in complexity in its social structure.

SPATIAL DIVISIONS OF THE VILLAGE

Before land registration, when the lands around Umm Qeis were farmed sporadically or seasonally, travellers' accounts indicate that the peasants lived in caves, in the Roman vaults, and in makeshift huts and temporary dwellings.[12] According to the oral tradition, in the period immediately following land registration the new landowners continued to live in similar dwellings or in simple houses built of stone with mud facing and mud mortar. By the 1880s and 1890s, however, after their fortunes had been firmly tied to the land, the people of Umm Qeis began to build more permanent stone dwellings. With the expansion of these fortunes, they began to expand their dwellings as well.

The two main sections of the Ottoman village can still be distinguished in present-day Umm Qeis. First, there was the area with the large dwelling-complexes where the major landowning families lived and which was called the *Hara al-Foqa*, or "Upper Quarter." This area was also known as the *Mil'aba*, from *mal'ab*, meaning "playground," in reference to the adjacent Roman theatre. Secondly, there was the *Hara al-Tahta*, the "Lower Quarter," where the poorer peasants, laborers, herders and craftsmen lived. This division illustrates a clear hierarchy within the Ottoman village (FIG. 8). In addition, although the dwellings in each quarter share some features of building style and technique, there are significant differences in the organization of space between them.

The Upper Quarter itself can be further divided as Figure 8 shows. There is a central cluster of eight large dwelling-complexes, some of them subdivided into smaller units at the very top of the hill (FIG. 9). These were the houses of the major landowners, the *mellakin*, and they are clustered together forming a closed circle.

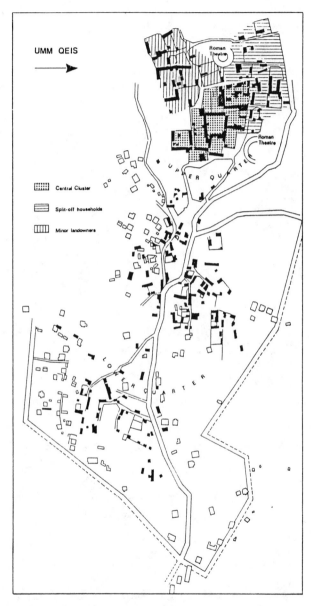

F I G U R E 8. Map of the first two sections of the village. The scattered nature of the *fellahin* dwellings is in contrast to the clustering of the *mellakin* dwellings. (D r a w i n g s : Ali Zeiadeh.)

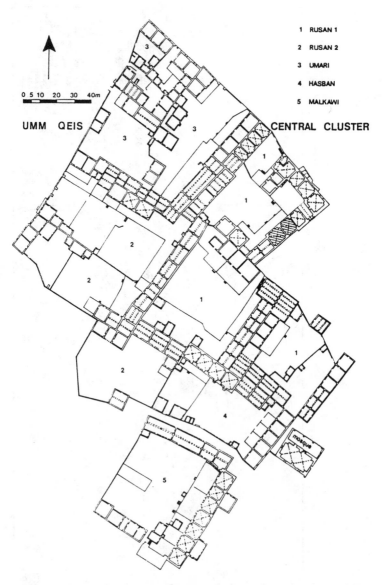

1 RUSAN 1

2 RUSAN 2

3 UMARI

4 HASBAN

5 MALKAWI

0 5 10 20 30 40m

UMM QEIS

CENTRAL CLUSTER

F I G U R E 9. The central cluster of the *mellakin* dwellings, showing the divisions and sub-divisions of dwellings according to the changing relations within the kinship groups. The vaulted rooms were built by professional masons. (D r a w i n g : Ali Zeiadeh based on the original by Heinz Gaube.)

The houses were not originally built in this manner, but because of attempts by families related by kinship to stay close together and because of the gradual increase in the number of houses, a solid cluster emerged. With one exception there are no streets between these houses, and they contain few windows or other openings to the outside except for heavily-built doors. At a later stage one or two of these houses had shops built into their walls but always in ways that prevented access to the house. Still later, in the 1920s and 30s, windows began to be installed as well as smaller doors. This may indicate that when the houses were first built they were designed to be easily defensible. This would have been an important consideration not only because of bedouin attacks during harvest-time but also -- as the people say -- to guard against theft by poorer peasants and general trouble-makers.[13]

In the same area but separated from the main cluster are houses of smaller landowners who obtained land in the village somewhat later (FIG. 8). These complexes appear to have originally been quite large and were built in the same courtyard style as those of the larger landowners, however the location of walls and dividers within them show that a great deal of subdivision occurred within the households that occupied them, and that this led to the division of space into quite small units. These houses are also not as well-built as those of the larger landowners, and they clearly represent less prosperous households than those at the top of the hill. Presently they are not as well-preserved as the other houses and many appear to have been abandoned earlier. On the periphery of the area of large dwelling-complexes are the houses of those families that split off from the households living in these complexes. These houses are smaller and well-preserved, and some were built as late as the mid-1940s. They were also built in the courtyard style.

In the Lower Quarter there are a large number of small houses which belonged to the *fellahin*, the "cultivators" as the local terminology designates them. Since this area of the village contains a mix of old houses and new concrete construction, it is not possible to estimate the actual number of *fellahin* houses at any given period.[14] It is clear, however, that each landowning family

must have employed a substantial number of poorer peasant laborers. These would have been seasonal workers, herders, plowers
and sharecroppers, although the number in this last category
appears to have been limited before the 1930s. Craftsmen and
some poorer peasant-landowners also lived in this quarter. The
term *fellahin* refers to social as well as occupational status. It
refers to the poorer inhabitants of the village who are also those
with smaller, less important kin groups and less general prestige.
Since these families worked as laborers for others or were specialized in craft production, they did not need to maintain large
households the way the landowners did.

The dwellings of the *fellahin* reflect all these conditions. They are
smaller and appear to have rarely included walled courtyards.
Most were scattered and stood alone in the open or with only
rudimentary enclosures. Clearly their inhabitants had little to fear
or protect. The differences in the dwellings of the *mellakin* and the
fellahin are directly related to the place of their inhabitants in the
system of production.

SOCIAL DYNAMICS IN THE VILLAGE

As described above, in the landowners' quarter we can see spatial
divisions that distinguish three variations on the same type of
dwelling. The political and social relations between the landowning families do not, however, simply follow the spatial divisions.
Although the houses of the landowners are similar in structure and
size, this does not mean that their inhabitants were equal in economic or political power. For example, since the central cluster of
dwellings distinguishes the most powerful landowning families, it
creates the impression that these landowners formed one political,
economic and therefore spatial bloc vis-a-vis the smaller landowners on the one hand and the laborers on the other. Yet this is not
accurate. Understanding the relationships that existed between the
landowning families requires that one examine the process of land
registration and use in the Ottoman period.

When peasants in the various villages of the area began to register land, a number of families were forced to leave their original villages and go to other areas to seek land.[15] In the case of Umm Qeis, the first to attempt registration were the Rusans, a kin group from the nearby village of Sama Rusan that was composed of five families divided into two descent groups (henceforth referred to as Rusan1 and Rusan2). The Rusans had previously cultivated land near Umm Qeis, though they only lived in the town seasonally.

Ottoman regulations required that a certain total amount of land be registered in each village, and incoming families could afford to register only a limited number of shares of the total amount. Under the new code the acquisition of land was no small burden, especially for peasants who were starting anew in the sense that they had lost the social and economic support of their original kinsmen and co-villagers. There was a registration fee and an annual tax to pay on each holding. In addition, there was a limit to how much land each family could cultivate without hiring laborers or giving land to sharecroppers, practices which both entailed risk. Therefore, in order to make up the total area of the village, the Rusans began to encourage other families to come to Umm Qeis.

The Umaris and the Malkawis were among those who followed the Rusans. They came from Sama Rusan and Malka respectively, driven out by the same forces that had driven out the Rusans, and they registered a large number of shares in Umm Qeis. Other families arrived later, although most of these only registered a small number of shares. Since this still did not make up the total number of shares required, the Rusans continued to recruit people -- even persuading a Lebanese Christian itinerant trader to register two shares. Eventually, however, their efforts fell short, and they had to register the remaining number of shares in their own name.

An interesting system of partnership evolved among this newly formed group of landowners. In spite of the individuation of land ownership enforced by the Ottoman code, the people of Umm Qeis continued to apply the *musha'a* system of land cultivation common to the region. Under this system village land is redistributed among village families every few years.[16] The lands of Umm Qeis were divided into six types according to the nature of the terrain and the quality of the land, and each family had a share in each type. Later, during the cadastral survey and final registration of land in the 1930s, this classification was simplified to three types of land: the plains, the foothills and the valley.

In the Umm Qeis variant of the *musha'a* system, the total amount of village land was divided into four equal shares distributed over the different types of land. These shares were called *rub'as*, or "quarters." Each *rub'a* was cultivated by a number of landowning kin-groups, with one kin-group holding the leading position. Leadership meant having the largest number of shares within the *rub'a* and hence the right to distribute actual plots to various families and have first choice in the distribution. The groups formed as follows: the Rusan1 with the Hasban; the Umaris with the Masarweh, Hawatmeh, Sharif and Sweiti; the Malkawi with the Khuluf; and the Rusan2 with the 'Ukush and "the Christian." The less shares of land the main landowning family owned, the more partners it had to find.

These *rub'as* became permanent partnerships, with the smaller landowners being known as the "followers" of the main landowners, and the partnership also being called a *rub'a*. The members of the *rub'a* helped each other in ploughing and harvesting seasons. They also stood guard over the crops together and regulated their herding so as not to harm each others' crops. Therefore these groupings came to form economically corporate groups as well as units for the redistribution of land. Social barriers, however, were maintained and marriages rarely took place between the leading and following families in each bloc, since they represented different economic statuses.

These relationships crossed the spatial boundaries of the village. Although the Hasban, for example, were "follower landowners," their house was one of the largest and was located in the main cluster at the top of the hill (FIG. 9). According to informants, there were several reasons for this. Although the Hasban registered only two shares of land, they were related by marriage to the Rusan

before they settled in Umm Qeis. In fact, it was this con-
sanguineous relationship that had led them to seek land in the
village. Furthermore, since the Hasban owned substantial amounts
of land elsewhere, they could comfortably be considered one of the
mellakin. Finally, since the Hasban made up only one household
in the village and had come somewhat later than the others, they
wished to build as close as possible to the Rusan for protection.

In contrast, the Malkawi house, belonging to one of the main
landowning families, was slightly separated from the main cluster
by a narrow alley. Family members explain this by saying that
they were strong enough and wealthy enough to defend
themselves. But the real reason may have been related to the fact
that while the Rusans, the Umaris and the Hasban were all related
by marriage, the Malkawis generally seemed to have kept
themselves apart and maintained a slightly oppositional manner to
the others. They even periodically challenged the village
leadership position of the Rusan1.

One example could go on to illustrate how social and political
relationships such as kinship, competition and cooperation all
played a role in determining where families built their houses.
One of the families of follower landowners, for example, lived in
the northeast, at the far edge of the Lower Quarter, completely
separated from the other follower landowners. This is explained
by the fact that they arrived in Umm Qeis seeking protection
because one of their members had committed a murder. Therefore,
although spatial divisions in the village as a whole do reflect
economic relationships, they also reflect a number of social and
political considerations.

THE *MELLAKIN* DWELLINGS

A closer look at the dwellings further clarifies the social structure
that was emerging in the late nineteenth century in Umm Qeis. As
mentioned above, due to the present semi-abandoned character of
the houses, it is only possible to construct a somewhat idealized
picture of the use of space in the dwelling-complexes of Umm

Qeis. Although many people have vivid memories and give colorful descriptions of the past, it is impossible to observe today a household composed of six married brothers such as the Melkawi dwelling once housed, or to observe a process such as that which led the Rusans to finally divide their courtyard in two. Also, depending upon the age of the informant, we would hear different stories concerning the use of rooms, who had lived in a household, and other subjects.

The houses of the landowners are large and built around courtyards (FIG. 9). As mentioned previously, most were built using stone from the Roman ruins, re-cut to smaller and more suitable sizes. This does not mean, however, that the houses were built by their occupants. In fact, the sophisticated way in which the Roman remains were utilized, both for functional purposes and for aesthetic value, clearly indicates that professional masons were employed (FIG. 3). The Roman remains were fully integrated into the structure of the buildings, and in one case a house was built on an ancient foundation. Furthermore, courtyards were designed to facilitate the re-use of Roman wells and cisterns.

The masons came from the town of Safad in Palestine and built the basic necessary structures of the dwelling. This included the cross-vaulted rooms and the simple double-vaulted rooms, typical of the region.[17] The building of these rooms would take several months, during which time the masons lived at the site and were provided with food and shelter in addition to being paid their regular costs and fees.

Understanding the use of space within the dwellings requires that one take into account the relationships of the people who inhabited them -- the nature of their domestic cycles as well as the nature of their work, or agricultural cycles. The area around the courtyard comprised multi-purpose rooms for general living, stables for various types of drought and transport animals, and storehouses for grain and other agricultural products (FIG. 10). Rooms were re-used for different purposes as the needs of the household shifted over time.[18] The basic requirements of a household included a room for every conjugal family. When a son married, a room would be

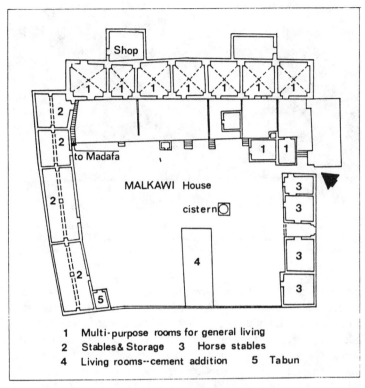

F I G U R E 10. The Malkawi house showing the function of the rooms in the late 1920s. Cooking was done inside the rooms or on the platform in front of them. (D r a w i n g : Ali Zeiadeh based on the original by Heinz Gaube.)

made available to the couple where they would live together with the children born to them. This was the main purpose behind the addition of new rooms to the dwelling. There also had to be a separate guest room, a *madafa*. The stables and storage rooms also doubled as living quarters for herders, since each landowning family hired several of these -- some seasonally and others on a permanent basis.

While the technically-complicated rooms were built by professionals, additional rooms were built by the inhabitants themselves, perhaps with the help of local laborers employed for

F I G U R E 11. The private space of a family unit in the Rusan house is defined through self-built mud structures. The low wall encloses a kitchen on the left and an outhouse on the right. Above rise the impressive arches built by professional masons.

the purpose. These rooms would be built out of a mixture of the basalt Roman stone and local white soft stone, using mud mortar and facing. In addition, households were constantly building additional structures out of stone and mud brick, or out of mud and straw. These structures included dividing walls within courtyards that defined boundaries between families and vital parts of the dwelling such as kitchens, outhouses, baking ovens (*tabun*) and poultry coops (FIG. 11).

These structures were built out of easily available materials, required less skill, and shifted as the use of the space changed with the changing relationships of the inhabitants. As a household grew, and new conjugal families were formed within it, low dividing walls were built to designate the private space of each family within the commonly shared courtyard. Figure 12 shows such a space in the Rusan house. If these families still formed one household in the sense that they still pooled their resources and cooked and ate together, then there would be one *tabun* and one kitchen shared among them. But if a family unit split off completely so that the major resources were no longer pooled, a high dividing wall was built and each family would have its own *tabun*, kitchen and poultry coops. When it became impossible to divide a courtyard any further, some families would split off and build a completely separate dwelling, although it was usually as close to the main dwelling as possible.

It is the mud structures which give the real picture of the use of the space as well as the structure of the household(s) inhabiting the dwelling. The professionally-built rooms were nothing more than the necessary backbone of a dwelling. What really made it livable and usable were the self-built structures. This illustrates that describing the structure of the houses at any given time requires taking into account the nature of domestic cycles. The relationship between the members of the household at any given time determined how the basic structure of the dwelling was modified.

The effect of agricultural cycles must also be kept in mind. The local system of agriculture combined dryland grain farming with irrigated vegetable and pulse production and herding. This meant that the property of each household was scattered in different locations in the surrounding area. Therefore, a single dwelling-complex could not fulfill all the needs of a peasant household. Part of the household had to live during the appropriate seasons near the particular fields being cultivated. Irrigated lands needed continual care, while the plowing and harvesting seasons on the plains required intensive communal labor. Herders needed to be constantly moving, especially during the spring and summer.

At any given time part or all the household would be living outside the main dwelling, in temporary structures and in goat-hair tents. This was the practice until recent times, even though after the 1940s irrigated lands in the valley and the foothills became increasingly allocated to sharecroppers. The main dwelling-complex then should be regarded as a sort of general headquarters from which the coordination of activities took place, and where produce was stored and redistributed. However, the needs of a peasant household exceeded that one main dwelling structure, and spatial extensions were made to it.

THE INTERRELATION OF THE MATERIAL AND THE SOCIAL

The above description shows a clearly complex relationship between material and social concerns. The emphasis on social and economic factors or determinants of the structure and use of space has not been stressed here to devalue the importance of purely architectural and technical features of the dwellings. Rather, this chapter has been aimed at highlighting those aspects of a particular historical context that played a major role in determining people's choices in structuring their physical surroundings.

The preservation of the old houses of Umm Qeis provides a unique opportunity to achieve a better understanding of the material expression of settlement processes. The physical structures disclose many aspects of society which would otherwise remain obscure, and they serve as a reminder of a period of great significance in the history of the region. Since it is also possible to reconstruct an image of the social dynamics of interaction in the village, many issues concerning the interrelation of spatial and social organization become further clarified.

REFERENCE NOTES

I would like to thank Cherie Lenzen, Martha Mundy and Lucine Taminian for their comments on earlier versions of this paper. I would also like to thank Ali Zeiadeh for doing the illustrations and for giving me technical advice.

1. *Tell* means a small hill in Arabic. The word has passed into archeological usage as referring to an artificial mound created by layers of earth and waste accumulated due to continuous human occupation.
2. The project started in 1984, and intensive work was carried out for six months. The principal investigators were Dr. Heinz Gaube of Tubingen University and Dr. Birgit Mershen and myself of Yarmouk University. The aims of the project were to record the architecture, material culture and social life represented at Umm Qeis, and at the same time to persuade the various authorities of the importance of preserving the village houses, which provide one of the few remaining examples of a concentration of Ottoman vernacular architecture in Jordan. Since then, the reconstruction of two of the largest houses has been undertaken by the German Protestant Institute for Archaeology in Amman. As the research project is an on-

going effort of the Institute of Archaeology and Anthropology of Yarmouk University, further research was carried out in the context of graduate courses.
3. For a critique, see Cherie J. Lenzen, review of F. Zayadine, ed., "The Jerash Archeological Project," in *Zeitschrift Fur Deutsche Palastinas-Vereins*, (henceforth, *ZDPV* (1989, forthcoming); Birgit Mershen and Axel E. Knauf, "From Gadar to Umm Qais," in *ZDPV* (1988, forthcoming), p. 104.
4. Bilad ash Sham, or Greater Syria, is the historic name of the area presently comprising Syria, Lebanon, Jordan and Palestine.
5. I have in an earlier paper sketched the factors that affected land-use systems in the Umm Qeis area. See Seteney Shami, "Umm Qeis -- A North Jordanian Village in Context," in Adnan Hadidi, ed., *Studies in the History and Archaeology of Jordan, Vol. III* (Amman and London: Routledge and Kegan Paul, 1987), p. 211-213. Also see Mershen and Knauf, "From Gadar to Umm Qeis." Further research, however, is needed to construct a comprehensive view of the land-use system in this region.   For one attempt to do so, see Leon Marfoe, "The Integrative Transformation: Patterns of Socio-Political Organization in Southern Syria," *Bulletin of the American Schools of Oriental Research*, Vol. 234 (1980), pp. 1-42. For a detailed study of the historical geography of the area, see Norman Lewis, *Nomads and Settlers in Syria and Jordan 1800-1980* (Cambridge: Cambridge University Press, 1987).
6. See Andrew M. Watson, *Agricultural Innovation in the Early Islamic World* (Cambridge: Cambridge University Press, 1983).
7. See Mershen and Knauf, "From Gadar to Umm Qais," for an analysis of the evolution of the name of the village.
8. For a detailed account of the settlements and production in southern Bilad ash-Sham in the sixteenth century as drawn from Ottoman tax records, see Wolf-Deitrich Hutteroth and Kamel Abdul Fattah, *Historical Geography of Palestine, TransJordan and Southern Syria in the Late Sixteenth Century* (Erlangen: Erlanger Georgraphische Arbeiten, 1977).
9. See Gabriel Baer, *Studies in the Social History of Modern Egypt* (Chicago: Chicago University Press, 1969); Philip S. Khoury, *Urban Notables and Arab Nationalism: The Politics of Damascus 1860-1920* (Cambridge: Cambridge University Press, 1983); Roger Owen, *The Middle East in the World Market 1800-1914* (London: Methuen, 1981).
10. For details of this process, see Shami, "Umm Qeis"; Mershen and Knauf, "From Gadar to Umm Qais." For in-migration to cities, see Owen, *The Middle East in the World Market*.
11. For an analysis of grain markets and prices in this period, see Owen, *The Middle East in the World Market*.
12. For travellers' accounts see, among others, James Silk Buckingham, *Travels Among the Arab Tribes Inhabiting the Countries East of Syria and Palestine* (London, 1825); John Lewis Burckhardt, *Travels in Syria and the Holy Land* (London, 1822); William Francis Lynch, *Narrative of the United States Expedition to the River Jordan and the Dead Sea* (London: Richard Bentley, 1849); Salah Merill, *East of the Jordan: A Record of Travel and Observation in the Countries of Moab, Gilead and Bashan* (London, 1881).
13. For a critique of the idea of Bedouin attacks as a "multi-purpose explanation" in the literature, see Owen, *The Middle East in the World Market*, p. 6.
14. Figure 7 represents an attempt to estimate the situation as it was in the 1930s. However, research in archival sources and land records is essential for this purpose.

15. See Shami, "Umm Qeis," for more details of this process. The following analysis is based totally on oral history and requires further corroboration through documentary and historical research.

16. For details of the *musha'a* system, which is as yet poorly understood, see Owen, *The Middle East in the World Market*; Ya'acov Firestone, "Crop Sharing Economies in Mandatory Palestine," *Middle East Studies* XI (1975), pp. 3-23.

17. See Tawfiq Canaan, "The Palestinian Arab House: Its Architecture and Folklore," *Journal of the Palestine Oriental Society*, XII and XIII (1932), pp. 223-247, 1-83.

18. See Mershen and Knauf, "From Gadar to Umm Qais," for a short account of the shifts over time in the functional use of rooms.

All photos are by the author unless otherwise indicated.

MIGRATION, TRADITION AND CHANGE IN SOME VERNACULAR ARCHITECTURES OF INDONESIA

ROXANA WATERSON

"Satingi-tini tabang bangau
Balik ka kubangan juo"

(However high the egret flies
It will still return to its pond) -- Minangkabau saying

In times of unprecedentedly rapid change, traditional styles of architecture in many regions of the world are under threat or have already disappeared. Tradition, all the same, remains a problematic notion, one that must be carefully addressed in any attempt to understand the forces that help or hinder the survival of indigenous architectures. This chapter seeks to examine some of the forces affecting the future of vernacular building styles in Indonesia. It discusses three examples: the Sa'dan Toraja of South Sulawesi, the Toba Batak of northern Sumatra and the Minangkabau of West Sumatra (FIG. 1).[1] All three cultures have experienced radical changes during this century, yet despite predictions that they are in decline, their traditional architectural styles still retain vigor, even if in slightly changed forms.

In examining why this should be so, I focus upon the phenomenon of migration, widespread within Indonesia today. Far from being a

F I G U R E 1. Partial map of Indonesia, showing peoples discussed in the text.

drain upon local cultures, migration tends to heighten the sense of ethnic identity in individuals as they encounter other ethnic groups in cities.[2] Those who migrate may feed considerable amounts of money and cultural energy back into their home communities, as they seek ways to reassert their cultural identity or convert new wealth into prestige. This has considerable importance for traditional architecture. In many Indonesian societies descent is traced through the house, and the house remains the proper site for storing heirlooms and conducting kin group rituals. As such, the impulse to maintain the house goes beyond any thought of inhabitation. Migrants are often prepared to spend large amounts of money on houses in which they have no intention of living.

In Tana Toraja the more times a house has been rebuilt the more prestige attaches to it as an origin-house. Among the Toba, less money is spent on houses than on elaborate house-shaped tombs which are the sites of secondary burial for the bones of a whole group of ancestors. Among the Minangkabau, too, there is currently considerable interest in the renewal of the houses, very often funded by migrants. In all three societies house- or tomb-building is accompanied by large-scale ceremonies. I shall argue that houses continue to be regarded as deeply significant structures, even as shifts take place in what the house is held to signify.

"TRADITION" VERSUS "MODERNITY"

Before going further, it is important to address the question of what tradition means, both to the investigator and to the cultures under investigation. This is a difficult question because the concept of tradition is inherently ambiguous. Western cultures are not alone in revering tradition as something which ought to be upheld without change. Tradition generally tends to become equated with stasis, while its implied opposite -- modernity or modernization -- tends to become equated with change. But the word tradition really describes a process of handing down, one that is just as dynamic and historical as any other social process. Meanwhile, the idea of tradition, and its clash with the ideology of modernization as often translated into action as national policies, is also part of the total social dynamic, and needs to be considered as such. Tradition, like history, is continually being recreated and remodelled, even as it is represented as being fixed and unchangeable.

Telling insights into the history of the word are provided by Raymond Williams. He observed that tradition is "a particularly difficult word" because its meanings have shifted over time. He noted that "tradition" came into English via old French in the fourteenth century. Its root was the Latin *traditionem*, from *tradere* -- "to hand over" or "deliver." Williams wrote:

> The Latin noun had the senses of (i) delivery, (ii) handing down knowledge, (iii) passing on a doctrine, (iv) surrender or betrayal. The general sense (i) was in English in mC16, and sense (iv), especially of betrayal, from 1C15 to mC17. But the main development was in senses (ii) and (iii) . . . . Tradition survives in English as a description of general process of handing down, but there is a very strong and often predominant sense of this entailing respect and duty . . . .

> It is sometimes observed by those who have looked into particular traditions, that it only takes two generations to make anything traditional: naturally enough, since that is the sense of tradition as active process. But the word moves again and again towards *age-old* and towards ceremony, duty and respect. Considering only how much has been handed down to us, and how various it actually is, this, in its own way, is both a betrayal and a surrender.[3]

Ambiguities are likely to arise wherever the concepts of tradition and modernization form part of the local discourse, particularly due to the difficulty of reconciling their implications. In today's world it has become virtually impossible to separate the idea of modernization from the idea of industrialization, and, in most instances, the idea of colonial and post-colonial Western influence. However, it is also likely that modernization may be identified with the goals of nationalist development. Traditions, particularly in a nation like Indonesia with its enormous diversity of cultures, have to be thought as multiple, whereas modernization is more likely to be conceived of as a unitary goal to which the whole nation aspires. Most of the peoples of modern Indonesia are engaged in lively debates among themselves about what the enduring and unchangeable elements of their own particular *adat*, or customs, should be. The Indonesian Constitution is designed to encourage respect and tolerance of different customs and religious beliefs, and "Unity in Diversity" is the national motto. At the same time, "development" and "modernization" are powerful key words in current Indonesian administrative ideology, words which inevitably have practical impacts on local cultures.[4]

Clearly, the impact of administrative attitudes on the maintenance of indigenous architectures may be either drastic or benign. Both colonial Dutch and post-Independence administrations have had their effects on local traditions, particularly where concepts of modernization, and related ideas such as hygiene, have been brought into play. At the local level, the application of policy can be very uneven, and does not always reflect the more sophisticated opinions of those in the higher echelons of the administration who believe in preserving Indonesia's diversity of cultural traditions. "Modernization" has sometimes been interpreted very literally as insistence on one particular building style (or mode of dress or type of religious belief). Fox, for example, reports that until the late sixties almost all houses on the island of Roti were built in traditional style. But between 1968 and 1975 local officials decreed that these houses should be pulled down and replaced with more "modern," "hygienic" houses built on the ground following a basically Dutch bungalow model. There are now scarcely any traditional houses left on the island.[5] By contrast, the government

FIGURE 2.
A Toraja origin-house
(*tongkonan*) at Lemo
village, recently
restored with the aid
of government
funds, but no
longer occupied.

has in other places given generously of funds to help preserve outstanding traditional buildings. Such is the case of the Minangkabau royal palace at Pagarruyung, rebuilt as a museum after it was destroyed by a fire (FIG. 6), the great house of Raja of Simalungun at Pematang Purba on the northern shore of Sumatra's Lake Toba, and some traditional origin-houses in Tana Toraja, which have been designated National Monuments (FIG. 2). It is possible, therefore, that part of the reason for the continued vitality of the architecture in the regions I am considering is that the people of these regions have not been demoralized by government interventions that might have led them to devalue their traditional forms. At the same time, one may note that a major motive behind government support for traditional architecture is tourism. Tourism is a significant income-earner in the regions I have mentioned but has yet to become significant in the remote islands of eastern Indonesia like Roti. As well as being part of the nation's cultural heritage, the restored buildings become designated "Tourist Objects." But clearly it is easier to destroy a tradition than bring it back or legislate against its disappearance. Admirable as it is, the preservation of a few outstanding buildings does not in itself ensure the maintenance of traditional ways among the populace at large. An examination of the interaction of some social processes determining the fate of indigenous styles is necessary.

MERANTAU AND ETHNICITY IN CONTEMPORARY INDONESIA

Indonesia, with its more than 350 distinct ethnic groupings, presents perhaps the greatest density of distinctive vernacular architectures in the world. These styles share a common heritage, evinced in such characteristic features as pile construction, saddle roofs, gable-horns, the dominance of roof over walls, and nail-less construction. The origins of this architecture can, I believe, be traced to the Austronesian peoples whose migrations into the islands of Southeast Asia began at least six thousand years ago, and which eventually carried them north to Japan, east into the Pacific as far as Easter Island, and west as far as Madagascar. The enthusiasm for migration has remained a fundamental feature of the cultures of many Austronesian-speaking peoples.

Familiar in Indonesian as *merantau*, "to leave one's home area go abroad" (*rantau* refers to the estuary of a river, or "foreign parts"), the concept of migration is particularly associated with the Minangkabau, who, as historical records show, have made a habit of it for centuries. But migration is equally established among other groups such as the Bugis, the Baweanese and the Banjarese.[6] During the colonial period even the more isolated hill peoples such as the Batak and the Toraja began to develop a more centrifugal orientation, as education, improved communications and the introduction of a money economy opened new opportunities for them beyond their homelands.[7] In modern Indonesia migration is more widespread than ever before, though exact figures are impossible to come by. Census data since 1960 have not included information about ethnic origins, but some rough estimates have been offered. As many as 10 percent of Jakarta's population of six million may be Minangkabau, and Kato estimates that one million, or approximately 25 percent, of the total population of Minangkabau are to be found in the *rantau*.[8] The proportion of Bataks on the *rantau* is not known, but Bataks are very strongly represented in Medan, Jakarta and other Javanese cities, including Bandung. No exact figures are available for Torajan migrants, but they are so numerous that in some districts where land shortages are acute, almost no young people are left in the villages. The amount of money entering Toraja as remittances from migrants through the bank, post office and other, informal channels is perhaps the single biggest factor in the development of the Toraja economy. Jakarta, the major destination for migrants from all over Indonesia, is so ethnically-mixed that it has been described as "a city of minorities." Much the same could be said of other major cities like Medan in Sumatra.[9] But migration is not restricted to destinations within Indonesia; eighty thousand Indonesians currently work in Saudi Arabia, and an uncertain number are employed in Malaysia and countries farther afield.

TORAJA

The Sa'dan Toraja, named after the major river running through their territory, occupy the administrative district of Tana Toraja in the northern highlands of the Province of South Sulawesi. Those living in Tana Toraja number around 340,000, and are largely subsistence farmers who grow wet rice in rain-fed hill terraces. They rear buffaloes and pigs, which are sacrificed during the many ceremonies which provide a major focus of Toraja social life, even for the perhaps 60 percent of the population who have become Christians. Most of the remaining Toraja adhere to a traditional set of beliefs which has gained official status as one of Indonesia's recognized religions. Christianity, modernization and another very different kind of migration -- tourism -- have all raised questions about which Torajan tradition should be maintained and which should be altered. At the same time, the flow of new wealth from the *rantau* has created a boom in expenditure on rituals, so that there is now what Volkman has aptly termed, "a simultaneous blossoming of ritual activity and doubt."[10]

When tourism first took off in the early seventies, the arrival of foreigners who had travelled thousands of miles to admire Toraja houses and witness Toraja funeral ceremonies caused many Torajans to reconsider the value of their traditions. This occurred at a time when most of these traditions were in decline or under attack from fundamentalist members of the Calvinist Toraja Church. Thus, although tourism certainly poses problems, it may not represent a wholly negative influence. In the same way, emigration may have a positive impact on the vitality of the home culture. Migrants from Toraja maintain remarkably strong ties with their homeland and typically make periodic visits, even from great distances and at heavy expense, in order to participate in ceremonies. The link with one's home village is even more importantly expressed through ties with family origin-houses, or *tongkonan*. These are the houses where one's parents, grandparents or more distant ancestors were born. At birth, a baby's placenta, which is regarded as a sort of twin, is buried on the east side of the house; Torajans say that however far they may roam, the placenta will always draw them back to their birthplace. One of the most prominent ways in which migrants spend money is on the renewal and ceremonial re-inauguration of origin-houses (FIG. 3). Nothing adds more visibly and enduringly to a family's prestige, or is better appreciated by fellow Torajans, than this type of expenditure. It is considered despicable to have a fine house in the city if one's origin-house in Toraja is dilapidated.[11]

Torajans recognize the changes taking place in their society, yet they often express the opinion that there is a core of tradition that will never change. When I asked about this core, Torajans most frequently told me it consisted of the ritual cycle, the ceremonial division and distribution of meat, and the *tongkonan*. In many respects, however, the role of the *tongkonan* has changed. In the past, the noble ruler of a community lived in an origin-house that dominated all the houses around it by its size and magnificence.

FIGURE 3.
The origin-house of Nonongan, decorated with heirloom valuables for the ceremony held to celebrate its re-building in January 1983. The ceremony was attended by many emigrant as well as locally-resident Torajans who trace descent through this house.

But the role of such a house as a concrete representation of aristocratic political power is no longer very relevant in an age of modern national administration. The resident of a noble *tongkonan* used also to hold certain ritual offices in the community, but nobles who are now Christians have for the most part ceased to function as ritual leaders. Ideas about comfort in everyday life have also undergone some change. Although the traditional house appears huge on the outside, its interior spaces are actually surprisingly limited. The interior consists of three narrow rooms with no furniture, lit only by very small window-openings. The doorway is a small square opening at knee height, closed by a heavy carved slab of wood. Many people find the old houses too cramped for modern living, and even those who have the right to inhabit an ancestral house often prefer to live elsewhere. New houses today often imitate the Bugis style of the lowlands. This style is characterized by slender stilts, a pitched roof, a very open plan, and large windows and doors. Most modern of all for those who can afford it, is a bungalow of stone or concrete in a style introduced by the Dutch. At a seminar held recently to discuss Torajan culture, a number of speakers expressed the opinion that builders and architects were much to blame for departing from traditional styles, and were "ruining the *adat*." But when one individual asked if anyone present would be prepared to live in a house of the traditional style, no one could bring themselves to reply in the affirmative.[12]

Those who are sufficiently wealthy may seek a compromise which enables them to enhance their social prestige both in terms of tradition and modernity. They may rebuild a traditional origin-house at great expense and with all the attendant ceremonies, and then leave it empty in order to live in a nearby modern stone house. In one district not far from the town of Rantepao stands a newly-constructed *tongkonan* with a line of six rice barns and a large stone bungalow beside them (FIG. 4). The *tongkonan's* builder, a man of noble descent, organized the construction as part of a large double funeral for his father and grandfather. The man lives in Jakarta and rarely visits Tana Toraja; but when he does, he and his family stay in the stone house. The rest of the time a caretaker lives in the stone house and looks after the *tongkonan*. A generator behind the stone house supplies electricity, and each of the rice barns is fitted with a light bulb. The caretaker is instructed to turn on the lights at dusk every night and leave them on until about 2 a.m. so as to impress the local populace with the heights to which his employer's fortunes have risen on the *rantau*.

Another innovation in style is the two-story wooden house (FIG. 5). The first floor is in Bugis style with a roughly square plan, spacious rooms, and large doors and windows, while the second floor is built entirely in traditional style, complete with wall carvings and a saddle roof. This represents an ingenious compromise between the desire for a more modern and convenient living space, and the desire to maintain the traditional form.

FIGURE 4.
Recently-built
tongkonan near
Madandan, Tana
Toraja, with modern
bungalow alongside
and row of rice barns
in front. The
undercroft of the
tongkonan has been
glassed in to form an
extra room beneath
the floor.

FIGURE 5.
Funeral guests dance
in front of a Toraja
house in the new two-
story style, whose
upper story retains the
traditional shape. The
structure on the left
holds the corpse.

Needless to say, this new creation is particularly decried by purists as a devaluation of the original style. But there are other, more subtle changes. One involves a standardization of carving styles.[13]

A centralization of carpenters in the main town of Rantepao seems to be causing the growing predominance of a Rantepao style of house, whose proportions are elongated and whose roof ridge is being exaggerated into longer and longer points. A certain rigidity seems also to be creeping into carving motifs. Furthermore, some carpenters prefer commercial paint to natural earth colors. With improved roads and communications, carpenters can easily move about to take commissions, and those people who want to learn the trade are more likely to go to Rantepao to do so.

In spite of these changes, traditional architecture in Tana Toraja is still very much alive. The 1950s and 60s in South Sulawesi were times of considerable economic hardship and social disturbance. World War II and the deprivations caused by Japanese occupation were followed in the 1950s by the struggle for Indonesian Independence and the incursions of Islamic guerrillas. The guerrillas burned villages, destroying a number of old *tongkonan*, and conscripted some Torajans into their forces. Not surprisingly, hardly anyone was in a position to carry out building projects under these circumstances, and there was almost no renewal of origin-houses. The 1950s and 60s also saw the emergence of the Indonesian Christian Party, the Parkindo, as the dominant force in Toraja politics. Its members, together with the Torajan Church, were hostile to many aspects of traditional culture, including the ceremonies associated with house-building. Anyone attempting to predict the future of Toraja architecture at that time would have painted a gloomy picture. However, by 1969 the traditional religion had received official government recognition, and Parkindo had suffered an overwhelming defeat in the elections of 1971, as Torajans voted for the government party, Golkar.[14] With the return of more peaceful and prosperous times, there was an immediate resurgence of building activity. I attribute this firstly to the continued centrality of the house within the Toraja kinship structure, and secondly to its continued importance as a ritual site.

Toraja ceremonial life is too culturally specific to translate easily to areas outside the homeland, just as houses outside Toraja are never thought of as origin-houses, and a house in traditional style would not mean the same thing elsewhere. Hence arises the

F I G U R E 6. The royal palace of Pagarruyung, Minangkabau, recently rebuilt after a fire with the aid of government funds, and now a museum.

compulsion to return to celebrate rites in a place where people understand and appreciate them. Visits home do not just reaffirm identity, however. Wealthier migrants often maintain considerable landholdings in Toraja and use the occasion of their return to check on their affairs or make new deals. Wealthy migrants may take land in pawn in exchange for loans and arrange for relatives and others to sharecrop it. At the same time, they want to make an impression, and the family origin-house is essential to family prestige.

In a broader sense, the house lends itself to interpretation as a convenient cultural symbol at a time when the definition of ethnic identity is becoming important in a modern, culturally-diverse nation. In spite of its close connections with ritual, most people agree that the house is a secular element of culture, and therefore less controversial than some other elements -- such as funeral ceremonies, the rectitude of which is still debated by some Christians. Even as some of the older significances of the houses are lost, it continues to function as a vivid and condensed symbol of what it means to be Toraja.

MINANGKABAU

The architecture of the Minangkabau represents one of the most graceful and striking variations on the theme of the saddle-backed roof in all Southeast Asia. The Minangkabau occupy the province of West Sumatra whose population in 1980 was 3.4 million. This figure does not include the one million or more Minangkabau who have probably left their homeland to trade or seek city jobs in other parts of Indonesia, or beyond.

Minangkabau, even more than other peoples of Indonesia, are much given to discussion and analysis of their own *adat*. Though they may tend to view their own adat as fixed and unchanging, that which "neither rots in the rain nor cracks in the sun," historical changes have in fact shaped and reshaped Minangkabau society, making it necessary to be especially cautious when speaking of "traditional" Minangkabau society. Although they have been Muslim for several centuries, the Minangkabau have maintained their matrilineal system of inheritance. Islamic and *adat* traditions are so integrated that, despite the efforts of various reform movements, most Minangkabau do not perceive any contradiction between the two.

Minangkabau women inherit and have control over houses and ancestral rice lands. Each house is known by the name of its leading and most active woman. Within a village reside the members of four or more matrilineal clans, or *suku*, each consisting of a number of lineages. A segment of a lineage is called a *saparuik*, meaning "one womb," and consists ideally of three generations of women and their families living in a large house, a *rumah gadang* or a *rumah adat*. This group has been described as "the most important functional unit" of Minangkabau society.[15] Although some formal leadership roles are given to men, the authority of women within their households is very great. In the past, Minangkabau great houses have lived up to their name by being large enough to accommodate huge numbers of people. A Dutch official in 1871 found over one hundred people residing in one such house in Alahan Panjang and between sixty and eighty people residing in another.[16] In the village of Sulit Air there still stands a magnificent longhouse of twenty apartments. It is 64 meters long, even though today it is only occupied by seven families. Construction of a house was traditionally accompanied by expensive ceremonies, and the house became the important ritual site for the descendants of those who built it.

The Minangkabau view their world, the *Alam Minangkabau*, as divided essentially into two areas -- the *darek*, the inner highlands of Minangkabau territory, and the *rantau*, the outlying frontier. Kato suggested that in earlier times *merantau* must have represented the movement of population into new areas of West Sumatra as villages grew and split to form new settlements. Later a "circulatory" pattern developed as men oscillated between their home villages and their various, relatively-close destinations -- mostly cities in Minangkabau or in other regions of Sumatra. But some went further afield, to Java, Malaya, eastern Indonesia and the Middle East. There were also movements of a more permanent nature, for example of settlers to the Negri Sembilan area of the Malay Peninsula during the seventeenth and eighteenth centuries. Nowadays many whole families reside permanently on the *rantau*, especially in Java. They maintain ties with their homeland through occasional visits and through the activities of vigorous Minangkabau associations.

Thus, the concept of an inner and outer territory of Minangkabau and the practice of migration itself have always been part of the Minangkabau world view. Returning migrants have always been a source of new ideas and information about the outside world, and the sense of Minangkabau identity itself is partly shaped by experiences on the *rantau*.[17] Several writers have suggested that an attitude of "romantic conservatism" characterizes those who settle permanently on the *rantau*.[18] Even though they have no desire to remain at home, the knowledge that their home villages continue to adhere to *adat* patterns is reassuring for migrants. Minangkabau associations perform many tasks in addition to channeling funds home to assist in the maintenance of their villages. They help arrange important ceremonies, especially weddings, for their members; they form art, dance and theater groups, which often make periodic returns to the homeland, and thus inject new energy into various uniquely Minangkabau art forms; and they publish Minangkabau newspapers and magazines.

The dynamic relationship between home-based and migrant Minangkabau is further reflected in the frequency with which migrants fund the rebuilding of houses-of-origin, either for their own matrilineal kin or for the kin of their wives. As with the Toraja, interest in the maintenance of these houses appears to have fluctuated but is currently enjoying a resurgence. During this century various disasters have caused the destruction of a great many older houses. In 1926, for example, a serious earthquake in Padang Panjang toppled many houses. Thousands more were destroyed by the Dutch in the War for Indonesian Independence (1945-1949) and in the warring factions by the unsuccessful PRRI Rebellion of the 1950s. Subsequently, it was too expensive to rebuild these houses and finance the necessary rituals accompanying their construction. In addition, deforestation has made it increasingly difficult to find trees large enough to furnish the great central pillars of the *rumah gadang*. Figures compiled by Kato suggest that in the early decades of this century there was still a very high proportion of buildings in *adat* style, while within the last generation or so the percentage has declined dramatically.[19] In recent years there has been a proliferation of individual family dwellings. In part this has reflected a growing preference for the greater privacy such houses afford, compared to the intense interaction of life in the multifamily *rumah gadang*. Nowadays one may even come across a large *rumah gadang* standing empty with the descent group occupying a number of small houses around it. In 1986 I stayed in a small village near Payakumbuh in a compound of seven houses built around a beautiful, old, traditional house (FIG. 7). The houses were occupied by a group of married sisters and daughters. Those who were better off had built themselves new, modern houses in stone and concrete, the latest of which was the pride of the compound, complete with balconies, net curtains and purple lamps. The old house was still occupied by the eldest sister, but the others privately felt sorry for her because she and her husband had not been able to afford a new house.

FIGURE 7.
The oldest house of a
matrilineal family
compound at Kampai,
near Payakumbuh,
Minangkabau. It is
surrounded by houses
of married sisters in
old and new styles.

Swift, writing on social change among the Minangkabau in the
1960s, suggested that being able to afford a new, stone house was
regarded as very prestigious, and that some houses were being
built with money earned on the *rantau* even if no one wanted to
live in them. He noted, however, that people were becoming
unwilling to spend large sums on the maintenance of traditional
houses, since this might mean foregoing the status of building a
modern house in order to add to the prestige of *adat* superiors and
elders. This sacrifice of prestige was resented, and, moreover,
people were beginning to find the traditional houses
uncomfortable. Furthermore, Swift suggested that the *rantau* was
tending to become a permanent, rather than an episodic, form of
migration, which was causing a loosening of ties to the home area,

particularly among second-generation migrants born in cities outside of Minangkabau.[20] Swift's predictions do not appear to be fully borne out, however. I have already mentioned the apparently strong continuation of ties to the home area even among permanent migrants. Houses are also still important as the proper sites for rituals and gatherings of the kin group, and people have emphasized to me that they would feel shame if the kin group were without such a gathering place. A number of researchers more recently have commented on the definite upsurge of interest in the rebuilding of traditional houses, or at least in the building of houses with traditional roof styles (though as yet this may be more obvious in some areas than in others). Persoon, for example, noted: "Many traditional *adat* houses of typical Minangkabau design have been nicely restored during the last 10 or 15 years with money earned somewhere on the rantau."[21] One may yet be justified in hoping that Minangkabau architecture will remain an active and living tradition.

TOBA BATAK

The Toba are by far the most numerous of the Batak peoples. They occupy the heart of the Batak homelands in northern Sumatra, centering around the island of Samosir in Lake Toba. The Toba region is a great mountain plateau with an altitude of three thousand feet. In this wild and beautiful landscape may still be seen large numbers of the traditional, finely-decorated houses and sculpted stone tombs of Toba. The pile-built Toba house with its elegantly upcurved roof shows clear similarities to the houses of the Toraja and Minangkabau, although the construction techniques of all three have unique features.[22] Fewer houses seem to have been destroyed by historical disturbances in the Toba area than in Tana Toraja or in Minangkabau territory. But it is the building of tombs which is the most eye-catching architectural activity at the present time.

During the late nineteenth century Toba culture began to be drastically altered. In 1860 a German Protestant mission was established, which resulted in mass conversions. Subsequently, the Dutch took over administration of the area, though they did not succeed in pacifying all the Batak lands until early in this century. Improved communications, education and the introduction of a money economy changed Toba society from an inward-looking one, distrustful of outsiders, to a centrifugal one from which many migrants began to move to cities in other parts of Indonesia. The traditional religion disintegrated under the impact of Christianity, and was abandoned. Nonetheless, elements of Toba culture have survived in a changed configuration, and the dynamic relationship between the Toba homeland and the Toba emigrants in Indonesian cities has fostered a new and vigorous ethnic awareness.

Toba are particularly numerous in Medan, as well as in Jakarta and other Javanese cities. They are extremely enterprising and hardworking, and some have built up highly successful businesses. Numerous clan, district and church associations provide points of contact for Toba in the cities; these were well described by Bruner in the 1950s and 60s and they are still very much a part of the scene in Medan today.[23] One woman, for example, told me that she attends a meeting of her clan association once a fortnight and is a member of two local ward groups who met regularly for prayer and choral practice. All told, she meets at least once a week with groups of fellow Toba. A wealthy Toba businessman and newspaper owner in Medan recently endowed a Batak University, the Universitas Sisingamangaraja, which includes a "Centre for Batakology." The center contains a small museum and has many plans to encourage the preservation of Batak culture and stimulate a sense of Batak identity among migrants and residents of the homeland. When the inaugural ceremony for the university was held in 1984, efforts were made to trace and invite all known Toba clan associations in Medan, and around eighty groups responded; it is possible that there are even more.

The Toba are divided into named patrilineal clans, called marga. Each of these has important links with other marga, to which they are related as either wife-givers, *hula-hula*, or wife-takers, *boru*. Each clan or clan branch has a special house, the *rumah parsangtian*, which is the birthplace of its founding ancestor. Tombs, echoing the shape of the houses, reflect both a belief in the

FIGURE 8.
Houses of the dead
and of the living echo
the same form.
Sangakl, Samosir
Island, Lake Toba.

FIGURE 9.
Concrete tomb in
church-like form at
Sangkal, Samosir
Island, Lake Toba.

necessity of providing the dead with homes, and the centrality of
the house in the social organization of the living.   Old stone
sarcophagi, with their curved lids, echo the form of the house in a

general way; in the past, some graves have also had miniature wooden houses built over them, called *joro*.[24]

Nowadays elaborate and expensive tombs may be built out of concrete, imitating in every detail the shape of the traditional Toba house (FIG. 8). The use of concrete began very early this century, for Bartlett comments on it. But the examples he recorded mostly predate World War I, and he noted that few had been erected in the period 1918-1927. He warmly admired the quality of their design, but interpreted this as only a last burst of creative energy in a culture that would inevitably die. "It appears," he wrote, "that the movement to create a new art in the spirit of the past was abortive. The forces bringing about cultural disintegration are too strong."[25]

As it turns out his prognostication was overly pessimistic, since one now sees concrete tombs all over the area. Some, moving away from the imitation of house forms, incorporate new views of the afterlife, with the inclusion of features such as church steeples (FIG. 9). The tombs, called *tambak* or *parholian*, are constructed by groups of patrilineally-related kin. These groups hold special ceremonies in which the bones of a number of ancestors of several generations are exhumed, regrouped and transferred into new tombs. This ceremony, today somewhat Christianized, will be attended by both wife-giving and wife-taking clans of the hosts. The survival of secondary burial in this form provides modern-day Toba with the opportunity to assert their continuity with clan ancestors, as well as gain prestige in the eyes of the community. The great expense of the ceremony, as well as the construction of the tomb itself, is frequently met by migrant clan members who will return long distances to attend this most important of Toba ceremonies.

Even more expensive and demanding an even bigger ceremony, is the erection of a kind of mausoleum or memorial monument which commemorates the founding ancestors of an entire clan. Such monuments are a new development, dating from only the 1960s. They are called *tugu*, an Indonesian word which refers to national monuments and obelisks such as those erected in large numbers in the post-Independence period. A *tugu*, I was told, should be tall, and some are of impressive size, reached only by flights of steps. They often incorporate portrait figures of the ancestors worked in painted concrete. The *tugu* is an interesting example of a highly traditional and distinctively local idea recast in a modern, nationalist idiom. It appears that it is in fact the clan associations on the *rantau* who are responsible for this new idea.[26] Toba investment of money, effort and artistic creativity in tomb-building is a remarkable example of the way a society undergoing far-reaching economic, political and religious change may nonetheless succeed in maintaining a thread of continuity through the creative reassembly of elements of its traditional culture.

THE RESILIENCE OF VERNACULAR STYLE

In selecting these three examples, I have attempted to give a picture of some architectural traditions which are truly active in Williams' sense of the word. The traditions are not fixed and immutable, and the societies which produce them are experiencing many forces of change, but the traditions have an undeniable vitality. In all three cases what keeps the tradition vital has as much to do with the ritual importance of houses or tombs and their place within kinship systems, as with any purely functional consideration.   Migration, a major factor affecting all three societies, is one source of change and new ideas. But migration also gives birth to a new search for ethnic identity. In this search, the house -- even as its traditional functions change -- can apparently become more important than ever as a symbol of what it means to belong to the society. Migration channels energy and resources back to a society as well as out to a wider world.

Two decades or more ago it appeared that the decline of the vernacular styles of all three societies was irrevocable. But this has not happened; in fact, the cultures have shown more resilience than would have been expected. They have flourished while adapting to new circumstances, and there has been a resurgence of building in traditional styles. But one may ask, what of second-generation migrants. There seems to be agreement that children born in cities outside the homeland do not experience the same feelings toward the place of origin, or the same searching for identity, that their parents experience. Indeed, they may feel uncomfortable in the villages, and may not even speak the language of origin. Nonetheless, the impact of this group on the overall dynamic should not be overestimated. There will always be a generation of first-time migrants over whom the origin-place will exercise its pull.

REFERENCE NOTES

1. I conducted fieldwork in Tana Toraja in 1977-1979 and 1982-83. My research was kindly sponsored by LIPI, the Indonesian Institute of Sciences, and was funded on the first occasion by the then Social Science Research Council of the U. K., and on the second occasion by a Cambridge University Evans Fellowship and a British Academy South-East Asian Fellowship. The continued generous support of these bodies has also enabled me to spend two years (1985-86) as a Visiting Fellow at the Institute of South-East Asian Studies, Singapore, researching the anthropology of traditional architecture in Southeast Asia. I should like to express my gratitude to these bodies for their support. In 1986 I visited Sumatra for several weeks in order to see and photograph traditional architecture.

2. A great deal of literature has shown how ethnicity operates as a boundary-defining mechanism and, as such, is likely to become important where ethnic groups most often come into contact with each other (as is likely to be the case in cities). See, for example, F. Barth, *Ethnic Groups and Boundaries* (London: Allen & Unwin, 1969); A. Cohen, *Urban Ethnicity* (London: Tavistock, 1974).

3. R. Williams, *Keywords: A Vocabulary of Culture and Society* (London: Fontana, 1976), p. 269. In very much the same way, the shades of meaning attaching to the terms modern or modernization have shifted over time. From the primary sense of "contemporary," they have acquired tones both favorable and unfavorable. Interestingly, Williams notes that the majority of pre-nineteenth-century meanings were unfavorable, while throughout the nineteenth and, still more noticeably, the twentieth century, "there was a strong movement the other way, until modern became virtually equivalent to improved, or satisfactory or efficient." (*Keywords*, p. 174).

4. M. van Langenberg, "Analysing Indonesia's New Order State: A Keywords Approach," *Review of Indonesian and Malaysian Affairs* 20/2 (1986), pp. 1-47. The concept of keywords was developed by Raymond Williams to refer to words which denote important cultural concepts whose meanings, although often taken for granted, have typically shifted over time; they are defined by him as: "significant, binding words in certain activities and their interpretation; they are significant, indicative words in certain forms of thought." (*Keywords*, p. 13).

5. James Fox (personal communication).

6. L. Castles, "The Ethnic Profile of Djakarta," *Indonesia* 3 (1967), pp. 153-204; J.

Lineton, "The Bugis of South Sulawesi: An Indonesian Society and its Universe" (Ph.D. thesis, SOAS, London, 1975); T. Kato, *Matriliny and Migration: Evolving Minangkabau Traditions in Indonesia* (Ithaca, NY: Cornell University Press, 1982); G. Persoon, "Congelation in the Melting Pot: The Minangkabau in Jakarta," in P.J. Nas, ed., *The Indonesian City: Studies in Urban Development and Planning* (Dordrecht: Foris, 1982), pp. 176-196.

7.   On changes in Batak society, see A. Viner, "The Changing Batak," *Journal of the Malay Branch of the Royal Asiatic Society* 52/2 (1979), pp. 84-112.

8.   Persoon, "Congelation in the Melting Pot," p. 181; Kato, *Matriliny and Migration*, p. 131. Naim suggests a much higher figure which Kato points out is inflated by the inclusion of neighboring districts, such as Kerinci, which are only distantly related to Minangkabau (M. Naim, "Merantau: Minangkabau Voluntary Migration" (Ph.D. thesis, University of Singapore, 1973).

9.   Persoon, "Congelation in the Melting Pot," p. 180.

10.   T. Volkman, *Feasts of Honor Ritual and Change in the Toraja Highlands* (Urbana: University of Illinois Press, 1985), p. 43.

11.   I have discussed elsewhere the role of the house in the construction of Toraja identity, as well as its significance within the kinship system and the manner in which rebuilding projects are organized. Torajans disagree about the length of time necessary for a house to come to be viewed as an origin-house by its descendants, but the basic rule seems to be that one rebuilding (i.e., two generations) is enough. This is fully in accord with Williams' definition of tradition as an active process. See R. Waterson, "Taking the Place of Ancestors: Ethnic Identity in Tana Toraja in the 1980s," in R. Waterson, *Ritual and Belief among the Sa'dan Toraja* (University of Kent Centre of South-East Asian Studies, Occasional Paper 2, 1984) pp. 34-72; "The Ideology and Terminology of Kinship among the Sa'dan Toraja," *Bijdragen tot de Taal-, Land- en Volkenkunde* 142/1 (1986), pp. 87-112.

12.   H. Setiono, "Arsitektur Tradisional Toraja sebagai Ungkapan Wadah Fisik Nilai Budaya Adat Toraja" (Traditional Toraja Architecture as an Expression in Physical Form of the Cultural Values of Toraja *Adat*) (Paper presented to a seminar on Toraja *adat*, Ujung Pandang, April 1983. p. 4.

13.   See R. Waterson, "The House and the World: The Symbolism of Sa'dan Toraja House Carvings," *RES* 15 (June 1988), pp. 35-60.

14.   For a fuller discussion of these events, see E. Crystal, "Cooking-pot Politics: A Toraja Village Study," *Indonesia* 18 (1974), pp. 119-151.

15.   J.P.E. de Josselin de Jong, *Minangkabau and Negri Sembilan: Socio-Political Structure in Indonesia* (The Hague: Nijhoff, 1952) p. 11.

16.   Kato, *Matriliny and Migration*, p. 45.

17.   The percentage of "return migrants" in West Sumatra (those who are living in their province of birth but who have lived elsewhere prior to that) is about 35 percent, higher than the national average of 21 percent. Sundrum, "Interprovincial Migration," *Bulletin of Indonesian Economic Studies* 12 (1976), p. 77.

18.   Kato, *Matriliny and Migration*, p. 232; Persoon, "Congelation in the Melting Pot," p. 189.

19.   Kato, *Matriliny and Migration*, p. 176.

20.   M.G. Swift, "Minangkabau and Modernization," in L. Hiatt and C. Jayawardena, eds., *Anthropology in Oceania* (Sydney: Angus & Robertson, 1971), pp. 259-60.

21.   Persoon, "Congelation in the Melting Pot," p. 188. The renewed interest in restoring old houses or building new ones in traditional style has been noted also by others (Audrey Kahin, Anton Alers, personal communications). The popularity of

Minangkabau roof forms in municipal buildings also reflects the appeal of this building element in particular as an instant statement of Minangkabau identity -- although in these cases, the roofs are usually made of zinc and not necessarily constructed according to traditional methods. In a development rather similar to that on which I have remarked in Toraja, Alers notes that the centralization of carpenters in the village of Pandai Sikat, near Bukittinggi, may be leading to a certain standardization of carving styles. Some of the carpenters work from stencils rather than freehand, which tends to introduce a certain rigidity to the style. They can now travel easily to other districts to execute commissions.

22. On the very different construction techniques of the Batak and Minangkabau, see D. Sherwin, "From Batak to Minangkabau: An Architectural Trajectory," *Majallah Akitek* 1:79 (1979), pp. 38-42. For architectural diagrams of Toraja house construction, see G. Domenig, *Tektonik im Primitiven Dachbau* (Zurich: ETH, 1980), p. 179.

23. E. Bruner, "Kin and Non-Kin," in A. Southall, ed., *Urban Anthropology* (New York: Oxford University Press, 1973), pp. 373-392; "The Expression of Ethnicity in Indonesia," in A. Cohen, ed., *Urban Ethnicity* (London: Tavistock, 1974), pp. 251-280.

24. H. Bartlett, *The Sacred Edifices of the Batak of Sumatra* (Ann Arbor: University of Michigan Press, 1934).

25. *Ibid.*, p. 29.

26. K. Sjahrir, "Asosiasi Klan Orang Batak Toba di Jakarta," *Prisma* 12/1 (1983), pp. 75-81. Sjahrir links *tugu*-building to an increased intensity of ritual performance as part of a "new social phenomenon" such as has never been seen before in the homeland, but which, on the contrary, has grown directly out of the urban experience of migrants.

All photos are by the author unless otherwise indicated.

TRADITIONAL VERSUS MODERN HOUSING IN BOTSWANA—AN ANALYSIS FROM THE USER'S PERSPECTIVE

ANITA LARSSON

In Botswana, as in many developing countries, housing moderniz-ation is a vital part of the national ambition for progress. Traditional ways of providing housing are consequently being abandoned and replaced by what is referred to as modern housing. An ongoing transition from traditional to modern housing is underway. Due to this transformation, many types of dwellings exist today in rural and urban areas of Botswana, ranging from the genuine traditional dwelling to the modern multi-room house with several amenities, and incorporating a wide range of dwellings with a mixture of modern and traditional elements in between.

Superficially, the ongoing transformation can be interpreted as an evolution from traditional to modern; that is, a linear transform-ation where traditional housing elements are gradually being replaced by modern -- better -- ones. This is, however, not the case. Housing modernization has, especially in the case of low-cost housing, led to the disappearance of qualities of utility characteristic of traditional dwellings. For the poor, the transition has in many respects meant change for the worse, not, as anticipated, for the better.

Housing modernization has created a great deal of confusion concerning the use of space in low-income dwellings. This confusion, however, is not primarily caused by a conflict between the needs and wants of low-income people and the housing policies of the government, an explanation that comes easily to hand. Instead, it is being caused by a contradiction between people's desires both for modernization and a better dwelling, and by the impact of the government's housing policy on the design and use of dwellings. The purpose of the following comparison between traditional and modern housing is to interpret this contradiction, in other words, to try to understand the impact of modernization on low-cost housing in Botswana and in other developing countries. This will be done by searching for and analyzing fundamental concepts intrinsic to housing in Botswana. The whole societal context is of importance. The role and responsibility of housing in relation to the place of men and women in the society will be found to be of special significance.

In order to understand how traditional housing differs from modern low-cost housing, a summary description and analysis of traditional housing as it exists today will be presented first. Traditional housing did not remain static prior to the introduction of modern housing. During the last hundred years or so there have been important changes that can be regarded as development. A look at the transformation that took place before the introduction of modern housing is essential for understanding the differences between the concepts of "traditional" and "modern," or for analyzing utility values. Many conditions in the development of housing, constituting the setting, are specific for Botswana.

THE SETTING

Botswana was once a protectorate of Britain. Colonial influence, especially compared to the other colonies, was limited, however. During British rule internal matters continued to be handled by Botswana's tribes under the authority of chiefs. Sectors such as health and education were severely neglected by the British, however.

This neglect did not mean that colonization had no impact on Botswana. The most important effect was undoubtedly caused by labor migration to South Africa. Though labor migration started about 1850, it became a necessity when Britain introduces taxation in 1899. Taxation affected many households, forcing young men to leave their home villages for contract periods of several months. Cash was introduced into the subsistence economy not only to pay taxes but also to buy goods in Botswana and South Africa. The introduction of the cash economy also had an impact on housing, and this impact is an underlying theme of this paper.

Britain's general neglect of Botswana did not have serious consequences in the field of housing; rather, the reverse was true. The Tswana[1] people had long since provided their own dwellings as part of their subsistence economy. Many nineteenth-century travellers, while making their way into the "interior of Africa," noted the high quality of Tswana housing.[2] Up to the time of Botswana's independence traditional housing was almost the only model available.

When Botswana gained independence in 1966, it was among the poorest countries in the world. Botswana has, however, since that time experienced very rapid economic growth. Through the customs union with South Africa, modern building materials and other industrial goods are available. But for many people, this availability is only in principle; most low-income people cannot afford industrial goods in any amount.

TRADITIONAL TSWANA HOUSING TODAY

Self-provided traditional housing is still the predominant form of housing for the majority of people in Botswana, despite the fact that nobody today can totally rely on the subsistence economy. Around 80 percent of the population live in rural areas, most of

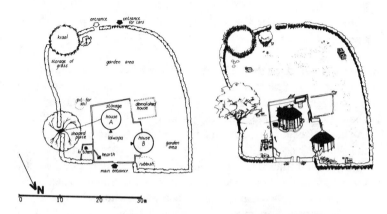

F I G U R E 1. The layout and use of space in a typical traditional dwelling. The whole yard makes up the dwelling unit or "house." The heart of the dwelling unit is the *lolwapa*, or inner courtyard, enclosed by a low mud wall. The houses, the *lolwapa*, and the different parts of the yard are the rooms of this dwelling. The *lolwapa* is the living room of the family; it is where children play, visitors are received, meals eaten, and where a fire is often lit on cold evenings and mornings. To have a beautiful *lolwapa* is the pride and joy of the wife. The design of its walls is the result of individual effort and creativity.

them in dwellings made partly or entirely from traditional materials.3

The layout of houses and yards, together with the fact that building materials are available, at least in principle, makes the dwelling adaptable to changes in the number and nature of household members. As a new house can easily be built when needed, over-crowding seldom occurs (FIG. 1).

Domestic activities take place indoors as well as outdoors, and large parts of the yard are utilized daily for domestic tasks. It is thus artificial to consider only indoor space when analyzing a dwelling with a traditional layout. This aspect of traditional housing is often neglected, perhaps because the actual use of the space has not been the object of investigation.

The type and standard of arrangements for different domestic activities vary considerably. Modern living patterns have been adopted for some domestic activities, while for others the traditional patterns still survive. Custom dictates that women's household work such as cooking, cleaning dishes and washing clothes is always done on the ground. There are few means to enable these chores to be done more conveniently. Storage space for everyday household goods is simple and sometimes inadequate. The presence of beds for sleeping and wardrobes and sideboards is the most frequent sign of an adaptation to modern living patterns (FIG. 2).

Traditional building methods, in their genuine form, require no capital expenditure. Mud, wood and grass, the main building materials, are collected from communal land, and the household itself constructs the dwelling in such a way that no advanced tools are needed.

Men and women have their respective tasks. All work in mud is done by women. They collect materials, and build and maintain walls, floors, skirtings and the inner courtyard, or *lolwapa*. Bricks for the walls are made of mud and water and dried in the sun. As the surface of a mud wall is easily eroded, walls have to be replastered every year. Women also thatch roofs in the traditional way. The poor quality of the grass used and the simple way the grass is fastened to the structure make for a roof of limited durability. On the other hand, the material is fairly easily obtainable and does not have to be purchased (FIG. 3).

Men collect materials for the roof structure, put that structure together and thatch the roof in the boer or Afrikaner way. For the boer type of roof, a stronger but rarer kind of grass is used. Today this type of grass is often purchased. In the boer thatching method, each layer of grass is carefully sewn onto the battens, not loosely spread out and simply fastened to the bottom batten, as in the traditional method. A boer roof will last as many as thirty years. To thatch the boer way has become a skilled craft for male villagers. Doors and windows are as a rule made by a local craftsman.

A general opinion holds that traditional houses have a short lifespan and little stability. However, houses more than twenty years

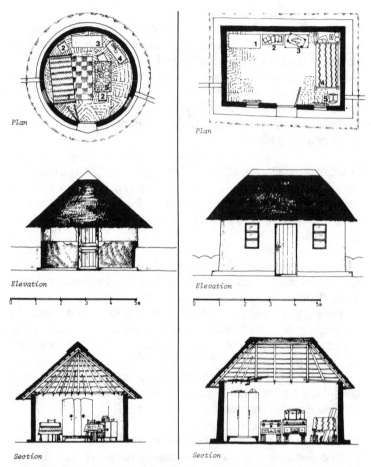

Plan

Plan

Elevation

Elevation

Section

Section

F I G U R E 2. Traditional houses. Houses are circular or rectangular with one, two or three rooms. Some houses have a proper verandah. Houses are generally about ten to twenty square meters in size. They are mainly used for sleeping and storage. The house on the left is that of a household's grown-up daughters: 1) bed, 2) chair, 3) wardrobe, 4) cabinet, 5) table. The house on the right is that of the sons of the same household who are working in South Africa: 1) wardrobe, 2) chest of drawers, 3) metal trunk on wooden chest, 4) bed, 5) sack and cardboard box. A bicycle is stored in the roof structure.

old are common, and houses more than fifty years old may be found. A mud wall is strong enough to carry the load of the whole roof.

There are, in addition to many merits, some disadvantages to traditional building methods. Regular maintenance and repairs at intervals are essential to ensure a long life-span. The quality of materials and techniques is, however, also important. For instance, wide skirtings and eaves protect the walls from heavy rains. Another constant threat is soil termites.

THE TRANSFORMATION OF TSWANA HOUSING SINCE 1900

Functional aspects of the Tswana dwelling correspond well to the needs of a rural household living mainly on subsistence farming. However, as has been pointed out by Rapoport, the important question was not what needs are fulfilled, since basic needs are always met, but how they are met. This is determined by the culture: "What is characteristic and significant about culture is this choice, the specific solution to certain needs . . . ."[4] The Tswana dwelling is no exception; it is determined by and an expression of the Tswana culture, still very much alive.

F I G U R E 3. Traditional thatching is collectively done by women. Bundles of grass are thrown on top of the roof and tied to it with tree bark strings.

Labor migration to South Africa and the introduction of a cash economy created new needs and wants. Material advancement, including better houses for the Tswana people, was explicitly supported by some chiefs. At the same time these chiefs did not want to see changes among their people that would result in alteration of "their personality, their spirit, their character as Tswana."[5]

According to Schapera, the consequence of new needs and wants in the 1930s was the elimination of self-sufficiency:

> Contacts with Western civilization introduced new commodities of many different kinds, whose acceptance drew the Kgatla [an ethnic group of the Tswana people,] into an elaborate system of exchange through which they are linked up with and even dependent upon the markets of the world. The early Boers in the Transvaal revealed to them new forms of dress, housing, transport, weapons and other instruments, ...[6]

Schapera further points out that it was necessary to find money not only to pay for the goods introduced by the Europeans but to pay the annual tax and to pay for school fees and medical treatment and water from bore-holes. The result was,

> . . . a greater differentiation in standards of living. Poor people on the whole still occupy the same kinds of huts as before, ... Many people, however, also acquire more and better clothes and implements, as well as . . . tables and chairs, . . . dwellings and furniture of European type.[7]

This material advancement led not only to increased numbers of cattle but also to houses and furniture becoming signs of progress. Schapera summarized the change:

> . . . cattle remain a symbol of wealth, but more perhaps for their trade value than for their traditional desirability. Brick houses, complete outfits of European clothing, wagons, . . . suites of furniture and . . . other objects like them, are today the visible indications of the man of property.[8]

These changes in material standards led to a gradual transformation and development of traditional housing, an interesting example of how traditional housing can undergo important changes that result in improvement and development.

When nineteenth century records are related to present-day Tswana housing, the transformation of building methods becomes very evident. Rectangular houses, pitched roofs, proper doors and windows, boer thatched roofs, roof trusses, and wide verandahs are the most important examples of how new elements and techniques have been integrated into the tradition. Such changes have been discussed by Hardie. By comparing photographs of the village of Mochudi taken in 1907 and 1930, he found differences in the appearances of houses:

> The roof design and roof materials used serve perhaps as the best barometer of change in these photographs. For instance, the most striking difference between the 1907 and 1930 photographs is the change in the method of thatching. In 1907 the thatch is held in place by a network of ropes [traditional thatching]. By 1930 it can be seen that most dominant style is that brought to the area by Boers and known as "Afrikaner" thatching.[9]

Rectangular houses and roof trusses must have been coeval changes. It is not easy to roof a rectangular house the traditional way by joining rafters at the apex while standing on a temporary scaffold. The introduction of trusses, including a crossbeam, was necessary. Such trusses are put together on the ground and then lifted up and placed on the walls. When such a house has posts, these support only those parts of the roof which extend beyond the wall, such as those parts over a verandah (FIG. 4). Usually the roof is double-pitched, and multi-room houses with such roofs are not uncommon. According to Hardie, this house-type is called "Meadowlands," after one of the original sections of Soweto in Johannesburg. He concludes that, "by its very name it reflects the desire to have the 'modern' house of the city."[10]

The above changes meant only technical improvements; nonetheless, they were important. For instance, they meant that the house received more light from outside, was easier to furnish with European-type furniture, and required less maintenance. Stronger roofs allowed for larger houses, whether the roofs were circular or rectangular (FIG. 5).

Initially, the improvements did not result in any important change in the ways space was conceived or used. In improved traditional

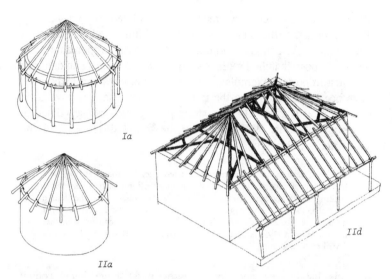

F I G U R E 4. The development of Tswana roof constructions. Two methods of building roof structures are practiced, those using posts and those not using posts. When posts are used, they are placed outside the wall and carry the whole load. Roof and wall are then not joined (Ia). When there are no posts, the roof structure rests on the wall (IIa). There is good reason to believe that the post support is the indigenous way. Rafters and battens do not form a stiff and strong construction. Proper roof trusses are generally used on rectangular houses (IId), and they provide a strong construction.

dwellings with one or two multi-room rectangular houses of mud and thatch and one or more one-room circular house, most daily activities still took place outdoors in the *lolwapa*. The interiors were still used mainly for sleeping and storage, even if a suite of living-room furniture could be found there.

The next step in the transformation of Tswana housing was the introduction of burnt bricks, cement blocks and corrugated iron sheets. These new materials did not have a serious impact on housing until the 1970s, however. Hardie, when comparing photos of Mochudi in 1971 and 1978, noted: "Rapidly over this short period a corrugated-galvanized iron sheet roofing material . . . has taken hold. Along with this development has been the introduction of the dry soil-cement block."[11]

The introduction of burnt bricks, cement blocks and corrugated iron sheets did not initially mean a change in the concept of housing (FIG. 6). There are many examples of dwellings in both

FIGURE 5. Examples of the development of traditional building techniques through contacts with Europeans in South Africa. Above is a rectangular two-room house with a wide verandah. Below is a circular house eight meters wide. Both are built with mud, wood and grass only.

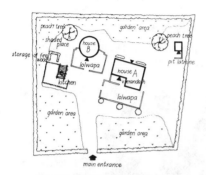 

FIGURE 6. A dwelling including both traditional and modern elements. Traditional concepts still dominate the use of space and the layout. The rondavel is mainly for visitors and for cooking during rains. Visitors are generally received outdoors. The modern house was built first, by the husband. Later, the wife built the rondavel because she had no savings for another house and wanted and indoor cooking area.

villages and urban squatter areas where traditional materials have been replaced by modern ones in one or two houses. The layout and the use of space are in principle the same as in the traditional dwelling.[12] This was one of Hardie's overall conclusions: "The concepts which underlie the internal organization of the house have not changed and thus neither the built expression."[13]

However, Hardie undertook his fieldwork ten years ago and mainly in a rural village, and his statement is no longer valid. The process of change has proceeded and now includes a change in the concepts underlying the organization and use of space. New concepts can be found mainly in the towns but also to some extent in rural areas, especially in the villages around Gaborone, the capital.[14]

It is tempting to look upon the replacement of traditional building materials by modern ones as still another development within a type of traditional housing. However, the use of a considerable amount of such materials requires a significant financial investment, and this in turn has had an important impact on housing. These changes are not always improvements; for the poor, the changes are for the worse. The introduction of such materials leads to a deterioration in the quality of housing, because the cost of modern building materials means that the plot-holder can no longer build a dwelling with the same floor area.

Perhaps the most important consequence of the introduction of modern materials has been to shift the responsibility for providing housing from the sphere of women to the sphere of men. Hardie fails to recognize this in his analysis of continuity and change, and consequently he also misses its implications. This shift has had important consequences for the concepts of traditional and modern housing in today's Botswana.

SOME CHARACTERISTICS OF MODERN LOW-COST HOUSING

Urban low-cost housing is supported by the government in Botswana through so-called self-help programs. This type of low-cost dwelling consists of a two-room core house on a plot that includes a pit-latrine, but which is much smaller than plots in villages. As in the villages, water is provided by a standpipe shared by several households, but there is no electric power supply. The core house can be extended or supplemented by another house through the plot-holders own efforts. Houses are normally built by a more or less skilled builder, always a man (FIG. 7).

The urban low-cost dwelling has little in common with the traditional dwelling. Not only the materials but also the layout and use of space have changed. A lot of traditionally outdoor activities have moved indoors. Some of the changes are adjustments to a modern way of life. For instance, socializing with family and friends may now take place indoors, and living room furniture for this purpose requires a lot of space. Other changes are requisite adjustments to urban life. For instance, the lack of firewood has moved cooking indoors to a paraffin stove, and the risk of theft has moved storage indoors -- despite the fact that no provision for either of these needs is made in the urban houses. Thus the demand for space increases as the cost of providing space also increases. The result is overcrowding and limited opportunities for

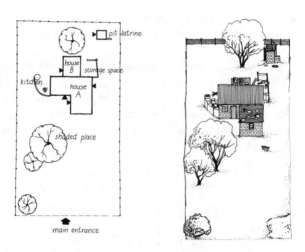

F I G U R E 7. A low-cost dwelling in a self-help housing area. It is planned with modern housing concepts in mind but provides inadequate space. Cooking is done outside over an open fire within a temporary kitchen area or indoors on a paraffin stove. The household of eight people uses one room. Two rooms are rented to tenants. The room at the back is for storage. Baths are taken by the pit-latrine for the sake of privacy.

maintaining traditional patterns in the arrangement of living and sleeping quarters.[15]

Modern housing within the framework of self-help projects is not a further development of traditional dwellings but the result of new concepts being introduced to modernize housing. A five-room house, including kitchen, living room and bathroom, built of durable materials, can easily be considered an improvement and a modernization. But when modern amenities and adequate space are lacking, the result is the deterioration of housing standards. For this reason the two-room core house is only quasi-modern.

Dwellings in squatter areas demonstrate a wide range of intermediate ways for using materials, and the layout and use of space. These are of interest when discussing the transformation to modern low-cost housing.[16]

TRADITIONAL HOUSING	MODERN LOW-COST HOUSING

THE CONTEXT:

mainly rural setting	mainly urban setting
subsistence economy	cash economy
women's responsibility	men's responsibility
the dwelling is regarded as a household utensil	the dwelling regarded as a commodity
status of dwelling related to women's world	status of dwelling related to men's world
symbol of family-identity	symbol of self-identity and status
the dwelling is simultaneously means and end	means and end of dwelling differentiated

THE BUILDING PROCESS:

the household has much knowledge of and influence on the design of dwellings	the household has little knowledge of and influence on the design of dwellings
materials of little or no cost: mud, thatch and grass	purchased materials: concrete blocks, zinc sheets etc.
maintenance (= household work) dominates	construction (= technical work) dominates
time a necessary resource	money a necessary resource

DESIGN OF DWELLING:

dwelling for owner household only	dwelling includes rooms for tenants
outdoor living mainly	indoor living mainly
high space standard indoors	low space standard indoors
much privacy	little privacy

T A B L E 1. Pairs of aspects related to traditional and modern housing respectively.

TRADITIONAL AS OPPOSED TO MODERN DWELLINGS

A comparison between traditional and modern low-cost dwellings has led to the identification the pairs of aspects listed in Table 1. These are of significance when analyzing the concepts intrinsic to traditional and modern housing. Some of the aspects represent the extremes in a continuum of forms; other are opposites. Few dwellings have the same degree of modernity in all aspects. Very often one finds dwellings that at first look seem to be a rather confusing mixture. This is especially true among dwellings in squatter settlements.

The terms traditional and modern do not refer only to the house or to its materials. In an extended form, these terms are also present in the whole context of housing as the listed pairs indicate. Many of the aspects are interrelated.

What follows is an elaboration on the aspects related to the transferral of responsibility for housing-provision from the domain of women to the domain of men. The implications of this shift are of primary importance. The historical and socio-cultural changes underlying this transformation will only be touched upon.

The relation between the male and the female is discussed by Rosaldo in a manner that usefully interprets my experiences of housing in Botswana. She proposes, ". . . a structural model that relates recurrent aspects of psychology and cultural and social organization to an opposition between the 'domestic' orientation of women and the extra-domestic or 'public' ties that, in most societies are primarily available to men."[17]

Rosaldo defines domestic as, "those minimal institutions and modes of activity that are organized immediately around one or more mothers and their children," and defines as public, "activities, institutions and forms of association that link, rank, organize, or subsume particular mother-child groups."[18] She argues that men always have a stronger position than women, which can be related to women's domestic sphere and men's public sphere. This asymmetry "appears to be universal," she concludes.[19]

Following Rosaldo's argument, housing in Tswana society has not only been transferred from the sphere of women to the sphere of men, but, more importantly, from the domestic sphere to the public sphere. There are many factors in this transformation which support this argument.

TRADITIONAL HOUSING AS PART OF THE DOMESTIC SPHERE

To understand the traditional role of housing, I will have to rely on the records of Schapera.[20] He does not treat housing and its meaning specifically,but the many details in his writings are very useful. Women in traditional society are subordinate to men. Their opportunities for acquiring property are limited; only houses, traditional pieces of furniture and household utensils are regarded as belonging to women and as being under their control. Imported objects like furniture, especially those purchased by the husband, belong to the husband. The woman's sphere consists of the necessary domestic work in a broad sense. It is in the execution of these duties that the woman has some power. She has all the responsibility for domestic work, including ploughing, harvesting and weeding, as well as for providing shelter for the family. Only in heavy work such as field clearance, ploughing with oxen and raising roof structures is she assisted by her husband.

The plot is allocated to the husband, and it creates the basis for his family-identity. To build a family and a home is one of the five "great works" that Alverson identified for a Tswana man. Alverson stresses that each of these works is "at once the means and the end of wanting-to-do. Each is both a resource and an asset. All are weal and wealth. To do these is to be a contented and fulfilled individual."[21]

The wife, however, is responsible for building the houses. From Schapera's writings it is evident that houses are on a par with household utensils, or rather, they are household utensils. Houses are under the control of the wife; she is regarded as their mistress and supervises everything connected to them. She gives her unmarried children sleeping quarters and allocates houses to visitors. Houses are as a rule referred to by the name of the wife occupying them.

But a house does not only provide shelter for the living members of the family; it also provides the place for reproduction in the biological sense. There are some statements by Schapera that underline the strong links between a house, the wife and the reproductive power of the couple. Schapera says that it was the duty of husband and wife when building new houses "to sleep in it before it is roofed in, so as to forestall others from doing so and thus injuring their reproductive power."[22] Scapera also says that a woman's blood is considered "hot" when she is mixing earth or smearing the walls and floors. Both men and women can sometimes have hot blood, and it may occur in connection with sexual activities, child birth, menstruation, or when somebody returns from a long journey or funeral.

Schapera does not give any interpretation for the existence of hot and cold blood. The common factor in the various situations when a person is considered to have hot blood seems to be that life is at the border of birth or death. If interpretation is correct, women's smearing the wall is not only a matter of maintenance but also a symbolic action: to keep the reproductive power of the family alive. The close relation between houses and reproduction is also underlined by the fact that afterbirth, as well as small children who die, are buried inside the house. This relation between housing and reproduction, the prime function of a woman, is perhaps the major reason for house-building being entrusted to a woman, therefore making it part of the domestic sphere.

MODERN HOUSING AS A PART OF THE PUBLIC SPHERE

Rosaldo makes a distinction between the ascribed status of women and the achieved status of men:

> A woman becomes a woman by following in her mother's footsteps, whereas there must be a break in a man's experience. For a boy to become an adult, he must prove himself -- his masculinity -- among his peers . . . . If "becoming a man" is, developmentally, an "achievement," social groups elaborate the criteria for that achievement and create the hierarchies and institutions we associate with an articulated social order. Insofar as achievement in this sense is a prerequisite of manhood, then men create and control a social order in which they compete as individuals.[23]

In Botswana cattle are traditionally associated with the status of men. Schapera wrote that before the coming of Europeans, the mere possession of cattle was in itself a source of status, for a man's wealth was estimated by the size of his herds, and a wealthy man was generally respected and able to exercise much influence in tribal affairs. For all these reasons cattle were sought after more eagerly than any other commodity, and their slaughter was normally reserved for festive or other occasions, the importance of which was enhanced by the magnitude of this sacrifice.[24]

The introduction of a cash economy and labor migration meant that a man could increase his power through money converted into cattle. Money was, and still is, more often earned by men, especially in the rural areas. The cash income is seldom equally shared by the whole household. Generally, the male cash-earner decides how to use what money remains after immediate needs are met.

Money has, however, not only been invested in cattle; for a long time, surplus money has been invested in housing improvements and furniture, as has already been described. This has led eventually to housing becoming the concern and responsibility of men, and thereby part of the public sphere. It is by becoming a symbol of self-identity, as opposed to family-identity in the traditional sense and of status, that the shift of housing into the public sphere should be understood. Houses have achieved a similar position to cattle. Even though the domestic sphere is still almost entirely the responsibility of women, it has been deprived of the task of providing housing.

The importance of the house as a symbol of progress is very evident. One man, when asked about his new modern house on a plot which previously contained only traditional houses, told me that "modern houses are for modern life." Hardie had similar experiences, and he concluded, "there is no doubt that the adoption of the zinc-roofed house with concrete block or brick wall . . . symbolically expresses the desire to be like the white man."[25]

The consequences of housing modernization are that a dwelling is no longer concomitantly a means and an end as in the traditional setting; means and end have now become two separate aims. The dwelling is an end in the sense of being a sign of progress. As a housing market has developed in urban areas, it has also become a means to achieve progress, mainly by renting rooms to homeless urban people. In this way a house owner can earn considerable extra money for further investment, often in the form of a dwelling in the home village.

Cattle have undergone a similar transition from being means and end simultaneously to being both means and end, but separately. Though today cattle are often raised to be sold on the market, cattle ownership is still associated with status, and is mainly a concern of men.

Many qualities of utility in the traditional dwelling disappear in the shift of housing from the sphere of women to the sphere of men, due to the sharp division between the two. Instead, the role of housing as a symbol of status, progress, self-identity and modern life, and as a means to acquire money, has been emphasized at the expense of qualities of utility.

But not all urban people fit the above description. According to traditional Tswana views, it is not possible to have tenants in a traditional dwelling, nor, for some people, in a modern one. When asked why he did not have tenants, a man living in a modern house in Francistown, a small town in northern Botswana, answered, "I do not want to capitalize on somebody. I want to stay with my parents and wife. I want those people to be under my influence; if you bring in tenants you get problems." He then added, "Francistown is like a home village." Modern people, however, especially in Gaborone, do not hesitate to have tenants.

A woman in a rural village explained to me why her husband had built a modern house on the plot: "The traditional houses we have here are enough, but we also want to develop as you do. I want to become a white lady; I want to become light-skinned in a modern house. I will continue to be a Motswana if I continue to live in this traditional house." But she assured me that she, as a "white lady," would maintain her very large rondavel with a thatched roof, because it is more pleasant to sleep in.

Thus, women, despite being responsible for the domestic sphere, do not hesitate to aspire to modern achievements. Very often they combine the two. Single women are much more concerned about providing houses for their families than men householders. Despite lower incomes and fewer economic resources, they invest more in housing. One may conclude that they have maintained their traditional responsibility for housing the family, despite the fact that the whole context has changed.[26]

THE DOMESTICATION OF WOMEN
THROUGH HOUSING MODERNIZATION

The reasons behind this investigation of the concepts inherent in traditional and modern housing were to understand the ongoing transformation of housing. To limit the interpretation to only building materials, or to the layout of dwellings and the use of space, is insufficient. A comprehensive understanding of the whole societal context has to be included that takes into consideration the role and responsibility of men and women in housing issues.

The transformation has, however, not only been created by actions at the household level. In shaping the independent state of Botswana, housing policies have to a considerable degree been decided by men in line with men's values. These are reinforced, perhaps unconsciously, by donors like the World Bank. Modern materials, used as security for a building loan, are emphasized at the expense of adequate space and other utilitarian qualities.

The common law of Botswana, based on the British model and introduced as a substitute for traditional customary law, definitely confirms the change. In a marriage according to common law, marital power over the house and the place of abode, power which cannot be excluded by any agreement, in general rests entirely with the husband. Without consulting his wife, a husband can make all important decisions about the house, including a decision to sell it. In other words, through the process of modernization the dwelling has acquired value mainly as property, and women have been denied one of their traditional duties and spheres of influence -- the provision of housing for their families. Thus, housing modernization is still another factor contributing to what Rogers has called the "domestication" of women.[27]

Though there are certain circumstances in the above description of housing transformation that are specific for Botswana, the country most likely shares patterns with other developing countries. Among all the Bantu-speaking people in southern Africa, women in the traditional model of society hold the responsibility for housing.[28]   This is also the case for women of many pastoral societies in Africa.[29]   There are few studies that are concerned with the roles of women and men in relation to housing and the impact of housing modernization.   Further studies in the field would probably prove that the case of Botswana is repeated else-where among developing countries.

A full understanding of the concepts intrinsic to traditional and modern housing is not only a matter of academic concern. It is of profound importance when developing housing policies, and when aid organizations aim at supporting housing in developing countries.   Which is to be supported, dwellings belonging to the domestic sphere or dwellings belonging to the public sphere?

REFERENCE NOTES

1. Botswana is the country; Tswana denotes the people of the main ethnic group and is also an adjective. A citizen of Botswana is called a Motswana -- in plural, Batswana. The language is called Setswana.
2. See, for instance, W.J. Burchell, J. Campbell, J. Chapman, H. Lichtenstein and W.C. Willoughby.   For detailed information, see James Walton, *African Village* (Pretoria: Van Schaik, 1956); Graeme John Hardie, "Tswana Design of House and Settlement -- Continuity and Change in Expressive Space" (dissertation, Boston University Graduate School, 1980).
3. For further details of Tswana housing, see Anita Larsson and Viera Larsson, *Traditional Tswana Housing -- a study in four villages in eastern Botswana* (Stockholm: Swedish Council for Building Research, Document D7, 1984). In fieldwork for this study some kind of distinction between traditional and modern layout and houses had to be made. A layout with several houses was considered

traditional, while one with a single multi-room house in the yard was regarded as modern. Houses with mud walls and a thatched roof were regarded as traditional, while purchased elements such as factory-made doors, panes of glass and wire fences were considered improvements.

4. Amos Rapoport, *House Form and Culture* (Englewood Cliffs, NJ: Prentice-Hall, 1969), p. 60.

5. Quotation of Chief Seepapitso by his son, in Isaac Schapera, *Tribal Innovators, Tswana Chiefs and Social Change 1795-1940* (Monographs on Social Anthropology, London School of Economics, University of London) (London: the Athlone Press, 1970), p. 257.

6. Isaac Schapera, *Married Life in an African Tribe* (Middlesex, England: Penguin Books, 1971), p. 109.

7. Schapera, *Married Life*, p. 112.

8. Schapera, *Married Life*, p. 113.

9. Hardie, "Tswana Design," p. 99.

10. Hardie, "Tswana Design," p. 101.

11. Hardie, "Tswana Design," p. 100.

12. Anita Larsson, *From Outdoor to Indoor Living. The transition from traditional to modern low-cost housing in Botswana* (Department of Building Function Analysis, R4:88, 1988), pp. 45-47.

13. Hardie, "Tswana Design," p. 199.

14. Larsson, *From Outdoor to Indoor Living*, Ch. 5.

15. Larsson, *From Outdoor to Indoor Living*, pp.57-63.

16. Larsson, *From Outdoor to Indoor Living*, pp. 51-55.

17. M.Z. Rosaldo, "Woman, Culture and Society: A Theoretical Overview," in M.Z. Rosaldo and L. Lamphere, eds., *Woman, Culture and Society* (Stanford, California, 1978), p. 17.

18. Rosaldo, "Woman, Culture and Society," p. 23.

19. Rosaldo, "Woman, Culture and Society," p. 19.

20. Isaac Schapera, *A Handbook of Tswana Law and Custom* (London: Frank Cass and Company, 1970); *Married Life*.

21. Hoyt Alverson, *Mind in the Heart of Darkness* (Johannesburg: Macmillan South Africa Publishers, 1978), p. 122.

22. Schapera, *A Handbook*, p. 154.

23. Rosaldo, "Woman, Culture and Society," p. 28.

24. Schapera, *A Handbook*, p. 214.

25. Hardie, "Tswana Design," p. 102.

26. Anita Larsson, *Housing Careers of Women Householders in Gaborone, Botswana* (Working paper, Department of Building Function Analysis, University of Lund, Sweden, 1987).

27. According to Rogers, the domestication of women is critical in the Third World development process. It is manifested by the extraction of the unpaid domestic or subsistence sector from the modern economy. Rogers, *The Domestication of Women. Discrimination in Developing Countries* (London: Tavistock Publications, 1982), p. 22.

28. Basil Sansome, "Traditional Economic Systems," in W.D. Hammond-Tooke, ed., *The Bantu-speaking Peoples of Southern Africa* (London: Routledge and Kegan Paul, 1974).

29. Aud Talle, "Women as Heads of Houses: The Organisation of Production and the Role of Women among the Pastoral Maasai in Kenya" and other articles, in *Ethnos 1-2* (1987).

All drawings by Viera Larsson, Stockholm .

DUALITIES IN THE STUDY OF TRADITIONAL DWELLINGS AND SETTLEMENTS: AN EPILOGUE

NEZAR ALSAYYAD

There are many approaches to the study of traditional dwellings and settlements, as the different contributions to this volume clearly demonstrate. Our theoretical constructs make these approaches possible and allow us to put together books like this. An important construct underlying this book is that of duality. To cope with complexity, we in academia inevitably revert to the practice of abstraction, which includes the classification of research subjects into polar opposites, setting up dualities without which our understanding would seem to be curtailed.

Duality in the study of traditional environments is based on the comparative premise that two subjects, X and Y, may have sufficient properties in common and/or properties that differ along specified dimensions to allow meaningful convergent conclusions.[1] This simplistic approach to comparative analysis can and has been labelled crude by scholars working in one particular discipline or another. And although these accusations are partially justified, this duality is accepted by most scholars because it leads to cross-cultural generalizations which could not have been arrived at otherwise.[2]

Another problem inherent to dualistic comparisons concerns methodology. We may ask, for example, why is it that two and only two entities are contrasted instead of three or four? Researchers of the vernacular, especially architectural historians and folklorists, have been accustomed to dual comparisons under the assumption that juxtaposition brings out the unique qualities of each of the compared entities. This approach appears to have been inherited from the Wofflinian art history tradition of comparing two artifacts from two different periods or cultures. The limitation of the approach is apparent in the desire to seek more by way of similarities and differences than is perhaps methodologically justified. It ignores, for example, the possibility that the two entities under comparison may represent entirely different economic conditions or production relations, or that they may be governed by completely different sets of socio-political values.

We must, of course, realize that all comparisons are limited from the outset by their own frameworks. I say this only as a word of caution, because I see a dangerous trend developing in the study of traditional dwellings and settlements that is primarily built on the acceptance of the concept of duality. At a more philosophical level, we may argue that duality is based on the concept of "otherness," or the belief that other people are substantially different enough from "us" to be classified as "others." If we accept this concept, we should continue to be concerned with the idea of capturing this "native's otherness," while still confronting the abstraction of our own "experience distant."[3]

At the heart of the matter lies the question of how we see the world. Each of our disciplines has its own orientation, methods, vocabulary and even world view. But does this mean that we all see different worlds? This, obviously, is not an easy question, especially when we are reminded that as academics we speak a different language from and live in different places than the people we study. Given these conditions, the question of whether we can intersubjectively communicate our disciplinary findings must remain open.

The division of environments into types (i.e. modern and traditional, urban and rural) should draw our attention to the many inconsistencies embedded in such systems of classification. For example, we may notice that it is always modern urban people who study traditional rural ones. This coincides with the fact that those who study usually come from, or are educated in, the First World, while those who are studied are primarily situated in the Third World. We may also observe that most researchers of traditional environments go elsewhere to study rather than focus on questions close to home. Why is this the case? The question of what motivates modern scholars to study traditional environments is not irrelevant because we cannot escape the issue of intellectual colonialism.

At the symposium out of which the chapters in this book originated, Roger Montgomery suggested that we must develop a more critical self-awareness as we go about the business of appropriating the worlds of relatively powerless people, and that we must understand our role in the apparatus of colonial and imperial domination. He suggested that we must be informed by ideas about ideological hegemony, about "the appropriation of culture as a source of intellectual power," and about "the imperialist's definition of the dominated person, the colonized other, to the point that his/her understanding of themselves becomes our own construct." Montgomery also pointed out that prowling into the traditional environments of the Third World to produce commodified research can be seen as part of a dominant society's need for interpretive work as "a way of sanitizing the class distinctions, of transmitting the class structure into tradition, and of turning Apartheid into vernacular."[4]

These valuable cautionary remarks should not lead us to condemn the study of traditional environments and deplore it as imperialistic. We have to remember that although the initial motivation behind many works may have been influenced by such imperialistic bias, we often empathize with our subjects and achieve a degree of unity seldom found in other scientific or humanistic discourses. As some of the symposium participants pointed out, researchers in the field often encounter an attitude of shame among the residents of traditional environments. "They are ashamed of what they have, because it is not like what we have in the modern Western world."[6] It is with regard to this point that we may have a significant positive role to play. Instead of thinking of ourselves as ugly imperialists, we may consider our responsibility as people committed to educating ourselves and explaining to the people who live in traditional environments why we value what they have. This is often something that the difficulties of day-to-day subsistence living may have caused them to forget.

Just as the use of environmental signs for identity varies in the analysis of the symbolic role of dwellings and settlements in traditional societies,[5] so does the desire to preserve or maintain traditional practices. In many parts of the Third World we see native peoples, especially those who have the choice, rejecting traditional forms. This apparent rejection among members of cultures which still adhere to established social norms may have been precipitated by the superimposition of modern practices which have automatically rendered traditional ways substandard.[7] We obviously cannot ignore the universalization of the world when we study traditional environments, and we should not try to isolate those international influences from the environments we study. We cannot continue to claim that we are taking a neutral position toward our subjects. There is an implied bias in our work toward preserving what can still be preserved of traditional dwellings and settlements. This bias seems to stem from the fear that if these environments change, as some of their residents may desire, we will lose our research subjects and hence our means of livelihood. As a discipline, the study of traditional dwellings and settlements, no matter how young, seems to have fallen into the trap of constructing a social reality dependent on its own particular jargon. In its attempt to preserve itself, the members of the discipline have concentrated on aspects of research which reaffirm the original basis instead of confronting new and changing paradigms.[8]

One of these new paradigms is the changing nature of traditional dwellings and settlements. In the not-so-distant past, these existed primarily in rural areas. Today this is no longer true. In Third World countries the overwhelming majority of urban poor live in traditional settlements. We often refer to these as "squatter" or "informal" settlements because we fail to see that behind those inadequate structures are traditional modes of existence, traditional lifestyles and traditional economies. In one view, these settlements are the closest thing we have today to traditional vernacular.[9] Many of the developing countries in which these settlements exist have reached the take-off point for economic development and market-oriented consumption, or what Ivan Illich has called "modernized poverty."[10] Now may be the appropriate time for us to look at these environments whose "rurban" people continue to live traditional lives while adapting to an ever-changing, modernizing world.

Another important paradigm that needs to be reconsidered involves methods. Regardless of the disciplines we come from, we all seem to fall into one of two groups: those who cannot take a first step without investing considerable time building taxonomies they hope will help them in the larger world even though this does not always happen, and those -- mostly romantics -- who reject all forms of structured inquiry and turn only to their cameras and pencils to snap photos and draw beautiful sketches without realizing that their contribution is severely limited by the very modes of representation they have elected. We must move beyond such simplistic approaches. Maybe we ought to pay more attention to those stories our people tell, the stories that represent the unique kind of knowledge that can only be acquired growing up in a certain culture.

We must realize, as Spiro Kostof has rightfully remarked, "that by studying other cultures and peoples, we are putting ourselves in context."[11] There is a point at which we must agree that the study of "others" is fundamentally for our own well-being, not for theirs. We must also stop lamenting the passing away of traditional environments, and instead accept this as a normally healthy process by which societies regenerate themselves. We must understand that tradition does not die, but simply takes different forms. As scholars from different disciplines, we cannot afford to let our approaches separate us any further, and we must realize that an enormous world of ordinary people will not have access to our knowledge or will not use it simply because they have more pressing priorities. Finally, and as one participant in the symposium put it, ". . . in all of this theorization in the study of traditional dwellings and settlements, there is a tendency to forget that it all began as a simple means to provide shelter. That column, that carved-out column, which has become enamored as a symbol of this and that, is basically there and was originally conceived to hold up the roof."[12] We should never lose sight of this immediate reality.

REFERENCE NOTES

This concluding note is based on discussions I had before, during and after the symposium with many of the participants. I wish specifically to acknowledge Norman Carver, Spiro Kostof, Roger Montgomery, Paul Oliver, Amos Rapoport and Davide Saile, whose remarks at the final plenary session may have set the tone for this epilogue.

1. J. Walton and L. Masotti, "The Logic of Comparisons and the Nature of Urbanism," in J. Walton and L. Masotti, eds., *The City in Comparative Perspective* (New York: Sage Publications, 1976), p. 3.
2. C. Pickvance, "Comparative Urban Analysis and Assumptions of Causality," in K. Brown, M. Jole, et al, eds., *Middle Eastern Cities in Comparative Perspective* (London: Ithaca Press, 1986), pp. 29-52.
3. Terms used by C. Geertz in *The Interpretation of Culture* (New York: Basic Books, 1973).
4. Remarks made by Roger Montgomery at the closing session of the symposium.
5. Remark made by an unidentified participant at the closing session of the symposium.
6. J, Duncan, *Housing and Identity* (New York: Holmes and Meier, 1982).
7. G. Payne, *Urban Housing in the Third World* (London: Leonard Hill, 1977).
8. In this sense the discipline of studying traditional dwellings and settlements may not be different from any other established discipline as discussed by P Berger and T. Luckmann in *The Social Construction of Reality* (New York: Anchor Books, 1967).
9. Remark by Amos Rapoport at the concluding session of the symposium. For more on this, refer to A. Rapoport, "Spontaneous Settlements as Vernacular Design," in C. Patton, ed., *Spontaneous Shelter* (Philadelphia: Temple University Press, 1988).
10. I. Illich, *Deschooling Society* (New York: Harper and Row, 1971).
11. Remarks by Spiro Kostof at the concluding session of the symposium.
12. Remark by Norman Carver at the concluding session of the symposium.

I   A   S   T   E

INTERNATIONAL ASSOCIATION
FOR THE STUDY OF TRADITIONAL
ENVIRONMENTS

The International Association for the Study of Traditional Environments (I A S T E) was established at the First International Symposium on Traditional Dwellings and Settlements held at Berkeley, California, in April 1988. I A S T E is an interdisciplinary forum where scholars from various disciplines and countries can exchange ideas, discuss methods and approaches, and share findings in a non-applied study of cultural aspects of design. Unlike disciplinary associations, I A S T E is primarily interested in the comparative and cross-cultural understanding of traditional habitat as an expression of informal cultural conventions. I A S T E's purpose is to serve as an umbrella association for all scholars studying vernacular, indigenous, popular and traditional environments.

Current activites of I A S T E include the organization of biennial conferences on selected themes in traditional environments research and the publication of *Traditional Dwellings and Settlements Review*, a quarterly journal that will act as a forum for the exchange of ideas and a means to disseminate information and report on research activity. Partially sponsored by the National Endowment for the Arts, the journal will be available through the Center for Environmental Design Research at the University of California, Berkeley.

For further information, contact:
I A S T E, Center For Environmental Design Research
390 Wurster Hall, Berkeley, CA, 94720.
(4 1 5)   6 4 2   2 8 9 6 .

TRADITIONAL DWELLINGS AND SETTLEMENTS: WORKING PAPER SERIES

In addition to its current activities, I A S T E will publish a working papers series, the first eighteen volumes of which include papers presented at the First International Symposium on Traditional Dwellings and Settlements. The papers were selected through a blind peer-review process and were revised and submitted by their authors in camera-ready form. The following is a list of papers in the first eighteen volumes of the series. They are available through I A S T E.

v o l . 1. TRADITIONAL FORM AS CULTURAL IDENTITY
1. Domestic Architecture and the Occupant's Life Cycle: Sudan -- *Natalie Tobert.*
2. Myth, Symbol and Function of the Traditional Toraja Dwelling -- *Eric Crystal.*
3. Safranbolu: An Anatolian Town with Roots in Urban Form -- *M. Bilgi Denel.*
4. Identity and Giove: Hill Towns Are Alive and Well in Umbria -- *Francis Violich.*
5. Procession and Urban Form in a Sri Lankan Village -- *William Bechhoefer.*

v o l . 2. METHODOLOGICAL ANALYSIS OF TRADTIONAL ENVIRONMENTS
1. Analyzing Aerial Photographs of Maroon Settlements -- *Anne Hublin.*
2. Pattern Language as a Method for Analysis: Case Studies of Roman Houses -- *Carol Martin Watts.*
3. Spanish Vernacular House Form: An Excersize in Comparative Analysis -- *Catherine Cresswell* and *William Widdowson.*
4. A Research Method for the Study of Traditional Dwellings: Case Studies of Indian Habitat -- *Madhavi Desai.*
5. A Methodological Scheme for a Systematic Study of the Evolution and Diffusion of Human Dwellings -- *Giancarlo Cataldi.*

v o l . 3. TRADITIONAL ENVIRONMENTS: INTERPRETIVE APPROACHES
1. Varieties of Tradition and Traditionalism -- *Gul Asatekin* and *Aydan Balamir.*
2. The Meaning of Traditional Dwelling in Gujarat Based on Language and Literature in Rural and Urban Environments -- *Miki Desai.*
3. Text Reading and Personal Expression -- *Josef Priyotomo.*
4. Interpreting Buildings as Interpretations -- Toward a Hermeneutics of Building -- *Georg Buechi.*
5. Comparing the Forms of Indigenous and Classical Architecture -- *Ralf Weber.*
6. The Meanings of Circular Forms in Buildings, Housing Settlements and Communities -- *Hugh Burgess.*

v o l . 15. TRADITIONAL FORMS AND ARCHITECTURAL DESIGN

1. Adaptabilty of Thai and Chinese Architecture -- *Amos Ih Tiao Chang.*
2. Type, Tradition and Design -- *Ludovic Micara* and *Attilio Petruccioli.*
3. The Evolution of a Traditional Architecture -- *Christos A. Saccopoulos.*
4. The Extent To Which Two Countries Consider Tradition in Designing New Housing -- *E. Raedene Combs* and *James J. Potter.*
5. Replication: The Key to Interpreting American Vernacular Architecture -- *Herbert Gottfried.*

v o l . 16. ARCHITECTS AND TRADITIONAL FORM

1. Metier: The Tradition of Dwelling -- *Gevork Hartoonian.*
2. Hassan Fathy and the Re-interpretation of the Traditional Environment -- *James Steele.*
3. New Gourna: Vernacular Remodelling of Architectural Space -- *Fekri A. Hassan* and *Christine Plimpton.*
4. Our Profession's Fascination with Traditional Dwellings and Settlements -- *Ali Faramawy.*

v o l . 17. TRADITIONAL CONSTRUCTION PRACTICES

1. The Evolution of French Colonial Architecture in the Mississippi River Valley -- *Edward J. Cazayoux.*
2. The Gable End -- *M.R. Austin.*
3. The Wood Framework of Traditional Dwellings in Southeast Asia -- *Yoshihito Katsuse.*
4. Traditional Wood Architecture of Cameroon -- *Wolfgang Lauber.*
5. The Pitches of the Timber Roof Construction in Eastern Europe -- *Kunio Ohta.*
6. Traditional Construction Practices Utilizing Unreinforced Masonry in Seismic Areas -- *Randolf Langenbach.*

v o l . 18. FORM, ENERGY AND CLIMATE

1. Climatic Response in a Traditional Settlement -- *Paul Gabriel* and *Davide Garda.*
2. Divergent Desert Dwelling Typologies: Arab Courtyard vs. U.S. Ranch House -- *Jeffrey Cook.*
3. Energy Use and Traditional Dwelling Form and Fabric -- *Madan Mehta.*

NOTE ON CONTRIBUTORS

Nezar AlSayyad is an Adjunct Professor of Architecture and a Research Associate at the University of California, Berkeley, USA.

Suzanne Preston Blier is an Assistant Professor of Art History and Archeology at Columbia University, New York, USA.

Botond Bognar is an Associate Professor of Architecture at the University of Illinois, Urbana-Champaign, USA.

Jean-Paul Bourdier is an Associate Professor of Architecture at the University of California, Berkeley, USA.

Sophie Clement-Charpentier is an ethnologist, an architect and a researcher at the Ecole des Hautes Etudes en Sciences Sociales, Paris, France.

Norma Evenson is a Professor of Architectural History at the University of California, Berkeley, USA.

Jerome Feldman is an Associate Professor of Art History at Hawaii Loa College, Kaneohe, Oahu, Hawaii, USA.

Aharon Ron Fuchs is an Israeli architect and a staff member of The Technion -- Israel University of Technology, Haifa, Israel.

Jana Hesser is an American anthropologist specializing in biological and cultural anthropology.

Ismet Khambatta is an Indian architect currently practicing in the United States.

Amr Abdel Kawi is an architect and a member of the faculty at Ein Shams University, Cairo, Egypt.

Spiro Kostof is a Professor of Architectural History at the University of California, Berkeley, USA.

Anita Larsson is an architect and a building function researcher at the University of Lund, Sweden.

Sang Hae Lee is an Associate Professor of Architecture at Sung Kyun Kwan University, Seoul, Korea.

Michael Linzey is a Senior Lecturer of Architecture at the University of Auckland, New Zealand.

Michael Meyer-Brodnitz is a member of the architecture faculty at The Technion -- Israel Institute of Technology, Haifa, Israel.

Paul Oliver is a folklorist and vernacularist specializing in architectural anthropology. He is currently affiliated with the University of Exeter, United Kingdom.

Eleftherios Pavlides is an architect and a member of the faculty of Roger Williams College, Bristol, Rhode Island, USA.

Amos Rapoport is a distinguished Professor of Architecture at the University of Wisconsin, Milwaukee, USA.

Seteney Shami is the head of the anthropology department at the Institute of Archeology and Anthropology, Yarmuk University, Irbid, Jordan.

Gunawan Tjahjono is an Indonesian architect and a member of the faculty of the University of Indonesia, Jakarta, Indonesia.

Jo Tonna is an Associate Professor of Architecture at the University of Malta, St. Andrews, Malta.

Yi-Fu Tuan is a Professor of Geography at the University of Wisconsin, Madison, USA.

Roxana Waterson is a social anthropologist and a Lecturer at the National University of Singapore.

John Webster is the Dean of the Environmental Design Division of the Tasmanian Institute of Technology, Australia.